The Greater Jesus

His glorious unveiling

JOHN NOĒ, Ph.D.

What They Are Saying Already

"John Noē is so right that we are misunderstanding the contemporary Christ in so many ways! . . . In this book he demonstrates that learning about the greater Jesus as He is today is the key to unlocking the mysteries of The Revelation, and this opens up numerous possibilities for experiencing the Person of Christ in one's life . . . . I encourage you to jump to *Appendix A* and read Noē's account of why he feels called to tackle such a mysterious book and why he has made it his life's work."
— Dave Shulse, Amazon.com Review

". . . a terrific and timely read. I enjoyed the hell (whoops!) out of it. . . . This his fourth and longest book in a new series may just be Noē's most dynamic and challenging. It presents what I hope will come to be recognized as a major contribution toward repairing the damage done to the Church by those who have claimed to speak with biblical authority about such doctrines as the Second Coming, the Rapture, a future Antichrist, and the Apocalypse. Jesus never left us, Noē insists, and He remains active in the spiritual realm for the benefit of believers. Noē presents a methodical yet readily understandable analysis, with particular emphasis on the Book of Revelation, that conclusively destroys the case for accepting these widely accepted ideas." **— John S. Evans, Ph.D., Amazon.com Review**

"Noē transcends the traditional, mild-mannered image of Jesus and unveils a realistic and wholistic word-picture of today's *greater Jesus* who emerges as the Warrior of God's Holiness that the Believer can experience. What a fantastic book . . . out of the park!" **— Benton Ruth, M. Div., M.A., D. Min., Amazon.com Review**

"This looks like a book that we have needed for a long time. I am excited to read it!" **— Edward J. Hassertt, JD**

"This book is of great interest to me, because I am developing a new course for Bible 10: 'Christ from Creation to Consummation.'" — **Robert Preston, M.A., M.Div., Bible Teacher at Liberty Christian School**

"This book is needed. I wish you well and much success in getting this out to thousands . . . hopefully millions." — **Jerry Bernard, BM, Ph.D., Phil.D., Litt.D.; Director of Research at Library in the Palms Research Center; VP of Scripture Research**

"It really and truly sounds very interesting and hopefully compelling . . . . Am looking forward to reading it." — **Miller Houghton, President, Houghton Oil Co.**

"You're getting pretty prolific with your output volume! This does sound interesting!" — **Harold Hoopingarner, Presbyterian Elder**

The Bad & Ugly — What Some Pre-Publication Critics Are Saying

"Somebody like John Noē is no place to learn the truth." — **prefers anonymity**

"The theme of Noē's material is undeniable — he thinks he is smarter than you. . . . people are stupid and he is here to educate you idiots. . . . This is what happens when a person has no peers . . . no accountability . . . . no restraining hand of people who might be able to tell him he is wrong . . . . I expect Noē will continue to produce books, papers, and other material that are simply arrogant and condescending diatribes telling everyone else how 'unaware' and 'uninformed' they are compared to the 'greater' John Noē." — **Roderick Edwards, Blogger, "The UnPreterist"**

The Greater Jesus

By John Noē, Ph.D.

Copyright © 2012 by John Noē.
All rights reserved.
Printed in the United States of America

No part of this publication may be reproduced, stored in a retrieval system or transmitted in any form by any means, electronic, mechanical, photocopy, recording, or otherwise, without the prior written permission of the author, except for brief quotations in critical reviews or articles.

Unless otherwise noted, all Scripture quotations are from the Holy Bible, *New International Version* © 1973, 1978, 1984 International Bible Society. Used by permission of Zondervan Bible Publishers.

Published by:

East2West Press
Publishing arm of the Prophecy Reformation Institute

5236 East 72nd Street
Indianapolis, IN 46250 USA
(317)-842-3411

Cover: Tom Haulter

ISBN: 978-0-9834303-3-9

Library of Congress Control Number: 2012946227

Jesus. Bible. New Testament Revelation. Prophecy. End Times.

Dedication

To the greater Jesus
whose greatness and grandeur
neither I nor anyone
will ever completely capture.
May your name be lifted higher and higher.

And to the greatest overcomer
I've ever met or known,
my wife and state representative,
Cindy Noē.
You are so amazing in so many ways!
Yes, you do live in and operate out of the Holy City,
and for the purpose of healing of our state and the nations.

Contact Us:

EAST2WEST PRESS
Pioneering the next reformation

www.east2westpress.org

Publishing arm of . . .

PRI
PROPHECY
REFORMATION
INSTITUTE

5236 East 72nd Street
Indianapolis, IN 46250
www.prophecyrefi.org
jnoe@prophecyrefi.org
Ph. # 317-842-3411

Contents

Author's Note – My Continuing Quest *ix*

Introduction – What Is Jesus Like and Doing Today? 1

PART I – UNLEARNING

Chapter 1 – Why You Don't Have to Wait Around for the 'Second Coming' or 'Return' 21

Chapter 2 – Confronting Centuries of Confusion 57

Chapter 3 – Unraveling the Mysteries of the Unveiling 81

PART II – NEW DISTINCTIVES

Chapter 4 – He Rides a Horse on the Clouds 121

Chapter 5 – He Still Comes in Many Wondrous Ways 155

Chapter 6 – He Hosts a Grand Banquet 189

Chapter 7 – He Fights the 'Battle of Armageddon' 221

Chapter 8 – He Plagues the Great Prostitute 251

Chapter 9 – He 'Raptures' a Remnant   291

Chapter 10 – He Wants You to Live in the City   339

Conclusion – He Stands Up for Heroes—the Ultimate Honor   391

Appendix A – My Patmos Pilgrimage and Revelation   397

Appendix B – My ETS Revelation Experience   413

More Books from John Noē   417

What's Next?   423

Scripture Index   425

Endnotes   441

Author's Note

My Continuing Quest

Thirty-some years ago, I began my quest for truth and understanding regarding the Bible and the Christian faith. In the Author's Note for my book, *The Perfect Ending for the World*, I wrote—"In retrospect, my journey has taken me to new heights of understanding, practical relevancy, and spiritual appreciation."[1]

During that time, one of the toughest questions I have sought to answer is this: *Who is Jesus in modern terms?* This book addresses that question. It is another product of my quest and another opportunity for you to travel along with me on a portion of that journey. As you do, I hope you will discover, as have I, that Jesus of Nazareth has changed. This revelation is the essence of this book and the basis for its title.

Accordingly, let me challenge you, as I have been challenged, to broaden your perception from the traditional way most people picture Jesus in their mind's eye and have come to know and follow Him, and to see Him as He really is today. The Bible—which I believe every word is true—clearly and emphatically reveals significant changes in Jesus. In the pages that follow, please read carefully, consider closely (even if you don't agree at first), and test and prove everything I present (1 Thess. 5:21).

Who is Jesus in modern terms?

What's So Unique?

Over the centuries, no idea has gripped the human imagination more firmly than the doctrine of a Second Coming and Return of Jesus Christ. Nor has any idea ever created more needless confusion, anxiety, or spiritual poverty among Christians and more discredited Christ's Church in the eyes of the world. As dates have come and gone, history has continually proven false those who have tried to predict when this most anticipated event will occur. Initially, this pursuit was considered a fringe movement or flat-out heresy. However, within the past sixty short years it has become a central tenet of American Protestantism and prime preoccupation of evangelical Christians. So we have seen a barrage of predictions, along with their missed times and dates. But with every war or global disturbance, a new wave of predictive books and materials suddenly appears. In their wake, all of these writers and teachers have been left with one thing in common: they have all been wrong. Unfortunately, this fact does not seem to deter the next wave of date-setters eager to capitalize on this fascination and fear.[2]

This book is timely because, once again, a new date is approaching for the apocalyptic end of the world as we know it—December 21, 2012 (based on predictions from the Mayan calendar). When this date comes and goes (and it will) and the dust settles, perhaps we earthlings will be more receptive to discovering some of the central truths contained herein.[3] I assure you; these revelations and realizations will not only transform your daily life, they will transform you.

Why I Wrote This Book

This book is not only a synopsis of some of the most relevant truths and empowering realities I have discovered during my thirty-some-year study and research into the Scriptures. It is also the product of ideas formed during my doctoral studies and in development and presentation of several theological papers over the past eighteen years. These efforts resulted in an article published in 2006 in the *Journal of the Evangelical Theological Society*. That article forms the theological basis for this book (See two personal interest stories on this background in Appendices A and B).⁴ Hence, you will find this book well-grounded in the ancient authority of the Bible and in the living Word of God, Who is Jesus Christ (John 1:1-2).

Some of the material in this book may seem familiar to those who read my book *The Apocalypse Conspiracy* (Brentwood, TN.: Wolgemuth & Hyatt / Word, 1991). But since its publication, I have made several changes, additions, and improvements in my theology. All this and more is contained herein, and, in essence, renders that previous book obsolete. I send this revised, enhanced, and expanded material forth to do what work it may; believing that the truth will prevail.

I further believe the time is at hand to move on from the well-trodden and exhausted search for the historical Jesus to a quest for today's Christ. Please be assured, however, that I am not recommending we abandon or diminish the former for the latter. As you will see, the historical Jesus was and is important—very important. But what is more important, is what Jesus is like and doing today. Thus, I am proposing a coming together, a synthesis, of the two.

For many of you this synthesis will require a radical reassessment of the image of Jesus you have crafted in your mind and a shift in your theological/spiritual paradigm. For those deeply entrenched in the historical Jesus tradition, this reassessment and shift will likely be uncomfortable, at least at first. For that reason, I pray you will test everything herein (1 Thess. 5:21), earnestly and honestly wrestle with the issues raised, and not allow your particular tradition to blind or confuse you (Mark 7:13; Matt. 15:6). Instead, be like the Bereans who were commended for being of "more noble character" because they "examined the Scriptures every day to see if what Paul said was true" (Acts 17:11). For non-Christians and those Christians who take Scripture as less authoritative than I, my presentation may be less persuasive. But, at the least, I trust you will find it thought-provoking.

As we go about our quest together, I do not intend to provide an exhaustive explanation of every word or verse in the Bible, or to cover everything that Jesus is or may or may not be doing today. If this kind of disclaimer was good enough for John (see John 20:30), it's good enough for me and I shall leave that task for others as they build upon this work.⁵

Also, I am not writing for scholars, *per* se; but I am writing for intelligent people who want to know more about Jesus and, possibly, follow Him as He is today. Hence, my primary goal is to encourage all of us to take a serious new look at Jesus Christ in his unveiled, revealed, and contemporary form. I believe this higher and greater perspective of Him will ring true and stir you on to greater heights of faith and the practice thereof. At the same time, however, I have utilized endnotes to provide additional details, references, and sources. They can be either read or ignored.

My further hope is this book will provide some common ground upon which Christians can come together to know, worship, and serve God in greater harmony and effectiveness. In recent decades, Christendom has experienced far too much confusion, conflict, and complacency. All this divisiveness has made a mockery of the Church in the eyes of the world.[6] Consequently, this book is offered in the same spirit Moses exhibited when he threw a tree into the bitter waters of Marah and made them sweet (Exod. 14:22-26).

For many of you this synthesis will require a radical reassessment of the image of Jesus you have crafted in your mind and a shift in your theological/spiritual paradigm.

Let us also remember, as Jesus commanded, that we are to love God not only with "all your heart and with all your soul" but also "with all your mind" (Matt. 22:37). As such, what matters here is not what I think or you think, or I feel or you feel. What matters is what does God's Word, the Bible, actually say and not say. My continuing prayer for you as you read through this book, and as it has been for me during my journey of discovery, is that you will learn to know, love, and follow Jesus more fully with all your heart, soul, *and mind*, and in greater ways than you have dreamed possible.

Yes, I know that one book won't suddenly wipe away all the doctrinal squabbles and long-running conflicts over the historical Jesus, his coming and comings, and his modern-day nature and activities. Admittedly, these have plagued the Church for decades, even centuries. And too often something we perceive as "new" is automatically resisted and rejected. Cindy Jacobs in her recent book, *The Reformation*

Manifesto, accurately describes why this tendency is so prevalent among Christians:

> There is too often a desire to resist something God is doing for the sake of traditions that are not found anywhere in the Bible. Others may want to keep their control and positions of power in a church body rather than letting God have His way.[7]

If this book does indeed enable the grandeur and sweetness of the greater Jesus to take out even a little of the bitterness, it will have been more than worth all my years of labor, prayer, study, and writing.

A Plea for Openness

As was and is true for my other books, I've had to face the possibility that this book may have the opposite effect from what I desire. It may be controversial and divisive. Some may be disturbed or even offended by the notion that Jesus could be any greater than the Jesus Who died for our sins. Others may try to brand me a heretic simply because the contents are so different from what they've been told and taught. Let me remind you that the dictionary defines heresy as "any belief that is against a belief of a church or most people." By that definition, Jesus was a heretic, and so was every New Testament writer. Certainly, they were anti-establishment in regards to the traditional religion of their day. But history has often proven that the majority is wrong. To those who would make the charge of heresy against me, I call you to come to the table with open Bibles and honestly, sincerely, respectfully, and in a civil manner discuss and debate the issues this book, and any of my other books, present.

Others—especially those who insist on a literal/physical interpretation of all apocalyptic symbols—may feel that I have greatly over-spiritualized the Bible's last Book of Revelation. They will argue (as one Bible scholar did) that, if you start spiritualizing a few things, pretty soon you'll have nothing to take literally.

Please be assured that I take plenty literally. But also, I did not start the process of understanding material and physical symbols spiritually. God did! Read the first five books of the Bible, and notice how often

God used physical objects—a rainbow, the blood of a lamb, a pillar of fire—as spiritual symbols. And look how often Jesus used physical/material objects—a coin, weeds, yeast—in his parables to teach and convey realities of the spiritual world.

The truth is, nearly everything in the Bible can be spiritualized, but the opposite is not true. You can attach a spiritual meaning to nearly every physical/material object or event in Scripture, and the writers of the Bible and the early Church very often did. Yet, you cannot always reverse the process. For example, Jesus spoke of being born again as a spiritual reality (John 3:3-21). But try to interpret that analogy literally and physically (as Nicodemus did) and you are re-entering your mother's womb, or reverse it (as some have), and you come up with reincarnation.

As you read this book, let me urge you to be open. Even if you disagree with some of my understandings of prophetic symbols, don't throw out the whole reality the symbols represent. Ask the Holy Spirit to reveal to you the intended meaning of those symbols within the contextual restrictions that a particular section of Scripture places upon itself.

If this book does indeed enable the grandeur and sweetness of the greater Jesus to take out even a little of the bitterness, it will have been more than worth all my years of labor, prayer, study, and writing.

In the final analysis, I am beholden and accountable to both and the one historical and greater Jesus and will be measured by his standard. Throughout my quest for truth and understanding, I have also consistently prayed for "the Spirit of wisdom and revelation, so that you (I) may know him (the God of our Lord Jesus Christ) better" (Eph. 1:17), as well as "know the hope to which he has called you (me)" (Eph. 1:18), and that I would neither add to nor subtract from the truths and realities presented herein—something clearly warned against (see Rev. 22:18-19).

I have also taken great effort to avoid getting caught up in the complex jargon and confusing rhetoric usually associated with writings about Jesus, biblical prophecy, the Book of Revelation, the end times, and other revelational topics. Instead, I've tried to offer here-and-now insights on how we can tap into tremendous power and the unveiled and revealed realities presented in both the Bible's Old and New Testaments. In so doing, I trust I can better present how we can overcome evil in both the spiritual and the physical/material world, here and now.

My hope for you is that this book will stimulate your hunger and thirst for a greater personal revelation of and relationship with the greater Jesus Christ (as He is today) and for the ever-present realities of the spirit dimension. If you come to this book with these expectations, it is my firm belief that you will be encouraged and emboldened to live a higher and greater life for Christ, will have a greater impact in our world, will bring more souls into a saving relationship, and will more greatly advance Christ's kingdom, here and now.

Lastly, I have and do consider it a high honor and privilege to have been enabled to write this book. Its development has also produced some tension. Nonetheless, this book may be my most significant yet or ever because it is about a Person and not a concept. But you be the judge.

So if you are ready for a great and grand adventure, let's begin our quest and journey together with this prayer: May the greater Jesus open our eyes to his glorious truth, "increase our faith" (Luke 17:5b), and his name be lifted higher and higher.

Introduction

What Is Jesus Like and Doing Today?

To get to know someone, anyone, it is important we learn about their past—what they were like and what they did. That's why employers seeking to fill a job position first ask to see a résumé.

But what is more important is what that person is like and doing now. Therefore, if interested, an employer will request a face-to-face interview. Why? It's because people change.

On my seventh birthday, my parents gave me a new baseball glove, uniform, hat, ball, and bat. They then drove me down to the Olin Mills Photography Studio to have professional pictures taken in my new attire to give to my grandparents. Today, a 5 x 7 picture is displayed in both our family scrapbook and a framed one once hung on a stairway wall of my son's home before his family moved. It shows me with a burr haircut in that baseball uniform, hat cocked on the back of my head, bat resting on my shoulder, and, of course, with a charming little smile across my face. My thirteen grandchildren love to make fun of that picture (and me) with teasing little comments like, "Hey, Papa John, you were cute back then." But guess what? I'm not like that anymore. Yes, I'm the same person, but I have changed. You, too, have changed since you were seven. The same is true of Jesus since He was seven, twelve, and thirty and thirty-three, and even before that.

Yet every week in churches around the world people gather to hear a story. For almost two thousand years that story has been told and retold.[1]

During the week, countless more gather in schools, universities, seminaries, conferences, and Bible study groups to hear and consider that same story. In modern times, this story has drawn millions more to the movies, to turn on their TVs and radios, and onto the Internet.

It's the story about a baby born under special circumstances, who was a renowned teacher at age twelve, cared about people, and taught thousands how to live better lives. Yet he was accused of being a heretic, received death threats, and suffered the ultimate penalty for standing up for what he believed. History has proven that this man was the greatest revolutionary the world has ever known. Consequently, this story has been dubbed "the greatest story ever told." It's about a man named Jesus of Nazareth—his birth, life, death, and resurrection.

In 1949, Fulton Oursler penned his timeless best-selling book, *The Greatest Story Ever Told*. In 1965, it was made into a movie with the same title. Both the book and the movie present a fictionalized narrative of the life of Jesus, and cover the time between the betrothal of Mary and Joseph, around 4 B.C., through his death and rumors of his resurrection in A.D. 30

Make no mistake, that story is important—very important. It's about a real historical human being—the historical Jesus—Who walked, breathed, and left huge footprints in the sand of history and in the lives of countless billions ever since.

But that story is also 2,000-year-old history!

How Do You Picture Jesus?

> *Just a closer walk with Thee,*
> *Grant it, Jesus, is my plea,*
> *Daily, walking close to Thee,*
> *Let it be, dear Lord, let it be.*

When many of us sing this classic hymn, "Just a Closer Walk with Thee," we experience a warm fuzzy feeling as we vicariously contemplate this special kind of a time with Jesus. But let me ask you a question. When you sing this hymn, or other hymns about Jesus, or when you pray, talk to, or think about Him, how do you picture Jesus in your mind's eye? If you are like most of us, your mental picture is probably of the historical Jesus of Nazareth, the one we read about in the Gospels, hear about in church services, and study in Sunday school classes. At Christmas time we might picture Him as the "Christmas Jesus," a sleeping and cuddly little baby lying in a manger; at other times, as boy growing up, or a young man ministering in Galilee, or as our Savior hanging on a cross at Calvary.

Over the past two-and-a-half centuries, a field of study has arisen that is termed the search for the historical Jesus. This search has produced thousands of books battling over and attempting to discover more about this Jesus of Nazareth. Some of these writers accept the Scriptures as authoritative, perhaps inspired, infallible, and inerrant, and proceed from there. Others do not, and see no reason to treat the Bible any differently from any other book. So they approach the scriptural accounts critically, preferring to augment or discredit them using other historical sources, human reasoning, and/or naturalistic speculations.

During the past twenty-plus years many more historical-Jesus books have been written on all levels and from different perspectives. Each specializes upon trying to find an alternative to the traditional Jesus, i.e., the "real," "true," "other," "third," "Rabbi," "a wild Messiah," "re-Judaized" Jesus or "the real story of Jesus," "Simply Jesus: A New Vision of Who He Was, What He Did, and Why He Matters,"[2] or "The Jesus I Never Knew,"[3] etc. This year (as I write) a new book has come out from a rabbi. It's titled *Kosher Jesus* and is causing quite a heretical stir in rabbinical circles as it insists that "Jesus lived the life of a devoted Jew. His rebellion was not against Jewish law, but mostly against Roman brutality."[4] Naturally, this book has already drawn a response book titled, *The Real Kosher Jesus*, which counterclaims that Jesus "was the most influential Jewish man who ever lived—and the most controversial."[5]

> **Over the past two-and-a-half centuries, a field of study has arisen that is termed the search for the historical Jesus.**

The bottom line—according to Philip Yancey in his highly acclaimed book, *The Jesus I Never Knew*— is "more has been written about Jesus in the last twenty years than in the previous nineteen centuries."[6] Hence, the historical Jesus remains a "hot topic."[7]

Some of the probing but contorted questions still being asked by many modern-day scholars further muddy the picture and produce a numbing effect. Questions like: Who really was this Jesus? What did He really say and do? How did He view Himself and his mission? Was He really crucified and resurrected from the dead? Was He human or divine? Did He really do miracles? And even, did He really exist?

Forensic scientists also participate in this search. The renowned Shroud of Turin, for example, has undergone recent testing to determine if the facial image found on its fibers is really the burial face of the historical Jesus of Nazareth, or a fake perpetrated by some clever artist. One thing all these efforts have in common is that they all focus on some portion of the thirty-three years of Jesus' earthly life almost 2,000 years ago. And once again, that life was and is important—very important.

Chances are, if you live in America, the image of Jesus most ingrained in your mind's eye is Warner Sallman's "Head of Christ" painted in 1941. Without a doubt, Sallman's painting has become "the most popular picture of Jesus of all time," having been reproduced "over 500 million times." In addition to hanging on the walls of many Sunday school classrooms and in church offices around the country, it has been "replicated in Bibles, Sunday school literature, calendars, posters, church bulletins, and even on lamps, buttons, and bumper stickers." Countless Christians and non-Christians, alike, would recognize this picture of Jesus. (To see this picture of Jesus and the source of these above quotes, go to www.godweb.org/sallman.htm.)

Sallman painted Jesus as a young, tender and slender, handsome, meek and mild, sensitive and serene, intelligent-looking, white, Anglo-Saxon man who is gazing up to heaven with expressive eyes, and long brown hair parted in the middle and flowing over his shoulders. His calm face is full of sweetness and love, without a blemish or wrinkle, with a faultless nose and mouth, and a nicely trimmed beard.

Whether this picture is an accurate representation of the historical Jesus' physical appearance is highly contestable. But the Bible offers scant description. Notably, not one New Testament author provides a physical description of the earthly, historical Jesus. We don't even know if He was tall or short. Also notable is that for more than 300 years after his crucifixion, church authorities forbade the making of any images of Jesus for fear they would be idolized. Instead, symbols were used, like a fish and Greek letters for fish, *ichthys*—the first letters of an acrostic meaning "Jesus Christ Son of God Savior." Islam, to this day, allows no images or cartoons of its prophet Muhammad, believing this constitutes blasphemy and requires death for anyone so doing.

Not surprisingly, some Christians have reacted strongly against Sallman's painting of Jesus because of its effeminate character, non-Jewish appearance (i.e., pink colored skin and blue eyes and long flowing hair), its soft lighting, and retouched commercial-studio-photograph likeness. Yet this ridiculously inaccurate caricature of a Jewish Jesus appeals to many who long for an intimate and personal relationship with a warm, friendly, and familiar face. And admittedly, it is hard to erase that picture from memory when it has been so deeply etched into our brain cells.

One of the problems this popular image of Jesus creates, as writer Brandon O'Brien points out, is that "a meek and mild Jesus eventually is a bore. He doesn't inspire us." Furthermore, this is "the aspect of church that men find least appealing." O'Brien insists that "Jesus is not a 'limp-wrist-ed, dress-wearing hippie'" and "men created in his image are not sissified church boys." Yet he contends that "allowing women to create Jesus in their image has emasculated him."[8]

Likewise, J.B. Phillips in his appropriately titled book, *Your God Is Too Small*, laments that we have spawned little nursery rhymes about Jesus that hundreds of thousands have learned in their childhood, and which have infected their minds with reductionistic visual images of Jesus, such as:

> Little Jesus, meek and mild,
>
> Look upon a little child.
>
> ~
>
> Christian children all must be
>
> Mild, obedient, good as He.[9]

Phillips criticizes "mild" as "the least appropriate" epithet for Jesus because it conjures up to our minds "a picture of someone who wouldn't say 'boo' to the proverbial goose; someone who would let sleeping dogs lie and avoid trouble wherever possible; someone of a placid temperament . . . someone who is a bit of a nonentity, both uninspired and uninspiring . . . . Yet it is this fatal combination of 'meek and mild' which has been so often, and is even now, applied to Him."[10] He sadly concludes that "we can hardly be surprised if children feel fairly soon that they have outgrown the 'tender Shepherd' and find their heroes elsewhere."[11]

Elsewhere in today's world also we find a number of other visual images of Jesus. They may be drawn from any number of ancient mosaics, paintings, frescos, drawings, sculptures, or stained-glass windows created by artists across the centuries as they imagined Him to have looked.

Or perhaps your mental picture may have been imprinted in your imagination from a movie—the latest being of a beaten and crucified Jesus hanging on a cross and portrayed by the handsome and blue-eyed James Caviezel in Mel Gibson's 2004 blockbuster film, *The Passion of the Christ*.

On the other hand, and if you are a college football fan, you have been treated to the sight of a somewhat-farcical, arms-raised "Touchdown Jesus" peering over the top of Notre Dame's football stadium from a giant mural painted on the side of a campus building.

With the possible exception of a crucified Jesus, the one thing all these modern-day pictures have in common is, they present Jesus in a safe, sanitized, soft, tame, and tender manner. Yes, we are comfortable by these "to-Thy-bosom" images. They soothe us even though they may be nothing more than projections of our own heart-felt wishes.

The world likes these nice images of Jesus as well. After all, who can object to a baby or a comely and sedentary Jesus relegated to live in the innocuous realm of human hearts and behind church doors? Practically speaking, the above images of Jesus fit quite well within societal norms and can easily be taken or left behind.

In other parts of the world, one can choose from a bewildering number of portraits of Jesus. Seems his physical appearance easily adapts to fit ethnic tastes. So in the Far East, Jesus is seen as an oriental; to the Indians, He's an Indian; to the Africans and some African-Americans, He's black; to the Chinese, He's Chinese.

Let's face it; all of us tend to gravitate toward identifiable and non-threatening pictures of Jesus. And since no actual paintings, drawings, or renderings of Him exist, nor were there cameras or video recorders back in Jesus' time, we feel free to impart our own image and/or latch on to whatever non-threatening one appeals to our whims—as we want Him to be. But the Apostle Paul warned about preaching another Jesus "other than the Jesus we preached" (2 Cor. 11:4a), i.e., the one revealed in Scripture. The f act is, the "Jesus" critical scholars write about is always less than the Bible's eternal God Who lowered Himself to become human flesh, lived on this earth, died for our sins, was resurrected, and ascended back to the Father in heaven.

In spite of these questionable depictions and characterizations of Jesus, the historical Jesus has proven to be the most challenging and controversial figure of human history. Consequently, many view the historical Jesus with contempt. Others dismiss Him as an ancient myth, culturally and contemporarily irrelevant. And some people in our "postmodern world. . . . [who] don't care about the historical evidence for Jesus anymore,"[12] nonetheless view Him as a pop-culture icon and wear Jesus and/or Christian paraphernalia or trivialize Him on fashionable T-shirts, bumper stickers, coffee mugs, or on the stage. Others freely use Jesus' name to curse by, but for some reason don't use the name of any other religious leader for this purpose.

In so many ways, over and over again, we see an awareness of Jesus throughout many different societies and areas of culture. It seems "we cannot get away from this man Jesus."[13] Thus, the historical Jesus remains important—very important. Again, this unique prominence is why volumes upon volumes continue being written and offering a wide variety of opinions about Him. Something about the historical Jesus transcends all this reality. And surveys continue to show that over 80 percent of Americans believe Jesus of Nazareth was God or the Son of God. But what is more important, and what we shall be exploring throughout this book, is, *He's not like that* (any of that) *anymore!*

Unveiling and Revealing Today's Jesus

If you want to see the latest and only full-blown, physically descriptive picture of Jesus we have today—one that is sharp, clear, true, authoritative, and more revealing and challenging than any of the above images—there is only one place you can go. That is to the greatly misunderstood and abused Book of Revelation.

Unfortunately, this last book of the Bible has both fascinated and frustrated Bible readers for centuries. Its apocalyptic content and symbolic style still confuse and frighten most readers. Hence, Philip Yancey terms it "a strange book by any measure."[14] But this book's first five words make it perfectly clear that its purpose and over-arching theme is not to satisfy our intellectual curiosity about distant, future events or the proverbial end of the world, but to unveil and reveal Jesus as He now is. It's "the revelation of Jesus Christ" (Rev. 1:1).

The apostle John, one of Jesus' original apostles, received this revelation from both an angel and from Jesus Christ Himself while exiled on the isle of Patmos in the Mediterranean Sea some time during the 1st century.[15] The Greek word translated "revelation" is *apokalypsis*. It's our word "apocalypse." The kind of imagery that comes to most people's mind in our day when they see or hear the word apocalypse is total devastation, a nuclear holocaust, or an exploding universe. That's why we have books and movies like *The Four Horsemen of the Apocalypse* and *Apocalypse Now*. But what did this word mean to John, who wrote down the Revelation, and to the Greek-speaking people he wrote and sent this book to nineteen centuries ago?

The Greek word *apokalypsis* simply means an "unveiling" or "uncovering" *of* Jesus Christ. Interestingly, the Greek preposition translated as *of*, contains two meanings—one meaning is *from*, the other meaning is *about*. Hence, the Bible's last book is not just *from* Jesus Christ, which gives it incontestable authority. It is also a visual allegory and unveiling and revealing *about* Jesus Christ in his present, ascended, exalted, glorified, transformed, transfigured, transcendent, apocalyptic, crowned, and cosmic form—who He now is, what He now is like and doing. It further reveals his past, present, and future involvement and interactions with both humankind and spirit-realm beings. Yet most current teachings, books, and movies on the Revelation conclude that the book is primarily about Satan, his cohorts, and an imaginary Antichrist and what they are supposedly going to be doing to our world at some future date.

A prime example is the runaway, mega-best-selling *Left Behind* series. This series of books and three spawned movies purport to be a fictional portrayal of the end times as described through the Book of Revelation. Its storyline is based upon the two authors' popular position that we are now living in the "the earth's last days," as the subtitle for their first book in this series states, *Left Behind: A Novel of the Earth's Last Days.*

Authors Tim LaHaye and Jerry B. Jenkins believe that the Revelation's message is this: soon, some day in the future, "in one cataclysmic moment, millions around the globe [will] disappear" in the Rapture.[16] Then the Antichrist will take over and wreck havoc throughout the world. Tellingly, their main character in their sensational series and three movies is the Antichrist and not Jesus. But I have searched in vain to find any mention of an Antichrist in the Book of Revelation.[17]

As we shall see throughout this book, i.e., the one you hold in your hands, such interpretations are gross distortions of God's Word, as well as a misrepresentation of the Revelation's stated purpose and content. Sad to say, the above Antichrist misunderstanding is the tip of the iceberg when it comes to the erroneous ideas many people have imported into this most important and last book of the Bible. And yet multiple millions of people, both within and outside the Church, believe such works as *Left Behind* are biblically accurate. Other Christians within the Church, and along with me, contest *Left Behind's* system of understanding the Scriptures, and rightfully so.

No wonder, however, millions are frightened by Revelation's prophecy and have missed its stated purpose. They also miss out on its promised blessings in this life, here and now (Rev. 1:3; 22:7). It seems the very trap the Revelation warns about—adding to or taking away from the prophecy of this book (Rev. 22:18-19)—has ensnared millions of people and thousands of churches. The result of disobeying this warning has been to strip the Apocalypse of its present reality and life-giving power.

And yet this bottom-line fact remains, if you really want to know and follow Jesus as He is today—what He's now like and doing—you must come, expectantly, to this last book of the Bible. The Book of Revelation is the climax, the completion, the pinnacle of God's progressive revelation to humankind. It is the only source that unveils and reveals Jesus of Nazareth in his present-day, pertinent, and full reality. It's the transformational vision of *the Jesus of the Apocalypse, the Christ in our midst today, and a much greater Jesus than most of us have been led to believe!* This is the more glorious Jesus each of us needs to meet, know, take seriously, and follow.

From within the pages of God's ultimate and climatic prophecy—shockingly for some, refreshingly for others—we can discover many amazing things about the unveiled and fully revealed Christ in our midst today, such as:

- He looks different than the way we usually picture and think of Him.
- He's not just sitting around up in heaven waiting to come back.
- He's in our midst all around the world.
- He drops in unexpectedly and occasionally.
- He still comes in many wondrous ways.
- He rides a horse on the clouds.
- He hosts a grand banquet.
- He fights the battle of Armageddon.
- He plagues the great prostitute.
- He raptures a remnant.
- He wants you to live in the city.
- He stands up for heroes.
- And much more.

Make no mistake, this is the living and active Jesus of today, Who also sits at the right hand of God (Rom. 8:34; Heb.8:1), is our High Priest (Heb. 4:14-15; 8:1), makes intercession for us (Rom. 8:34; Heb. 7:25), is our "mediator between God and men" (1 Tim. 2:5), and much more as the New Testament Scriptures reveal. But the above bulleted points will be our delimited scope and focus in this book as we attempt to unearth key distinctives about *the greater* Jesus—Who is in the world, in our midst, and functions in a *much greater* manner and in *much broader* capacities than most of us have been led to believe.

No longer is this ascended, exalted, glorified, transformed, transfigured, transcendent, apocalyptic, crowned, and cosmic Christ of the Revelation the earth-bound, historical Jesus we have come to know and love. No longer is He the sleeping baby in the manger we celebrate every Christmas, or the boy who played in Galilee, or the man they hung at Calvary, or even the lamb who died for you and me. Simply put, those views of Jesus are out-of-date and inadequate. *No, He's not like that anymore.*

And yet, He's the same Jesus Who was equal in every way with the Father and made the whole creation (Col. 1:15-17), but Who willingly surrendered aspects of his divinity, left the glory of heaven, lowered Himself to take on human flesh, was born of a virgin, raised as a boy, ministered throughout Judea, suffered scorn and rejection, endured the agony of the cross, and died for you and me. Without this historical Jesus we would still be lost in our sins (1 Cor. 15:17). So we must stay grounded in this historical Jesus Who was "made a little lower than the angels" (Heb. 2:7, 9) and "made Himself nothing, taking the very nature [form] of a servant, being made in human likeness" (Phil. 2:7) in order to show us God, bring in the everlasting form of God's kingdom, and provide the perfect sacrifice. We must never diminish this Jesus.

But He did not stay lowered or confined in an earthly human body. Nowadays, He is both the same and the greater Jesus. Why is this so? It is because after his birth, earthly life, death, burial, resurrection, and ascension, "God exalted him to the highest place and gave him the name that is above every name that at the name of Jesus every knee should bow, in heaven and on earth, and every tongue confess that Jesus Christ is Lord, to the glory of God the Father" (Phil. 2:8-11; also Eph. 1:20-23). "So he became as much superior to the angels as the name he has inherited is superior to theirs" (Heb. 1:4).

Simply put, those views of Jesus are out-of-date and inadequate. *No, He's not like that anymore.*

Today, we must also recognize that the divinely determined mission of Jesus—his leaving heaven, lowering Himself, coming to earth, and going back to heaven—was a massive change in both his bodily form and ministerial capacities. Thus, Revelation's last revealed form of Jesus is a more glorious and complex Jesus than during his earthly ministry. Whether you agree or disagree with me on this point at this time, one thing is for sure. This same Jesus has changed somehow—from before creation to cradle to cross to coronation. Perhaps the one thing we can now agree upon, and hopefully you will be able to fully agree after you read the rest of this book, is that this Jesus today, Who is in our midst, is a *much greater* Jesus than has been and is generally being presented, preached, and perceived.

The tragedy for many people in most churches today is, they are missing out on this greater Jesus. They don't know Jesus in the greater way the Revelation unveils and reveals Him. In my opinion, this deficiency accounts for much of the lack of faith and power in the Church and its effectiveness in the world today. Yet every year we present to Christians and non-Christians alike the ever-so-popular image of baby Jesus—so tiny, so adorable, and so helpless. Frankly put, fixating on and perpetuating this 2,000-year-old image of the historical Jesus, or any image of Him during his earthly life, is, at best, a partial view.

T. M. Moore strongly voices this condescending problem in a recent article titled, "The Jesus We Preach at Christmas," in Chuck Colson's *BreakPoint Worldview* magazine:

> What bothers me more and more each year is the way Jesus is presented to the masses . . . . as though Christ's coming on that first Christmas were the end of the story, rather than its beginning . . . . a seasonal dose of peace and goodwill, expressed in a veritable shark feed of gifts and giving . . . . Many Christians go along with . . . downplaying their faith at Christmas time. They don't want to offend unsaved family members . . . . [or] those twice-a-year visitors . . . . We will only recover the true meaning of Christmas when preachers begin proclaiming the whole message of Christ from their pulpits.[18]

In my opinion, that "whole message of Christ" must include an accurate and up-to-date presentation of Jesus as He is today—not only during Christmas time to the masses, but all year long to the regulars. I also believe a change of this magnitude would change many things for the better. For one, the Bible's last book teaches that the more you know and follow Jesus as He now is, the Jesus of the Apocalypse, the more spiritual blessings and power will be unleashed in and through your life.

Hence, this book, the one you hold in your hands, is your opportunity to discover some of those wondrous truths about the greater Jesus in our midst today and to enable you to appropriate the blessings and power promised in the Revelation (Rev. 1:3; 22:7). My prayer, therefore, is that your heart will be stirred, your mind challenged, your faith awakened, your emotions fired, and your intentions refueled to know and follow the

Christ in our midst as He is today, to worship Him more devotedly, and to serve Him more obediently and effectively, so help you God.

'But He's Not Like That Anymore!'

Verse 1 *It's Christmas morning everyone*
Time for joy and time for fun
With Mom and Dad and family
We gather 'round the Christmas tree

Verse 2 *But remember Jesus He was born*
Long ago one Christmas morn
He lived a blessed life on earth
That's why we celebrate Jesus' birth

Refrain:

But He's not like that anymore
No, He's not like that anymore
He's glorified in the highest
He's not like that anymore
No, He's not like that
No, He's not like that
No, He's not like that anymore

Verse 3 *The babe the son of Mary*
The boy who played in Galilee
The man they hung at Calvary
The Lamb Who died for you and me

Repeat Refrain

– Lyrics and music by John Noē

So if you are ready for this great and challenging experience, let's take an introductory look at Jesus as He is today, a Jesus Who is much greater than most of us have been led to believe!

The Latest Picture of Jesus

The first chapter of the Book of Revelation (the Apocalypse) unveils and reveals the latest and only full-blown, physically descriptive picture of Jesus in the Bible. By inspiration, John records what he heard and saw when Jesus literally and physically came, appeared, touched, spoke to, and commissioned him on the island of Patmos over nineteen hundred years ago:

> *I, John, your brother and companion in the suffering and kingdom and patient endurance that are ours in Jesus, was on the island of Patmos because of the word of God and the testimony of Jesus. On the Lord's Day I was in the Spirit, and I heard behind me a loud voice like a trumpet, which said: "Write on a scroll what you see and send it to the seven churches: to Ephesus, Smyrna, Pergamum, Thyatira, Sardis, Philadelphia, and Laodicea.*
>
> *I turned around to see the voice that was speaking to me. And when I turned I saw seven golden lampstands, and among the lampstands was someone "like a son of man," dressed in a robe reaching down to his feet and with a golden sash around his chest. His head and hair were white like wool, as white as snow, and his eyes were like blazing fire. His feet were like bronze glowing in a furnace, and his voice was like the sound of rushing waters. In his right hand he held seven stars, and out of his mouth came a sharp double-edged sword. His face was like the sun shining in all its brilliance.*
>
> (Revelation 1:9-16)

Make no mistake; this is Jesus *as He is now!* We are not told the meaning of the sword coming out of his mouth or why his hair is white and his eyes like blazing fire. Nor are we told why a crown of thorns no longer encircles his head. But one thing is sure. He is no longer the Jesus of popular thought and tradition. He is that, of course, but He is now much more.

Grasping the full reality of this divinely revealed and new image of Jesus and knowing and serving Him as He is today, and as He requires, are essential prerequisites if we hope to hear the words someday, "Well done, good and faithful servant" (Matt. 25:21, 23; Rev. 1:3; 22:7). Anything less is less. But where is this image of Jesus being presented, nowadays? Where is this picture of today's Christ hanging on a wall? Where is this present-day and pertinent perspective being taught, studied, and worshiped?

Since the time John personally saw and experienced Jesus like this, Jesus has not changed. Therefore, we can definitely affirm that "Jesus Christ is the same yesterday and today and forever" (Heb. 13:8). That is, He is the same in his Personhood and divinity—the second Person of the Trinity.

Critical Objection: Some theologians contend that the word "yesterday" means Jesus has never changed from his preexistence before creation and ever since.[19] That assertion, however, is only partially true as William Hendriksen properly explains, "He is the same Savior, yet different from the days of his humiliation."[20]

Sadly, a partial truth parading as a whole truth is a lie! The testimony of Scripture is, Jesus *has changed*—in major, magnificent, and significant ways—from his preexistent form, into a babe, into a boy, into a man, into a dead man, into a resurrected body, and onto being the ascended, exalted, glorified, transformed, transfigured, and transcendent, crowned, and cosmic Christ, the *Jesus of the Apocalypse!*

Another factor these theologians overlook is, more than 12,000 literal "yesterdays" have transpired between Jesus' ascension and glorification in A.D. 30 (see Dan. 7:13-14) and the time of the writing of this verse in the book of Hebrews circa A.D. 65-67. Thus, and for more reasons we shall cover shortly, we can both affirm that Jesus "is the same yesterday and today and forever" and yet He has changed. For one, and as most Christians will agree, Jesus is now interceding for us (Rom. 8:34). Well, that's a change, isn't it? He wasn't doing that before his birth and earthly ministry days, was He?

So how did John respond after seeing and hearing Jesus this way in the Revelation? Remember, John had personally known and served Jesus during his earthly ministry, had stood at the foot of the cross, and even saw Jesus after his death in his post-resurrected form. Yet this Jesus of the Apocalypse was so different, so awesome, and so much greater than John had previously known that he reports, "When I saw him, I fell at his feet as though dead" (Rev. 1:17a).

Ask yourself, how would you respond if Jesus suddenly appeared to you face-to-face, like this, and in this form? Well, if you have the eyes of faith, i.e., spiritual eyes to see, He just did. Otherwise, these words in the first chapter of the Revelation are only ink on a page. One of the blessings the Book of Revelation offers is for Jesus to appear to you, personally, face-to-face, here and now, as He is today, through these inspired words.

Prior to being exiled on the isle of Patmos, John had written, "But we know that when he appears [is made known / is manifested] . . . we shall see him as he is" (1 John 3:2). Once again, this unveiling and revealing is the primary purpose of the Book of Revelation. And when we let Jesus appear to us this way, by what we might call spiritual reading, we can come to know and have communion with Him as He is today—and not just know about Him as He was some 2,000 years ago.

Given this insight, we shall no longer be limited to view Christ only from a worldly or fleshly perspective but rather in an apocalyptic, heavenly light (see 2 Cor. 5:16). Not everyone, however, will accept nor will they receive this unveiled and revealed experience of Jesus. Why not? It is for the same reason Jesus pointed out when his first disciples asked Him, "Why do you speak to the people in parables?" (Matt. 13:10). He responded:

> *'Though seeing, they do not see;*
> *though hearing, they do not hear or understand.'*
> *In them is fulfilled the prophecy of Isaiah:*
> *'You will be ever hearing but never understanding;*
> *you will be ever seeing but never perceiving.*
> *For this people's heart has become calloused;*
> *they hardly hear with their ears,*
> *and they have closed their eyes.*
> *Otherwise they might see with their eyes,*
> *hear with their ears,*
> *understand with their hearts*
> *and turn, and I would heal them.'*
>
> (Matthew 13:13-15, from Isaiah 6:9-10; also see Ezekiel 40:4; John 12:39-41; Acts 28:25-27)

So, how about you? Can you now see Jesus in this different way? Later in the Revelation, John will see Him several more times in different but visionary forms. After John is transported to the throne room of God in heaven, Revelation's vision portion commences (Rev. 4). John will see Him as: a slain lamb standing with seven horns and seven eyes (Rev. 5); then perhaps as a mighty angel holding a little scroll (Rev. 10); next as a male child Who was to rule all nations with a rod of iron (Rev. 12); then sitting on a white cloud wearing a golden crown and holding a sharp sickle (Rev. 14); next as a rider on a white horse with the armies of heaven following Him (Rev. 19); and lastly on a great white throne from whose face the earth and the heaven fled (Rev. 20).

Each of these visionary and symbolic glimpses of the Jesus of the Apocalypse gives us a different perspective on Jesus today—i.e., portraying via metaphors the broad range of what He's like and doing. The fact is, we have no other language with which to convey the present-day realities of a transcendent God.

Much more is waiting for us to unveil and reveal regarding this same but *greater Jesus*. Admittedly, these picturesque glimpses of Jesus of the Apocalypse are symbolic. But they do reveal awesome truths about his glory and power. Please keep in mind that behind every biblical sign or symbol is a practical and relevant reality—more practical, more relevant, and more powerful than if these images were merely understood literally and futuristically. So what do they mean? When correctly understood, one thing they mean is, Jesus of Nazareth has changed, and yet He is still the same Person.

So, how about you? Can you now see Jesus in this different way?

After John personally saw Him like this, face-to-face, in Revelation's first chapter, this greater Jesus placed his right hand on John, comforted, and commissioned him to "Write, therefore, what you have seen, what is now and what will take place later" (Rev. 1:19). This is how and why we have the Book of Revelation today. Again, it is the ultimate, the pinnacle, the climax of God's progressive revelation to humankind. Honestly, it unveils and reveals a lot more pertinent, here-and-now truths and realities than most Christian prophecy teachers, Bible commentators, and preachers have conveyed to us. Revelation's first chapter sets the stage. But there is much more to be unveiled and revealed about this Jesus of the Apocalypse, the greater Jesus of today. While in a fleshly human body, He was restricted in what He could do. But no longer.

Before we get into more of the present-day reality of this greater Jesus, however, we must unlearn some things. Alas, unlearning can be the hardest form of learning. And yet with all the confusion surrounding Jesus, the proper interpretation and understanding of the Bible's last Book of Revelation is absolutely necessary if we want to know and follow Jesus as He really is today. Therefore, our first three chapters will address this task of unlearning—"for," as Jesus said, "there is nothing hidden that will not be disclosed, and nothing concealed that will not be known or brought out into the open" (Luke 8:17).

So if you are ready for an apocalyptic adventure of transcendent proportions, and unlike any you may have encountered before, read on! Prepare to be challenged, stirred, and perhaps frightened. John was, when He saw Jesus like this. But this greater Jesus is the Jesus of today, and a *much greater and more glorious Jesus* than most of us have been led to believe, than we celebrate every year at Christmas time, and than we worship almost every Sunday. We need to stop seeing Jesus only as Jesus of Nazareth—because He's not like that anymore. We need to get a bigger picture of Jesus, to lift his name higher, and to step up our faith. There is only one place we can go to do this. We've got to start seeing, proclaiming, and following Him as John the Revelator saw, proclaimed, and followed Him.

So which Jesus is the Jesus you follow?

Revelation's first chapter sets the stage. But there is much more to be unveiled and revealed about this Jesus of the Apocalypse, the greater Jesus of today.

Let's continue our quest and our journey together by first examining the issue you might have the most trouble unlearning—why you don't have to wait around for the so-called "Second Coming" or "Return" of Jesus.

Part I – UNLEARNING

Chapter 1

Why You Don't Have to Wait Around for the 'Second Coming' or 'Return'

So much is riding on this unlearning issue that we shall start this book with this chapter.

Newspapers have a special name for their largest and boldest headline type—the type used only for the biggest stories they will ever be called upon to report. They call it *second coming type*.

One of the milestones in the advance of "Second-Coming" doctrine from the fringe to the status quo in recent history was the publication of *The Late Great Planet Earth* by Hal Lindsey (1970). In it (and in a raft of sequels), Lindsey made the bold assertion that we are living in "the terminal generation" preceding Jesus' Second Coming. Although, he was not so bold as to set a specific date, others have not been so careful.[1]

Fifty-some years ago, some Christians who believed that "Jesus was coming again soon" began purchasing wall plaques reading PERHAPS TODAY! Today, they claim "the signs described in the Bible," which were so obvious 50 years ago, have only grown in intensity and "are coming to pass at a rapid rate."[2] Surely, the Lord's Second Coming is not only soon and getting sooner, they surmise, but we are living in "Earth's Final Moments . . . as we look forward to Jesus' return."[3] And even though the nineteen-centuries-and-counting trail of speculative and failed predictions has had a profoundly negative effect upon the Church and upon the credibility of Christianity as a whole, this nonoccurrence factor is ignored in favor of *now* being the right time.

But try this headline as one worthy of the biggest and boldest second-coming type: *"Second Coming Exposed!"*

In this chapter, that's exactly what we'll do. We'll discover from God's Word that the so-called "Second Coming," as well as the "Return" of Christ, are actually biblical misnomers, additions to and subtractions from the book of prophecy (Rev. 22:19), and a highly misleading doctrine. Some, I'm sure, will find this statement to be the most provocative and controversial of this book. Therefore, I feel compelled before continuing to clarify an important point and to affirm to you my belief on this subject.

First, I believe every word the Bible says about the coming of the Lord—but not what most tradition-bound preachers say about it. Secondly, and in the words of the Nicene Creed, "I believe . . . He [Jesus] shall come again with glory to judge both the living and the dead; Whose kingdom shall have no end." As a matter of fact, and as we shall soon see, this creed's phraseology only conveys part of the story. "Now," as the late radio news commentator, Paul Harvey, was so fond of saying, "for the rest of the story"—a much-needed correction and re-direction to a field that is plagued with human-caused problems.

Try This Little Exercise

One of my favorite ground-breaking exercises before beginning a lecture or a Bible study on the topic of this chapter is to ask the following question of any group that feels they have above-average knowledge of the Bible. How would you answer it?

QUESTION: IN YOUR OPINION . . . OVER THE ENTIRE COURSE OF HUMAN HISTORY – PAST, PRESENT AND FUTURE – HOW MANY COMINGS OF JESUS ARE THERE?

ANSWERS: A) ONE? B) TWO? C) THREE? D) FOUR? E) MORE?

Circle the answer you believe is correct.

The responses and reactions this survey question elicits are quite interesting. Some look offended by just its asking (I am aware of how uncomfortable even the asking of these questions can be). A few others act baffled, become defensive, or sit silent thinking it's a trick question. Almost all, however, are amazed by the variety of answers and reasoning that arises from within their own group. Overall, this little exercise serves as an attention-getter and mind-opener causing the participants to take off the blinders and reconsider with me from the Scriptures just what is and what is not true concerning this important, doctrinal tenet of the Christian faith—the coming of the Lord. After all, the Bible does tell us to "test" and to "prove all things" (1 Thess. 5:21). The coming of Jesus is certainly part of "all things."

What answer did you pick? Most people pick "B) Two," because nothing has been more strongly emphasized throughout Church history than the so-called, "Second Coming" of Jesus Christ and its implied limitation of only two comings. But the biblically correct answer is "E) More." Yes, you may be amazed—I was when I first discovered it—at how little knowledge most of us have about the Bible and the Christian faith in this fundamental area.

But try this headline as one worthy of the biggest and boldest second-coming type: *"Second Coming Exposed!"*

Consequently, I want to begin to move you onward and upward from waiting only for the Second Coming to begin to see, through God's Word, the full and glorious reality of Jesus' many comings (plural). Hopefully, this will clear up many misconceptions and open the way for us, as Christians, to unite and stop limiting his comings to merely a past event or a future hope!

Of course, it's not what I or any other human being says about the coming of Jesus that counts, but what the Word of God says about it. So let me urge you to get out your Bible and test everything you read in this chapter—and everywhere else in this book as well.

Neither the Second Coming nor Return of Christ Fits the Terminology of Scripture

Popular TV evangelists, Bible teachers, and church pastors commonly claim that the Bible speaks extensively about the Second Coming of Christ, mentioning it many times in the New Testament.

Billy Graham, for instance, in one of his crusades and in a January 2004 article in his *Decision* magazine titled, "The End of the World," claimed, "the Bible speaks extensively about the Second Coming of Christ, mentioning it more than 300 times in the New Testament. By comparison, repentance . . . is mentioned about 70 times, and baptism . . . is mentioned about 20 times." He concluded, "It is obvious, then, that the Holy Spirit, who inspired the Scriptures, places great importance on the return of Jesus Christ."[4]

With all due respect for Dr. Graham, do you know what the Bible actually says (literally mentions) about a "Second Coming?" Nothing! Nowhere does the Bible use the term *Second Coming*. It's a non-biblical term. Nor does the Bible use the term *Return* in direct association with Jesus.

Factually, the Bible contains many references to many different comings of Jesus, but none to a single "Second Coming." Please be assured that by pointing out this biblical fact, I am not intending to diminish, detract from, or mock the "promise of his coming" in any way. Rather, I'm justifying why the doctrine of a "Second Coming" and "Return" must be faced anew.

Most everyone recognizes that words matter and wording is important. With this in mind, the late-great theologian, George Eldon Ladd, in his highly acclaimed book, *The Blessed Hope*, acknowledged something very important: "The words 'return' and 'second coming' are not properly speaking Biblical words in that the two words do not represent any equivalent Greek words."[5] This is a major admission with huge implications. Another fact is, we Christians have been hamstrung for centuries with these two non-scriptural expressions and unscriptural mindsets. As we shall soon discover, biblically, the idea that Jesus is off somewhere waiting to come back at some future time, as well as the idea of limiting the comings of Jesus to only two or three times, or to any at all, is man's idea and not God's.

The closest we can come to the phraseology of a "Second Coming" is in Hebrews 9:28: "so Christ was sacrificed once to take away the sins of many people; and he will appear *a second time*, not to bear sin, but to bring salvation to those who are waiting for him" (italics added). Contrary to popular belief, this scripture does not limit, number, or confine Jesus' comings to only two times. Rather, it highlights two specific and significant comings, among many (see a partial list in 1 Cor. 15:5-8 for instance), and for a special salvation-fulfillment purpose. This "second-time" coming follows the typology of Israel's high priest on the Day of Atonement, which occurred every year. And Christ as both our sacrifice and our High Priest (see Heb. 7:27-28; 9:11-15) had to come and fulfill this typology, perfectly (see Heb. 8, 9, and 10).[6]

But here's a real shocker of a headline that certainly deserves the use of second-coming type: "Second Coming Reported in Ancient Religious Courtroom!"

Far-fetched? Think about it! If we persist in limiting the comings of Jesus to only two times and in calling the babe in the manger the "first coming" of Jesus, as so many do, that means the "Second Coming" is over. Chronologically, it happened after Jesus was crucified and ascended to heaven, when He came and appeared to Stephen during his trial before the Jewish Sanhedrin (Acts 7:55-56). Or, it happened when Jesus came and appeared to Saul on the road to Damascus (Acts 9:1-8), or to John in the Revelation (Revelation 1 and John 21:22-23). How do you count or discount those comings of Jesus? And, as we shall see shortly, there are many more comings of Jesus.

At this point, you may be feeling a bit perplexed by my last few statements. Or, you may be upset. But before you react in a knee-jerk fashion (again, I know how emotional this can be), let's define what we mean by "a coming of Jesus." Then we'll consider the biblical evidence. Please don't dismiss any of this too quickly, and until you've considered it all.

My working definition for "a coming of Jesus" is this: it's a personal and bodily intervention and/or manifestation of Jesus into the life of an individual, a group, a church, or a nation on this earth. As we shall see, there are many different types of comings for different purposes, and they occur at different times and places. Some are visible appearances; some are invisible interventions. Some are physical (seen, heard, felt); some are spiritual (an internal illumination or revelation); and some are combinations. Theologian Henry A. Virkler calls them "a special manifestation of His presence."[7] Also, there may be other types of comings of which I am not aware, if for no other reason than not everything Jesus did was written down (see John 21:25).

He Never Left

While God's Word clearly documents and teaches that the comings (plural) of Jesus run like a thread throughout both the Old and New Testaments, the word "return" is also never used. Like the expression "Second Coming," it is non-scriptural terminology, an unscriptural concept, and a non-event.[8] To this point, I submit that authentic Christianity does not stand for a departed and absent Christ—absent the entire length of the Christian age! Paradoxically, it stands for a departed but still present and active Christ who never left and has truly, wholly, and totally been *with* his Church and people for over nineteen centuries and is still *with* us today. How do I know He never left? He told us so.

Of course, at one point early in his earthly ministry, Jesus also told his disciples that a time would come when He would be "taken from them" (Mark 2:20). Then later, toward the end of his ministry, Jesus said He was "going there [heaven] to prepare a place for you." And, He promised to "come again" to "take you to be with me that you also may be where I am." (John 14:2-4). He said his going away (John 16:5, 16) was required and the decisive factor for the coming of the Holy Spirit (John 16:7). But also, in what may seem to be a contradiction, He told them that "I will not leave you as orphans" (John 14:18). And then, at the end of his famous Great Commission in Matthew 28:18-20, He also assured his 1st-century followers that He would be *with* them, "And surely I will be *with you always*, to [until] the very end of the age" (italics added, Matt. 28:20b).

In a similar manner, Jesus previously had promised, "For where two or three come together in my name, there am I *with* them" (Matt. 18:20 – italics added). So how can Jesus *go* somewhere, i.e., depart, and still be *with* them? Can these two seemingly paradoxical notions be reconciled?

The traditional explanation has been that what Jesus was really saying was He would be *with* them in the future in the Person of the Holy Spirit, Whom He was to send at Pentecost (see Acts 2). The verse, "the

Lord is the Spirit," is cited in support (2 Cor. 3:17). But the outpouring of the Holy Spirit was a separately and distinctly prophesied event from the Old Testament (see Ezek. 36:26-27; 37:9-14; 39:29; Joel 2:28-32) and a singular happening in the New Testament (see Acts 2). Furthermore, did Jesus really mean He had to "depart" to send Himself back? No New Testament text written twenty or more years later ever acknowledges this outpouring of the Spirit as a coming again of Jesus. To the contrary, many subsequent, New Testament texts, again written after that event, were still anticipating this coming of Christ as yet future.

Besides, if what Jesus really meant was "the Holy Spirit would be with them always," why be so cryptic? He wasn't cryptic anywhere else when He spoke about the Holy Spirit. In John 14, for instance, Jesus spoke, distinctively and by name, about the Holy Spirit and the Holy Spirit's coming (see John 14:15-29). He clearly differentiated between Himself and the Holy Spirit by using the personal pronouns "I" and "him." Moreover, He spoke, clearly and plainly, in the rest of his Great Commission. So why not so in verse 20 as well?

. . . authentic Christianity does not stand for a departed and absent Christ —absent the entire length of the Christian age!

I believe there is a much better explanation. That is, Jesus did speak, clearly, plainly, and distinctively. He meant exactly what He said. He, Jesus, the second Person of the Godhead, would both leave them to go to heaven *and* yet always be with them, and with us today as well, as opposed to the popular idea that He is currently *absent* from this present world and waiting to unscripturally return.

Most notably, when we compare different Bible translations with the original and literal Greek language, we find something quite interesting. For instance, in the popular *New International Version (NIV)*, the phrases "when he returns," "I will come back," "I am coming back," "going back," "until I return," and "Jesus . . . will come back" are found in only seven places in the New Testament (see Matt. 24:46; Luke 12:43; John 14:3, 28; 16:28; 21:22-23; and Acts 1:11, respectively). The problem is, the words "return" and "back" are not in the original language. And the word "back," when added, unfortunately, conveys a nuance of being away and necessitating a "return." But Jesus never said He would "come back" or "return." Correctly translated, his words are "cometh," "come again," "come again," "go to," "till I come," and just "come," respectively. The *King James Version KJV* translates these phrases correctly. Big difference! See this comparison in the table below:

COMPARATIVE

NIV	Literal Greek	*KJV*
(Incorrect trans.)		(Correct trans.)
"when he returns" (Matt. 24:46)	"coming"	"cometh"
"when he returns" (Luke 12:43)	"coming"	"cometh"
"I will come back" (John 14:3)	"again I come"	"come again"
"I am coming back" (John 14:28)	"I . . . come"	"come ag*ain*"
"going back" (John 16:28)	"go to"	"go to"
"until I return" (John 21:22-23)	"until I come"	"till I come"
"Jesus . . . will come back" (Acts 1:11)	"will come"	"shall so come"

Also, three of the above phrases (John 14:3, 28; Acts 1:11) are in a future-deponent-indicative verb form. Hence, they convey a dualistic sense of an in-process action of coming and/or a present and continuous activity of coming.

Another revealing tidbit comes from Jesus' unveiling in the Revelation's first chapter. Here, John (and we) see Jesus not off somewhere waiting to return someday, but instead, He's standing "among [in the midst] the lampstands" (Rev. 1:13, [KJV]). Jesus explains that "the seven lampstands are the seven churches" (Rev. 1:20b). This is more evidence that Jesus did not *leave* them but was *with* them, i.e., *with* the churches, in their *midst*.

Also notable, in my opinion, was the question Jesus' disciples ask Him the week before his crucifixion, "what will be the sign of your coming" (i.e., the Greek word translated as "coming" here is *parousia* and literally means "presence" as opposed to absence – Matt. 24:3). They did not ask Him "what will be the sign of your return?" or "what will be the return of your presence?" Why not? It is because, in this context, his presence would remain with them and a return was not required. (In Chapter 4, we'll see what the sign was, past tense.)

Perhaps, the reason so many of us have misunderstood this seeming conundrum and paradox of Jesus' departure and yet remaining *with* them is because of our physical/material mindset. It blinds us to the realities of the spirit realm. (We shall explore this hindrance in our next chapter.) However, Scripture makes it clear that both are true and real. But still, how can this be? Here's how. By inspiration, the writer of Hebrews not only informs us that "we are surrounded by such a great cloud of witnesses" (Heb. 12:1) but he also tells us who is in this cloud. It contains "thousands upon thousands of angels . . . the church of the firstborn, whose names are written in heaven. . . . God . . . the spirits of righteous men made perfect, to Jesus . . . ." (Heb. 12:22-24; also compare with Psa. 125:1-2). Of course, this revelation is only of the good side of the spirit realm. Quite simply, Jesus would be leaving them in the physical/material realm via his death on the cross and after his resurrection and ascension to heaven, but He would continue being with them in the spirit realm that both surrounded them and would be in them as it similarly is with us today. Get it?

Consequently and rightly, *Jesus never left*. He remained with them— as He had said, "I will be with you always."[9] Thus, there is no reason for Scripture to speak of a "coming back" or a "return." This terminology would be totally inappropriate and is therefore not used. He doesn't have to "come back" from anywhere and "returning" makes no sense. Even Jesus *cannot and will not return* to someplace He *never left*. Get it? He simply promised, "I will come to you" and "you will see me" (John 14:18, 19; also John 16:16). As we will see, He did and they did. Several times after his death Jesus "came" to them and they saw Him (see John 20:24, 26; 21:1, 14).

Likewise, today, we have no scriptural warrant, necessity, or language for a return. It is just as an angel of the Lord told Joseph at Jesus' birth, "'and they will call him Immanuel'—which means, 'God with us'" (Matt. 1:23); and as the Jewish people of that time expected of the Messiah, "We have heard from the Law that the Christ will remain forever, so how can you say, 'The Son of Man must be lifted up'?" (John

12:34). Hence, after Jesus' ascension and as "the disciples went out and preached everywhere . . . the Lord worked *with them* . . . ." (Mark 16:20 – emphasis added).

So it has been ever since. Even after the end of the age (see Chapter 4), He is still here with us! But many of us are impaired by the Church's traditional "Second Coming" and "Return" teachings and our physical/material mindset. Consequently, we have difficulty thinking in terms of spirit and the spirit realm. So we imagine Jesus as being off in some distant place waiting to come back, to return. And we think that He cannot be here with us, at least not totally, unless He has literally and bodily returned in the flesh, and is physically resident and visible someplace on this earth. And yet, as we shall continue to explore, this return terminology and concept is not found in the Bible and is inconsistent with what Jesus actually said—it is totally inappropriate.

Likewise, today, we have no scriptural warrant, necessity, or language for a return.

When I started studying the presence of Jesus and his many comings several years ago, no one could (or would) answer my questions about why the "Second Coming" wasn't mentioned in the Bible. Most pastors and professors I asked merely beat around the proverbial bush and tried to avoid exposing what they did not know. But each of them assured me the Bible clearly taught it.

More recently, I asked a seminary professor who teaches theology to show me a single scripture to support the idea of a single, future Second Coming. Together, we examined all the classic Second Coming scriptures, one by one. But none of them literally spoke of a "Second Coming." "I agree . . . I agree . . . I agree," he said on each. "But," he lectured me, "I still believe Jesus has left this world, hasn't come back yet, and there will only be one coming—the final Second Coming—at his return."

With all due respect to this precious man of God, such a response is an emotional reaction that grows out of a lifetime of doctrinal conditioning and not from the Word of God. Yet a literal "Second Coming" or a "Return" of Christ is considered a "core" belief that is persistently adhered to, perpetuated, and passed on by learned people with many degrees and much professed wisdom. It is also the central event around which conflicting and divisive systems of eschatological (end-times) views are conjoined.[10]

Do you see a problem here?

Obviously, old habits are hard to break. But this improved understanding is indispensable to a correct understanding of the New Testament and for grasping the reality of the contemporary Christ, the greater Jesus. As we shall further see, the idea that Jesus is off somewhere waiting to return to planet Earth at some future time is just as erroneous as the notion of limiting the comings of Jesus to only two or three times, or to any at all. It's a classic case of the traditions of men "nullify[ing] the word of God" or making it of "none effect" (Mark 7:13; Matt. 15:6 – NIV/KJV).

I believe it is time for this non-biblical, unbiblical, and yet long-perpetuated tradition to give way to revealed truth. We must not be hamstrung by its artificial terms, human constructs, or preoccupations any longer. These human terms and inventions have only obscured the reality of the greater Jesus and his many comings (plural). It is a destructive habit we must break, i.e., using the unscriptural phrases "second coming" and "return" of Christ and lamenting that *Jesus hasn't come back yet* when the truth truly is, He never left, as He said, and He comes, as He said He would. It is a major piece of unlearning we must accomplish.

What's at Risk Here?

What's involved here is much more than semantics or a doctrinal dispute over some insignificant issue, like the ancient squabble over how many angels can dance on the point of a pin. What's at risk here is plenty and everything. With close to one-third of the whole Bible and two-thirds of the New Testament[11] devoted to the subject of end-time prophecy, the main theme of which is the Lord's coming, we cannot afford to be misinformed or confused about this important element of biblical faith.

Yet with all the false pronouncements over the centuries of Christ's soon "Second Coming" and "Return," and the unprecedented level of apocalyptic frenzy that heated up around the recent turn-of-the-millennium, Christianity has lost much of its credibility and is mocked as a joke by many in the world. If these predictions persist, some feel Christianity may be in danger of someday being considered a false religion.

Despite all the failed predictions of the past, an imminent "Second Coming" and "Return" of Jesus Christ remains a dominant theme in Christianity and a prominently recognized concept throughout the world. But for almost two millennium, so many have been wrong so many times that it would seem that the 1st-century scoffers who denied the imminence (nearness) of Jesus' coming again were right after all! "Where is this 'coming' he promised?" they contested over nineteen centuries ago (2 Pet. 3:3-4; Jude 17-19).

One must wonder if there is any way we can effectively counteract the ongoing claims that Jesus' "Second Coming" and "Return" will finally occur in 2012, 2014, 2018, or whenever, without having to endure the embarrassment and further discreditation of more "nonoccurrence?"

So how can we know? The answer is, we can never know from the future, because the future never arrives. Thus, the dates for Jesus' supposed and so-called "Second Coming" or "Return" keep getting revised and reset. It's a perpetual "theology-around-the-next-corner" shuffle. Nothing can ever be refuted by the future. It's always future. But we can correctly know from the PAST! So let's explore some history.

Why Jesus' Birth Is Never Called His 'First Coming'

Have you ever wondered why Jesus' birth (around 4 B.C.) is never called his "first coming" in Scripture? It's for a good reason—it wasn't. This misconception only leads to the improper numbering of another coming as his "second coming"—which it isn't either. The whole idea that Jesus is off somewhere waiting to return to planet Earth at some future time is just as erroneous, biblically, as the notion of limiting his comings to only two, three, or to any at all. Again, it's the classic case of the traditions of men that "nullify the word of God" or make it on "none effect" (Mark 7:13; Matt. 15:6 – NIV/KJV).

God's Word clearly documents and teaches that the comings (plural) of Jesus run like a thread throughout both the Old and New Testaments. Usually, Jesus came to individuals; He came suddenly, unexpectedly, and unannounced; He came to bring aid, to judge, to assign a task, or to proclaim a message. Often his coming and appearing was recognized only by the person for whom it was intended. These comings produced profound, life-altering impacts upon those who received them, and in turn upon other people and nations who were touched by that person's subsequent life and ministry.

Many Comings of Jesus in the Old Testament

Consider, for example, several of the Old Testament comings of Jesus that will document and well make our point here. Theologians technically refer to them as theophanies, meaning "a physical appearance, divine visitation, or vision of God to a person or persons." The word "theophany" is from the Greek *theo* (God) and *phaneia* (to reveal oneself). Some, however, count the times when God spoke to people—such as in the Garden of Eden, or to Moses on Mt. Sinai, or to Noah. Or they count times of other physical manifestations, such as lightning, thunder, a cloud, a consuming fire, fire, a rainbow in the clouds, or radiance, which were the appearance of the glory of the Lord but not a literal, physical, bodily appearance of the Lord Himself.[12]

For our purposes, and based upon the following nine reasons, we'll only count and document visible appearances of the person of deity in human form as theophanies of Jesus (with one exception):

1) Since the Bible states that "no one has ever seen God [the Father], but God the only Son, who is at the Father's side, has made him known" (John 1:18; also 1 John 4:12; Matt. 6:6; 1 Tim. 6:16—with the possible exception of Exod. 24:10-11; Isa. 6:1; Heb. 11:27; and "face to face" in Exod. 33:11; Num. 14:14; Deut. 34:10, which is a Hebrew idiom that does not necessitate a visual seeing but rather means "to be in front of, before, to the front of, in the presence of, in the face of, at the face or front of, from the presence of, from before, from before the face of"[13]);

2) Since the Lord, God the Father, told Moses, "you cannot see my face, for no one may see me and live" (Exod. 33:20, 23; also 19:21; Heb. 11:27);

3) Since there are two Lords in the Old Testament—"The Lord says to my Lord: 'Sit at my right hand until I make your enemies a footstool for your feet'" (Psa. 110:1); the first "Lord" is *Jehovah*—the Jewish national name for God; the second is *Adown*—meaning sovereign;
4) Since Matthew, Mark, and Luke report that Jesus directly applied Psalm 110:1 to Himself (Matt. 22:41-46; Mark 12:35-37; Luke 20:41-44);
5) Since Peter confirms to us in Acts that Jesus has been "exalted to the right hand of God" in fulfillment of Psalm 110:1, which he quotes (Acts 2:32-36; also see Rom. 8:34; Eph. 1:20; Col. 3:1 Heb. 1:13; 8:1; 10:13; 12:21; 1 Cor. 15:25);
6) And since the Holy Spirit has never been seen, as far as we know (John 14:17);
7) These above six reasons leave only one Person in the Godhead (the Trinity) as being the viable candidate Who could have been seen in human or physical form. Therefore, these physical appearances of the Person of God are reckoned by many scholars—including Eusebius, a 4th-century Christian leader and writer, who is often called "the father of Church history" (as we shall see shortly)—to be comings of the preincarnate Son, Jesus. I use the word "reckoned" here, advisedly, because we cannot be dogmatic about this.

Nevertheless, we also have the physical appearances of one called "the angel of the Lord" in the Old Testament—as opposed to just "an angel of the Lord" in New Testament. Many scholars also reckon this angel to be Jesus for these two additional reasons:

8) This angel receives worship, something regular angels refuse to receive. See, for instance, Revelation 22:8-9 where John falls "down to worship at the feet of the angel" who had been showing him spectacular things. The angel emphatically commands him, "Do not do it! I am a fellow servant with you and with your brothers the prophets and of all who keep the words of this book." Then the angel instructs John about this saying, "Worship God!" This is the second time John made this mistake for only God is to receive worship (see Rev. 19:9-10).

9) This angel is called "Lord."

Given these above nine reasons, let's begin our exploration into several prominent Old Testament theophanies and probable comings of Jesus. With only a few possible exceptions, these theophanies were *non-prophesied* comings. Jesus just showed up.

Genesis 17:1-2: Jesus came and appeared to Abram —"When Abram was ninety-nine years old, the Lord appeared to him and said, 'I am God Almighty; walk before me and be blameless. I will confirm my covenant between me and you and will greatly increase your numbers."

Exodus 3:2-15: In a similar encounter, Jesus came and appeared to Moses in the burning bush.

(In verse 2)—"the angel of the Lord appeared to him in flames of fire from within a bush."

(In verse 4)—the angel is called *both* "the Lord" (*Jehovah*—the Jewish national name for God) and "God" (*Elohiym*—a plural form).

(In verse 5)—He commanded Moses "not to come any closer" and to "take off your sandals, for the place where you are standing is holy ground." The taking off of his sandals is an act of worship in the presence of deity.

(In verse 6)—He identified Himself as "I am the God of your father, the God of Abraham, the God of Isaac, and the God of Jacob." Jesus alluded to this identification in John 8:58 when He said, "Before Abraham was, I AM."

(In verse 8)—He stated that He has "come down to rescue them [my people] from the hand of the Egyptians." Therefore, this is certainly a coming.

(In verses 14-15)—He again identified Himself as the eternal "I AM" This is the same identification He gave for both God the Father and Himself in Revelation 1:8 and 21:6, and 22:12, "I AM the Alpha and Omega . . . who is, and who was, and who is to come, the Almighty." (Also see Acts 7:30-34; Rev. 4:8.)

Hence and later, it was said of Moses . . .

—"whom the Lord knew face to face" (Deut. 34:10; also 5:4).

—"he [Moses] saw him who is invisible." (Heb. 11:27).

Exodus 17:1-7: Jesus was the rock that Moses struck, and from which life-giving water flowed. That rock was a real, physical, and visible rock. Then how do we know this rock was Jesus? The Apostle Paul by inspiration told us so in 1 Corinthians 10:4, ". . . that rock was Christ." Notice that Paul did not say the rock represented, symbolized, or was a type of Christ. He said it *was Christ*. Two verses later, he states that "these things occurred as examples" (1 Cor. 10:6).

Exodus 24:9-11: "the God of Israel" appears to "Moses and Aaron, Nadab and Abihu and the seventy elders of Israel." That's 74 people at one time. And they visibly and physically "saw" Him for Moses further recorded that "under his feet was something like a pavement made of sapphire, clear as the sky itself" and "they saw God."

Judges 6:11-26: Jesus appeared to Gideon, twice—under an oak and later that night. Here, too, "the angel of the Lord" is equated with being "the Lord" (vss. 14-22) and received worship (vss. 18-19; also see Psa. 34:6-8).

2 Chronicles 7:12f: Jesus, the Lord, came and appeared to Solomon at night and told him, "I have heard your prayer." Then Jesus gave him the famous admonition, "if my people who are called by my name will humble themselves and pray and seek my face and turn from their wicked ways, then will I hear from heaven and will forgive their sin and will heal their land (2 Chron. 7:14) . . . . But if you turn away and forsake the decrees and commands I have given you and go off to serve other gods and worship them, then I will uproot Israel from my land, which I have given them, and will reject this temple I have consecrated for my Name. I will make it a byword and an object of ridicule among all peoples" (2 Chron. 7:19-20).

Twice, this uprooting and rejection happened at another and different coming of the Lord:

1) Solomon's temple was destroyed by the Babylonians in 586-587 B.C. and many Jews were taken into captivity.
2) Herod's temple was destroyed by the Romans circa A.D. 70 and many Jews also taken into captivity.

(More on this type of coming in Chapter 4.)

Daniel 3:24-27: Jesus came and appeared in the fiery furnace with the three young Hebrew friends of Daniel. "Did not we cast three men bound into the midst of the fire?" King Nebuchadnezzar asked (v. 24, KJV). "Lo, I see four men loose, walking in the midst of the fire . . . and the form of the fourth is like the Son of God" (v. 25, KJV). Many Bible scholars believe that fourth man, Who was seen, presents another coming of Jesus.

Daniel 10:1-21; 11:1-2f: More certainly, it was Jesus Who later appeared to Daniel and gave him the prophetic vision and message of his chapters 10-12. This includes "the time of the end" prophecy (Dan. 12). It is argued that this Person could not be the angel Gabriel, who appeared and gave Daniel his prophecy of "70 weeks" in Daniel 9 because Gabriel is not described the way this Man is described (compare the description in Daniel 10:5-12 with similar language describing Jesus' appearing to John in Revelation 1:12-17).

Next, we come to Eusebius, a 4th-century Christian leader and writer who is often called "the father of Church history." Eusebius cited three more Old Testament comings of Christ, Whom he refers to as the "second Lord after the Father" (referencing Psa. 110:1-4; Gen. 19:24):

Genesis 18:1f: Eusebius writes: "Thus the Lord God is said to have appeared as an ordinary man to Abraham as he sat by the oak of Mamre, yet he worshiped him as God, saying, 'O Lord, judge of all the world, will you not do justice?' [Gen. 18:25]. Since reason would never permit that the immutable essence of the Almighty be changed into human form . . . who else could be so described as appearing in human form but the preexistent Word [Jesus], since naming the First Cause of the universe [God the Father] would be inappropriate?"

Genesis 32:30: Eusebius writes: "Then too: 'Jacob called the name of that place 'the Vision of God,' saying, 'For I saw God face-to-face, and my life was spared."

[Author Note: Jacob not only saw this man but wrestled with Him and had his hip physically wrenched (dislocated) by Him (Gen. 32:22-29). This man also blessed Jacob and changed his name to Israel. This coming of Jesus dramatically altered Jacob's life as well as the course of redemptive history. In confirmation, Hosea 12:3-5 declares that this man was "the angel" and none other than "the Lord God Almighty." Evidently, this is why Jacob/Israel names the place where this happened, "Peniel," which means "the face of God." As he declared, "It is because I saw God face to face, and yet my life was spared" (Gen. 32:30). Don't you think this angel just might have been the same angel of the Lord as appeared to Abraham, Moses, Joshua, and Daniel, i.e., the Lord Jesus? Further notable, God appeared to Jacob again at Bethel (see Genesis 35:9-10).]

Joshua 5:13-15: Eusebius writes: "Joshua too saw him only in human form. For it is written:

> When Joshua was at Jericho, he looked up and saw a man standing before him with a drawn sword in his hand. Joshua approached him and said, 'Are you for us or for our enemies?' He replied, 'It is as commander of the Lord's army that I have come.' Then Joshua fell to the ground, face downward, and asked, 'Master, what do you command your servant?' The commander of the Lord's army replied, 'Take off your shoes, for the place you stand is holy.'"

Eusebius compares this coming and appearing of Jesus to Joshua with a prior coming of Jesus to Moses by writing "the words themselves will show you here too that this was none other than the one who spoke to Moses" in Exodus 3:2-15 (see again above at the burning bush where Moses was also commanded to perform the same act of worship—to take off his shoes).

Eusebius puts down any attempt to diminish these comings with this argument, "to suppose that these recorded theophanies were appearances of subordinate angels and ministers of God cannot be correct, for whenever these appear to people, Scripture distinctly declares in countless passages that they are called angels, not God or Lord"[14]

In conclusion, Eusebius emphatically clarifies his position, "But clearly they knew the Christ of God, since he appeared to Abraham . . . spoke to Israel [Jacob], and conversed with Moses and the later prophets as I have shown."[15]

Space will not permit us to explore in detail other possible Old Testament comings of Jesus. Likely, there were many more (see also Gen. 12:7; Exod. 33:11, 20-23; Isa. 6:5; and more) and as the prophet Micah said, "whose goings forth have been from of old, from everlasting" (Mic. 5:2 KJV).[16] Especially note here the use of the plural for Jesus' "goings forth." The more literal Hebrew is "goings out."[17]

I also encourage you to look up these additional Old Testament appearances of "the angel of the Lord" (theophanies), which most interpreters conclude was the "preincarnate Christ" (see for example: Gen. 16:7-14; 21:17ff.; 22:11ff.; 31:11ff.; Exod. 3:2ff; Judg. 6:11ff.; 13:2ff; Zech. 1:10-13; 3:1-2, where this angel either identifies Himself with the Lord and/or those to whom He reveals Himself recognize Him as God).[18]

> **"But clearly they knew the Christ of God, since he appeared to Abraham . . . spoke to Israel [Jacob], and conversed with Moses and the later prophets as I have shown."**

Please remember, all of these comings serve as examples for us (1 Cor. 10:6). Even back in Old Testament times, Jesus was a frequently present and active God, was He not? Another point I must again emphasize is that none of these above comings were foretold in advance. They were all physical incarnations that just happened as and when God the Father and/or Jesus chose. But all this was about to change.

At the tail end of the Old Testament time period, we have the birthing-incarnation event itself—the coming of the promised Messiah born in Bethlehem of Judea. The exact location of his birth was prophesied by the prophet Micah eight centuries earlier (see Micah 5:2). The exact time of his birth in 4 B.C. occurred precisely as prophesied by Daniel six centuries earlier (see Dan. 9:24-27).[19] That's why the Apostle Paul was prompted by God's Spirit to write these time-sensitive words: Jesus Christ was born "when the time had fully come . . . to redeem those under the law" (Gal. 4:4). He also wrote that Jesus died "at just the right time" (Rom. 5:6); and "who gave himself as a ransom for all men – the testimony given in its proper time" (1 Tim. 2:6).

As decisive and significant as the babe-in-the-manger coming of Jesus was, Scripture never terms it his "first coming"—and for good reason, as we have begun to see. Nor would it be his only coming in that same 1st-century A.D. time period.

Many Documented Comings of Jesus in the New Testament

Hundreds witnessed Jesus' death on the cross. But on the third day He arose and during the next 40 days hundreds more witnessed his physical presence. As a result, their lives were dramatically changed. They now knew that there is life beyond the grave. After his resurrection, the writers of the New Testament documented many post-Resurrection, pre-Ascension and post-Ascension comings and appearings of Jesus.

Critical Objection: These appearances were not comings.

My Response: Jesus said they were comings: ". . . I will come to you . . . . you will see me" (John 14:18-19). That's good enough for me.

1 Corinthians 15:5-8: "and that He [Christ] appeared to Peter, and then to the Twelve. After that, he appeared to more than five hundred of the brothers at the same time, most of whom are still living, though some have fallen asleep. Then he appeared to James, then to all the apostles, and last of all he appeared to me also, as to one abnormally born." That's a lot of comings/appearings. Some were private; some were public.

Acts 1:3: "After his suffering, he showed himself to these men and gave many convincing proofs that he was alive. He appeared to them over a period of forty days and spoke about the kingdom of God." More documented comings—such as:

1) To the two on the road to Emmaus; "Then their eyes were opened and they recognized him, and he disappeared from their sight" (see Luke 24:13-32).
2) To his disciples on the shore as they saw, talked, and ate with Him (see Luke 24:36-49; also John 21:4-14).
3) To his disciples, and notably Thomas, in the upper room when "Jesus came and stood among them" and talked to them (see John 20:26-29).

Jesus said they were comings: ". . . I will come to you . . . . you will see me" (John 14:18-19). That's good enough for me.

Acts 7:55: "But Stephen, full of the Holy Spirit, looked up to heaven and saw the glory of God, and Jesus standing at the right hand of God." This was not a dream. Whether it was a coming or a vision of Jesus, Stephen actually *saw* Him. Perhaps, this was like Elisha's servant in 2 Kings 6:17 whose eyes were opened and saw the angelic army above the hills.

Acts 9:4-5: "He [Saul] fell to the ground and heard a voice say to him, 'Saul, Saul, why do you persecute me?' 'Who are you, Lord?' Saul asked. 'I am Jesus, whom you are persecuting.'" That's a coming and appearance of Jesus, no question about it. See Paul's later account of this event in Acts 26:12-16 for further confirmation that Jesus actually did appear here to him while the others with Saul only witnessed something supernatural—"a light from heaven, brighter than the sun, blazing around me and my companions." And they "all fell to the ground."

Acts 10:13-15: "Then a voice told him, 'Get up, Peter. Kill and eat.' 'Surely not, Lord!' Peter replied. 'I have never eaten anything impure or unclean.' The voice spoke to him a second time, 'Do not call anything impure that God has made clean.'" Again, that's probably a coming of Jesus, even though this text only says this manifestation was a voice.

Acts 22:17-18: "When I [Paul] returned to Jerusalem and was praying at the temple, I fell into a trance and saw the Lord speaking. 'Quick!' He said to me. 'Leave Jerusalem immediately, because they will not accept your testimony about me.'" If your doctrine demands it, you can call that a vision. I'm comfortable calling it a coming of Jesus. (Also see Acts 9:9-16; 18:9-11).

Acts 9:10-16: The Lord appeared to Ananias "in a vision" and gave him instructions to go to Saul. This definitely was a vision, as stated, and not a coming.

Acts 18:9-11: The Lord also spoke to Paul "in a vision" and comforted him. Yes, another vision and not a coming.

Acts 23:11: "The following night the Lord stood near Paul and said, 'Take courage! As you have testified about me in Jerusalem, so you must also testify in Rome!'" This was a visual/physical coming and not a vision.

Matthew 17:1-3: "After six days Jesus took with him Peter, James and John the brother of James, and led them up a high mountain by themselves. There he was transfigured before them. His face shone like the sun, and his clothes became as white as the light. Just then there appeared before them Moses and Elijah, talking with Jesus." Then, Moses and Elijah disappeared leaving only Jesus. Truly, something powerful, glorious, and unveiling happened on that mountain. Peter, who was one of the eyewitnesses to this event, may have referred to this experience as a "coming" (*parousia* – see 2 Pet. 1:16-18). Certainly, it was a "preview of coming attractions," so to speak. As we shall see in Chapter 4, the presence of Moses and Elijah here was most significant. It prefigured, or foreshadowed, the very essence of the nature of what many people consider to be Jesus' most, or second most, important coming—his *parousia* coming. This transfiguration was also another indigenous component of the expansion of the kingdom of God (Isa. 9:6-7)—the comings of Christ in his kingdom (Matt 16:28b). And as we have already seen, Jesus followers were to witness many of his comings in his kingdom [post-resurrection] some of which, but most likely not all, are recorded for us in the Bible (John 20:30).

Revelation 1:17: "When I saw him, I fell at his feet as though dead. Then he placed his right hand on me and said: 'Do not be afraid. I am the First and the Last.'" In this coming, Jesus not only appeared and spoke to John, He also touched him. This all happened on the island of Patmos and for the purpose of giving him the Book of Revelation.

When we consider the symbolic names that refer to Jesus, we shall find other New Testament comings and appearings: to Philip (Acts 8:26), to Cornelius (Acts 10:1-6), and again to Peter (Acts 12:7). With the lone exception of Jesus' birth, none of these other and documented comings in the New Testament were specifically prophesied in terms of time, place, or recipient. At best, they were only generally prophesied (see John 14:18-19; 16:16).

Question: Which of the above comings of Jesus was or is the "Second Coming?"

Question: So far, how many possible, historical, and biblical comings of Jesus have we already identified?

Depending on how we count them, it's between 30 to 40 comings of Jesus. And we're not done. There's much more. But doesn't this listing of up to 40 possible and historical comings of Jesus give you more appreciation for why God's Word never uses the expression "second coming" and why the Church's doctrine of a "second coming" will not stand up to an honest, sincere, and objective test of Scripture?

Surely, by now we can recognize that nowhere do the Scriptures limit the comings of Jesus to a single, "Second Coming" event, nor to a "First Coming." Instead, both the Old and New Testaments clearly document many comings of Jesus. He came in many different ways, at special and quite unexpected times, and to both those who sought Him and those who did not. All this (and more) happened exactly as Jesus had told them, "You also must be ready, because the Son of Man will come at an hour when you do not expect him" (Luke 12:40).

What's more, innumerably more comings are taught and promised.

The Many Promised Comings of Jesus

Sad to say, many Bible interpreters believe that all the New Testament verses speaking of or promising the coming of Jesus refer to a single event. For some, that event is past and over; it happen circa A.D. 70. For most, it's still future and unfulfilled, and to happen at the unscriptural end of the world, the end of time, or before, during, or after a seven-year period of Tribulation.[20] Obviously, someone or ones are greatly mistaken.

Of course, it's easy to read Bible passages for years, and given an *a priori* assumption, to never fully realize what's actually being said or not said. And limiting the Lord's coming again to a single event definitely has an appeal of simplicity. On the other hand, why should we assume singularity when the pattern of his coming throughout the Scriptures is just the opposite—many comings? Surely, we need to rise above our preconceived and limiting notions and submit to the authority of Scripture. Therefore, let's see if there is a better way to further sort out the whole thing as we re-explore some of the promised comings of Jesus:

But doesn't this listing of up to 40 possible and historical comings of Jesus give you more appreciation for why God's Word never uses the expression "second coming" . . .

John 14:1-3: "Do not let your hearts be troubled. Trust in God; trust also in me. In my Father's house are many rooms, if it were not so, I would have told you. I am going there to prepare a place for you. And if I go and prepare a place for you, I will come [*erchomai*] again [not 'back'] and take you to be with me that you also may be where I am."

This promised coming is often read at funerals as an assurance that Jesus personally comes at the death of each of his saints to receive them into heaven—perhaps angels do, too (see Heb. 1:14). No one can dogmatically deny or prove this one way or the other. But Jesus' promise also bears relevance to his coming to fulfill and finalize all things: "so Christ was sacrificed once to take away the sins of many people; and he will appear a second time, not to bear sin, but to bring salvation to those who are waiting for him" (Heb. 9:28). If, however, Jesus has not come in this way—as He promised in John 14:1-3 above, as was being anticipated by his disciples twenty and thirty years later (see 1 Pet. 1:5; Luke 21:27-28), and as most popular views today still hold—then the unpleasant, inescapable, and present-day consequence is this. Heaven must not yet be prepared and open, even yet. Remember, Jesus also said, "No one has ever gone into heaven except the one who came from heaven – the Son of Man" (John 3:13; also see 13:33, 36). Thus, this supposed "nonoccurrence" poses quite a dilemma for modern-day preachers, if they're honest about it. There's more.

John 14:18-23:

> Verse 18: "I will not leave you as orphans; I will come [*erchomai*, not 'come back'] to you." Come to whom? Who is the "you?" It's not some future, unborn generation. It's his disciples with whom He's talking at the Last Supper.

> Verse 19: "Before long, the world will not see me anymore, but you will see me. Because I live, you also will live." The fact is, Jesus came and appeared to them, and they visibly saw Him, several times following his resurrection.

> Verse 20: "On that day [the day I come to you] you will realize that I am in my Father, and you are in me, and I am in you [in the spirit]."

> Verse 21: "Whoever has my commands and obeys them, he is the one who loves me. He who loves me will be loved by my Father, and I too will love him and show [or manifest, *emphanizo*] myself to him." This verse implies an inward illumination and/or a relational coming for an individual. It, too, can be considered part of this coming even though the word "come" is not specifically used here.

> Verse 23: is similar ". . . If anyone loves me, he will obey my teaching. My Father will love him, and we will come to him and make our home with him." Here, again, the word "come" (*erchomai*) is used. By the spirit the whole Godhead—not just the Holy Spirit as

many have assumed[21]—comes, indwells and manifests perhaps in ways and dimensions beyond our comprehension.

And wow! What a promise this is! It is certainly not a promise of a visible coming or a coming in judgment. This promise is for a spiritual coming. It is addressed to individuals and is unlimited—"whoever . . . if anyone." Jesus fulfilled that promise within a few days; He came to those very same people (see John 20:19-31). Moreover, this promised coming is contingent upon meeting certain conditions of love and obedience—big "ifs." Then, and only then, has He promised to manifest Himself, personally, in this manner. The word "manifest" in the original Greek means: "to exhibit (in Person) or disclose (by words): – appear, declare, inform, show, signify." Although it's true that God does this by his Word, the Bible, that is not the intent of this coming's promise. It's a personal revelation of Jesus Himself, like the type of revelation shared between the closest friends or intimate lovers. Again, some feel this coming is of the Holy Spirit and not the same as a coming of Jesus, *per se.* But that is not what this verse says. Evidently, and since then, this coming has occurred many, many times, all over the world, wouldn't you think?

Acts 1:9-11:

Verse 9: "After he had said this, he was taken up before their very eyes, and a cloud hid him from their sight." This cloud may have been an ordinary cloud. Or it could have been the same Shekhinah glory cloud that was in the Temple, the one the Jews followed through the wilderness by day and/or that in which Moses and Elijah appeared in the Transfiguration.

Verse 11: "'Men of Galilee,' they said, 'why do you stand here looking into the sky? This same Jesus, who has been taken from you into heaven, will come in the same way you have seen him go into heaven.'" Again, the Greek word for "will come" is *erchomai.* Remember, biblical Greek is a much more elaborate language than modern English. This word actually means "to come or go (in a great variety of applications, lit. and fig.).":"[22] In this instance, it was a going.

The operative phrase we want to focus on here is "in the same way," or in other translations, "in like manner." Mostly, it has been taught that this means Jesus' return to earth has to be in an identical manner, i.e., identical in every detail, except in reverse order. So since He ascended in a visible resurrected body, He must come back in that same form, physically and visibly. If that is true, then must He also come back to that exact same location on the Mount of Olives? How far do we press this similarity? If we are consistent, doesn't this interpretation methodology require that his so-called return will not be seen by every person on earth, since only a handful of disciples saw Him go? Or, must He return to only to those very same people who saw Him ascend and without any fanfare? Obviously, traditional explanations contain numerous problems when you critically think about it. Others, on the other hand, argue for an invisible nature of his return based upon this same account. They reason that since his ascension into heaven was not visible, but hidden from their eyes by the cloud, so shall be his return to earth from heaven, i.e., not visible.

Additionally troubling are these factors. If "in like manner" means "in exactly and literally the same way," how would Jesus come back from heaven riding "a white horse" (Rev. 19:11) and leading "the armies of heaven" (Rev. 19:14, or "with thousands upon thousands of his holy ones" (Jude 14), or "as the lightning comes from the east and flashes to the west" (Matt. 24:27), or "with a loud command, with the voice of the archangel and with the trumpet call of God" (1 Thess. 4:16), or "in blazing fire" (2 Thess. 1:7)? Clearly, these other traditionally taught Second Coming passages in no way resemble Jesus' ascension going and disappearance.

More to the point, the two angels ("two men dressed in white") (v. 10) did not say Jesus would come in a like "body," or the same "body," or to the same "place," or to those witnessing his ascension. The emphasis is on the *manner* of his coming. Contrary to most popular teachings, "in like manner" does not limit Jesus to coming in only a physical/visible mode, nor to that same geographic location from which He ascended, or to a small group. The proper focus here is on *how* He comes. What we can legitimately ascertain from some of his comings we've reviewed so far in this chapter is, Jesus both comes and goes as the Greek word used here (*erchomai*) allows. He comes out of the spirit realm, manifests Himself in the physical realm, then goes back into the spirit realm. That has been the means and manner of his visible and physical comings and goings. They are documented throughout both the Old and New Testaments. With the lone exception of this birth coming, He moves out of one dimension into another and goes back again. His form, the place, the recipients, and the purposes vary. *Erchomai*—comes or (and) goes—is the general, overall manner in which his many visible comings have and do occurred. Angels also have this same capability (Heb. 13:2), do they not?

Revelation 1:7-8:

Verse 7: "Look, he is coming [*erchomai*] with the clouds, and every eye will see him, even those who pierced him; and all the peoples of the earth will mourn because of him. So shall it be! Amen."

The declaration, "Look, he is coming" or "cometh" [*KJV – King James Version*], is explicitly descriptive and revealing. It will become a major theme throughout the Book of Revelation and concerns something Jesus was, is, and will continue doing "yesterday and today and forever:" We shall explore it, and other related verses, more fully later in this book. But one aspect to note, here and now, is in the original Greek language, in which the Revelation was written, the verb "is coming" is a present deponent indicative. Since Greek is a more elaborate language than English, this verb tense is used to convey either an in-process action or a present and continuous action. In other words, it expresses Jesus as either in the process of getting ready to come at a specific and future time and place and/or many ongoing, present, and future comings. In other words, "Look, he is coming, and coming, and coming, again, and again, and again!"

Twice, in the Revelation's last chapter, Jesus uses this same verb form and sense of meaning: "Behold, I am coming soon! [quickly]"

(Rev. 22:7, 12). In light of all that's promised herein and revealed elsewhere in Scripture, both meanings—in process of coming and/or a continuous activity of coming—are supportable, scripturally and historically. As we shall continue to see, the future coming(s) of Jesus cannot be limited to a single historical event, close to or far removed from Revelation's writing. Nor are his comings (plural) confined to a single geographic location or restricted to a single timeframe. This revelation is both an historical and yet an ongoing and cosmic aspect of the greater Jesus, the contemporary Christ, and its relevance is far greater than many have known before.

He comes out of the spirit realm, manifests Himself in the physical realm, then goes back into the spirit realm.

What do you think the phrases "every eye will see" and "all peoples of the earth will mourn" mean? Literally, these phrases mean exactly what they say. But they have been differently interpreted for centuries as a single, worldwide coming visible *only* to those people living on planet Earth at that particular moment in history, or at the end of history. Especially singled out, however, are the 1st-century Roman guards who physically "pierced" Jesus during his crucifixion in A.D. 30 (John 19:34-37; Psa. 22:16; Zech 12:10-14). Others also must be included: those who "pierced" Him by their participation in his sentencing and the Jews who accused Him in the first place (Matt. 27:25; Acts 2:36). The full realization of this promised, universal coming for "every eye" and "all peoples of the earth," must, therefore, have started in the 1st century. (More on this in Chapter 5.)

Verse 8: "'I am the Alpha and the Omega,' says the Lord God, 'who is, and who was, and who is to come [*erchomai*], the Almighty.'" Just as God the Father comes (notice the similarity with verse 4) and as the beast comes (notice the similarity with verse 17:8), so comes Jesus (Rev. 22:12-13, 20). Perhaps, the "is" is the present coming of Jesus to John on the island of Patmos; the "was" are his many past comings; and the "is to come" are his many future and promised comings.

As we discussed in this book's Introduction, the Book of Revelation enables us to see the greater Jesus fully unveiled and revealed. By divine design, its words allow this contemporary Christ to appear (come) to its reader, as He came and appeared to John. Why? It's because "the word of God is living and active. Sharper than any double-edged sword, it penetrates even to dividing soul and spirit . . . ." (Heb. 4:12a), if we so allow it to function. Yet most people see only beasts, plagues, earthquakes, locusts, torment, and end-of-world cataclysms. What a shame! But to those who would read, hear, i.e., with understanding, and obey the words of this prophecy—all of it (Rev. 1:3), it's a total personal unveiling of Jesus Christ in his greater form and position. That's another coming. As we've also seen, the transliterated Greek word in Revelation 1:1 that is translated "revelation" is *apokalypsis*. Primarily, it means an "unveiling" or an "uncovering" of Jesus. But its other meanings are a "manifestation, the coming, the appearing, the seeing" of the greater Jesus in all his glory—to you and me as a reader of the Revelation! That's why Jesus said after each of the messages to the seven churches, and to us today as well, "Let him who has ears hear." It's an individual and continuous refrain throughout Revelation chapters 2 and 3.

Revelation 2 & 3: The focus of these two chapters in the Apocalypse is not on a Christ who is away and waiting to come back but on the greater Jesus Christ Who is in the midst of these churches (Rev. 1:13, 20) and comes. So here, first of all, we find a collection of different types of comings that were relevant for and applied to these seven churches and their individual members. Yet these comings were for various reasons and purposes. Some of them you would not want to have happen to you.

Verse 2:5: "Remember the height from which you have fallen! Repent and do the things you did at first. If you do not repent, I will come [*erchomai*] to you and remove your lampstand from its place." Here Jesus threatened a special coming(s) in judgment to this particular church in Ephesus and to the individuals (the "he" who has

Why You Don't Have to Wait Around for . . . 51

an ear) in all of the seven churches (plural) (Rev. 2:7). Note, this promised but conditional coming is not directed toward the world or to nonbelievers. Also, these churches were located throughout Asia Minor (the modern-day country of Turkey) and were not in Jerusalem.

Verse 2:16: "Repent therefore! Otherwise, I will soon come [*erchomai*] to you and will fight against them with the sword of my mouth." It's another promised and conditional coming(s) of Jesus to that church and to persons in the other six churches as well.

Verse 2:25-26: "Only hold on to what you have until I come [*heko*]. To him who overcomes and does my will to the end, I will give authority over the nations"—an individual coming(s) of reward for faithfulness. (Also see Rev. 22:12).

Verse 3:3: "Remember, therefore, what you have received and heard; obey it, and repent. But if you do not wake up, I will come [*heko*] like a thief, and you will not know at what time I will come to you." It's another unexpected coming(s) in judgment and with consequences best to avoid.

Verse 3:11: "I am coming [*erchomai*] soon. Hold on to what you have, so that no one will take your crown." Crowns in Scripture are only given to individuals. It's another imminent coming(s) of reward for perseverance.

Verse 3:20: "Here I am! I stand at the door and knock. If anyone hears my voice and opens the door, I will go in [*eiserchomai*] and eat with him, and he with me." What a wonderful promise of his coming(s) to individual believers.

First and foremost, these descriptions of Jesus' corporate and individual comings in judgment, reward, or the continuance or withdrawal of his presence in Revelation chapters 2 and 3 were promised to these seven churches. They are not the subject of a single, universal event, but of a pertinent and conditional reality in the lives of these believers at that time. But the relevance of these comings is more than that and for a profound exegetical reason that we shall layout in Chapter 3.

Revelation 22:7, 12: Twice in the last chapter of Revelation, Jesus admonishes, "Behold I am coming soon," or "quickly." The verb formed used here is the same present deponent indicative used in Revelation 1:7 (see above). Again, it conveys the dual meaning of Jesus being in-process of coming and/or a present and continuing action of coming—both are supportable and viable.

Some claim that "soon" or "quickly" does not mean soon and quickly, as we humans normally understand these words. Translating the Greek word, *tachu,* as "soon," and remaking it to mean "far" by stretching its fulfillment nineteen-centuries-and-counting has been an all too common and avoidance practice. Those interpreters base this difference of time perspective on the passage, "One day is with the Lord as a thousand years and a thousand years is as a day" (2 Pet. 3:8; Psa. 90:4). Of course, God does not view time as we humans do. But He created time for us to understand and use (Gen. 1:14). Actually, this Second Peter passage describes God's eternal character. To use it to relativize the meaning of time language between God and human beings is an abuse and a theological cop-out. In his Word, God always uses precise time terminology that we humans are to understand from a human point of view, and not from some ethereal God perspective, as many errantly surmise.[23] For God the Father or Christ the Son to change the normal meaning of time-statement words would be deceitful and give Scripture a character of deception rather than revelation, thereby making these words utterly mystifying, meaningless, and irrelevant. The Greek word *tachu*— translated as "soon," "quickly," "shortly," or "suddenly"— means exactly what it means in normal and ordinary usage. It does not mean "speedily" or "fast"—i.e., whenever this event happens someday, still-yet-future, it will happen in a flash or in a brief moment. Not only would Christ come "soon" to Revelation's first readers, but also "unexpectedly" (see Luke 12:40). The unveiling of this central truth and original-audience relevancy flows throughout the Book of Revelation and all of the New Testament. Failure to grasp this dualistic dynamic of his coming and comings is one of the reasons this last book of the Bible and most of the New Testament has been so misapplied and misunderstood.

> **For God the Father or Christ the Son to change the normal meaning of time-statement words would be deceitful and give Scripture a character of deception rather than revelation . . .**

He Comes in a Variety of Ways

Doesn't the realization of the many past and promised comings of Jesus we have been re-exploring in this chapter give you a new appreciation for Jesus' admonition, "You also must be ready, because the Son of Man will come at an hour when you do not expect him" (Luke 12:40)?

Of course, we have much more to cover and expound upon regarding the many past, present, and future comings (plural) of Jesus. The Bible's Book of Revelation is loaded with both past and contemporary relevance in this regard, as well as being the Bible's climactic revelation of other spirit-realm/physical-realm truths and realities.

Unfortunately, the most contested aspect of Jesus' earthly ministry has been his numerous predictions and supposed failure to come again within the lifetime of his contemporaries. These predictions and this supposed "nonoccurrence" charge have troubled Christianity and the world for centuries. No more!

By now, I hope you are beginning to get a glimpse of the big picture. If we sincerely search the Scriptures for what they say and don't say, there is no legitimate, scriptural, or historical way we can limit the comings (plural) of Jesus to a single "Second Coming" event—past or future. This popular, two-advent mindset does not fit Scripture's terminology, teaching, or testimony.

Also by now, I trust it's more than evident that the correct, biblical, and historical answer to the question I asked at the beginning of this chapter is "E) MORE." Since the greater Jesus, the contemporary Christ, has shed the hindrance of human limitation, He can come any time He wants and do much more than He could during his earthly ministry.

Shouldn't we, therefore, desire for Him to come and do great things in our day and time? As we will see, He does in many wondrous ways.

In concluding this chapter, let's call it like it is. "Second Coming" and "Return" terminology makes no textual, historical, logical, grammatical, or biblical sense. It is totally inappropriate and brings reproach upon the name and integrity of Jesus Christ and his Church. Neither expression is a valid scriptural term or concept.

It is truly amazing, when you stop to think about it. Many people, who focus on a single, future Second Coming, support their doctrine by saying you have to take the Bible literally. Yet, if you take it literally, not one single verse ever makes reference to a "Second Coming" or a "Return," nor do any of the historic creeds of the Church. Perhaps, it's our traditions that have led us astray?

(NOTE TO READER: Out of 97 Old Testament prophecies of Jesus Christ's birth-coming, life, death, and resurrection that are quoted in the New Testament, "only 34 were directly or literally fulfilled, which is only 35.05 percent!" The rest were fulfilled in a "typical," "analogical," and "according to sense" manner.)[24]

Indeed, that is exactly what has happened. "Second Coming" and "Return" expressions are contrived terminology and reductionist ideas that have been read into the Bible and handed down for centuries. They have hamstrung and harmed the Church long enough. The historical and biblical reality of Christ's many comings is a contradiction of the limited, misleading, and deceptive idea of a single "Second Coming." And the fact that He never left, renders a "Return" totally inappropriate. That is why this language is never used in Scripture. Get it yet?

What's at risk here is plenty and everything! The continued use of this non-biblical terminology is another classic example of the traditions of men dumbing down, diluting, devaluing, and depreciating authentic biblical Christianity (Matt. 15:6; Mark 7:13). And since words mean things and wording is important, we cannot afford to be misinformed or confused about such an important element of our faith. It is paramount, therefore, that we in the Church be clear on and control our word usage, i.e., use Bible names for Bible things. Would you now agree?

Oh, I'm sure Satan and his cohorts would love to keep God's people busy looking for just a single Second Coming and Return, somewhere up in the sky, off in the future. Why? Because it distracts them from tapping into spiritual dynamite,[25] from worshipping the greater Jesus, the contemporary Christ, in all his unveiled reality, and from doing the kingdom works of and greater works than Jesus (John 14:12) in the full power of his Spirit, today.

"Second Coming" and "Return" expressions are contrived terminology and reductionist ideas that have been read into the Bible and handed-down to us for centuries.

In my opinion, the Christian faith cannot and will not progress as quickly, and as effectively as it is capable of doing, until its proponents begin to speak out the biblical truth of what Jesus is like and doing today, especially regarding his presence and many countless comings. Yes, this is a credibility, reliability, relevance, and practical issue. So where am I wrong on this, or on any of it, so far?

My Recommendation—a Purging

Since Scripture instructs us to "demolish arguments and every pretension that sets itself up again the knowledge of God" (Heb. 10:4b-5a), I recommend that we'd be well advised to start right here by dropping the non-scriptural use of both "second coming" and "return" terminology and purging it from our vocabulary. Let us also cast aside the unscriptural and arbitrary idea of limiting the comings of Jesus to two, or three, or to in any at all. It's dishonoring to Christ. Whenever a tradition of men is proven ungrounded in Scripture, it must be purged and no longer allowed to weaken, hinder, or undermine the progress and effectiveness of the faith. All this and much more is what's at risk and at stake.[26]

I further suggest that we seriously consider whether or not we have been "carried away" by "strange doctrine" (Heb. 13:9) that has "deceived even the elect – if that were possible" (Matt. 24:24). The presence of the greater Jesus and many countless comings are two beautiful truths of Scripture and a long-precedent reality of history. We shall never properly understand or fully appreciate the greatness of our faith and the reality of the greater Jesus, the contemporary Christ, if we are boxed into, or intimidated and brainwashed by, an erroneous and limited mindset in this matter.[27]

Oh, I can hear the cries of the H-word ("heresy") already arising from those unwilling to honestly and sincerely contemplate the abundant biblical and historical evidence for the presence and many comings of Jesus, from those who fear such a change would do great damage to the faith of the "fragile," and from those who will not want to give up, for any reason whatsoever, their two- or three-advent hope, mindset, and limited view. But please don't misinterpret my motives. If we are truly sincere about seeking after, knowing, and following Jesus as He now is, that means it's time for serious reflection and repentance. The time has come for us in the Church to honestly reconsider exactly what is heretical, unbiblical, and even anti-biblical in regard to the presence and many comings of Jesus.

Therefore, dear saints, let us jettison these expressions which are totally foreign to God's Word, as well as to the major creeds. So much is at stake. Again, the presence and many comings of Jesus are such beautiful truths and historical realities. It's time these plain, simple, yet precious truths and realities be proclaimed in scriptural terms. Stop limiting his comings! Amen. Come, Lord Jesus! As we will continue to see, He has; He still does; and He will!

In our next chapter of unlearning, let's continue our quest and journey in searching out the Revelation's infinite riches by examining how you can avoid being taken in by confusion.

I recommend that we'd be well advised to start right here by dropping the non-scriptural use of both "second coming" and "return" terminology and purging it from our vocabulary. Let us also cast aside the unscriptural and arbitrary idea of limiting the comings of Jesus to two, or three, or to in any at all. It's dishonoring to Christ.

Chapter 2

Confronting Centuries of Confusion

Another perplexing question I have wrestled with over the past thirty-some years in the theological area known as eschatology (the study of last things) has been: Why is there so much confusion, controversy, and conflict among Christians and churches over the Book of Revelation—whose stated purpose is to reveal Jesus Christ as He is today? Why, for instance, can't a typical, ordinary layperson, like I was when I began and during much of my quest, study this prophecy and trust the Holy Spirit to guide him or her into its truths?

"Oh," my professors and several pastors cautioned, "it's all very complex . . . . First, you'd need years of education in such subjects as hermeneutics, theology, ontology, biblical and contemporary history, millenarianism, literary and form criticism, apocalyptic imagery, and so on. Plus, you'd have to have an in-depth knowledge of at least the ancient Hebrew, Chaldee, Greek, Aramaic, and Latin languages."

Wait a minute, I thought. The guy who wrote the Book of Revelation was a commercial fisherman—an unschooled and ordinary man, according to the religious leaders of his day (see Acts 4:13). What he had going for him was a personal intimacy with Jesus Christ, a sincere heart, and the anointing of the Holy Spirit.

What's more, the Apostle Paul (a trained theologian) didn't tell the Ephesians he was praying that God would open the door for them to go to the best theological seminary in the world. Instead, he told them that God had "made know to us the mystery of his will" (see Ephesians 1:3-10). He thanked God for their faith and said, "I keep asking that the God of our Lord Jesus Christ, the glorious Father, may give you the Spirit of wisdom and revelation, so that you may know him better" (Eph. 1:17). This verse still is a personal favorite of mine and one I frequently pray.

Besides, the very Person the Revelation reveals, Jesus Christ, promised that "the Holy Spirit . . . will teach you all things and will remind you of everything I have said to you" (John 14:26).

So, with an open and hungry heart, I began an in-depth, exhaustive study into the Revelation and related prophetic Scripture. To my great delight, the Holy Spirit began to open up their mysteries to me. I began to discover that the Revelation message was not so much a prediction of distant, future events, but vital and vibrant descriptions of then-present realities and impending events that would soon take place, back then and there. Later on, I began to see that it not only painted a most hopeful picture for the immediate future of its original recipients, but also an equally relevant reality for every generation since then as well as for each of us in our daily lives—here and right now!

Why Don't Most Christians Know This?

"Why don't most Christians know the pertinent truths and empowering realities the Revelation teaches?" I began to ask.

After all, if the stated purpose of the book is to unveil Jesus Christ and what He says has, is, and is to take place; and if it promises blessings to those who read it, hear it, heed it, and obey it; and if there are severe warnings to and consequences for those who don't (see Rev. 1:1-3, 3:22; 22:7, 18, 19); why are most Christians either ignorant, confused, or deceived about its contents? It's as if someone had taken the veil that had been removed by God and laid it right back over this prophecy.

Gradually, I began to see that this is exactly what has happened. Like the people of John's day, I think you, too, will be "astonished" (Rev. 13:3; 17:6-7). Below are six major reasons, or hindrances, why for centuries most people (Christians included) have not and today still do not understand, heed, and obey this prophecy—which, again, is the only place the greater Jesus, the contemporary Christ, is unveiled and revealed. Consequently, and as we shall see in our next chapter, they have not and do not receive its wisdom and promised blessings. So prepare yourself for what might be a rude awakening as we begin to unlearn and rediscover how far off track many of our current understandings about the prophecy of the Revelation truly are.

Reason #1 – They Are Hamstrung by a False Paradigm

A frequent question people ask after I teach from the Book of Revelation or on other related prophecy is this: "Doesn't the Bible say that God is someday going to destroy the world and set up a new heaven and earth?" In my opinion, this false, "end-of-the-world" or "end-of-time" paradigm is, by far, the number one reason so many have been hamstrung in their understandings of the Book of Revelation and end-time prophecy as a whole.

A classic example occurred during 2006 when I was able to fulfill a long-held dream. My wife and I were invited to join a group of confessing Methodists on a tour of Greece and the Greek Isles. This tour was billed as "In the Footsteps of St. Paul." For me, however, its major attraction and highlight was a half-day visit to the island of Patmos, where St. John received the Book of Revelation from Jesus and an angel.

Here's a short section from the account of my visit (for the full account see Appendix A).

Around nine o'clock groups began disembarking our cruise ship onto tender boats that ferried us to shore. On shore, we boarded buses that took us to the Monastery of the Apocalypse. This monastery, built around the 11th century, surrounds the cave, or the Sacred Grotto as the Greeks refer to it, in which St. John received the Book of Revelation. By the time my group arrived, several other tour buses had already unloaded and a long waiting line to get into the monastery had formed.

While we waited, the young Greek lady who was our tour guide told us that "during the reign of the Roman Emperor Domitian in A.D. 95 the Apostle John was banished to Patmos, where he was held for two years.

It was here that he received the inspiration for the Book of Revelation from his professor, Jesus Christ. It contains prophecies about the end of the world."

When she finished her prepared spiel, I stepped out of line, worked my way over to her and asked, "How do you know the prophecy of Revelation is about the end of the world?"

"This is the interpretation I was told," she frankly replied.

Fact is, the Book of Revelation continues to be viewed as a guide to the end of the world by many today who grapple with its violent apocalyptic imagery. Scholarship, on the other hand, has been moving away from this direction, and rightly so.

So what does the Book of Revelation say about the end of the world? The answer is *nothing*![1] What does the whole Bible say about the end of the world? The answer again is *nothing*! That's right—just like the historic creeds. *Nothing*! Many Bible teachers like to qualify the End they think the Bible proclaims by telling us that someday the world and human history will certainly end in its present form or, "as we know it."[2] What do these qualifying phrases mean? They don't know. Nobody knows. Yet they keep telling us this line, over and over. Another fact is, the world is always changing or coming to an end in its present form or as we know it, and a new one is continually coming into existence. Ask your parents or grandparents, if they are alive, or yourself, hasn't the world as they or you knew it changed?

So what does the Bible actually say about the world ending as we know it or in its present form? Again, *nothing*! What did Jesus say about it? *Nothing*! What does the Bible say about an end of time or end of human history? Again, *nothing*! Not a single text, taken in a literal, plain, straightforward context, declares the world will ever end. As unpleasant as this truth may be for some, the end of the world is simply a false and pagan doctrine that has been dragged into the Church and read into the Bible. This revelation should be a major wake-up call to all endsayers.

But wait a minute! you protest. I've been reading Billy Graham's newspaper column for years and he says the Bible says "the world will definitely end some day[3] .... When Christ comes again[4] .... [and] this world is only temporary."[5] With all due respect to this revered man of God, and one with whom I agree on so many other points of faith, the emphatic answer to that assertion is, *it does not*!

Moreover, relying on who says what will not settle this matter. Only specific statements from Scripture will do, as we agree to "test everything. Hold on to the good" (1 Thess. 5:21). Nothing is exempt from this scriptural admonishment. And the facts are that there is no clear statement in the Bible that teaches an end of the world, an end of time, or an end of human history. *None!*[6]

Likewise, not one iota of evidence exists that 1st-century Jews, the early Christians, or any New Testament writer (men guided by the Holy Spirit, according to John 16:13) anticipated an end to the human race or the demise of planet Earth. It is not, as some believe, a profound and glorious doctrine of the Church, even though many throughout Church history have espoused it.

So what does the Book of Revelation say about the end of the world? The answer is *nothing*!

Many cite isolated verses of Scripture to support their final-destruction doctrinal preference. They might, for instance, take a verse out of context, such as, "Heaven and earth will pass away, but my words will never pass away" (Luke 21:33; Matt. 24:35). "See," they'll exclaim, "that's a clear prediction that the earth is going to pass away!" They ignore Jesus' main point: that his words are more eternal than the heavens and the earth, and that He has just given (in the preceding verse) his word that the generation He's speaking to will not pass away until all the things He's predicting have happened.

Another factor missed by those subscribing to this termination belief, is the knowledge and awareness that there are three different entities in the Bible termed "heavens and earth." They are:

1) Planet Earth and the cosmos creation (Gen 1:1; Isa. 51:13).
2) The old world empire of Babylon (Isa. 13:13, 19-22).
3) The Old Covenant creation (Deut. 32:1; 31:28; Isa. 1:2-3; 51:15-16; Heb. 12:26-27 from Hag. 2:6-7)

Two of these "heavens and earth" entities have already ended. The other, as we are about to see, never ends. Question: So which one of these creations was the one to pass away and be made new as spoken of in the Book of Revelation (Rev. 21 and 22) and in the Old Testament book of Isaiah (Isa. 65:17-18; 66:22) as well?

Since I have written about this topic extensively elsewhere,[7] for now let us simply re-address this issue in a recapping and condensed manner. The biblical truth about the proverbial "end of the world" is contained within the biblical phrase "world without end, Amen." The Bible says that the world had a beginning, but is without end . . . "from the beginning of the world . . . . throughout all ages, world without end. A-men. (Ephesians 3:9, 21, KJV)

The Gloria Patri, the famous doxology and confessional of the historic Church, emphasizes and confirms this same biblical truth:

> Glory be to the Father, and to the Son, and to the Holy Ghost.
> As it was in the beginning, is now and ever shall be.
> World without end, Amen.

A pastor friend of mine declared in astonishment one day, "I've said and sung this doxology so often in church and never stopped to realize what it meant." He added, "it's tragic that so many of us, so often, have repeated this biblical phrase in our services without ever stopping to consider what it means."

What does "world without end, Amen" mean, anyway? It means exactly what it says: the world (or age) is not going to end! It's endless. Earlier I said that the truth about the end of the world is contained within this biblical phrase. I stated it this way because in the original Greek, the phrase translated as "world without end" in the King James Bible is an idiom and is translated differently in other, more modern translations. Some versions read, "throughout all generations (ages) for ever and ever!" Literally, it's "into all generations of the age of the ages." As an idiom, the actual meaning of the phrase is greater than, and cannot be directly understood, from its literal words. But every translation of this Greek idiomatic phrase contains the same basic truth.

The meaning of the word translated as "age" (*olam* in Hebrew and *aion* in the Greek) is "an indefinite and/or unknown period of time." And, of course, every age has a beginning and an end and a duration that could be either long or short. Therefore, an age does not mean "forever." In Ephesians 3:21, however, the verse contains both the singular "age" and the plural "ages." The reason for this double employment is because neither the Hebrew nor Greek language had a separate word for the concept of eternity, foreverness, or endlessness. That's why, throughout the Old and New Testaments, both of these ancient languages used a range of phrases employing the word "age" in a hyperbolic and idiomatic fashion.[8] The more this word was employed in a phrase, the more intensified was the meaning of what might best be translated as *forever*. Examples of these phrases in an increasing and intensifying order are:

- "unto the age" (singular)
- "unto the ages" (plural)
- "unto the age of the age" (double singular)
- "unto the age of ages" (singular and plural)
- "unto the ages of the ages" (double plural)

Hence, this double use of age (singular) and ages (plural) in Ephesians 3:21 is a way of saying forever. One thing, however, is for sure. This idiom cannot mean its opposite. Therefore, "world without end" or "for ever and ever" are preferred translations that emphasize the concept of permanence, eternalness, endlessness, everlastingness, perpetuity. These translations clash with any idea of an end of the world, end of human history, or end of time.[9] The world, time, and the present new-covenant age simply do not have an end.[10]

The translation "world without end" is also a contrapositive. In literary style, a contrapositive is used to make the meaning more emphatic, like John F. Kennedy's famous phrase, "ask not what your country can do for you . . . ." Biblical statements, too, are sometimes made more powerful by using a negative. Are they not? Instead of strengthening a point by using a superlative, the statement is emphasized by using a negative. "I am not ashamed of the gospel of Christ" (Rom. 1:16 KJV) is an example. What it really means is, I am exulting in it, I am proud of it.

The "amen" following "world without end" makes the phrase even more emphatic. Amen affirms the contrapositive proclamation and adds the meaning, "so may it be in accordance with the will of God." What we end up with, then, is a double strengthening and emphasis of the certainty of this Greek idiom that the world (or age) is without end, i.e., is going to continue forever and ever.

Over the centuries, many attempts have been made to evade the plain meaning of certain biblical phrases. This one is no exception. Contrast this message from God's Word to the many voices that keep trying to predict the proverbial end of the world. Doesn't this explain the reason why endsaying prophets of doom throughout history have continually been proven wrong? It's not their timing that is wrong. It's their concept that is wrong. As failed prophets of a false premise, they have been continually trying to predict something that's not going to happen. In their folly, they've ignored or rejected the transcendent truth of the Bible and the historic proclamation of the Church that "the world is without end, Amen."

Consequently, endsaying (saying "the end is near") can be compared to crying wolf when there is no wolf. In this case, they've been crying End! End!" but there is no end of the world. It's a basic foundational flaw of all endsaying and a concept that's headed for the scrap heap of history. We've been programmed by it for too long. The world is never, repeat never-ever, going to end. We live in a never-ending world. How can we be so sure? We can repeat the old rhyme, "How do I know? The Bible tells me so." Count on it—Hal Lindsey and his book, *The Late Great Planet Earth*, and John Hagee and his book, *Earth's Final Moments*, opinions notwithstanding.

In dramatic contrast, the Bible emphatically and directly tells us that "generations come and generations go, but the earth endures [remains] forever" (Eccl. 1:4).[11] The Psalmist confirms that the earth is established forever (Psa. 78:69) and that the earth and its foundations shall not be removed, ever (Psa. 104:5; see also Psa. 93:1; 96:10; 119:90). This applies to the whole material universe that God created, as well. Both moon and sun are eternally established as faithful witnesses in the sky (Psa. 89:36-37), as are the highest heavens (Psa. 148:4, 6). Eternalness is not only an attribute ascribed to God and his glory, it's also an attribute ascribed to his creation. That's one reason why Psalm 19:1 states, "The heavens declare the glory of God; the skies proclaim the work of his hands."

God's plan has never been to deal with human sin by eliminating the human race or by destroying his creation. If we think otherwise, we've misunderstood his plan of redemption. "For God so loved the world that he gave his one and only Son . . . For God did not send his Son into the world to condemn the world . . . " (John 3:16a, 17a). And neither should we condemn it by saying it's going to end when Scripture clearly states that it's without end and therefore not ever going to end.

Rest assured that the future stability and everlasting nature of the earth and the cosmos are secure. They are grounded in the trustworthiness of God and his Word, the Bible.[12]

The recovery of a world that is "without end, Amen" is an idea whose time has come. Victor Hugo said it well:

> There is one thing stronger than all the armies in the world; and that is an idea whose time has come.

The power of this idea to influence the human psyche and thus the future course of history cannot be overestimated. In this author's opinion, the unleashing of this truth is destined not only to change the way we view the Book of Revelation, but also to change the cultural and theological landscape. Entire schemes of religious and non-religious teaching focusing on a future end of the world (or end of time) have run their course; their prophecies have not come true. Instead of striving to hang on till the end, we can have a strong reason to undertake dynamic roles in the present, both individually and corporately, for a better future and for the benefit of coming generations.[13]

God's plan has never been to deal with human sin by eliminating the human race or by destroying his creation.

Unfortunately, pioneering a new, counter-traditional idea is rarely popular, at least at first. Historically, the "powers that be" have usually reacted angrily whenever confronted with an upsetting truth. Voltaire, the 18th-century French philosopher, hit it on the head when he surmised, "Our wretched species is so made that those who walk on the well-trodden path always throw stones at those who are showing a new road."

This road I am showing is really not new, but so old and so neglected that it seems new. Thus it will suffer the usual reaction of anger and disbelief. But after a reformational idea bursts onto the public scene and awareness spreads and people at the grassroots level begin to realize how much the value of the new outweighs the detriments of the old, a paradigm shift begins to take place.

This new, open-ended paradigm of a world without end will force us to reexamine and rethink other end-time assumptions, prophecies, and beliefs as well. It will also guide us into a better understanding of the Book of Revelation and its stated purpose of unveiling and revealing the greater Jesus, the contemporary Christ—what He is like and what He is doing today.

Furthermore and finally, if this world is, indeed, a world without end that was eternally established by a Creator God isn't our role in taking care of it, and of each other, even more significant? Doesn't this provide more reason and responsibility to pass it along to future generations in a better condition than we found it?

Reason #2 – The Church Is Confused

Traditionally, people have looked to the Christian Church for answers in confusing and troubled times. After all, if anybody should understand where the future is going and how we should prepare for it, it should be the institution that claims to have an inside track with the Creator and Controller of the Universe.

It makes sense, doesn't it, that people would turn to the one source which should be able to interpret the confusing language and imagery of prophetic writings to give them some clues about what to expect in the future and how to prepare for it?

Unfortunately, when people turn to the Church today for answers about the future, especially regarding the Book of Revelation, they simply find more confusion.

First, they don't find one Church speaking with a unified voice. Rather, they find literally thousands of denominations and countless independent churches, each interpreting the Scriptures in its own way.

Second, even within denominations (and often within the same local church) they find more controversy than agreement over what the Bible says about the future and how to prepare for it in the present.

Third, they may have a hard time finding out what a church really believes about prophecy. Most churches seem to have a chronic case of prophetic laryngitis, especially regarding the Book of Revelation, which they themselves often don't understand.

Fourth, they may turn to the media. Unfortunately, in the absence of a clear and cohesive message from the Church, anybody who can put together enough words to write a book or raise enough money to get on radio or television to talk about prophecy can quickly become identified as the authentic voice of the Church. And most of the prophetic long rangers of the last three or four decades have been so far afield that they've made a laughing stock of the Church.

Fifth, since bad news sells and good news doesn't, they find only the more dire predictions and dramatic timetables in the media versions. Thus, they rarely hear the more responsible prophetic voices.

All this disunity leaves the majority of people to fend for themselves at a time when they desperately need guidance and hope. So people cope (or fail to cope) in a variety of ways.

Reason #3 – Most People Simply Ignore Prophecy

Most people are so confused by the so-called apocalyptic imagery of many prophetic scriptures that they ignore their teachings and busy themselves with the daily concerns of their lives.

I recently heard about a new convert who began immediately plowing through the Bible, starting with the New Testament. Several weeks later, a fellow Bible student noticed a bunch of staples in the new convert's Bible, thought it odd, and asked, "Why have you put staples in your expensive new Bible?"

"Oh, that," replied the novice Christian. "That's Revelation."

"But why the staples?" his friend pursued.

"Look," he said flatly, "My pastor can't understand anything in that book, my Bible teacher can't understand it, and I certainly can't figure it out. So I just stapled it shut."

Imagine! Here was a Christian at the beginning of the 21st century stapling shut a book that was dearer than life itself to Christians during the second half of the 1st century! Surely, a book that once brought so much comfort and life, a book that God saw fit to preserve as part of the Canon, cannot have lost all its meaning for our generation!

Reason #4 – Most Churches Neglect Bible Prophecy

Perhaps another big reason most people no longer look to the Church for answers to questions about the future is that many churches avoid biblical prophecy like the plague.

Since most Bible scholars push the fulfillment of prophecy either back into the past or out into the future, it has little relevance to the here and now. Many ministers I've questioned about the Book of Revelation quite frankly admit they just don't know what to do with it.

"There are sixty-five other books in the Bible," one minister opined, "so why do we even need to talk about Revelation?"

"I recently took an informal poll in my church and asked about what book of the Bible people would like most to study," an announcer from a radio station in my area told me during a interview program a while ago.

"And what did you find?" I asked.

"To a person, they all said they'd like to study Revelation," he answered.

"That's interesting," I replied. "Then what did you do?"

"I went to my pastor and told him what I'd found. I asked if he would teach some classes on Revelation."

"What was his answer?" I queried.

"He told me he'd rather not."

"But why?" I wanted to know.

"He said studying Revelation is too divisive . . . that he knows a number of churches that have split wide open over such a study."

Can you believe that—churches splitting over a book that was given by the Holy Spirit to bring unity of heart and spirit to the Body of Christ? Yet it has happened.

Reason #5 – Some People Get Carried Away with Dramatic Predictions

It's not surprising that most people, at the mere mention of the Book of Revelation, start conjuring up mental images of grotesque beasts, global devastation, and vanishing loved ones. Virtually all of the popular books on biblical prophecy focus mainly on such themes, and many have gained credibility by basing their predictions on recent news events and people.

Since we humans are naturally curious about the future, and many are also quite fearful about coming events, it's not hard to convince many people that the world is quickly coming to an end.

This common countdown-to-doomsday approach causes people to react in several destructive ways:

Some are immobilized by anxiety and depression. "Look, man," a blurry-eyed street person told a volunteer in a shelter for the homeless, "we're all gonna be blown away one of these days .... What's the use in trying?"

Many psychiatrists now routinely ask depressed patients about their views on biblical prophecy. They've found that fears about the end of the world frequently appear as symptoms of a mental breakdown.

Some lapse into escapist lifestyles. Some people are convinced that the end of the world is just around the corner but that they're going to be removed from planet Earth in time to escape the holocaust. They develop what we called in the military service a FIGMO (**F**orget **I**t **I**'ve **G**ot **M**y **O**rders) attitude and become "short" sighted.

"The Rapture could occur at any moment," a woman in a troubled marriage told her pastor, "it's all foretold. So I find it hard to even think about my work or raising my children or paying bills or getting along with my unbelieving husband .... Praise Jesus, it won't be long until I leave all this pain and sorrow behind me."

Others are simply looking for an easy way to push aside what they fear will inevitably be their own destruction. "Why not live it up?" they ask. "Living it up" may involve substance abuse, sexual promiscuity, extreme materialism, or a host of other modern-day magic carpets that whisk people away to exotic states. "Don't Worry, Be Happy," proclaimed the title of a Grammy-winning song of the late eighties. And that's exactly the philosophy many have adopted.

Some retreat into cynicism. "When I was a little boy, I used to go to church and hear preachers telling hair-raising tales about how the Second Coming could happen that very night," said a cynical humanist to a friend of mine. "They'd show all these charts from the Book of Revelation about the Millennium and frightening pictures of beasts and swarms of locusts.

"I'd go down to the altar and cry my eyes out and confess every sin I'd ever thought of committing, but it never seemed to help," he continued. "I'd still get up and go home scared half to death and lie awake until I saw the morning sun peeping through the windows.

"All night long, I'd keep tiptoeing into my mother's room to see if she was still there . . . . I figured if anybody was going to get raptured it would be her.

"Gradually," he continued, "it began to dawn on me that as soon as Adolph Hitler was disqualified by death as a candidate for the Antichrist, the preachers would replace him with a Joseph Stalin or a Henry Kissinger or a Ronald Reagan, or whoever seemed to be the biggest threat to them at the moment. The absolutely certain dates for the Rapture kept slipping further and further into the future.

"Eventually," he chuckled, "I just dismissed the whole business as superstition born of ignorance."

"Has that eliminated your anxieties about the future?" my friend questioned.

"No . . . not really," the skeptic replied thoughtfully. "I don't think you can be certain about anything. But, at least I don't go to bed with goose bumps all over me anymore."

Perhaps most people are simply indifferent to biblical prophecy. Part of it stems from the fact that most of us have about all we can deal with each day. With all of our family needs, job demands, and other concerns, we never seem to have time to sort through all the confusion about prophecy.

This common countdown-to-doomsday approach causes people to react in several destructive ways:

Besides, there seems to be no place a person can turn in order to get straight answers about all the conflicting views of various prophetic Scriptures. Even churches, teachers, and theologians seem to be at odds over what prophecies all mean.

So most people take the attitude, "Okay, you guys figure it all out, and when you agree, let me know."

Reason #6 – Some Use Scare Tactics to Get People Converted

Many churches and prophecy teachers use apocalyptic imagery to frighten people into what they call "making decisions for Christ." Very often, their hearers do not truly convert; they merely make a profession of faith to escape impending damnation. As soon as the fear factor is discredited (as with specific predictions that don't come true) and the apocalyptic heat wears off, the so-called decisions often lose their meaning.

Falling stars, bloody moons, darkened sun, shaking earth, and signs in the sky are some of this apocalyptic language. But this collapsing-universe, cosmic-cataclysm language is employed throughout the Bible. In our modern-day minds it sounds like the end of the world. But scattered throughout biblical history, and mostly overlooked by the popular prophecy writers of today, are numerous uses and fulfillments of this apocalyptic language. Knowing the nature of these previous uses and fulfillments will enable us to make proper sense of this biblical language.

The popular stream of endsaying pundits, however, has assumed that the Bible's apocalyptic language must now be interpreted literally and physically; and since no one has witnessed a cataclysmic, earth-ending event of this nature, its time must lie in the future. The shock value of earthquakes, exploding stars, cosmic eclipses, and nuclear holocausts is awesome. Thus, a literal/physical rendering of the Bible's apocalyptic texts serves the purpose of endsayers, and has become fixed in the minds of millions.

> **Many churches and prophecy teachers use apocalyptic imagery to frighten people into what they call "making decisions for Christ."**

The problem with this line of thought is that no biblical grounds exist for this assumption. What's worse, it's an obviously flawed method of interpretation. It ignores a long biblical precedent and pattern of many uses and fulfillments of this language. This is not the way to approach the Scriptures. When we fail to give proper attention to these historical uses and fulfillments, we do a grave injustice to understanding the Bible's employment of apocalyptic language.

Long Biblical Precedent and Pattern of Uses and Fulfillments

Let take a brief look at the pattern of judgment-comings of God in Scripture, i.e., the Bible's apocalyptic prophecies and descriptions of cosmic disaster and how they were actually fulfilled. This type of de-creation language has always been associated with another major Old Testament theme: the coming of "the day of the Lord." Only when we view these poetic figures of speech from within their numerous historical contexts can we properly apply them to our time. Without this historical perspective, we are guaranteed to misinterpret their meaning, committing the error of eisegesis—reading one's own preconceived ideas back into the text. This is not wise if one sincerely desires to know what the text is talking about.

As we allow the Bible to shed light on itself, we'll see that this type of apocalyptic language always depicted a coming judgment of God. Its use and this mindset were in full bloom in Bible times. Jesus used this same language, as did many New Testament writers, as well as John the scribe of the Revelation, and added no disclaimers that they were using it any differently. Its roots are in the Old Testament, and 1st-century Jews were steeped in it, not only from ancient Scriptures but also from inter-testament literature dating back to the 4th century B.C. Consequently, they expected apocalyptic fulfillments to be quite different from what most of us today have been led to believe. Here are some examples from the Old Testament:[14]

> **Isaiah 13:9-10, 13.** "See, the day of the Lord is coming – a cruel day, with wrath and fierce anger – to make the land desolate. The stars of heaven and their constellations will not show their light. The rising sun will be darkened and the moon will not give its light . . . . Therefore I will make the heavens tremble; and the earth will shake from its place at the wrath of the Lord Almighty, in the day of his burning anger."

Fulfillment. The prophet was *not* speaking of the end of the world, the final judgment, or a solar or lunar eclipse. He was giving a figurative prediction of the literal destruction of Babylon by the Medes in 539 B.C. (Isa. 13:1). The use of cosmic language means the presence of God was involved and revealed in this judgment upon these people.

Isaiah 34:4. "All the stars of heaven will be dissolved and the sky rolled up like a scroll; all the starry host will fall like withered leaves from the vine, like shriveled figs from the fig tree."
Fulfillment. This was *not* the end of the world, or the end of the cosmos, but a figurative description of the coming divine destruction of Edom in the late 6th century B.C. (Isa. 34:5).

Ezekiel 32:7, 8a. ". . . I will cover the heavens and darken their stars; I will cover the sun with a cloud, and the moon will not give its light. All the shining lights in the heavens I will darken over you."
Fulfillment. This prophecy was God's warning to the Pharaoh of Egypt of his impending fall in the mid-6th century B.C. (Ezek. 32:2).

Nahum 1:5. "The mountains quake before him and the hills melt away. The earth trembles at his presence, the world, and all who live in it."
Fulfillment. The subject is God's coming in judgment on the city of Nineveh, and not the physical world, in 612 B.C. (Nahum 1:1).

Isaiah 40:4. "Every valley shall be raised up, every mountain and hill made low; the rough ground shall become level, the rugged places a plain."
Fulfillment. This is not a reference to a giant excavation job, but a description of the 1st-century ministry of John the Baptist (Matt. 3:1-3).

Joel 2:30, 31. "I will show wonders in the heavens and on the earth, blood and fire and billows of smoke. The sun will be turned to darkness and the moon to blood before the coming of the great and dreadful day of the Lord."

Fulfillment. Joel was not describing the end of the world. He was giving a figurative description of the actual events accompanying the coming of the Holy Spirit on the day of Pentecost. Peter said it was fulfilled in their day (Acts 2:16-21). We'll see that this "day of the Lord" (actually, "the day of Christ") followed less than forty years later.

The Old Testament pattern of figurative and de-creation language usage and numerous fulfillments by literal, real, momentous, and divine judgment events sets the precedent. If the words of these passages were to be taken literally, it would mean that massive changes or destructions of the cosmos and earth occurred numerous times. But the language transcends its literalism and has to be understood figuratively. It's associated with, and really and truly describes, the literal coming of God's judgment upon a people or nation.

Next let's look at some uses found in the New Testament. These prophesied another, soon-coming-judgment event:

Matthew 24:29. ". . . the sun will be darkened, the moon will not give its light; the stars will fall from the sky, and the heavenly bodies will be shaken."
Fulfillment. Jesus is speaking in the same apocalyptic terms drawn from the language of the prophets cited above, a language very familiar to 1st-century Jews. As we shall see in Chapter 4, He was figuratively describing the coming judgment and fall of Jerusalem circa A.D. 70—an event as serious and severe (if not more so) as God's judgments upon people and nations in the Old Testament.

2 Peter 3:10, 11a. "But the day of the Lord will come like a thief. The heavens will disappear with a roar; the elements will be destroyed by fire, and the earth and everything in it will be laid bare. Since everything will be destroyed in this way, what kind of people ought you to be?"
Fulfillment. Again, Peter is employing the same common apocalyptic terminology of his day (see 2 Pet. 3:2). His words are no more to be taken literally/physically than are any of the others above. As we shall see in Chapters 4, 7, and 10 the figurative fulfillment about which he was warning came upon his contemporaries in a way

(nature) totally consistent with all the other apocalyptic fulfillments cited above.

So what should we learn from the above perspective? One thing is for sure—the Bible's use of this collapsing-universe, cosmic-cataclysm, apocalyptic language is well-developed, consistently employed, and highly pragmatic! No disclaimers, qualifications, or changes are ever recorded or hinted at by Jesus or any New Testament writer who used this similar kind of language. What, then, would cause us to interpret this apocalyptic symbolism differently today? If we do so, without legitimate justification, isn't this interpretation by exception and a violation of proper and honest interpretation? Or, perhaps, it's even worse? Let's see:

> **Revelation 6:12-17.** "I watched as he opened the sixth seal. There was a great earthquake. The sun turned black like sackcloth made of goat hair, the whole moon turned blood red, and the stars in the sky fell to earth, as late figs drop from a fig tree when shaken by a strong wind. The sky receded like a scroll rolling up, and every mountain and island was removed from its place.
>
> "Then the kings of the earth, the princes, the generals, the rich, the mighty, and every slave and every free man hid in the caves and among the rocks of the mountains. They called to the mountains and the rocks, 'Fall on us and hide us from the face of him who sits on the throne and from the wrath of the Lamb! For the great day of their wrath has come, and who can stand?'"
>
> **Fulfillment???** Five years ago a prominent pastor and friend of mine, with whom I enjoyed many extensive, one-on-one, and open-Bible lunches discussing issues contained in this book and other of my books, was teaching through the Book of Revelation in a weekly Bible study group of about fifty to seventy people, which I regularly attended and participated therein quite actively. When he arrived at these verses, he made this statement, "I believe this is literally going to happen someday." At which point I raised my hand. Somewhat reluctantly, he acknowledged me.
>
> I asked, "Are you aware that this type of language has a long history of uses and fulfillments in the Old Testament and never once was it literally fulfilled and never once during all its various fulfillments was the physical creation ever altered one iota? To

which he sharply quipped, "Well, I believe it will be someday." Then he abruptly moved on to the next verse terminating any further conversation on this issue.

Two months later he became sick. A month later he collapsed while teaching this Bible study and we had to call 911 and have him taken to the emergency room. But the doctors could find nothing wrong. During the next few months he kept getting worse, had to stop teaching our Bible Study, and was hospitalized. Then he died. It all transpired over a period of about six months. Our local paper carried a large, front page article and picture eulogizing him. Twice, in this article it reported that he "died of an undiagnosed illness . . . . Despite several tests, doctors could not diagnose his illness." What had happened? Perhaps, and as I discussed privately with the associate pastor who took this pastor's place in leading our weekly Bible study group during this time period, it relates to this warning the Book of Revelation places upon its own prophecy:

> *I warn everyone who hears the words of the prophecy of this book: If anyone adds anything to them, God will add to him the plagues described in this book. And if anyone takes words away from this book of prophecy, God will take away from him his share in the tree of life and in the holy city, which are described in this book* (Rev. 22:18-19; also see Deut. 4:2; 12:32; Prov. 30:6; and 1 Cor. 11:27-32)?

But I was essentially ignored, dismissed, and advised to not pursue this line of thought or to discuss it with others—to which, at that time, I submitted.

One thing, however, is for sure. This experience with this pastor, whether it was a valid or invalid application of Revelation's warning and plagues, has further ingrained within me the seriousness with which anyone must approach the teaching of and/or writing about the prophecy of the Bible's last Book of Revelation.

Many more examples of uses and fulfillments could be cited, but that would belabor the point. Even though it sounds like the end of the world, this apocalyptic language of the Bible is a common and frequently used linguistic style. It's the language of the prophets, and it's employed throughout the Old and New Testaments in an identical and consistent manner. It's the Bible's method of metaphorically describing actual, literal events—specifically, God's coming judgments upon nations, peoples, or cities that have been enemies of his people, or his judgment upon his own people, Israel. The physical means employed are always those of invading foreign armies or natural disasters. These many biblical judgments are also events of international and/or eschatological importance. In every instance, the "worlds" (social, political, religious) of those receiving this judgment of God were ended or dramatically changed. So complete and comprehensive was each judgment event that it was appropriately spoken of in hyperbolic, world-ending terms. Speaking appropriately does not require that one speak literally. Please note, once again, that in none of these historical fulfillments did the physical nature of literal heavenly bodies or the earth change *one iota*.

Even though it sounds like the end of the world, this apocalyptic language of the Bible is a common and frequently used linguistic style.

And yet you might legitimately ask if it is possible—and as many have been led to believe—that a literal/physical, time-ending, universe-destroying, cosmic-crashing event can be an additional fulfillment? Can apocalyptic language using symbolism and poetic imagery be taken both figuratively and literally? Some theologians argue that it can, terming such a case a double or multiple fulfillment. But is this possible here?

Certainly, a future cosmic destruction would be within the sovereignty and capability of a God who many (me, too) believe spoke the world into existence in the first place (see Genesis 1). But to break the pattern of biblical precedent by suddenly literalizing apocalyptic terms and phrases and applying them to the destruction of the physical universe, *without an expressed biblical warrant to do so*, is to misunderstand the Bible on the Bible's own terms.

The Jews of the 1st century did not understand apocalyptic phraseology as literally ending the world. And neither Jesus nor any New Testament writer amended this common Jewish understanding when employing this linguistic form. Doing so in our day is totally arbitrary and reprehensible. It only confuses and leads readers away from what this kind of language always meant and how it was consistently fulfilled when it was used. Nor is a literal rendering in harmony with the scriptures we have cited that proclaim the eternalness of our world. With all due respect, this is another classic case of the traditions of men "nullify[ing] the word of God" or making it of "none effect" (Mark 7:13; Matt. 15:6 – NIV/KJV). It is time for this false tradition to give way to revealed truth. We mustn't be hamstrung by it any more.

On the other hand, when God wanted to express his blessings upon a nation or a people, the same apocalyptic language is used, but in positive terms. Instead of the earth or the universe pictured as collapsing or destroyed, they're shown to be abundant, flourishing, and more strongly established. Note the following:

> **Isaiah 30:26; 60:19-20.** "The moon will shine like the sun, and the sunlight will be seven times brighter, like the light of seven full days, when the Lord binds up the bruises of his people and heals the wounds he inflicted . . . . The sun will no more be your light by day, nor will the brightness of the moon shine on you, for the Lord will be your everlasting light, and your God will be your glory. Your sun will never set again, and your moon will wane no more; The Lord will be your everlasting light, and your days of sorrow will end."
> **Fulfillment.** Portrays the blessings promised to Old Covenant Israel if they submitted to God and were obedient to their covenant.
>
> **Isaiah 35:1, 6.** "The desert and the parched land will be glad; the wilderness will rejoice and blossom. Like the crocus, it will burst into bloom; it will rejoice greatly and shout for joy . . . . Then will the lame leap like a deer and the tongue of the dumb shout for joy. Water will gush forth in the wilderness and streams in the desert."
> **Fulfillment.** The figurative language describes actual kingdom blessings brought by Jesus. He proclaimed them in like manner when He declared, "'Whoever believes in me, as the Scripture has said, streams of living water will flow from within him.' By this he meant the Spirit, whom those who believed in him were later to receive." (John 7:38, 39a).

Thus, both positive (blessings) and negative (judgment) symbolism were well understood in the Temple and the synagogues of the 1st century. Like them, we Americans use symbols that we well understand. For example, if I said that I love the Colts, the Bears, the Bulls, or the Dolphins, would you think I was an animal lover? Or, if I showed you a cartoon of an elephant and a donkey fighting each other, what would that mean to you?

The interpretation of apocalyptic language is taught to us by the Bible itself. This precedent should serve as a caution to any modern-day interpreter toying with the idea of breaking this consistency of use and fulfillment.[15] With a proper historical understanding of the Bible's consistent use of apocalyptic language in mind, we moderns would be wise to follow it. We must conclude from the Bible itself that God isn't going to destroy the world. That leaves only us. Could we destroy it? That's highly doubtful. And if we tried, God would likely thwart our plans. Why? It is because his Word teaches that our world is without end.[16] All the above is part of the reason why the Book of Revelation is not about an end of the world.

Clearly, Something Is Wrong

If the measure of a message's validity is the fruit it produces (Matt. 12:33), it's pretty clear that something is drastically wrong with the way many Christians are handling biblical prophecy, and especially its climactic book, the Book of Revelation.

Thus, both positive (blessings) and negative (judgment) symbolism were well understood in the Temple and the synagogues of the 1st century.

Perhaps this is why much of the Church is muddled in such a mess of confusion and mediocrity. Such misuses of prophecy—failed attempts to predict historical events and dates for the end of the world, fighting over when Jesus will return, or neglecting the prophetic message altogether—produce the bad fruit of divisiveness, fear, confusion, and escapism. Furthermore, this kind of misuse discredits the entire gospel message and emasculates the effectiveness of the Church and its people. Moreover, this bad fruit is not unique to our generation. Misuse of prophecy has been a pastime of many in the Church for centuries.

Not What God Had in Mind

As we'll continue to explore, the Book of Revelation was given to produce precisely the opposite effect in the Church. It was given to produce good fruit like unity, comfort, faith, understanding, personal and corporate power, obedience, and more.

The Church of the 1st century, to which the Revelation was originally addressed, as well as through two more centuries, was under severe persecutions from the religious Jews and from the Roman government. Historical accounts show that in many parts of Europe and Asia, Christians were brutalized and killed by the thousands because of their faith in Christ. And despite their prayers and trusting in Christ, the persecution, or tribulation, seemed to grow worse every day.

"Where is God while all this is happening?" any Christian back then would have had good reason to ask.

John's prophetic message, the Revelation, provides God's resounding and timeless answer to that question.

The Bottom Line

The bottom line of the Revelation is that God has removed the veil from the full, present-day reality of Jesus Christ, enabling believers to overcome the world, to live in perfect fellowship with the greater Jesus, and to reign and rule with Him, here and now, on this earth, via the kingdom of God, and in his Holy City.

The Revelation ends on this triumphant note. And since it is not a prediction of a disastrous end of the world, but a proclamation of a glorious beginning, let us continue to search out its infinite riches. Next, we need to unlearn and discover how to place the Book of Revelation, i.e., the greater Jesus' unveiling and revealing, in its proper fulfillment and relevance context for its original audience, for us today, and for the future.

Chapter 3

Unraveling the Mysteries of the Unveiling

The Book of Revelation is not placed last in the Bible for nothing. It's the pinnacle of God's progressive plan of revelation to humankind and, therefore, the climax of all prophecy. So if this climactic prophecy is all about unveiling and revealing the greater Jesus as He is today and what He is doing, why does it use such bizarre creatures, descriptions, and symbols to tell its message? If God had something important to tell us, why didn't He just come right out and say it in simple, everyday language?

In fact, God does have something very important to tell us in the Revelation, and He did say it clearly and simply. The problem is, most interpreters have garbled his message by attaching their own meanings to it and taking it out of its divinely determined time and relevancy context.

Let me ask you an unsettling question: How much of your belief about the Book of Revelation is based on your personal study and search of the Scriptures, and how much is based on what others have told you?

When I began to seriously study the Revelation and other biblical prophecy some years ago, I quickly discovered that I had picked up most of my beliefs from other people, and not from direct reading and study of God's own Word. Quite frankly, I soon discovered that much of what I had been told and taught did not square with the Bible.

Please hear what I am saying, and don't infer what I'm not saying. I don't at all mean to imply that we shouldn't listen to teachers and read other books on the subject. But listening to others and reading books about the Bible cannot take the place of our personal reading and study on any subject, including prophecy. We each have the responsibility to measure everything we hear and read (including this book) against God's Word (see Acts 17:11; 1 Thess. 5:21).

Once again, I must emphasize that unlearning is the toughest part of learning. But be assured if you have had trouble unraveling the mysteries of the Revelation, you're not alone. Bible scholars over the centuries have been puzzled by the book's strange symbolism and what theologians call its apocalyptic imagery.

Martin Luther, for instance, felt that the book should be dropped from the Canon because it was too different from the other New Testament Scriptures and neither taught nor acknowledged Jesus Christ. John Calvin, another leading 16th-century reformer, refused to write a commentary on it. Ulrich Zwingli, the 16th-century Swiss reformer and Bible translator, called it insignificant and refused to concern himself with it.

I certainly don't claim to have any direct new revelation from God, or even inspiration beyond what's available to any Christian. It's just that I have examined carefully the Revelation and discovered that this vital book has always been God's present-day message to his Church. What's more, the Book of Revelation explains itself, if we will just listen to it.

In this chapter, that is exactly what we will do. We'll examine seven keys you can use to textually, systematically, consistently and properly unlock the mysteries of this vital book, unlearn many popular misconceptions, and unravel its unveiling. As we shall see, the approach one brings for interpreting Revelation is, indeed, critically important. Grant R. Osborne concurs: "Perhaps more than any other book, our understanding of the meaning of Revelation depends on the hermeneutical perspective we bring to bear on it."[1] Unfortunately, many have been *consistently wrong* in their interpretive approach.

[NOTE TO READER: The content of some of these seven keys was originally published in the *Journal of the Evangelical Theological Society*, Vol. 49, No. 4 (Dec. 2006) in an article by John Noē and titled, "An Exegetical Basis for a Preterist-Idealist Understanding of the Book of Revelation." It is posted on PRI's website. Go to: www.prophecyrefi.org. Also see, Appendix B regarding how this article came to be.]

Key #1 – The Revelation Uses Figurative Language and Symbols to Reveal Spiritual/Physical Events and Realities

Very few, if any people take the Bible literally across the board. How many people do you know, for instance, who read the Old Testament in Hebrew and the New Testament in Greek? Most people read translations; and since it is impossible to translate literally from the ancient languages, any translation *is*, to some extent, an interpretation.

Or how many people do you know who are walking around half-blind because they've gouged out their right eye (see Matt. 5:29), or one-handed because they've cut off their right hand? (see Matt. 5:30).

Why is it that so many people can readily accept as figurative such metaphors as the gouging out of eyes and the cutting off of hands but insist on taking literally all of Jesus' references about his comings? Why do we readily accept such terms as *born again, the bread of life,* or *living water* as symbols yet refuse to accept *come again* or *wedding banquet, comes in glory, riding a horse,* or *coming on the clouds* as symbols illustrating real but greater, spirit-realm/physical-realm realities?

Why then did Jesus use physical/material symbols to convey spirit-realm/physical-realm realities?[2] It is because we humans have no frame of reference to enable us to understand the realities of the spirit realm. We can only relate what we don't know to what we do know.

Hence, the strange imagery of the Revelation is not God's way of keeping us confused. Rather, it represents the efforts of an infinite God to communicate with finite human beings about truth and reality in both the spiritual and physical realms. In other words, it's a behind-the-scenes peek at the invisible-spirit-realm reality behind the visible-physical-realm reality, the unseen world behind the seen natural world; and the great things taking place in the invisible spirit realm and how these interact with and manifest themselves in the visible physical world.

Of course, God knows that trying to figure out full spiritual/physical reality using earthly wisdom is like plugging your computer directly into a nuclear power plant—the source overloads the receiver's capacity. But the natural world is only part of God's creation. And the unseen world, which He created as well, is just as real, has a powerful effect on the seen world, and plays an active role in individual lives and in human history.

The trouble lies not with the way God has chosen to convey his message but with the way we humans try to grasp it. We simply cannot grasp invisible spiritual reality in the same way as scientific or historical knowledge. Spiritual reality can only be grasped by faith, and through spiritual ears (see 1 Cor. 1:18-25; 3:19; Rev. 2:7; 2:11; 2:17; 2:29; 3:6; 3:13; 3:22) and eyes (Matt.13:13-15, from Isaiah 6:9-10).

But the natural world is only part of God's creation. And the unseen world, which He created as well, is just as real, has a powerful effect on the seen world, and plays an active role in individual lives and in human history.

God has not chosen to complicate "the Revelation of Jesus Christ." Mostly, He speaks in figurative language, signs, and symbols to reveal spirit-realm/physical-realm realities. Many today, however, try to understand his meanings in purely physical/material terms.[3] But be forewarned, any one-sided attempt—all literal and physical or all symbolic and spiritual—is literally foolish.

Our Physical/Material Mindset

Jesus often encountered a physical/material mindset during his earthly ministry. Constantly, He spoke about the kingdom of God in very simple terms, using parables and metaphors such as water, seeds, coins, and fish. But the people who heard Him kept trying to interpret and understand his parables and symbols literally instead of spiritually.

For example, Jesus explained the most basic spirit-realm/physical-realm reality—the new birth—to a searching Pharisee named Nicodemus. Unable to grasp Jesus' message, Nicodemus talked about re-entering his mother's womb and asked, "How can this be?" Jesus exclaimed, "I have spoken to you of earthly things and you do not believe; how then will you believe if I speak of heavenly things?" (see John 3:1-13).

Remember, when the people asked Jesus why He spoke in parables, He said of the Pharisees, "Though seeing, they do not see; though hearing, they do not hear or understand" (Matt. 13:13).

We need to interpret and understand the stories and imagery of the Revelation just as we interpret and understand the parables and symbols Jesus used in the Gospel narratives—figuratively, as metaphors and similes that express both spiritual and physical realities. The visual parables and symbols of the Apocalypse become complicated and frightening only when we take the book's language literally, purely physically—something that God never intended for us to do.

Revelation's very first verse *literally* stipulates this communication style, "and he [God] sent and signified it by his angel unto his servant John" (Rev. 1:1 KJV). The word "signified" (Greek word, *semaino*) most graphically means "sign-ified," i.e., making known or communicating with signs and symbols.[4] Hence, if we take the Revelation precisely for what it is, visual parables of spiritual/physical reality, any sincere believer can understand and obey it.

But the physical/material mindset—the so-called scientific approach—denies or ignores the dimension of the spirit and blinds us to the spirit-realm and -world realities of the Revelation. Once we accept that God is speaking in spirit-realm/physical-realm terms using signs and symbols, however, the Revelation begins to open up its treasures to us.

Why Bother about Spirit-Realm Realities?

All this talk about the spirit realm may make you uncomfortable. The fact is that most people in our culture, and in the Church, get up every morning and go through the whole day without the slightest thought of what is going on in the spiritual dimension. To them, angels, demons, and other spirit-realm beings are little more than eerie creatures in science fiction or horror movies. Or they may think of everything that lies beyond the material realm as paranormal—something we humans may someday be able to explain in purely scientific terms.

For such people, the supernatural is not real and certainly not a touchable, squeezable, and graspable reality. For them, the Revelation presents only a confusing set of riddles that have little meaning for their daily existence. Simply put, they can take it or leave it. If this realm enters their consciousness at all (perhaps through a television episode about the occult), it lingers only until their attention is redirected to something they find more interesting.

"Why bother about the spirit realm?" they would ask if confronted with questions about it.

Here are four very important reasons why we humans need to grasp spiritual reality.

(1) God is spirit. Many in the Church have been doing a fairly good job of convincing most people—even Christians—to think of God only in physical terms. How? One way is by making an idol of the Church itself—by letting the Church, a human organization, usurp the rightful place of the Lord Jesus Christ as the focal point of worship and kingdom activity. That is why, today, many Christians talk about doing the work of the Church, being committed to the Church, making great sacrifices for the Church. Some even act as if the buildings, rituals, and doctrines of their churches are sacred themselves.

But Jesus said, "God is spirit, and his worshipers must worship in spirit and truth" (John 4:24). And while God is spirit, He is also literally God. The Greek word, *aletheia*, translated as *truth*, means "unveiled reality, the reality pertaining to an appearance."[5] Do you see the trap? When we absolutize the Church, we worship the appearance, not the reality behind it. Moreover, how can we worship in spirit if we don't or can't think in terms of spirit?

The Apocalypse (the Revelation) unveils and reveals the spirit-realm reality of the greater Jesus Christ—here and now. Hence, God invites us to look beyond Jesus' earthly appearance to see Him in all his present, glorious reality. That is not pie-in-the-sky-by-and-by. It was at hand, back then. It is at hand, right now.

That's what makes the Revelation message so vital for us today, in this present world. It lifts the veil and enables believers to get beyond Jesus' earthly ministry so that we can live daily in perfect fellowship with Him as He is today.

And remember, as we saw in Chapter 1, the writer of Hebrews not only informs us that "we are surrounded by such a great cloud of witnesses" (Heb. 12:1), but he also tells us who is in this cloud. It contains "thousands upon thousands of angels . . . the church of the firstborn, whose names are written in heaven. . . . God . . . the spirits of righteous men made perfect, to Jesus . . . ." (Heb. 12:22-24). Of course, this is only the good side of the spirit realm.

(2) Humans are spirit beings. Jesus made a very startling statement in one of his synagogue teachings: "Unless you eat the flesh of the Son of Man and drink his blood, you have no life in you" (see John 6:47-65).

"This is hard teaching. Who can accept it?" his disciples complained. It was so hard, in fact, that many of them "turned back and no longer followed him."

When Jesus became aware that his disciples were grumbling about his statements, He explained, "The Spirit gives life; the flesh counts for nothing. The words I have spoken to you are Spirit and life."

Why is spirit such a hard concept for us humans to grasp? It's because most of us do not recognize our spirituality. We can take in the idea that we have a body, a mind, and emotions, because we can prove them scientifically. But we can experience our spirits only through an awakening of our spirits to the realities of the spirit dimension—a dimension where God the Father, Jesus, the Holy Spirit, Satan, and other competing spirit-realm beings reside. Only we humans were created with this dimension and capability. No animal can perceive the spirit realm or desires knowledge of something beyond this visible, material world.

The night before Jesus was crucified, his disciples demonstrated their complete lack of understanding of the spirit dimension that's typical of most humans. When He told them that He was going to die, they protested vehemently. To them, his physical presence was everything. They wanted Him *with* them in his human flesh, but He longed to be *in* them in their spirits (see John 16:5-16). Likewise, humanity has continually attempted to discredit and despiritualize the spirit-realm/physical-realm message Jesus and his angel gave to John through visual parables in the Revelation.

Because we are so attuned to the material world and our flesh, we long for a physical rapture, for a physical and visible return of Jesus, for a physical and visible New Jerusalem, for a physical and visible wedding supper with Christ—someday, somewhere, yet to happen. As we shall see, the unadulterated message of the Revelation is that we don't have to wait—spiritually, truly, and really, we can dwell and dine with Jesus in his Holy City right here, right now.

"Yes, but we humans are also flesh and bone," you might protest, "and we live in a world of time, space, and matter." That brings us to the third reason we need to be concerned about the spirit realm.

(3) The kingdom of God is a spirit-realm/physical-realm kingdom of both blessings and battles. When the Pharisees asked Jesus when his kingdom would come, He replied, "The kingdom of God does not come visibly, nor will people say, 'Here it is,' or 'There it is,' because the kingdom of God is within you" (see Luke 17:20-21). The better translation, however, is "among you" or "in your midst." Why? It's because the kingdom of God was not *within* those unbelieving Pharisees.[6] Rather, the kingdom, in all its fullness, was both spiritually and physically standing right there among them, in their midst, in the form of Jesus Himself (see Col. 2:9). Thus, when Jesus comes in the spirit realm to indwell a believer at the point of their being born anew, his kingdom also enters him or her.

But the Pharisees and the temple rulers and teachers who constantly challenged Jesus refused to allow the spirit-realm/physical-realm kingdom of God to enter them or them enter it and tried to keep others from entering as well (see Matt. 23:13-14). How? By reducing everything to a mere physical/material plane, they sought to obtain the blessings of God by doing the works of the flesh.

Yet, the teachings of Jesus—and especially in the Revelation—repeatedly promise God's blessings to those who enter the kingdom of God's spirit realm and reign and rule with the greater Jesus, here and now, in this physical realm. That's where the power is! For instance, Jesus said:

- "Blessed is the one who reads the words of this prophecy [the unveiling and revealing of the greater Jesus] and blessed are those who hear it and take to heart what is written in it, because the time is near [at hand]" (Rev. 1:3).
- "Blessed is he who stays awake [spiritually] and keeps his clothes [garments of righteousness] with him" (Rev. 16:15).
- Blessed are those who wash their robes, that they may have the right to the tree of life and may go through the gates into the city" (Rev. 22:14).

As we shall soon see, those three promised blessings and much more were at hand for 1st-century believers; they have been at hand for believers of all generations ever since; and they are all available for believers today and will be for future generations as well. But the key to receiving them is to enter, reign, and rule with Christ via the spirit realm now—not to wait around for physical events to happen someday out in the future.

As far-fetched as it might seem, God has chosen human beings as the earthly seat of his kingdom. Within human beings the spirit world (both good and evil) and the material world connect. The fact that the spirit realm is invisible doesn't mean that it doesn't exist; the spirit dimension is just as real as the physical world we experience through our five senses. Thus, when we deny, ignore, or minimize the spirit realm, we simply diminish our ability to see it (through our spiritual eyes), to operate in it, and be blessed by it. What's more, we shall never be able to fully understand the physical world, and to effectively rule and reign with the greater Jesus, the contemporary Christ, here and now, until we recognize and attempt to understand the world of the spirit.

It is crucial that we recognize how spirit-realm forces influence the behavior of individuals, groups, nations, and even churches, and how they shape events in the material world. We must acknowledge that we can only overcome and live victoriously in the material world when we are energized by the Spirit of God within and among us.

Likewise, John's prophetic message in the Revelation explains that the horrors the original recipients of that book were experiencing in the material/physical realm, as well as some of us today, directly resulted from spirit-realm activities. Thus, it uses visual parables to show us these spiritual/physical realities. But Revelation also makes it clear that, no matter what the situation might look like at any moment in the visible world, God is in charge. Jesus Christ is the King of kings and Lord of lords (see Rev. 1:5; 17:14), and his kingdom belongs to those who have experienced the new birth, enter in, and follow Him. Yes, it takes all three (see Rev. 1:6; 5:9-10; 21:7). Further, it shows that those who obey and remain faithful in the midst of great troubles will receive the power to overcome the worst that Satan and his cohorts can do to them (see Rev. 12:10-12).

What a glorious reality!

(4) 'For the testimony of Jesus is the spirit of prophecy' (Rev. 19:10b). Prophecy declares what we cannot know by natural means. It can either predict or it can speak forth the mind and counsel of God—past, present, or future.

The very spirit and life of all biblical prophecy is Jesus. In fact, it is safe to say that all biblical prophecy is the ongoing disclosure of Jesus. To see this is to understand prophecy; not to see it is to miss its richest meaning.

"My purpose," the Apostle Paul said, "is that they may be encouraged in heart and united in love, so that they may have the full riches of complete understanding, in order that they may know the mystery of God, namely, Christ, *in whom are hidden all the treasures of wisdom and knowledge*" (Col. 2:2-3, emphasis added).

Thus, Revelation depicts the greater Jesus as the present-tense fulfillment of all prophecy:

- It is the greater Jesus Who stands among the lampstands and speaks with absolute authority to the seven churches of Asia (see Rev. 2-3).
- It is the greater Jesus alone Who is worthy to break the seven seals and open the scroll (see Rev. 5 and 6).
- It is the greater Jesus Who rides the white horse and defeats the enemies of God (see Rev. 19).
- It is the greater Jesus Who shares the wedding supper with the overcomers (see Rev. 19:6-9).
- It is the greater Jesus Who fights the battle of Armageddon (Rev. 16:14-16).
- It is the greater Jesus Who sends plagues upon the great prostitute (Rev. 17 and 18).
- And so much more.

Perhaps the most profound truth in the Revelation is that this greater Jesus freely receives worship—attesting to his deity (see Rev. 7). This is not a new pattern. Ten times in the New Testament people worshiped Jesus, and not once did He restrain them.

What is new in the Revelation is the degree to which He is exalted as "King of kings and Lord of lords" (Rev. 19:16). He is the conquering

"Lion of the tribe of Judah" (Rev. 5:5); He is in the midst of the majestic throne (Rev. 5:6); and He is the source from which the river of life flows (Rev. 22:1).

Yet, He has not lost any of his attributes as Savior. At least thirty times in the Revelation John calls Jesus the Lamb, and he often refers to the marks of death that Jesus still bears. Make no mistake about it; this is the same Jesus Who died on the cross.

So there is really only one major mystery in the Book of Revelation—Jesus Christ, Himself—and He is fully unveiled and revealed in his glorious and final form. The veil of his earthly flesh is removed so that we can see Him in all his spirit-realm reality and as the ultimate, timely, and precise fulfillment of all biblical prophecy.[7]

Thus, the Jesus of the Apocalypse is the same Jesus, but He is different from the Jesus of the Gospels because He is ascended and glorified. He is spirit and life to those who receive Him (see Matt. 13:11-17). Indeed, this is a profound mystery, which we can understand only by "the Spirit of wisdom and revelation" as we seek to "know him better" (Eph. 1:17), and not by the reasoning of men.

As we shall see throughout the pages of this book, all this is not to say that we should restrict Jesus' activities and impact to some past or future date or limit them to only the spirit realm. His presence visibly impacts the physical/material world right now, and it always will.

Hence, the Apocalypse reveals that "the testimony of Jesus *is* the spirit of prophecy" (Rev. 19:10, emphasis added). *Testimony* literally means evidence given. It comes from the Greek *martyria* from which we get our word martyr. Therefore, the testimony of Jesus is, as evidenced by his works, what He has done and continues to do, acting both alone and through his servants.

Spirit-Realm Reality Can Only Be Received Spiritually

Since the Bible is a supernatural book, uniquely inspired by the Holy Spirit, you simply cannot study it like any other book. And since it is a supernatural book, we can only receive its realities supernaturally, as they are made alive to us by the Holy Spirit.

But how do we do that? Jesus gave us a simple formula to follow. "Blessed are the *poor in spirit*," He said, "for theirs is the kingdom of heaven" (see Matt 5:3, emphasis added).

As we come in poverty of spirit (as opposed to coming with intellectual, religious, or prideful arrogance), we recognize that the only hope of solving humankind's two biggest problems—sin and death—lies in the earthly ministry of Jesus Christ. But in the Revelation we see Christ in all his present, spirit-realm reality. No matter how brilliant we may be, we shall not see Him this way or the kingdom of God until we approach the Word of God in spiritual poverty. Sad to say, many of us are like the blind fools or the kingdom killers, the Pharisees of the Gospels' era (see Matt. 23:17).

"You diligently study the Scriptures because you think that *by them* you possess eternal life," Jesus chided the teachers of the law. "These are the Scriptures that testify about me, yet you refuse to *come to me* to have life," He lamented (John 5:39-40, italics added).

If we read the Revelation with the eyes of the flesh, we can see only a physical Second Coming, a material global destruction, a geographical New Jerusalem, and a set of interruptible and deferrable time periods. If, however, we approach it in poverty of the spirit and allow the Holy Spirit to lift the veil by the Word of God, we can see and enter the spiritual dimension of God's kingdom.

But in the Revelation we see Christ in all his present, spirit-realm reality.

Again, Jesus explains how to do that: "Unless one is born again, he cannot *see* the kingdom of God," He told Nicodemus (John 3:3, emphasis added – NASB). That's the first step; we have to be born again to even *see* the kingdom of God. But He doesn't stop there. "Unless one is born of water and the Spirit, he cannot *enter* into the kingdom of God" (John 3:5, emphasis added – NASB). Even after this, however, we may not have entered as Paul explains about himself and to the believers in Antioch, "We must go through many hardships to enter the kingdom of God" (Acts. 14:22 – notice the plural "hardships").[8]

Unraveling the Mysteries of the Unveiling 93

So, the Spirit of God reveals the kingdom of God. Don't expect to comprehend all this with only your intellect; spirit-realm reality must be received spiritually, too.

Try as we may, we cannot figure out the mystery of spirit-realm reality by reducing it to a physical/material plane. But, if we are willing to come to the Bible in poverty of spirit and use the first key—recognizing that God uses figurative language and symbols to convey spiritual/physical realities and truths—the Revelation begins to open to us its bounteous treasures.

The bottom line is this. According to the entire Bible, spiritual forces exert major influence on people and events in the physical world. Consequently, we shall never be able to understand the visible world until we recognize the invisible realm of the spirit. The Book of Revelation is specifically designed to enable us to do just that, if we have ears to hear and eyes to see. Do we? Do you?

Nancy Pearcey in her book, *Total Truth*, articulates another reason:

> The only way the church can establish genuine credibility with nonbelievers is by showing them something they cannot explain or duplicate through their own natural, pragmatic methods—something they can explain only by invoking the supernatural.[9]

So if this last book of the Bible utilizes a combination of literal and symbolic images and language, how does one determine what is literal and what is symbolic?

Key #2 – The Revelation Most Likely Was Written Prior to Jerusalem's Destruction circa A.D. 70

When (the date) the book of the Revelation was actually given to John on the island of Patmos may not be the most exciting of these seven keys for you, but it is of critical importance in unlocking its mysteries. Unfortunately, scholars have reached different conclusions after assessing the dating evidence. The majority contend for a date around A.D. 95 or 96. This date is termed the "late date." But a sizeable and growing minority feel Revelation was written prior to Jerusalem's and the Temple's destruction circa A.D. 70. This is termed the "early date."

Adherence to the late date effectively rules out any contemporary and significant historical event(s) as the soon-coming fulfillment, or any relevance to the original and named recipients. But acceptance of the early date opens the possibility that it describes those events leading up to and including Jerusalem's fall and the destruction of the Temple in A.D. 70.

Without getting bogged down in scholarly discourse, and since I've written more extensively on this topic elsewhere, we shall only look at a few of the major issues in this debate.[10]

Notably, Philip Schaff, who wrote *History of the Christian Church* in eight volumes, and in the Preface to his Revised Edition, admits that "on two points I have changed my opinion – the second Roman captivity of Paul . . . and the date of the Apocalypse (which I now assign, with the majority of modern critics, to the year 68 or 69 instead of 95, as before)."[11]

Interestingly, the major piece of dating evidence cited by the popular late-date theorists is an ambiguous and questionable passage written by Irenaeus, one of the early church Fathers who wrote around A.D. 180-190. But translation difficulties preclude this passage from being used as evidence. Moreover, Irenaeus said nothing about the date of the writing of Revelation. The bigger issue with Irenaeus, however, is his credibility. He claimed that Jesus' earthly ministry lasted approximately fifteen years and that Jesus lived to be almost fifty years old. Thus, the difficulties with Irenaeus' writings in this dating matter are many and varied.

On the other hand, and in my opinion, arguments for the early date are superior, both quantitatively and qualitatively, to those advanced for the late date.[12] For example, of the two types of dating evidence, scholars generally acknowledge internal evidence (contained inside a document) as preferable and taking precedence over external evidence (what others have said about a document, like Irenaeus).

John A. T. Robinson in his book, *Redating the New Testament*, points out that Revelation, along with all New Testament books, say nothing about the destruction of Jerusalem in A.D. 70. He terms this omission as "one of the oddest facts," and questions why this event "is never once mentioned as a past fact" by any New Testament book, even though it is "predicted" and "would appear to be the single most datable and climatic event of the period."[13]

This omission propelled Robinson's redating study. His hypothesis and eventual conclusion was that "the whole of the New Testament was written before 70." He places the writing of Revelation in A.D. 68.[14] Admittedly, Robinson's argument is an argument from silence. But those who claim that Revelation was written in A.D. 95-96 do have major difficulties explaining this glaring omission.

Another piece of dating evidence that strongly favors the early date is also taken internally from the Revelation. Since many late date theorists believe that the symbol of Babylon in Revelation 18—which was yet to be destroyed—represents Rome, New York City, or any city anywhere, or commercialism in general, we shall use the basic interpretative principle of letting "Scripture interpret Scripture" to prove that it actually represented, first and foremost, 1st-century Jerusalem. This can be aptly demonstrated with four simple syllogisms:[15]

> **Major premise #1:** Five times this Babylon is called "O great city" (Rev. 18:10, 16, 19; 16:19; 17:18). Twice it is called "great city" (Rev. 18:18, 21).
> **Minor premise #1:** "The great city" is "where also their Lord was crucified . . . which is figuratively called Sodom . . . ." (Rev. 11:8). And Jerusalem is the only city ever metaphorically called Sodom (Deut. 32:32; Isa. 1:10; Ezek. 16:44-58).
> **Conclusion:** Jerusalem is Revelation's Babylon.

~

> **Major premise #2:** Babylon was guilty of "the blood of the prophets" (Rev. 17:6; 18:24; 16:6).
> **Minor premise #2:** According to Jesus and Paul, only Jerusalem killed the prophets (Matt. 23:34-37; Luke 13:33; 11:47-51; 1 Thess. 2:15-16).
> **Conclusion:** Jerusalem is Revelation's Babylon.

~

Major premise #3: John's people are commanded to "Come out of her, my people, so that you will not share in her sins, so that you will not receive any of her plagues" (Rev. 18:4).
Minor premise #3: The only city Jesus ever commanded his followers to flee from is Jerusalem—when they saw two specific signs (Matt. 24:15-16; Luke 21:20-21). Early church Father Eusebius recorded that this departure happened and that no Christians were trapped and destroyed in the siege and destruction of Jerusalem in AD 70.[16]
Conclusion: Jerusalem is Revelation's Babylon.

~

Major premise #4: This Babylon would be destroyed (Rev. 18:2, 8, 10, 11, 17, 19-23).
Minor premise #4: The only city Jesus said would be destroyed was Jerusalem—it would be "left to you desolate" (Matt.23:38) with "not one stone . . . left on another" (Matt. 24:2).
Conclusion: Jerusalem is Revelation's Babylon.

David Chilton concurred and proclaimed that "the evidence that the prophetic Babylon was Jerusalem is nothing short of overwhelming."[17]

Theologian Donald Guthrie suggests that "the symbol of Babylon was chosen because it stood for the oppressors of God's people."[18] McKenzie agrees and adds that "Harlot Babylon represents those of the old covenant community who rejected Jesus in favor of the temple system."[19]

The bottom-line is this. The proper identification of the doomed harlot-city Babylon sets the fulfillment and understanding context for the whole Book of Revelation. In 1st-century Jerusalem, apostate Judaism was persecuting God's emerging Church. And only one city in the world, at only one time in history, ever matched or will match Jesus' instruction to flee and these above descriptions. It was the city in which the "Lord was crucified." That city—and the apostate religious system it represented—was the city God was calling his people to "come out of."[20]

For these and many other reasons, I agree with a growing number of reputable scholars, who have seriously studied the dating issue that "a date in either AD 65 or early 66 would seem most suitable."[21] In my opinion, the weight of evidence greatly favors a pre-A.D.-70 writing. Therefore, as Reformed theologian R.C. Sproul has suggested, "if Revelation was written before A.D. 70, then a case could be made that it describes chiefly those events leading up to Jerusalem's fall."[22] This brings us to our third key for unlocking the mysteries of the prophecy of the Revelation.

Key #3 – The Revelation Is Time Restricted

Real estate agents have a comical but serious saying. They insist that the three most important factors in selling a property are: "Location! Location! Location!" In a similar fashion literary scholars maintain that the three most important rules for properly understanding the meaning of any piece of literature, including the Bible, are: "Context! Context! Context!" The point I wish to emphasize here is this; without establishing and honoring the context intended by the author, one creates a pretext. A pretext allows the reader to make a text mean almost anything he or she desires by lifting it out of its context. As a result, the intended and true meaning is distorted or missed entirely.

Much of the conflict and confusion over the Revelation stems from just such a practice of taking part or all of this prophecy out of its divinely determined time context, stretching it like a rubber band by nineteen centuries and counting, plopping it down out into the future, and creating a pretext for its fulfillment. But disregarding or abusing context is not the prerogative of any sincere reader or honest interpreter.

The Book of Revelation places its own direct and contextualizing time statements upon the *whole* of its prophecy. Like bookends at its beginning and end (its first and last chapters / introduction and conclusion / prologue and epilogue), these time statements establish the historical framework for the soon and now past fulfillment of the *whole* prophecy. Their strategic placement brackets the entire prophecy and was done, no doubt, to avoid confusion. But most commentators and prophecy teachers have missed, dismissed, or ignored these time and contextualizing statements, as well as their strategic placement:

- "what must soon [shortly] take place" (Rev. 1:1; 22:6 [KJV]).
- "Blessed is the one who reads the words of this prophecy . . . who hear it and take to heart [obey] what is written in it" (Rev. 1:3; 22:7 [KJV]).
- "the time is near [at hand]" (Rev. 1:3; 22:10 [KJV]).
- "Do not seal up the words of the prophecy of this book" (Rev. 22:10). Note: Daniel was told to "close up and seal the words" of his book "until the time of the end" (Dan. 12:4). In the Revelation, that time was now "near" or "at hand."
- "Behold, I am coming soon [quickly]!" (Rev. 22:7, 12 [KJV]).
- "Yes, I am coming soon [quickly]." (Rev 22:20 [KJV]).

Once again, these full-content-bracketing time statements establish the immediate historical context for the fulfillment of the whole of the prophecy. When ignored, as so many have done, it's easy to lose sight of the proverbial "forest for the trees."

We'd all be well-advised to be intellectually honest and honor these passages. They tell us that very significant events were to occur within a very short time and certainly within the lifetime of the book's original and primary recipients. These passages are also stated in simple terms—so simple, in fact, that people who won't take "soon," "shortly," "at hand," "near," and "quickly" literally must read their own non-literal meanings into these declarative statements. And yet these words are used hundreds of times and in a consistently literal manner throughout the New Testament. Everywhere else they mean what they mean in natural everyday speech.[23] Therefore, without a clear warrant to do so (none exists), there is no justification to assume special or unique meanings here. God is not that careless with language.

Hence, to look for a distant, future fulfillment (almost two thousand years removed from its writing) of part or all of this prophecy, as most commentators and modern-day prophecy teachers still do, is to ignore this book's plainest teaching and to engage in pretext. This common trait then demands manipulation of Scripture and ensures misconception and misunderstanding. The reader who does not hold fast to the Revelation's own contextual guidelines will infallibly lose himself in a labyrinth of conjecture and wild speculations.

David Chilton captured this anachronistic tendency quite well in writing:

> The futurists would have it that St. John was warning the Christians of his day mostly about things they would never see—meaning that the Book of Revelation has been irrelevant for 1900 years! To claim that the book has relevance only for our generation is egocentric; and it is contrary to the testimony of the book itself. . . . what purpose could it have answered to send them [the seven churches] a document which they were urged to read and ponder, which was yet mainly occupied with historical events so distant as to be beyond the range of their sympathies, and so obscure that even at this day the shrewdest critics are hardly agreed on any one point?[24]

Consequently, Revelation's prophecy only becomes difficult, if not impossible to understand, when it is lifted out of its self-declared, 1st-century time context. Sad to say many scholars, beholding to their deferment and futuristic interpretative positions, disagree. To justify their system of fulfillment, they are forced to interpret these above simple words and time-restricting phrases figuratively, or to undermine their meaning with unnatural treatments, or to ignore them entirely and jump right into fancy futuristic charts and timelines.

For instance, 2 Peter 3:8 is frequently cited as a dismissal justification: "But do not forget this one thing, dear friends: With the Lord a day is like a thousand years, and a thousand years are like a day." It is then concluded that we can "get around" or dismiss all New Testament time statements since God is not bound by time, as we humans are, and that He measures time differently than we do (even though He created time – the sun, moon, and rotation of the earth). These time statements, it is further insisted, must be seen from God's perspective, i.e., are "soon" in God's sight, and not from our human viewpoint. Thereby, they are relativized, elasticized, or otherwise distorted and made obscure in meaning. But no Scripture supports this dismissive contention.

Rather, the Book of Revelation was clearly written to us humans "to show his servants what must soon take place" (Rev. 1:1). What could be more plain and natural than that? Yet many are forced by their traditions to change or deny what the Bible clearly says.

Others explain that these words really refer to the speed with which these events will be carried out once they begin, i.e., speedily. Some others suggest that these words merely convey certainty—that someday all these things are certain to happen, or that those prophetic events are always viewed as being near. In other words, they are saying that the meaning of the time statements is literally meaningless. As a result, the time of fulfillment is stretched like a rubber band far out into the future and a pretext fulfillment created.

> **Consequently, Revelation's prophecy only becomes difficult, if not impossible, to understand when it is lifted out of its self-declared, 1st-century time context.**

These tactics are only the tip of the iceberg of the widespread and non-literal tampering and tinkering that has been perpetrated upon the time texts in Revelation (as well as on other similar time texts in the New Testament) by those driven to find a meaning in keeping with their futuristic, yet-to-be fulfilled interpretations. But this type of manipulation simply puts an intolerable strain on the plain and natural meaning of commonly used and normally understood words. The bottom line is that these avoidance tactics of trifling with words, and the Word of God, has produced an incredible amount of conflict, anxiety, and confusion.

Ironically, one fact that all nearness-evading and word-manipulating theorists recognize, is that the Revelation's original recipients did not understand these simple words and phrases in the manner these theorists are now suggesting. 1st-century believers were expecting the occurrence and fulfillment of all these things within their lifetime. And who could blame them?

Theologian Gary DeMar is right on target about these nearness avoidance tactics in his book, *Last Days Madness*, where he appropriately quips, "this is surprising since this line of argument is most often put forth by those who insist on a literal interpretation of Scripture."[25] He further condemns this treatment of the time statements because it "calls into question the reliability of the Bible and makes nonsense of clear statements of Scripture."[26]

On the other hand, if the Book of Revelation was written prior to the destruction of Jerusalem in A.D. 70, these time statements make perfect sense and make a distant fulfillment untenable. This, then, is the time context the Book of Revelation places upon itself. Who are we to ignore it, deny it, or remove it?

The 19th-century, English theologian J. Stuart Russell succinctly summarized the importance of honoring the Revelations' time statements this way:

> It may truly be said that the key has all the while hung by the door, plainly visible to every one who had eyes to see; yet men have tried to pick the lock, or force the door, or climb up some other way, rather than avail themselves of so simple and ready a way of admission as to use the key made and provided for them.[27]

In sum, the Revelation was addressed to a contemporary audience—seven real 1st-century churches (Rev. 1:4; 2:1-3:22).[28] People in those churches were expected to read, hear (with understanding), and take to heart, i.e., keep, heed, obey, the things in this prophecy—the whole of it—if they wanted to receive the first of seven blessings scattered throughout this book,[29] and because of the nearness of its events (Rev. 1:1; 22:6, 10). Please note that it takes all three to qualify for this promised blessing: reading, hearing with understanding, and obeying:

- "Blessed is the one who reads the words of this prophecy, and blessed are those who hear it and take to heart what is written in it, because the time is near [at hand]" (Rev. 1:3)
- "Blessed is he who keeps the words of the prophecy in this book" (Rev. 22:7)

Once again, as you can see, this promised blessing is used at both the beginning and the end of Revelation. Why? These blessing-bracketing passages emphasize the wholeness of the prophecy. To *keep* means to heed, to hold fast, to obey. It should not be too difficult for the reader to understand, therefore, that in order to keep, heed, or obey *all* of this book, it must *all* be "keepable," "heedable," and "obeyable" in their lives, back then and there. This obvious dynamic is simply called audience relevancy. If, however, as the modern-day group of end-timers tell us, Revelation's prophecies refer only to distant, future historic events nineteen centuries and counting removed from the original audience, what could people back then or since then have kept, heeded, or obeyed? Oh yes, it may have satisfied an intellectual itch for some to know what will be happening out in the distant future, but what relevance would it really have had in how 1st-century believers lived their lives or received comfort from their persecutions?

... it must *all* be "keepable," "heedable," and "obeyable" in their lives, back then and there.

The best principle to apply for understanding these commonly used and normally understood words is comparing "Scripture with Scripture." When we use it, we find that these words are decisive and their meaning is not up for debate. *At hand* and *near* do not become *distant* and *far*. "At hand," for example, includes meanings such as graspable, squeezable, within reach, and close enough to take hold of—not something that will happen over nineteen hundred years later. Jesus used this same expression in Matthew 26:46 to describe Judas Iscariot's proximity to Himself, saying "behold he is *at hand* that doth betray me" (emphasis added – KJV). The same expression is also used at the outset of Jesus' ministry to describe an approaching event; "And the Jews' Passover was *at hand*" (John 2:13, emphasis added – KJV).

Nor do *soon* and *quickly* signify *distant* and *far off*. Once again, the first hearers and readers of the Revelation did not understand these words this way. They understood them as relevant and pertinent for them—not a message about something(s) that would happen many centuries later. Perhaps, for a moment, 1st-century readers (like us today) could have misconstrued one phrase, like "the time is at hand," as meaning thousands of years away. But when placed with the phrase "which must shortly come to pass," each so interprets and clarifies the other that to make these words stretch two thousand years is utterly ridiculous.

First and foremost then, we should accept the Revelation on its own terms, as a book for its own time and for an original audience. The widespread emphasis today on interpreting the Revelation as a message only or mostly about *our* future is a far cry from what God intended.

Secondly, the Revelation's primary focus was given to reveal, and not to conceal, "what must soon take place" (Rev. 1:1; 22:6). These words are the book's overarching time and context-setting statement. They, too, are contained in both the Revelation's prologue and epilogue and encompass the *whole* of the prophecy. Ask yourself, What other words could John have used to better speak of contemporary relevance than those found in Revelation 1:1, 3, and 22:6, 10? Therefore, one's interpretation of this book must begin by looking at the *whole* of the prophecy before exploring any of its parts. Quite basically, this is what we today call grasping the "big picture."

Another context difficulty stumbled over by many interpreters is Revelation 1:19. Here John is told to "Write, therefore, what you have seen, what is now and what will take place later." Futurist-deferment interpreters claim that this verse sets forth a chronological division for the fulfillment of the prophecy into three consecutive, exclusive, and historical time periods—past, present, and future. Their overriding contextual problem, however, is where and how to divide the book— what part(s) to the past, what part(s) to the present, and part(s) to the future? Do you divide it after chapter 3, 6, 19, in the middle of 20, or just anywhere you desire?

What is ignored, once again, is that Revelation 1:19 is part of the *whole* of the prophecy and located within this book's overarching time parameter of the things that "must soon take place" (Rev. 1:1; 22:6). Hence, this book-ending and full-content embracing phrase is the controlling, contextualizing, and structural-determining statement. Fulfillment of Revelation's entire prophecy is either all or nothing. Any bifurcation of this prophecy would be arbitrary and a violation of this and other time-sensitive parameters the book places upon itself. The fact is, there is no justification for dividing this book's prophecy anywhere into two or three widely separated time periods. Its fulfillment unity is self-imposed and must be honored.

Thirdly, another highly significant factor is the angel's instruction to John to "do not seal up the words of prophecy of this book" (Rev. 22:10). This instruction stands in stark contrast to God's command to the prophet Daniel to "close up and seal" (Dan. 12:4, 9). Why? It is because in Daniel's time, the words of his prophecy and its time of fulfillment was not "at hand" but in the "distant future (Dan. 8:26).[30] In Daniel's time, the fulfillment of the end-time portion of his prophecy was some six hundred years away. But in John's day, as we shall see, that time of fulfillment was "at hand" (Rev. 1:3; 22:10), i.e., very close, a mere two to seven years hence, depending upon the actual time of its writing. If we fail to see this relevancy, and stretch the fulfillment of all or some of John's vision out for almost two thousand years away from its divinely determined time period, we are, in essence, re-sealing the prophecy for John's generation and all subsequent generations since John's day—except for one yet-future generation someday.

While trifling with the time-statements or assigning specialized meaning to ordinary and well-understood words violates commonly accepted principles of hermeneutics (the art or science of literary interpretation) and basic rules of grammar, the vast majority of interpreters simply choose to ignore them completely or flat out claim there are no specific time indicators at all. These nearness-avoiding devices and denying tactics are "standard tools of the trade" necessitated by particular theological positions. But taking fulfillment of any passage out of its self-imposed historical and time-sensitive context strips the Revelation of its intended meaning. All such approaches must be discarded if we truly desire to unravel the mysteries of the prophecy of the Revelation and unveil and reveal the greater Jesus, the contemporary Christ, as He truly is today.

What is needed is a careful, honest, and consistent approach—one that preserves the integrity and harmony of the *whole* of the prophecy and its associated events. Arbitrary divisions and specialized or alternative meanings of common and ordinarily understood words have no part in this process. The simplest solution is to recognize that the *whole* of the prophecy was written, first and foremost, to 1st-century Christians. Its book-ending and full-content-bracketing time statements must be taken literally and plainly, and honored seriously. They make perfect sense and bear witness to this book's unity and original audience-relevancy. (When, for example, did you ever write someone a letter using words you did not expect them to understand?) If this contemporary relevancy is not true, then it is simply incredible, if not inexplicable, why this book's original recipients were never informed of this fact. If true, this non-mentioning omission would give the Revelation the character of deception rather than of revelation. I think not. They were emphatically told just the opposite that the time was "at hand" for when this Jewish apocalypse would "soon take place."

Key #4 – The Revelation Is Fulfilled

The Book of Revelation does not contain end-of-the-world predictions or events, as is commonly held. Rather, it fully predicted and described, symbolically and accurately, the events leading up to and including the fall of Jerusalem and the Temple in a coming of the day of the Lord, in judgment, and in the change of covenants circa A.D. 70. All this and more occurred "soon" and "shortly," i.e., within two to seven years, depending upon the exact date of this book's writing. Any interpretation of its fulfillment that lies beyond the time frame of its original hearers and readers is, at best, suspect.

All attempts to place the fulfillment of the Book of Revelation beyond A.D. 70 have brought nothing but chaos and embarrassment to the Church over the centuries and still today. The problem is that most Christians have and still are reading the signs of the times of the 1st century as our times today. Popular end-times author and futuristic proclaimer, John MacArthur, Jr. represents a classic case illustrating this anachronistic problem. With the release of his book inappropriately titled, *Because the Time Is Near* (2007), he argues that "the end of the world is coming . . . . All of this is laid out in the Book of Revelation."[31] One reviewer, Thomas Albrecht, insightfully retorts, "The irony of the title is that Dr. MacArthur discounts the time texts in the Book of Revelation and their relevance to the first century believer to whom the letter was written."[32]

Again, first and foremost, the Book of Revelation described a local series of events very near to its writing and intended for an original and primary audience. These all occurred. Mistakenly, however, many feel that these events were only local and not worldwide. But just like the birth, life, death, resurrection, and ascension of Jesus, which were also all local events, the Revelation's fulfillment has universal applications and implications. Locally is just how God chose to fulfill his plan of redemption. These events ended forever biblical Judaism, its age, and the Old Covenant system (Heb. 8:13; 9:10).

Reluctantly, the late, renowned, and futuristic theologian George Eldon Ladd conceded that "there must be an element of truth in this approach for surely the Revelation was intended to speak to its own generation."[33] Indeed, it did! Mistakenly, however, he and many others feel that if this prophecy is totally fulfilled, this makes it meaningless to modern-day Christians. As we shall see next, Revelation's past fulfillment does not exhaust its meaning, relevance, and symbolism. In fact, just the opposite is true. Past fulfillment makes this prophecy *more meaningful* for us today, and not less. Why? It's because the Revelation is much more than a tract for its own times. How can we know this extended relevance is true? It's not some doctrine I have dreamed up, which leads us to our fifth key for unlearning many popular misconceptions and unlocking the mysteries of this vital book.

Key #5 – The Revelation Is Timelessly Relevant

Most of us have been conditioned to put everything in the Revelation on a timeline and think of its events and realities as either totally past or mostly future. Yes, a few Christians believe all its fulfillment and relevance lies in the past. The entire message, they say, was written to encourage the saints of the 1st century who were under severe persecution. Once that Roman persecution ended, the book lost all prophetic value and has no future component. Its only value now is in the principles or lessons it contains. What these principles or lessons are and how they are relevant for us today has never been defined or clarified.[34]

On the opposite extreme are most evangelical churches that say that the events and realities of the Revelation occur in stages. Of course, they differ widely on the timelines of various stages but usually agree that part of the book depicts literal, historical events of the past; part deals with literal events in the present; but most of it deals with literal, future events and realities that have still not taken place. The timelines on which these divisions are based also call for wild speculation as to which literal, historical events apply to which scriptural symbols.

In my estimation, both the exclusively past- and mostly future-fulfillment positions are contrived doctrines of men, and not of God. Tragically, they rob the Revelation of its present spirit-dimension/physical-dimension reality and much of its intended prophetic and practical impact.

Why can I take such a firm stand in opposition to the vast majority of commentators, interpreters, and prophecy teachers? It's because I have a strong, textual, and exegetical basis for doing so.

In the middle of the unfolding apocalyptic drama of the breaking of the seals, the sounding of the trumpets, and pouring out of the vials, is a drastic and dynamic instruction given to John that is either ignored or downplayed by most commentators. In Revelation chapter 10, the mighty angel of the Lord instructs John to *eat the scroll* (Rev. 10:9b). This is the same sealed scroll handed to the Lamb for Him to open in Revelation chapter 5.[35] Why was he told to perform such a graphic and grotesque act? (Have you eaten any good books lately?)

Let's not forget that this instruction is contained in a book filled with signs and symbols. The reason is, as we shall see, God did not intend the prophetic message in this scroll (the Book of Revelation) to be limited to one particular time period and one particular people, i.e., for John's original audience, the seven churches and the Christians of that 1st century alone. Fact is, the physical act of eating and ingesting something always transforms it. And so the whole of the prophecy of the Book of Revelation is thusly transformed.

Tragically, they rob the Revelation of its present spirit-dimension/physical-dimension reality and much of its intended prophetic and practical impact.

Immediately after John ate the scroll, he was commanded to regurgitate it, if you will; but this time the whole of Revelation's prophecy is redirected to a different audience. The angel told him, "You must prophesy again about/before many peoples, nations, languages, and kings" (Rev. 10:11). When you couple this statement with the angel's later instructions to John, "do not seal up the words of the prophecy of this book, because the time is at hand" (Rev. 22:10), it should soon become clear that the Revelation's prophecy was not exhausted in its circa A.D. 70 fulfillment. Its relevance was thereby broadened from its primary fulfillment audience (the seven churches) and refocused to a different and universal audience.

Below are six additional insights supporting a universal application and timeless relevance of this prophecy beyond its circa A.D. 70 fulfillment. This is what theologians call a *sensus plenior*—i.e. "a fuller sense . . . . the possibility of more significance to . . . [a] passage than was consciously apparent to the original author . . . ."[36]

Again, and *first and foremost*, it cannot be overemphasized, the *whole* of this prophecy, from first to last, was written to encourage its original audience.[37] They were under severe persecution and in need of relief. This is the Revelation's primary focus. The *whole* of it, therefore, is rooted, time-restricted, and fulfilled in one, immediate, specific, and real coming of Jesus Christ in judgment circa A.D. 70. As we shall see in our next chapter, "the coming of the Lord is its grand theme."[38] That contemporary and historical setting was Revelation's one and only fulfillment. In theological circles, this position is called the Preterist view. Preterist means "past in fulfillment." And this historical fulfillment "must play a controlling role"[39] as we explore a *sensus plenior*.

Secondly, John's prophesying "again about many peoples, nations, languages and kings" (Rev 10:9-11), is clearly a different and broader group of recipients of this "again" prophecy than John's original area and audience of the seven churches (Rev 1:4, 11). Traditionally, however, commentators have tried to minimize the meaning of the dramatic symbolism of John's eating the scroll and prophesying again. They contend it only meant a personal application for John. Suggested applications (in italics), along with my comments, include:

- *John must yet receive the rest of the prophecy (chapters 11-22).* But John was not going anywhere. He was there on the island of Patmos for the duration. This explanation is not only highly reductionistic; in comparison with the dramatic symbolism used, it is superfluous and weak.
- *John would later travel throughout the area of the seven churches sharing this prophecy verbally (a book tour, of sorts).* But it was not necessary for John to travel about doing this. That was the purpose of sending the letters. They were intended to be read aloud in the seven churches. John personally going to each church and reading them was not required.
- *This was a commissioning for John.* But John had already been commissioned on at least two previous occasions (see Rev. 1:10-20 and 4:1-2), and also in Revelation 1:19. Therefore, another commissioning would be unnecessary and overly redundant.

Thirdly, similar expressions are found five other times in Revelation 5:9; 7:9; 13:7; 14:6; and 17:15 (also see Rev. 22:9 and Dan. 4:1; 7:14). In

Revelation 5:9, for example, this expression universalizes the application of Jesus' sacrifice: "And they sang a new song; 'You [Jesus] are worthy to take the scroll and to open its seals, because you were slain, and with your blood you purchased men [and women] for God from every tribe and language and people and nation." Rightly, G. K. Beale terms this a "phrase of universality"[40] as it universalizes the application of Jesus' sacrifice. That means this phrase and reality includes me, and hopefully you as well, does it not?

Fourthly, if this expression's use in Revelation 10:11 is consistent with this book's other five uses and we employ the interpretative principle of letting "Scripture interpret Scripture," then it must carry the same universalized and timeless meaning here.

Beale willingly acknowledges this "widening application,"[41] which gives us the textual/exegetical rationale for reapplying the *whole* prophecy beyond its circa A.D. 70 fulfillment. Hence, the words of this climatic prophecy refer and pertain "to all peoples throughout the world" from that time on.[42] We must also specially note that in Revelation 10:11, "kings" replaced "'tribes' as the fourth element in the quartet. In Revelation 1:6 and 5:10, believers are called "kings." Thus, the Apocalypse is concerned with the whole of humankind from both a corporate and an individual sense. This universal and timeless application, beyond its fulfillment, is the most natural way to understand a consistent use of this terminology. In theological circles this position is called the Idealist view. It sees this prophecy as representing the ongoing battle between good and evil. Unfortunately, most Idealists put the end at the wrong end—out in the future instead of back in the past.

Fifthly, the Revelation's fulfillment (its realities, blessings, judgments, principles, and portrayals, which cannot be limited to a one-time, historic, and static eschatological fulfillment for its own day, which it was, or to someday still out in the future) serves in a typological and controlling manner. Thus, this fulfillment of Revelation's imagery and visions now serves as a type for repeating patterns of the greater Jesus' ongoing involvement and activity in history and in individual lives. In other words, John's prophecy now transcends its fulfillment time and context into new historical, personal, and global, but secondary applications. Post A.D. 70, this prophecy is not only timeless but also multifaceted. This position is what I now term the Preterist-Idealist view.[43]

Ongoing relevancy and timeless, and universal, but secondary applications, are part of the Revelation's uniqueness, and further differentiate it from Jesus' Olivet Discourse in Matthew 24, Mark 13, and Luke 21. All four books cover the same fulfillment time frame and events. However, the Revelation's ongoing aspects resist predictability because John's prophesying "again" was general and not time-sensitive or place-specific. The whole prophecy echoes this relevancy theme that it is for all who live and die for Christ from that time on (Rev. 14:12-13).

Post A.D. 70, the Revelation is still an open book and meant to be kept open from the time of its writing forward and forever. Its exciting message proclaims the ongoing involvement of the greater Jesus in the struggles of the spirit realm and the physical/material realm for all ages. Such a reformed application can help us better understand the rise and fall of empires, the history of nations, the lives of people, and the comings and goings of groups, institutions, churches, and other corporate bodies. They are controlled by God and his Christ (see Dan. 2:21). And there is much more as we shall continue to see in later chapters. But this textual understanding of Revelation's ongoing relevance and timeless applications secures its meaningfulness from the time of its fulfillment onward for all periods of Church and world history.

Thus, this fulfillment of Revelation's imagery and visions now serves as a type for repeating patterns of the greater Jesus' ongoing involvement and activity in history and in individual lives.

The Revelation also warns, "If anyone adds anything to them, God will add to him the plagues described in this book. And if anyone takes away from this book of prophecy, God will take away from him his share in the tree of life and in the holy city, which are described in this book" (Rev. 22:18-19).

Let me urge you to constantly make sure that no message you believe or present adds to or takes away from the content and the spirit of the Apocalypse. These two dire warnings and consequences are just as relevant for us today as they were for the Revelation's original audience. If not, they are toothless. In my opinion, any modern-day interpretation that relegates the relevance of all or any portion of this prophecy solely to the past or mostly to the future is at risk of violating these warnings and suffering their consequences. (See again my story in Chapter 2, pp. 75-76).

Moreover, this ongoing relevancy also perfectly corresponds with God's redemptive grace and purpose. While totally local in fulfillment, all redemptive and historical events are universal (worldwide) in goal, scope, and application. Seen in this manner, the Revelation is truly a prophecy of "the eternal gospel to proclaim to those who live on the earth – to every nation, tribe, language and people" (Rev. 14:6).

Sixthly, there is no suggestion of a termination of these applications. The popular terminology of a "final" or "last judgment," a "final blessing," a "final coming," a "final day of the Lord," or a "final Antichrist" is non-scriptural and unscriptural. The facts are that in the prophecy of the Book of Revelation, we moderns have real, ongoing blessings, warnings, comings, judgments, and interactions of the greater Jesus and spirit-realm antagonists with which to be personally involved and concerned (Rev. 1:3; 22:7, 14-19). Yet there is no "Antichrist" contained therein. That notion has been imported into this book. Rather, "many antichrists," who fit the descriptions found *only* in 1 John 2:18, 22; 4:3; 2 John 7, still roam the earth today, as they did in the past and will continue to do so in the future.

Make no mistake; this realization of the Revelation's ongoing relevancy is not a lesser reality or a second-rate option in comparison with solely past or mostly futuristic fulfillment views. In effect, it is more significant than any single view. Through the Revelation, God is equipping believers of all generations with an understanding of how the world of the spirit operates and interacts with and influences the material realm. This revelation is the highest form of revelation and knowledge. It is just as pertinent today as it was in the past and will be in the future. It is the revelation and knowledge of how the kingdom of God functions and how we can enter and live in it in this present world, effectively and victoriously.

Thus, nowadays, the entire vision of the Revelation is past, present, and future. It is the timeless unveiling and revealing of the greater Jesus, the contemporary Christ, as He is now and what He is doing, and not a timetable of yet-future events. To see this vision is to understand the Revelation as it was intended and to receive one of its blessings; not to see this divine perspective is to miss its richest and deepest meaning, for in this historical and greater Jesus Christ "are hidden all the treasures of wisdom and knowledge" (Col. 2:3).

Idealist William Hendriksen certainly saw this significance, even though he subscribed to the late date for its writing and placed its fulfillment out into the future at "the great consummation." And yet in his highly acclaimed book, *More Than Conquerors*, he rightly maintained:

> A sound interpretation of the Apocalypse must take as its starting-point the position that the book was intended for believers living in John's day and age. . . . we should give equal prominence to the fact that this book was intended *not only* for those who first read it, but for all believers throughout this entire dispensation.[44]

Our recognition of *both* the total fulfillment and total relevancy of "the revelation of Jesus Christ" (Rev. 1:1) in our lives and world, here and now, should create a greater sense of responsibility, a greater motivation for obedience, and a greater desire to worship the historical and greater Jesus than the traditional deferment views—past or future. God through Christ continues to act in history and in the lives of his saints in an apocalyptically revealed manner.

Key #6 – Let the Bible Interpret Itself

English poet Alexander Pope said, "A little learning is a dangerous thing." If that is true, then unbridled personal revelation is catastrophic. I cringe every time I hear someone say, "The Lord told me . . . ." People who cut loose from the Scriptures and live by their own visions and insights tend to bend truth to their own whims.

Nowhere is this tendency more prevalent than in the interpretation of Bible prophecy, especially the Book of Revelation. True prophetic revelation, however, is always anchored solidly in Scripture. As we study the Revelation in poverty of spirit, the Holy Spirit, the spirit of prophecy, reveals to us the spirit-realm/physical-realm realities it contains.

Sometimes, this last book of the Bible is straightforward. For example, Revelation's "at hand" time-restrictive theme, which spans the entire prophecy, is stated in simple terms. It does not mean nineteen centuries away and counting. In other instances, direct statements made in the context interpret many of the strange symbols of the Revelation.

Consider, for instance, these simple explanations:

- "The seven stars are the angels [literally, messengers] of the seven churches, and the seven lampstands are the seven churches" (Rev. 1:20).
- "Each one [of the four living creatures] had a harp and they were holding golden bowls of incense, which are the prayers of the saints" (Rev. 5:8).
- "The great dragon was hurled down—that ancient serpent called the devil, or Satan, who leads the whole world astray. He was hurled to earth, and his angels with him" (Rev. 12:9).

As you can see, each of these symbols introduced in the Revelation is explained in context. If a symbol is not explained in its context, you can be sure it refers to something that is illuminated elsewhere in Scripture. We have been and shall continue utilizing this key of letting "Scripture interpret Scripture" frequently in this book.

Likewise, no Scripture verse stands alone or contradicts any other Scripture. Thus, any interpretation of Scripture must be confirmed by other Scriptures. But please don't misunderstand what I am about to say. I believe that the Bible in its original form is the inspired, inerrant, and infallible Word of God. The problem is that the Bible was written in ancient languages. Therefore, it has to be translated into our and other languages before it can have meaning to us for our daily lives. As a result, one of the burning controversies of our day still rages around the question of whether the Bible should be taken *literally* or *figuratively*. Actually, it is to be taken both ways because that is how it is written. But I believe that God is much more concerned that it be taken *seriously*— that we take it to heart.

We don't, however, need a dictionary or an encyclopedia or tomorrow's newspaper to interpret and understand Bible prophecy. The Bible interprets itself. If we let the Bible interpret itself and study it diligently enough to know clearly what it says, we don't have to rely on other people to unlock the mysteries of the Revelation—we can unravel this unveiling ourselves. And that is exactly what we shall be doing in the pages ahead.

Key #7 – Judge Any Interpretation by the Fruit It Produces

Jesus warned that many false prophets would try to deceive the masses (Matt. 7:16-19). He cautioned, "Thus, by their fruit you will recognize them" (Matt. 7:20).

Unfortunately, most popular end-times teachings create the negative fruits of conflict, anxiety, and confusion. Receiving the full Revelation message as "at hand," fulfilled, universal, and timeless, on the other hand, produces the good fruit that comes from entering and living daily in the unique blessings and empowerment this prophetic book offers.

Let's examine some of this fruit.

Good Fruit: Worshiping God

When we receive the full pertinent reality of the Revelation message, we can see the greater Jesus, the contemporary Christ, in all his present glory and majesty. Seeing Him as *He is* creates a sense of awe and reverence that produces authentic and spontaneous worship. It removes any need to work up some emotional response or to go through some ritual.

The widespread emphasis on Jesus as friend in churches of our day leads many people to think of Him as a pal or a buddy. But one glimpse of the unveiled greater Jesus with a face beaming like the sun, eyes like blazing fire, and feet glowing like white hot brass (Rev. 1:12-16), and it quickly becomes obvious that this is no mere human friend.

As we have seen, the Apostle John knew the earthly Jesus. He shared his struggles, walked the dusty roads of Galilee with Him, leaned against his breast during the Last Supper, and saw Him crucified. He knew the Jesus of the Gospels intimately as friend, teacher, and savior. He even knew the post-resurrected Jesus. Yet, when he came face to face with the unveiled Jesus in the Revelation, he was overwhelmed. "When I saw him, John exclaimed, "I fell at his feet as though dead" (Rev. 1:17).

Once we have truly encountered the greater Jesus as He is today, no one will ever again have to tell us we ought to worship Him. We shall worship Him in total surrender of our wills as we partake of his reality and respond to Him in love and adoration.

Good Fruit: Godly Character

The unveiling of the greater Jesus, the contemporary Christ, doesn't stop with feelings of awe and reverence. When we heed, keep, and obey the message of the Apocalypse, we find it profoundly impacting our daily lives. We develop godly character, not so much by our efforts but by our exposure to Christ.

As we enter into and live daily in a relationship with Him, as He is now, we begin to share his values, his traits, and his ways. I don't mean in any way to imply that we become little gods, as some teach today. The idea of our taking on the divinity of God came from Satan (see Gen. 3:5), not from any word of the Lord in Scripture. Certainly, we are enjoined to rule and reign with Him, but there is never any doubt as to Who is sovereign.

Instead, we take on both his historical and apocalyptic character. John wrote in one of his letters, "We know that when he appears, we shall be like him, for we shall see him as he is" (1 John 3:2). This seeing Him and living in intimate, daily fellowship with Him, as He is now, has a way of removing all thoughts of being like anybody else but Him.

The popular end-times doctrines, which exclusively shove the reality of his appearing out into the future, tend to make the development of godly character a chore, a product of human effort. Furthermore, as we shall see in our next two chapters, the Revelation makes it clear that some of his comings and appearings (plural) are glorious present-tense realities that have a profound impact on those who receive them. They, too, produce the fruit of godly character.

Good Fruit: Expansion of God's Kingdom

As we worship the greater Jesus, as He is now, and develop his character, we begin to do the works of Jesus and even greater works (see John 14:12). Thereby, we actually become a part of the ongoing testimony of Jesus.

The 1st-century disciples proved to the world that the Jesus they preached was alive because they lived as He lived and did the same works that He had done (see 1 Cor. 11:1; 1 Thess. 1:4-8). This combination of proclaiming the full gospel of the kingdom and of salvation, living the life of Christ, and demonstrating the power of Christ led to the rapid expansion of Christ's kingdom (see Acts 2:47-4:4).

In the same way, when we grasp the present reality of the Revelation's full message today, we produce the good fruit of expanding his kingdom. The fact is, Jesus calls all of his followers "to be a kingdom and priests to serve our God" and to "reign on earth" (Rev. 5:10; also see 1:6).

Worshiping God, developing godly character, and expanding his kingdom are the kind of fruit God sought to produce by giving us the Revelation, and not the bad fruits of conflict, anxiety, confusion over the future and/or apathy over the present.

To Sum It All Up

Our difficulty in unraveling the unveiling of the Revelation is not in the book's strange symbols and language. Rather, our problem is that most of us have been conditioned to think of the Revelation as only a literal book about the future. We have not been taught about its primary focus, original audience, past fulfillment, and timeless relevancy. Nor have we been told that its primary purpose is the unveiling and revealing of the greater Jesus as He is today, and secondarily its revealing of the invisible realm of the spirit as a present, ongoing reality—all of which have been made known by way of signs and symbols.

God does have something vital to say to us through the Revelation, but we can never grasp or understand it through a physical/material mindset. Many people who heard Jesus' parables during his earthly life failed to see the spiritual/physical reality behind them (see Matt. 13:34-43; John 3:3) and misunderstood their meanings. Even today, the pertinent and ongoing reality of the Revelation remains hidden except to those who receive it through spiritual eyes and ears (see Rev. 2:7, 11, 17, 29; 3:6, 13, 22).

The many teachers who have interpreted the visual images of the Revelation as distant, one-time events to support their theories about

God's timetable and specific future plans, are like the Samaritan woman at the well who totally missed the point of Jesus' teachings. When Jesus promised to give her water that would forever quench her thirst, she quickly pointed out that He had no bucket to draw with and that the well was deep (John 4:4-26). He was speaking to her on a spiritual level, but she was trying to understand his words merely on a physical/material level.

Many of the popular ideas about the end times have grown out of such misinterpretations of the Revelation and other prophetic Scriptures. Consequently, over the centuries, we Christians have built layer upon layer of faulty theories over these flawed, theological, and out-of-context pretexts. Often, we have been so busy looking for what was not in the Revelation (the Antichrist, for instance) that we've overlooked what God actual put there. In short, we've complicated the simple by over-simplifying what appeared to us to be complicated!

God does have something vital to say to us through the Revelation, but we can never grasp or understand it through a physical/material mindset.

Most significantly, at the very end of the Revelation, Jesus issues the personal invitation "Come!" and "take the free gift of the water of life" (Rev. 22:17). The water of life was *at hand*, it was present then, it is present now, and it will continue to be present in the future. This invitation comes from the unveiled greater Jesus, the contemporary Christ, Who proclaims Himself to be "the Alpha and Omega, the First and the Last, the Beginning and the End" (Rev. 1:8; 22:13). The ancient Greeks used the idiom *alpha to omega* to express completeness. The Hebrews expressed completeness as *from aleph to tau*, or *the first to the last*. These parallel our expression *from A to Z*, meaning everything or all.

Just as we do not mean to drop all things that represents the letters between *A* and *Z*, Jesus is not implying that He was active at the beginning and will show up and be active at the end, but is inactive in between. He is both complete (needing nothing) and eternally present. He has been, He is now, and He always will be involved with humanity. The Revelation conveys, via powerful signs and symbols, some wonderful truths of Who Jesus is today and what He is literally doing—more powerfully than if these realities were interpreted literally. For sure, this greater Jesus, the contemporary Christ, is a much greater Jesus than most of us have been led to believe.

Rightfully so, many Christians throughout the centuries have drawn strength, faith, and courage from the Revelation as a message that was within reach for their times, as with all other New Testament writings. To limit its symbolic imagery to speculation about single historical events that have either already occurred or future events that might someday occur is to rob this vital book of its pertinent reality and practical guidance for our daily lives, here and now.

Remember and use these seven keys to unlock the mysteries of this vital book and unravel the unveiling of the greater Jesus, the contemporary Christ, as we progress through this book's remaining chapters. The Book of Revelation truly does explain itself:

1. The Revelation uses figurative language and symbols to reveal spiritual/physical events and realities.
2. The Revelation most likely was written prior to Jerusalem's destruction circa A.D. 70.
3. The Revelation is time restricted.
4. The Revelation is fulfilled.
5. The Revelation is timelessly relevant.
6. Let the Bible interpret itself
7. Judge any interpretation by the fruit it produces.

I firmly believe that if we in the Church would stop all the end-time speculation and recognize the soundness and integrity of the Book of Revelation that everything in it was at hand in the 1st century, is at hand for us today, and will be at hand for future generations—i.e., the Preterist-Idealist view—this could usher in a Scripture-based, Revelation revival that could make the Protestant Reformation look mild by comparison. And just because this level of relevancy may be foreign to our traditional beliefs that doesn't mean we can simply dismiss it.

In our next chapter we'll begin Part II – New Distinctives – and continue our journey by examining what the Bible has to say about what many consider Jesus' biggest coming of all (next to his birth-coming, of course)—his riding a horse on the clouds.

Part II – NEW DISTINCTIVES

Chapter 4

He Rides a Horse on the Clouds

Long muscular legs, pounding hoofs, flowing mane, flying tail, stately forehead, large penetrating eyes, strong upright neck, and a swayed back perfectly suited for a rider—such a noble animal. For thousands of years, we humans have been infatuated by the horse and held its beauty, power, and usefulness in high regard—in war, in work, in recreation, and in sport.

First used in warfare over 5,000 years ago, "horses once provided the fastest and surest way to travel on land."[1] And the horse remained a major instrument of war and work until largely phased out in the 20th century. But historically . . .

- Soldiers charged into battle on horses.
- Knights clad in heavy armor jousted atop opposing horses.
- Horses pulled chariots into warfare and raced in games.
- Hunters on horseback chased and killed animals for food or sport.
- The pioneers utilized horses to settle the American West in the days of stagecoaches, covered wagons, and the Pony Express.
- Farmers used horses to clear land, prepare fields, and perform other farm work.

No question, the horse is legendary, still greatly admired, and popular. Nowadays, however, horses mostly perform in circuses, rodeos, parades, and horse shows. But ranchers still round up cattle with horses.

Nevertheless, this fact remains. Throughout history, the horse has proven to be our most valuable and, arguably, most intelligent animal. For example, horsemen know that horses are eager to please their owners, trainers, and riders, have good memories, are quick to learn, and can easily be trained to obey commands. These attributes were especially important for the horse's use in battle where "much training is required to overcome the horse's natural instinct to flee from noise, the smell of blood, and the confusion of combat."[2] Furthermore, "people have improved the natural qualities of the horse by breeding various kinds of horses . . . to produce an animal that has both speed and power."[3]

But a horse on its own is worthless. A human being is required to direct the animal. And those people throughout history who have mastered the art of riding and managing a horse, termed *horsemanship*, have also been highly esteemed. For instance, to be effective in battle, a war horse needs to be "trained to be controlled with limited use of reins, responding primarily to the rider's legs and weight. . . . and learned to balance under a rider who would also be laden with weapons and armor. Developing the balance and agility of the horse was crucial."[4]

Today, "more than 150 breeds and types of horses and ponies"[5] fill the barns and stables of the world and continue to captivate the minds and imaginations of many people. It seems that our romance with the horse and its rider has not worn off in modern times.

The Rider on the White Horse

In Bible times, "Israel was forbidden the use of more than a limited number of horses (Deut. 17:16), since horses were the offensive weapon of ancient warfare."[6] Nonetheless, another visionary way we see Jesus in the Apocalypse (the Revelation), is as an awesome, conquering warrior wearing many crowns and riding a white horse of war. Once again, his eyes are blazing like fire and a sharp sword is coming out of his mouth.

But there is more:

> *I saw heaven standing open and there before me was a white horse, whose rider is called Faithful and True. With justice he judges and makes war. His eyes are like blazing fire, and on this head are many crowns. He has a name written on him that no*

one but he himself knows. He is dressed in a robe dipped in blood, and his name is the Word of God. The armies of heaven were following him, riding on white horses and dressed in fine linen, white and clean. Out of his mouth comes a sharp sword with which to strike down the nations. "He will rule them with an iron scepter" [from Psa. 2:9]. *He treads the winepress of the fury of the wrath of God Almighty. On his robe and on his thigh he has this name written:*

KING OF KINGS AND LORD OF LORDS.

(Revelation 19:11-16)

Make no mistake; "I saw heaven standing open" indicates another special view into the invisible spirit realm and visionary revelation of the greater Jesus—a crowned Christ coming out of heaven and down to earth in judgment and to do battle. The symbol of a white horse has been used before in John's prophetic book to represent a conqueror (Rev. 6:12).[7] William Hendriksen correctly advises that "In Scripture the horse is generally mentioned in connection with the concepts of strength, terror, warfare, and conquest (see Isa. 30:16; 31:1; Job 39:22-28). In the Apocalypse we have the same association of ideas (Rev. 9:7; 14:20; 19:11)."[8] McKenzie adds, "a white horse is what a Roman general would ride when he celebrated a great victory. . . . it shows a victorious rider."[9]

But no one else in history has ever been, or will ever be, like this Rider on the white horse. His names and descriptions make it clear (see John 1:1-5, 14). There can be no doubt that this Rider in Revelation 19 is the greater Jesus Christ, the Conqueror, in all his spirit-realm reality and apocalyptic glory.

Yet He's not alone. He leads the armies of heaven against the nations. They, too, are riding white horses and are wearing "fine linen white and clean." But heaven does not literally contain stables or house horses. Therefore, these white horses are symbolic of God's victorious armies overcoming and conquering via "the blood of the Lamb and by the word of their testimony" and by "their lives" because they did not "love their lives so much as to shrink from death" (Rev. 12:11). Some commentators feel these armies are comprised of angels. Others believe they are saints, because of the fine linen they are wearing. Previously, we were told in this same chapter that "the bride has made herself ready.

Fine linen, bright and clean, was given her to wear" which is symbolic of "the righteous acts of the saints" (Rev. 19:7-8). Another reason these armies might be comprised of earthly saints is because they and we are viewed as being in heaven since "God raised us up with Christ and seated us with him in the heavenly realms in Christ Jesus" (Eph. 2:6). Perhaps, these armies are comprised of both angels and, as we shall discuss in Chapter 7 and 10, overcoming believers.

Also, let's recall that early in his earthly ministry, Jesus told his disciples that God the Father "has entrusted all judgment to the Son" and "has given him authority to judge" (John 5:22, 27). No doubt, this is why "on his robe and on his thigh he has this name written: KING OF KINGS AND LORD OF LORDS" (Rev. 19:16). We can understand why He might have this monogram on his robe. But why would the same monogram be engraved on his thigh? One possibility is that, in the thick of a 1st-century battle, foot soldiers might confuse the identity of a rider on a horse. The name on his thigh, however, would be at eye level and easily recognizable.

There can be no doubt that this Rider in Revelation 19 is the greater Jesus Christ, the Conqueror, in all his spirit-realm reality and apocalyptic glory.

Additionally, and for the second time, we see Jesus with a sword coming out of his mouth and eyes like blazing fire (Rev. 1:14-16). Again, however, we are not told the meaning. We do know from other scriptures, however, that "the sword of the spirit" is symbolic of "the word of God" (see Eph. 6:17) which "is living and active. Sharper than any double-edged sword, it penetrates even to dividing soul and spirit, joints and marrow; it judges the thoughts and attitudes of the heart." (Heb. 4:12). Hence, and most likely, this is no ordinary sword. It also kills "the flesh of kings, generals, and mighty men, of horses and their riders, and the flesh of all people, free and slave, small and great" (Rev. 19:18, 21). Nor are his blazing eyes ordinary eyes, for "nothing in all creation is hidden from God's sight. Everything is uncovered and laid bare before the eyes of him to whom we must give account" (Heb. 4:13). The "many crowns on his head" may symbolize, as McKenzie suggests, the "many realms in his universal kingship"[10] as the "Supreme Ruler."[11]

But one thing is for sure. This greater Jesus is, once again, being revealed as a combination of both God and man. And this symbolic representation of Who He now is, is more powerful than any literal interpretation. Make no mistake, this greater Jesus is not an easy-going, meek-and-mild baby or sheep shepherd Whom everyone wants to love, talk to, and be buddies with. This Jesus is far different and greater than his portrayals in the Gospels. This Jesus is the conquering Son of God, Who sovereignly rules the world from behind the scenes in the usually unseen spirit realm.

Likewise, and most significantly, Jesus' first followers were accused of turning the world of their day "upside down," as they were doing battle and "defying Caesar's decrees, saying that there is another king, one called Jesus" (Acts 17:6-7). No doubt the vision of the Jesus they were serving and, perhaps, riding with was in stark contrast to the popular, modern-day image of Jesus as painted by Warner Sallman in 1940 or the modern-day and popular notion that Jesus is not yet King.

Tim LaHaye, the creator of the ever-so-popular *Left Behind* series, I'm sorry to report, insists that Jesus has not ridden this horse yet. But some day He will. In LaHaye's own words, "When Jesus comes, He is going to be 'King of kings and Lord of lords' . . . to say Christ is ruler now is a statement that reaches almost blasphemous proportions."[12]

To the contrary, however, the Book of Revelation and many other scriptures refute LaHaye's futuristic-deferment-and-reductionistic contention. In the Revelation's most uncontested portion, John writes that Jesus Christ "*is* [not someday will be] the faithful witness, the firstborn from the dead, and the *ruler of the kings of the earth*" (Rev. 1:5; also see 1 Tim. 6:15; Rom. 8:34; Heb. 2:9; 10:13; Matt. 28:18; 1 Cor. 15:25; and many more).

Furthermore, if Jesus was not, back then or now, ruler and King, as LaHaye would have us believe, what is the meaning of:

- Jesus sitting at the right hand of God (Rom. 8:34; Eph. 1:20; Col. 3:1; Heb. 1:13; 8:1; 12:2l; Acts 2:33-36; Psa. 110), Who is seated on his heavenly throne (Psa. 2:4; 11:4; 22:28; 47:2, 8; 103:19; Prov. 8:13; Isa. 66:1)?
- Jesus "now crowned with glory and honor" (Heb. 2:9)? Or, is Jesus merely sitting passively waiting to reign someday?

- Peter's declaration that Jesus is sitting there "at God's right hand – with angels, authorities and powers in submission to him" (1 Pet. 3:22)?
- Jesus' Great Commission and past-tense statement that "all authority in heaven and on earth has been given to me" (Matt. 28:18)?
- Paul's present-tense statement that "he must reign until he has put all his enemies under his feet" (1 Cor. 15:25; Heb. 10:13)?
- Jesus presently "sustaining all things by his powerful word" (Heb. 1:3)?

Perhaps, it is LaHaye whose contention is "almost blasphemous," if not outright blasphemy.

In contradistinction, theologian A. A. Hodge offers a more scripturally sound conclusion on this matter in writing, "In the strictest sense we must date the actual and formal assumption of [Christ's] kingly office, in the full and visible exercise thereof, from the moment of His ascension into heaven from this earth and His session at the right hand of the Father."[13] Another respected theologian, Authur F. Glasser concurs that after Jesus completed his atoning work, ascended, and was seated at the right hand of the Father, "the reign of the risen Christ had now begun."[14]

Unfortunately, LaHaye's contention is only the tip of the iceberg of poor understandings and deceitful attempts by some to explain away and dumb down "the revelation of Jesus Christ" and other related prophecy and scriptures from their intended meaning and relevance. Ironically, once again, this undermining comes from people who claim to be interpreting the Bible literally, faithfully, and accurately. They do nothing of the sort. Gary DeMar laments and poignantly points out that while "a majority of evangelicals believe LaHaye based on the millions of copies of Left Behind sold . . . . It's a shame that this type of nonsense is continually promoted by Christian publishers that know better . . . ."[15]

Once more, let's reemphasize that Jesus' riding of this white horse of war and coming in judgment was part of the *whole* of Revelation's prophecy. It was "near," "at hand," and part of the "things that would shortly take place" (Rev. 1:1, 3; 22:6, 10). Also, part of these happenings is the vision of Jesus "seated on a white cloud with a crown of gold on his head and a sharp sickle in his hand." Then John sees an angel come out of the temple and call to Him saying, "Take your sickle and reap, because the time to reap has come" (Rev. 14:14-15). Given the high likelihood that the Book of Revelation was written prior to A.D. 70, there can be little doubt as to the fulfillment of this historical judgment and how it was delivered.

But since we live in a day and time in which most people have been told this coming of Jesus in judgment has not yet happened, the burden of proof lies on those of us who proclaim its past fulfillment. For this reason, a further background review of some more Old and New Testament knowledge is necessary before we get into how all this was fulfilled. Since I have written extensively on these issues in my book *The Perfect Ending for the World*, the rest of this chapter will be mostly a compilation of excerpts from that book, along with a few endnote references, but also with *some significant additions*. For those desiring a more detailed and expansive treatment on the issues we'll be raising ahead, please see the references provided.

A Long Biblical Precedent of Divine Judgment

During the last days of his earthly ministry, Jesus specified exactly *how* He would come again in judgment riding this white horse. Twice, in his most dramatic prophecy, given on the Mount of Olives to his disciples, and pronounced one week before his crucifixion in A.D. 30, He said He would come "on the clouds" (Matt. 24:30; 26:64; Rev. 1:7). What did that mean?

If you were a 1st-century Jew raised in the synagogue, you would have known exactly what it meant. How is this so? It is because this type of coming had a long biblical precedent. To appreciate the rich Jewish terminology for cloud-coming, we must reenter the mind of a 1st-century Jew. If we look at these things only through 21st-century eyes, we'll become prisoners of what has become the traditional mindset of literalistic misunderstanding and confusion.

Christ's "coming on the clouds" is a common metaphor borrowed from Old Testament portrayals of God (the Father) descending from heaven and coming in power and glory to execute judgment on a people or nation. In all the historic comings of God in judgment, He acted through human armies or through nature to bring destruction ("the Lord is a man of war" [Exod. 15:3 KJV]). Each was a direct act of God and each was termed "the day of the Lord." These days were always described with figurative language and empowered by supernatural support. They brought historical calamity to Egypt, Edom, Assyria, Babylon, and even on Israel itself (see again Chapter 2, pp-72-74).

Stephen, for instance, during his speech at his trail before the Sanhedrin and in quotation of God speaking to Moses stated: "I have indeed seen the oppression of my people in Egypt. I have heard their groaning and have *come down* to set them free . . . ." (Acts 7:34; from Exod. 3:7-8). (Of course, this phrase does not mean God has to leave heaven or anywhere else in order to "come down" to earth since He is omnipresent.)

The Jews of Jesus' day had studied these "day of the Lord" occurrences and were familiar with "cloud-coming" phraseology, as well as the application of one with the other.[16] The Hebrew Scriptures are rich in similes and figurative language that poetically portray a heavenly perspective of God coming among men in judgment, protection, and/or deliverance in history:

- See, the Lord rides on a swift *cloud* and is coming to Egypt (Isa. 19:1). (For the earthly fulfillment, see Isa. 20:1-6)
- Look! He advances like the *clouds,* his chariots come like a whirlwind (Jer. 4:13).
- For the day is near, the day of the Lord is near—a day of *clouds*, a time of doom for the nations (Ezek. 30:3).
- Sing to God, sing praise to his name, extol him who rides on the *clouds* . . . (Psa. 68:4).
- . . . He makes the *clouds* his chariots and rides on the wings of the wind. He makes winds his messengers, flames of fire his servants (Psa. 104:3-4).
- Also see Ezek. 30:18; Psa. 18:9-12; 2 Sam. 22:10-12; Nah. 1:3; Joel 2:1-2; Zeph. 1:14-15).

Clouds used in this way are figures of speech and symbolic of God's majesty, power, glory, and elevated position. T. Everett Denton, however, advances a further insight. He claims that "the use of 'CLOUD' for a mass of people became an idiom: Homer wrote of 'a cloud of footmen, a cloud of Trojans,' and Themistocles referred to

Xerxes' army as 'so great a cloud of men.' Why? Probably because of the cloud of dust that armies of men, horses, and chariots created in those days of dusty roads."[17]

On the other hand, and with familiar cloud-coming imagery, Daniel prophesied the coming of the Son of Man into heaven (Dan. 7:13). Jesus, by deriving his "coming on the clouds" phrase directly from Daniel in his most dramatic prophecy, was revealing Himself as God and the promised Messiah— "At that time the sign of the Son of Man will appear in the sky, and all the nations of the earth will mourn. They will see the Son of Man coming on the clouds of the sky (heaven) with power and great glory" (Matt. 24:30).

When Jesus made this same claim to the high priest, Caiaphas, he immediately understood this claim of Jesus to be a claim of Deity and immediately responded, "He has spoken blasphemy!" (Matt. 26:64-65). In both of these verses, Jesus was applying his coming in judgment and power of war in the *same* technical way as the Father had come down from heaven to earth in the spirit realm many times before:

Look! The Lord is coming from his dwelling place; he comes down and treads the high places of the earth (Mic. 1:3).

See, the Lord is coming out of his dwelling to punish the people of the earth for their sins (Isa. 26:21).

But your many enemies will become like fine dust, the ruthless hordes like blown chaff. Suddenly, in an instant the Lord Almighty will come with thunder and earthquake and great noise, with windstorm and tempest and flames of a devouring fire (Isa. 29:5-6).

Add to this these Old Testament passages where God is said to have "come down" or "comes" (Gen. 11:5, 8; 18:21; Exod. 3:8; 19:11; Num. 11:16-17; Deut. 33:2; Isa. 31:4; 64:3; Psa. 18:9; also see: Isa. 40:10; 66:15; Psa. 46:8-9; 50:3; 96:13; Hos. 8:1)

Because of this Jewish background, Jesus' disciples would have understood what He was talking about in his Olivet Discourse, i.e., "coming on the clouds" (Matt. 24:30). The high priest also understood it.

That's why he was so offended and accused Jesus of blasphemy (Matt. 26:64-65). Let's also note that Jesus made no disclaimers to change the meaning or nature of this type of coming, and neither should we.

Another important factor is that in all these real and biblical comings of God in the Old Testament the Person of God was *never physically visible*; He was unseen by human eyes! Thus, cloud-coming is the language of divine imagery. It denotes divine action. In every instance, some humans were fully aware of God's presence and personal intervention in those events of history.

> **Because of this Jewish background, Jesus' disciples would have understood what He was talking about in his Olivet Discourse, i.e., "coming on the clouds" (Matt. 24:30).**

Obviously, this Jewish perspective is quite different from the way we moderns have been conditioned to think of Christ's coming on the clouds. We imagine his coming to be spectacularly visible on the tops of literal fluffy cumulus clouds gently transporting Him down to earth. To be consistent, shouldn't we also think of Him coming on a white horse (Rev. 19:11), as riding on a literal four-legged steed? Yet every biblical instance of a cloud-coming was a real coming and violent intervention of God. Jesus employed the same figure of speech for his end-time prophecies. Thus for Jesus and a 1st-century Jew, "coming on the clouds" was not a claim to come visibly to the human eye.

The Emphatic Time Statements of Jesus

Jesus also specified exactly *when* He would come on the clouds in this judgment event. Frequently, Jesus left no doubt that something truly significant was about to happen. Although his prophetic words have puzzled scholars for centuries, they need not. We have only to take Him at his word to arrive at his intended meaning. Thus, these time-restrictive statements provide the strongest possible evidence confirming the certainty and faithfulness of his end-time coming and the setting of its time parameter, i.e., within the lifetime of his contemporaries. His words were clear, concise, and unequivocal. He didn't say "maybe" or "possibly" or "someday" or "one day" or "in 2,000 years" or "in 10,000 years." Jesus spoke in a plain, straightforward manner to the ordinary people of his day, not in a complex manner only understood by trained theologians or linguists. When taken at face value, his words concerning this coming are some of the clearest in the New Testament. Only when forced to mean something else, do they become puzzling. As you read the following verses, imagine yourself being one of his 1st-century disciples. How would *you* have understood Jesus' words, especially concerning the *time* of his coming?

Matthew 26:64. Quoting from the prophet Daniel, Jesus responded to and forewarned Caiaphas, the high priest, and the Sanhedrin saying, *". . . in the future you will see the Son of Man sitting at the right hand of the Mighty One, and coming on the clouds of heaven."*

When Jesus said "you," He meant the people He spoke to. He spoke in the first person directly to Caiaphas, the high priest, and all present. They were familiar with this apocalyptic language, and would be the ones who would "see" (meaning to recognize or comprehend, "you see?") his coming in catastrophic judgment. How could Jesus possibly have been describing an event some 2,000 years later? The text demands fulfillment in their lifetime, not deferment to a people far removed or to times hundreds or thousands of years later. That would have meant nothing to them.[18]

Matthew 10:23. While talking with his disciples, Jesus promised, *"When you are persecuted in one place, flee to another, I tell you the truth, you will not finish going through the cities of Israel before the Son of man comes."*

Was Jesus lying or misleading them here? Was this part of a clever way of keeping them faithful and devoted by giving them false hope? Or were these words spoken to real people in that "you" group living in the 1st century? They were the ones to evangelize those cities of Israel. Jesus' obvious intent was not to deceive but to assure his disciples that during the persecution that was soon to come upon them, they would not run out of places to flee for safety before He came in this way. Furthermore, didn't Jesus' words have to be fulfilled before Israel ceased to exist as a nation circa A.D. 70? If He was inspired and telling the truth, they were fulfilled.[19]

Matthew 16:27-28. He informed his disciples, *"For the Son of Man is going to come in his Father's glory with his angels, and then he will reward each person according to what he has done. I tell you the truth, some who are standing here will not taste death before they see the Son of Man coming in his kingdom."*

Here again, Jesus is describing the same, singular event with a definite time-frame limitation. As we shall see, a forty-year period was to transpire between his ascension into heaven and this "coming in his kingdom" (also see 2 Tim. 4:1). During that time some of his disciples would die, but others would remain alive. If this event has yet to take place, then shouldn't we have people living today who are almost 2,000 years old? But that is ridiculous. Rather, why not accept Jesus' words at face value and leave this coming in the time context in which He clearly and emphatically placed it? Yet many Bible commentators have stubbornly resisted the plain and common-sense meaning of these words.[20]

John 21:22. *"Jesus answered, "If I want him to remain alive until I return* [the NIV here is a bad translation. Correctly translated is, "till I come" – see again Chapter 1, pp-27-28], *what is that to you? You must follow me."*

Here Jesus suggested that the Apostle John could be, but not necessarily would be, alive when this coming took place. It's another confirmation that a 1st-century timeframe is the only one Jesus ever intended. As far as is known, John was the only original Apostle who survived beyond the destruction of Jerusalem.

Jesus' Most Dramatic Prophecy

The week before his crucifixion in A.D. 30, and while sitting on the Mount of Olives looking across the valley at the beautiful Jewish Temple, Jesus stunned his disciples by prophesying that this entire complex of buildings, an awesome structure "famous throughout the world" (2 Maccabees 2:22 NRSV), would be totally destroyed: "I tell you the truth, not one stone here will be left on another; every one will be thrown down" (Matt. 24:2).

His disciples asked, "When will this happen?" (Matt. 24:3); and He answered, again using oath language, "I tell you the truth, this generation will certainly not pass away until all these things have happened" (Matt. 24:34). Not only was something significant about to happen; it was to happen in their lifetime. To top it off, He told them about many other events that would take place within that same time period. Included in Jesus' "all these things" were:

- The end of the age and the sign of his coming *(parousia)* (v. 3)
- The gospel preached in all the world . . . to all nations (v. 14)
- The end will come (v. 14)
- The abomination of desolation standing in the holy place (v. 15)
- The hearers fleeing for their lives (vv. 16-20)
- A great tribulation, unequaled in history before or after (v. 21)
- False Christs and false prophets appearing, performing great signs and miracles and deceiving even the elect–if that were possible (v. 24)
- The coming *(parousia)* of the Son of Man (v. 27)
- The sun and the moon darkened, stars falling from the sky and the heavenly bodies shaken (v. 29)
- The sign of the Son of Man appearing in the sky (v. 30)
- Them seeing the Son of Man coming on the clouds (v. 30)

This passage of Scripture is recognized as Jesus' longest and most dramatic prophecy. It is also his most problematic and contested teaching. It contains the promise of what many consider to be his biggest, baddest, and best coming of all. Scholars call it the Olivet Discourse, since Jesus gave this end-time prophecy while sitting on the Mount of Olives and during the last week of his life. I suggest you read the full text of Jesus' prophetic words for yourself. Three similar but slightly different versions are recorded in Matthew 24-25, Mark 13, and Luke 21.

Today, millions of Bible readers and scholars continue to be baffled and confused by Jesus' allegedly cryptic words and his emphasis that some of those who were there with Him at the time would witness all these climactic end-time events, i.e., "all these things." Most of the debate centers on what generation Jesus was really talking about when He referred to "this generation." As with his other time statements, many have employed a variety of side-stepping tactics and slick literary devices in attempting to get around the plain, natural, and consistent meaning of these words.

One of the most common of these tactics is to claim that Jesus was actually talking about some future and yet unborn generation. But this tactic is highly problematic since the pronoun *this* has no textual antecedent, and no preceding verse ever mentions a future generation. Most naturally, Jesus is speaking in the first person to *his* generation. Therefore, *this generation* simply refers to the people of that time.[21]

The fact is, Jesus frequently spoke of his contemporaries as *this generation*. And everywhere else in the New Testament where the phrase "this generation" is used (seventeen times), it always means the contemporaries of the writer or person speaking. Stretching out the meaning to some future, unborn generation over two thousand years removed from Jesus' time, or to mean a race or type of people, would, at best, be an interpretation by exception. Furthermore, the writer of Hebrews quotes the Old Testament Psalm 95:7-11 and strongly insinuates that "a generation" is "forty years" in length (see Heb. 3:9-10, 17).

Notably in Matthew 23, spoken only a few hours earlier on that same day, Jesus sets the stage and historical context for his Matthew 24 prophecy. He pronounces seven "messianic woes" on the Pharisees. He calls them "You snakes! You brood of vipers!" (Matt. 23:33). He says, "upon you will come all the righteous blood that has been shed on earth . . . ." (Matt. 23:35). Then He makes the identical time statement, "I tell you the truth, all this will come upon this generation" (Matt. 23:36). What generation did He mean here? The answer is, the same one He intended in all his other identical uses of the word "generation" and phrase "this generation." There are no exceptions.[22] Here are a few more examples of the consistent usage of this language:

* The same "wicked and adulterous generation" who was asking for a sign (Matt. 12:39; 16:4).
* The same one He calls an "unbelieving and perverse generation," of which He asks "how long shall I stay with you? How long shall I put up with you?" (Matt. 17:17).

- * The same one that would reject God's only Son: "But first he must suffer many things and be rejected by this generation" (Luke 17:25).
- The same one to whom John the Baptist came and about which Jesus lamented, "To what shall I compare this generation?" (Matt. 11:16-24).
- The same one who would crucify Him: "Therefore, this generation will be held responsible for the blood of all the prophets that has been shed since the beginning of the world . . . .Yes, I tell you, this generation will be held responsible for it all" (Luke 11:50, 51b).
- They were worse than all previous generations "more wicked . . . . That is how it will be with this wicked generation." (Matt. 12:45).
- And the same one Peter warned his contemporaries about: "Save yourselves from this corrupt [perverse] generation" (Acts 2:40; from Deut. 32:5, 20).
- As far back as the Song of Moses in the Old Testament, which prophesied what the end of Israel would be like, God spoke through Moses of this same perverse generation, thusly: "I will hide my face from them . . . and see what their end will be for they are a perverse generation, children who are unfaithful . . . . I will heap calamities upon them and spend my arrows against them" (Deut. 32:20, 23).

Those 1st-century Pharisees knew that Jesus was speaking to them and prophesying a judgment that was to come upon them (Matt. 21:45; 23:29-38; Mark 12:12). They were the generation who shouted out, "Crucify him . . . crucify him" and "let his blood be on us and on our children" (Matt. 27:22-25).[23] They were the ones who would personally experience the horrors of these end-time events. They were the ones upon whom would "come all the righteous blood shed upon the earth . . . ." (Matt. 23:35), not some unborn yet-future generation or people of the Jewish race in a far distant time. Jesus further prophesied to them, "Look, your house is left to you desolate" (Matt. 23:38).

> **Jesus frequently spoke of his contemporaries as *this generation*.**

There is no need to explain away Jesus' use of the word generation or mutilate its normally understood and consistent meaning. Nor is there a need to extend it beyond a scriptural forty-year period. In perfect harmony with this relevance, Brian L. Martin in his book, *Behind the Veil of Moses*, places Jesus' "this-generation," 1st-century, and judgment event into a striking and paralleled perspective:

> The first generation of the nation of Israel stood at the threshold of entering the Promised Land, but due to unbelief, failed to do so. Judgment was pronounced upon *that* generation, and *that* generation perished. The judgment was completed within forty years of being decreed, the span of one generation. . . .
>
> The last generation of national Israel (and the first generation of spiritual Israel) stood at the threshold of entering the Promised Land, via a new covenant mediated by their Messiah, but due to unbelief, failed to do so. Judgment was pronounced upon *that* generation, and *that* generation perished in AD 70. The judgment was completed within forty years of being decreed, the span of one generation.[24]

History records that circa A.D. 70, exactly forty years, and within one generation after Jesus gave his powerful end-time prophecy, Jerusalem, the Temple, and the whole of biblical Judaism were utterly destroyed and left desolated. No longer of a time span than one generation transpired between the decree and the inflicting of judgment for *either* that first or last generation of biblical Judaic Israel.

Only one generation in history was Jesus' "this generation." That generation was a contemporary group who had become the most evil, ungodly, rebellious generation of Jews ever. That generation of Jewish people filled up their cup of iniquity by rejecting and crucifying the promised Messiah and persecuting God's emerging new people. No other generation comes close! No other generation makes sense of the time-limited and time-sensitive meaning that Jesus gave it. Consequently, this judgment of coming on the clouds and its fulfillment *does not* pertain to a yet-future generation of Jews. Israel's worse days are behind them and not ahead of them.

Jesus also warned his first hearers, "Watch out that no one deceives you" (Matt. 24:4). His warning is just as relevant today. So if we take Jesus at his literal word (as they did) and hold to a high and authoritative view of Scripture, "all these things" must have occurred within the lifetime of his disciples exactly *as* and *when* Jesus said. Nothing short of the credibility of Jesus Christ is at stake. Surely Jesus didn't make a mistake or intend to mislead his disciples and other followers. The only other alternative is that He spoke truly, just as He said He did.

What Should We Learn from Jesus' Time-Restricted Prophecies?

Today, we would be well advised to follow Jesus' lead and his consistent and obvious use of terminology. How could He have made it any plainer?

Jesus divinely linked the time of this judgment coming to the destruction of Jerusalem and the Temple and inseparably named it as part, i.e., within the context, of "all these things" (Matt. 24:34). Can you seriously doubt that any of Jesus' disciples or hearers would have placed this coming in glory outside the lifetime of some then present? A well-established pattern of historical precedent and consistency of 1st-century imminency dominates Jesus' words.

Yet these statements of Jesus concerning the imminence of this coming have proven especially perplexing for all postponement and futuristic traditionalists. But why fight them? Why twist them? Why not just take Jesus' time-restricted words at face value, literally and naturally? Most scholars agree that every New Testament writer, the early Church believers, and even the unbelieving Jews (scoffers) did exactly that. They never imagined that Jesus might be referring to a distant event 2,000 years removed. So why can't we just take Jesus at his word and leave this most-magnificent eschatological event in its proper timeframe and historical context where it rightly belongs?

Critical Objection: A.D. 70 was only a local coming of Jesus in judgment and not worldwide.

My Response: Not only were Jesus' birth, life, death, resurrection, and ascension also only local events, the Garden of Eden, the Jewish prophetic tradition, the Temple, and entire Old Covenant system were also local, as was almost everything else recorded in the Bible, with two exceptions—creation and the flood.[25] But all had universal applications and implications. Locally is just how God chose to set up, implement, and fulfill his plan of redemption. The fact is, the local events circa A.D. 70 ended forever biblical Judaism, its age, and the Old Covenant system (Heb. 8:13; 9:10).

Thus, the 1st century should confirm when everything Jesus promised either did or didn't come to pass. If He was wrong, then He was neither inspired nor a Prophet of God (Deut. 18:21-22), nor the Messiah. There is no valid escape from this predicament. The texts demand it. Even appealing to the statement, "No one knows about that day or hour" (Matt. 24:36; 25:13) doesn't mean knowing the time was a futile task, nor does it override the nearness and time-restriction imposed by Jesus Himself. No one knows the day or hour of the birth of a baby following a nine-month gestation period either. And Jesus compared this coming to just that (Matt. 24:8). But that's why He gave two prime warning signs (see Matt. 24:15-16; Luke 21:20-21). By watching for these signs and obeying his instructions to flee, his disciples could know that the tough times of unequalled tribulation would not last forever and that his coming in judgment was very close.[26]

Consequently, we'd be well-advised to reconsider the words of the old hymn, *Tis So Sweet*.

> "Tis so sweet to trust in Jesus,
> Just to take Him at his word,
> Just to rest upon His promise,
> Just to know, "Thus saith the Lord."

Unfortunately, the overwhelming majority of Christians since Bible times have not been willing to just take Jesus at his word. They no more believe that Jesus' words of imminence applied to the time of his first disciples than did the scoffers of that day (see 2 Pet. 3:4). So we've employed every means imaginable to sidestep or distort their natural and time-restricted meaning. The fact is, these timeframe manipulations are necessitated by our preconceived notions about the nature of this coming. Since we haven't seen anything resembling what we've been told to look for (end of the world, end of time, a visible appearance), we've abandoned a literal time hermeneutic and postponed its occurrence to the future—now nineteen centuries and counting. So, does this mean that those 1st-century scoffers have been proven right?[27]

Ironically, profound things can be simple. And apparently Jesus wanted to keep his statements simple. Otherwise, why say them? We know that "the common people heard Him gladly" (Mark 12:37 KJV). But the traditions of men can make the word of God of little or no effect (Mark 7:13; Matt. 15:6). It was true back then. It's still true today. Think about it, though. Why complicate Jesus' words? Why not keep them simple and just honor their plain meaning and adjust our notions of the nature of fulfillment. Maybe, just maybe, Jesus Christ knew in what generation He would be coming on the clouds and riding on Revelation's white horse in judgment and in war and taught that very thing using words and meanings his hearers could easily grasp. And maybe, just maybe, it's the uninspired historic Church, its creeds, and our favorite theologians and pastors who have made the mistake.

Essentially, we should be able to stop right here and rest our case. Again, if you had heard Jesus' teachings first-hand, how would you have understood his words? Who would you have thought He was talking to and about? Then why should we believe any differently today? Why must we make excuses for Him? If Jesus said it, shouldn't we believe it, and that settles it? This is our first and strongest evidence of this coming's timely arrival. Even if it isn't sufficient to "prove" our point, there's more, much more.

Further Proof—Intensification of Nearness Language

Scholars almost unanimously agree, Jesus' 1st-century followers expected Him to come on the clouds in the manner mentioned above and within their lifetime. And why shouldn't they have so believed in this way? In the words of the respected Christian apologist C.S. Lewis, "their Master had told them so."[28]

But there is another reason for their heightened air of expectancy. One I think you will find equally compelling. According to the Bible, Jesus' first followers, including the inspired writers of the New Testament books, were guided into all truth and told the things that were yet to come by the Holy Spirit (John 16:13). Obviously, their expectations were formed by this divine guidance. But here's the rub. If their Holy-Spirit-guided expectations for Jesus coming on the clouds within their lifetime have been proven false by nineteen centuries and counting of human history, how can we trust them to have conveyed other aspects of the faith along to us accurately, such as the requirements for salvation?

Another factor well worth serious consideration is this; no Holy-Spirit-guided, New Testament writer ever corrected these 1st-century-fulfillment expectations. Nor did they compromise or contradict Jesus' teachings regarding the timeframe for this coming—"this generation." In fact, they did just the opposite.

As Jesus' literal, forty-year, "this generation" time period wound down (from A.D. 30 to A.D. 70), the sense of nearness language in the New Testament dramatically ratcheted up.[29] This intensification provides further proof that Jesus' first followers understood his words to come on the clouds as applying to them, then and there.

No Holy-Spirit-guided, New Testament writer ever corrected these 1st-century-fulfillment expectations .... they did just the opposite..

Approximately nineteen years after Jesus delivered his Olivet Discourse, the writers of the New Testament began writing their epistles—what we now call the books of the New Testament. The intensification of their nearness language is most evident. In my book, *The Perfect Ending for the World*, I dramatized this proofing dynamic with chronological-countdown language using "T" minus the number of years remaining in Jesus' forty-year, this-generation time period, along with the approximate dates when these works were written. I recommend that amplified treatment to your attention. I won't take the time and space to duplicate it here[30]—with this one exception.

According to Jesus, no one at the time (including Jesus and the angels) knew or could know the "day or hour" (Matt. 24:36; 25:13).[31] But that did not mean they, and we, could not know the time at all. Demons even knew "the appointed time" (Matt. 8:29). This prohibition on knowing was only against knowing the day or hour, not the week, month, year, or generation. Therefore, knowing was not and is not a futile task. In A.D. 66 - 70, this knowing was a matter of life and death, and claiming to not know was not a viable excuse. That's the reason Jesus gave two prime warning signs.[32] Amazingly, however, some thirty-seven years after Jesus' death, resurrection, and ascension, and in A.D. 67 – 68 with the guidance of the Holy Spirit (John 16:13), John emphatically knew and twice proclaimed it with this bold and double statement "this is last hour . . . . it is the last hour" (1 John 2:18).

In the Same Way for the Same Purpose

The bottom line is, the most undeniable aspect of Jesus' Olivet Discourse prophecy is the historical fact that Jerusalem and the Temple were destroyed and left totally desolate exactly *as* and *when* Jesus had prophesied. The problem has been that some, many, or most of the other things that He predicted would occur at that same time supposedly failed to occur. Nor have they yet occurred, according to the most popular view in the Church today. But, and once again, documentation for the fulfillment of all these other things is systematically presented in my book, *The Perfect Ending for the World*. I recommend it to your attention.

Surely, however, with just the time and precedent consistencies presented in this chapter of this book, we can see the Lord Jesus riding Revelation's white horse of war and coming on the clouds in judgment, forty years after his Mount of Olives prophecy, in the events of the Roman-Jewish War, and in the destruction of Jerusalem and the Temple circa A.D. 70.

The respected Reformed theologian R. C. Sproul in his book *The Last Days According to Jesus* affirms that "the coming of Christ in A.D. 70 was a coming in judgment on the Jewish nation, indicating the end of the Jewish age and the fulfillment of a day of the Lord, Jesus really did come in judgment at this time . . . ."[33]

Using the language of the Prophets, and comparing it with the biblical precedents of a coming "day of the Lord," we can document how Jesus' coming was accomplished. He came in exactly the same *way* ("on the clouds"), for exactly the same *purpose* (judgment), to accomplish exactly the same *thing* (destruction of a nation). Just as the cloud-coming Jehovah God came many times in Old Testament times, Jesus came as

He said, "on the clouds" (Matt. 24:30) and "in the glory of the Father" (Matt. 16:27). But what does this second and often-ignored phrase mean?

Many times in the past, and from his heavenly perspective, Jesus had seen the Father come out of heaven and go down to the earth on the clouds and in the glory of a literal, destructive, and historical judgment upon a nation or a city. It was termed a Day of the Lord. Therefore, in like manner and same nature as previous comings of the Lord, Judge Jesus came in that same glory as belongs to the Father utilizing the armies of Rome to deliver his people, the Church, from their Jewish persecutors. And in keeping with the Old Testament pattern, He was not physically seen.

Two other important facts to reflect in this judgment-coming event and "in the glory of the Father" are the change of covenants and change of the Person of the Godhead implementing judgment. Therefore, "the day of the Lord" (Jehovah) of the Old Testament became "the day of Christ" (*Christos* 2 Thess. 2:2; *kurios* 2 Pet. 3:10) in the New Testament. This was because, as Jesus told this disciples, "the Father . . . has entrusted all judgment to the Son" (John 5:22b). In the New Covenant economy, Jesus the Son would now be the Person of the Godhead Who would come and judge as the Father had done many times before. But the purpose of this action remained the same.

Throughout the Old Testament, God's often-stated purpose in acting or intervening in this manner was to "be a sign and witness to the Lord Almighty" and for the Lord to "make himself known," i.e., to manifest his sovereignty and majesty as the true God to a particular group, people, nation and among the nations (Isa. 19:20-21; 37:20; 64:2; plus 74 times in Ezekiel, and many more). In so doing, his name was glorified and men and women of discernment could understand Who He is. Hence, the Psalmist advises, "tell of his wonderful acts. Glory in his holy name; . . . Remember the wonders he has done, his miracles, and the judgments he pronounced" (Psa. 105:2-5).

And in keeping with the Old Testament pattern, He was not physically seen.

Likewise, Jesus' coming on the clouds in judgment circa A.D. 70 involved both visible and invisible aspects.

First and foremost, history records, quite literally, that Jerusalem and the Temple were burned and totally destroyed by invading Roman armies in A.D. 70 - 73. "Not one stone [was] left upon another," just as Jesus had perfectly prophesied (Matt. 24:2). Jesus had inseparably connected his age-ending coming with this dramatically visible, historical event (Matt. 24:1-34). This linkage of time, event, and place in the Olivet Discourse prophecy cannot be overstated. Even the 1st-century scoffers knew that the Temple's destruction was the corresponding physical event that signaled this coming (see 2 Pet. 3:3-4).

In this coming, Jesus was not only vindicated in the same arena of his humiliation and his prophesies fulfilled, but He was also be revealed as God, not man. Hence, He came "in the glory of the Father," riding a white horse on the clouds of judgment, showing Himself to be the King of kings and Lord of lords, and triumphing over those who had slain him. Following his circa A.D. 70 coming in judgment, Jesus now shares that authority and glory of the Father, not as a man, but as the One true God (Joel 3:15-17; 2 Thess. 1:7-10).

Second, the prophet Ezekiel said that in the latter days God would come up against Israel "as a cloud to cover the land" (Ezek. 38:9, 16; see also Zech. 12-14). New Testament writers confirmed they were then living in those "last days" (Heb. 1:2; Acts 2:17; 1 Tim. 4:1; 2 Tim. 3:1; Jas. 5:3; 2 Pet. 3:3; 1 Pet. 1:5, 20; Jude 18; 1 John 2:18). At this time, Isaiah had prophesied, the Messiah would come robed "with the garments of vengeance for clothing" (Isa. 59:17f; see also Rom. 12:19), and He would proclaim not only salvation, but "the day of vengeance of our God" (Isa. 61:2). Jesus' statement in Luke's account of the Olivet Discourse contains this very wording: "When you [Jesus' present audience] see Jerusalem surrounded by armies, you will know that its desolation is near . . . flee . . . For this is the time of punishment [*these be the days of vengeance*] in fulfillment of all that has been written" (Luke 21:20-22 [in KJV]). The immediate historical setting and explicit framework for these happenings proved to be the Jewish-Roman War of A.D. 66 – 70. After circa A.D. 70 - 73, the biblical "last days" were over.

Third, Isaiah also foretold that during this time Israel would fill up the measure of her sin and she would be destroyed (Isa. 65:6-15) by the Lord, Who would come with fire and judgment (Isa. 66:15f). Jesus said that this time of filling up would "come upon this generation" (Matt 23:32-36). As far back as Moses, God had instructed the people of Israel about a coming Prophet and warned that if they refused to listen to Him, they would be held "to account" (Deut. 18:15-19). Most of them didn't listen, didn't believe, and they were held to account—severe account.

Hence, the Apostle Paul confirmed that Jesus would be "revealed from heaven in blazing fire" (2 Thess. 1:7). That 1st-century apostate Jewish nation, with its city and Temple, had become the great enemy of God's emerging new people, the Church. And as Isaiah also proclaimed, "But the Lord of hosts shall be exalted in judgment . . . . (Isa. 5:16 KJV).

Jesus, Ezekiel, Isaiah, and Daniel all precisely pinpointed when everything promised would come to pass.[34] If they were wrong, they weren't inspired. There is no valid way to escape this conclusion. As the time of fulfillment approached, James said, "The coming of the Lord is at hand" (Jas. 5:8 NAS). Paul reminded his first readers that "the time is short" (1 Cor. 7:29). Peter proclaimed, "The end of all things is at hand" (1 Pet. 4:7 KJV), and warned, "For the time has come for judgment to begin at the house of God" (1 Pet. 4:17). Urgency permeates Peter's sense of expectation. He is emphatic, "The time has come!" John wrote, twice, "It is the last hour!" (1 John 2:18). How many "last hours" can there be? How long is short? How could these statements have been any clearer? How many more declarations of Scripture are required before we can believe this inspired imminency?

Fourth, the awe-inspiring, "mountain-top experience" of Jesus' transfiguration was a vision or preview of what was to come. It foreshadowed the nature of his coming judgment at his *parousia*. On that mountain, Jesus' disciples were amazed as Jesus' countenance changed dramatically before them. And they were terrified. Here's part of the account:

> *"His face shone like the sun, and his clothes became white as the light. Just then there appeared before them Moses and Elijah, talking with Jesus . . . . a bright cloud enveloped them, and a voice from the cloud said, 'This is my Son, whom I love; with him I am well pleased. Listen to him!' When the disciples heard this, they fell facedown to the ground, terrified. But Jesus came and touched them. 'Get up,' he said. 'Don't be afraid.' When they looked up, they saw no one except Jesus"* (Matt. 17:2-3, 5-8).

Indeed, something truly powerful, glorious, and unveiling happened on that mountain. What they saw was not Jesus being revealed as a special man, but as the Son of God—as Deity. Then why were Moses and Elijah there with Him? And why did they disappear leaving only Jesus?

Peter, who was an eyewitness of this event, may have referred to this experience as "the power and coming (*parousia*) of our Lord Jesus Christ" (2 Pet. 1:16). But in my opinion, the reason Moses and Elijah appeared is they represented the entirety of the Old Covenant—Moses as the Lawgiver to whom was given the Ten Commandments of the Law (Exodus 20) and Elijah the great prophet and precursor of the Messiah (Mal. 4:5-6).

Hence, what Peter and the others witnessed on that mountain top was a foreshadowing of Jesus' *parousia* coming in judgment, the fading glory and passing away of the Old Covenant, Mosaic era and world, along with the surpassing and transcending glory of the New Covenant of Jesus, which remained. This change of covenants is exactly what was prophesied and happened with the fall of Jerusalem and the Temple circa A.D. 70. It's also what all end-time prophecies are all about—this change of covenant and not a change of cosmos.

Notably, and to their credit, the scoffers of 2 Peter 3 knew this change of covenants would be the nature of Christ's *parousia* coming as they scoffed, "Where is this 'coming' (*parousia*) he promised? Ever since our fathers died, everything [i.e., the Old Covenant system] goes on as it has since the beginning of creation" (2 Peter 3:4). Jude tells us those scoffers were present just before the destruction of Jerusalem (see Jude 18-19).

Fifth, the visible "sign" of his invisible coming on the clouds would be: "Do you see all these things?' he asked. 'I tell you the truth, not one stone here will be left on another; every one will be thrown down" (Matt. 24:2).

The destruction of Jerusalem and its Temple was the "sign" that signaled Jesus' age-ending coming on the clouds in judgment and the sign of his presence (Matt. 24:3). At that time, almost everyone, if not everyone, in "the land" of Judea and Jerusalem saw this sign.[35] It was not a worldwide sign because it was not a global event, as many over the centuries have been mistakenly led to expect. But, and once again, neither were Jesus' birth, anointing, crucifixion, resurrection, or ascension global events. All were local events with universal significance and relevance.

Some six-hundred years earlier, the prophet Ezekiel prophesied of this sign when he was told to "take a clay tablet, put it in front of you and draw the city of Jerusalem on it . . . . It will be under siege . . . . It will be a *sign* to the house of Israel" (Ezek. 4:1, 3 – italics added). Similarly, and at about the same time, Daniel prophesied that the defining characteristic and immediate historical setting for the one and only "time of the end" would be "When the power of the holy people has been finally broken . . . ." (Dan. 12: 4, 7).[36] The "sign of the Son of Man . . . in the sky" [in heaven] (Matt. 24:30) could have been the massive plumes of smoke arising from the burning fires of the whole city that rose high into the sky for days above the mountain plateau on which Jerusalem sat (Mark 10:33).[37]

The destruction of Jerusalem and its Temple was the "sign" that signaled Jesus' age-ending coming on the clouds in judgment and the sign of his presence.

Even more astonishing, both Josephus, the Jewish/Roman historian and eyewitness, and Tacitus, the Roman historian, recorded the sighting of chariots and armed soldiers (angelic armies) riding about in the sky just before the first siege of Jerusalem in A.D. 66. This, too, could be interpreted as "the sign of his coming," since Jesus is the commander of the heavenly hosts and had prophesied of "great signs from heaven" (Luke 21:11). Josephus and Tacitus also reported a star in the shape of a sword that stood over the city, and a comet that continued for a year before Jerusalem's destruction.[38] Jesus had also prophesied of "signs in the sun, moon, and stars" (Luke 21:25).

In a similar fashion, the Old Testament prophet Joel had prophesied that God would "show wonders in the heaven above and signs on the earth below . . . . before the coming of the great and glorious day of the Lord" (Acts 2:19-20 in quoting Joel 2:30-31). Correspondingly, Josephus writes of several other strange, if not bizarre, oracles that appeared in the city before the first siege of Jerusalem and foretelling its impending devastation: a brilliant light around the altar at night, a cow that gave birth to a lamb, and the hearing of voices in the inner court of the Temple, saying, "We are departing hence."[39]

In his wisdom, God had set Jerusalem on a high place (Psa. 48:1-2; Isa. 2:2-3) at the crossroads of the world (three continents) and "in the center of the nations, with countries all around her" (Ezek. 5:5-17). He had a definite purpose (see Ezek. 5:8-17) and specifically declared through the Old Testament prophet Ezekiel, "I will display my glory among the nations and all the nations will see the punishment I inflict and the hand I lay upon them" (Ezek. 39:21). After the fall of circa A.D. 70, transcontinental traders and travelers from near and far could readily see that something significant had happened. News of the devastation of God's chosen people, their Temple, and the entire nation thus spread rapidly throughout the Roman world. In this manner and in perfect consistency and harmony of fulfillment, "the Lord Jesus is [was] revealed from heaven in blazing fire with his powerful angels" (1 Thess. 1:7).

A disclaimer: In Jesus' prophetic statement that "At that time the sign of the Son of Man will appear in the sky [in heaven] (Matt. 24:30), the better translation in line with the literal Greek is "in heaven." Yet "in heaven" (or "in the sky") does not modify the sign. Consequently, Jesus was not saying that a sign would appear in heaven or in the sky. He was only saying that they would see a sign proving He was in heaven and sitting at his Father's right hand (Acts 2:30-36). The destruction of Jerusalem, as with other day-of-the-Lord occurrences, would be that sign. It confirmed his enthronement as "King of kings and Lord of lords" (Rev. 19:16) and proof that He is exactly Whom He claimed to be and that Christianity is true. It's the empirical proof of the divine, timely, and precise fulfillment of prophecy (see Isa. 41:22-23; 42:9; 44:6-8; 45:21; 46:10-11; 48:4-6; Rev. 19:10b).

Sixth, Jesus had stated that a particular prerequisite must take place before his coming on the clouds and the end could occur. It was, "And this gospel of the kingdom will be preached in the whole world as a testimony to all nations, and then the end will come" (Matt. 24:14). Many futuristic interpreters cannot fathom how this preaching could have possibly been fulfilled before or during A.D. 70, when the gospel had not yet been preached in the Western Hemisphere? After all, the great missionary movement of the 18th and 19th centuries hadn't taken place, worldwide communications hadn't been developed, and many nations and people groups in remote tribes had yet to hear the gospel. This fact alone, critics contend, should stop dead in its tracks any idea that Jesus came and the end was reached in circa A.D. 70.

But as we've seen before, the Bible must be understood on its own terms and in the context of its original hearers. Only then can we properly understand what any portion really means for us today. Therefore, let's carefully note that the inspired writers of the New Testament, using the same or similar words that Jesus used, confirmed that Jesus' prerequisite was accomplished in their day:

- In the context of the Jewish worldview, "every nation under heaven" was assembled on the day of Pentecost (Acts 2:5).
- The Apostle Paul, thirty-one years later, confirmed that "all over the world this gospel is producing fruit and growing . . . ." (Col. 1:6) and "the gospel that you heard . . . has been proclaimed to every creature under heaven" (Col. 1:23), and that "your faith is being reported all over the world" (Rom. 1:8). This was not Paul's opinion. It is inspired Scripture.
- For more confirmations, read: Rom. 10:18; 16:26; Acts 1:8; 24:5; Jude 3; also compare with Dan. 2:39; 4:1, 22; 5:19; 7:23; Luke 2:1, 30-32; 24:47; Rev. 3:10.

Why is this scripturally documented fulfillment of Jesus' prerequisite so hard to believe? The answer is simply, once again, the power of the traditions of men riding roughshod over the Word of God (Mark 7:13; Matt. 15:6). According to the Bible itself, and prior to A.D. 70, the gospel was preached to all nations and to the world. The Greek word translated "world" in Matthew 24:14 is *oikoumene*, meaning "land (i.e., the [terrene part of the] globe, specifically the Roman Empire)." In this commonly used and restricted sense, the then-known Roman world, or the civilized world of that time, was also the "world" of the Jews into which they had been scattered. If the entire global earth was meant, the Greek word *kosmos* would have been used, as it is in Matthew 24:21. But it wasn't.

Hence, Jesus' end-coming condition had been scripturally met. This is a truth that has been lost or ignored by many today. But it wasn't lost on or ignored by early Church father Eusebius (A.D. 260 – 341). He clearly understood this linkage and its significance as he confirmed that both the worldwide preaching of the gospel and this end of biblical Judaism were fulfilled:

> Moses had foretold this very thing and in due course Christ sojourned in this life, and the teaching of the new covenant was borne to all nations, and at once the Romans besieged Jerusalem and destroyed it and the Temple there. At once the whole of the Mosaic law was abolished, with all that remained of the Old Covenant . . . . [40]

Let's further note that the fulfillment of this world mission was an absolutely necessary part of God's plan. Since Jews had been scattered over the known world (Jas. 1:1), they all had to have the opportunity to accept or reject the gospel and persecute its proclaimers. In this way, they would "fill up, then, the measure of sin of your forefathers" (Matt. 23:32; Isa. 65:6-12). That's why the gospel had to go out into "the whole world." The previously cited verses verify this accomplishment. These verses cannot be lightly dismissed. So let's just believe what inspired Scripture writers said. God allowed one generation of time—Jesus' "this generation"—for the completion of this missionary task. Once completed, the stage was set. The end Jesus spoke of could now come. It did, perfectly, precisely, and right on time. It was the end of the Old Covenant, biblical Judaic system, and not the end of the physical creation, which will never end because it has no end.[41]

Hence, Jesus' end-coming condition had been scripturally met. This is a truth that has been lost or ignored by many today.

A Caution: Many Christian evangelists and preachers fear that the recognition of this scripturally documented and 1st-century fulfillment of Jesus' worldwide, gospel-preaching prerequisite will cause the Church to lose motivation for evangelism and we'll fail to complete this task in our day and time, or in the future. Of course, this fear is based on the belief that the preaching of the gospel to all the nations is still necessary to hasten the so-called and futurized "Second Coming" and "Return" of Christ, i.e., the sooner we get this done, the sooner this will happen. But as we have seen in Chapter 1, this, too, is a mistaken notion and unscriptural concept.

So is the mission mandate a completable, once-for-all task? Let's recall that this mandate neither originated nor terminated with Jesus' Matthew 24:14 statement nor with his Great Commission "to make disciples of all nations" (Matt. 28:18-20). Why not? The mission mandate for world evangelism has always been the responsibility of those who are called to God, and always will be.

Four thousand years ago, God called Abraham and made a covenant with him. Not only did God promise to bless Abraham, and all families of the earth through him (i.e., through his seed), He also instructed him and his descendants to actively be a blessing to others (Gen. 12:1-4). Hence, God's covenant with Abraham was the origin of the mission mandate. It is frequently referred to and enlarged upon throughout the Old Testament. For example, God's people were to be priests and to minister to others (Exod. 19:4-6). Make "your [God's] ways known on earth, your salvation among all nations" (Psa. 67:2; also Psa. 98:3; Isa. 49:6; Acts 13:47). Be "a light for the Gentiles" (Isa. 42:6). "You are my witnesses" (Isa. 43:10, 12; 43:8), and "they will proclaim my glory among the nations" (Isa. 66:19). "Make known among the nations what he has done . . . tell of all his wonderful acts . . . proclaim his salvation day after day. Declare . . . his marvelous deeds among all peoples" (1 Chron. 16:8-9, 23-24). Thus, Israel's mandate to witness was grounded in her covenant with God and applies to every child of Abraham (Gal. 3:7)—by blood and/or by faith—and it never ceases (Gal. 3:15-19f).

Sadly, the Old Covenant Jews failed to take God's blessings to the Gentiles. Instead, they hoarded these blessings for themselves. In our day, if God's people desire his promised Abrahamic blessings through Christ, we must not keep his blessings for ourselves either. We, like they, are responsible to pass them on, to be a blessing to others and all nations, to be "witnesses" (Acts 1:8), to be "fishers of men" (Matt. 4:19), and to "produce the fruit" of the kingdom we've been given (Matt. 21:43). This missionary mandate hasn't changed since the days of Abraham. What has changed is that God's blessings are greater and the known civilized world is much bigger. We are to bless all the nations with "the eternal gospel" (Rev. 14:6), just as Jesus' contemporaries did in their day and time.

Beyond Contestable

No, Jesus did not physically ride a literal white stallion on top of literal fluffy cumulus clouds across a literal blue sky in circa A.D. 70. Physical eyes could and would have seen that spectacle. But what clearly must be considered beyond contestable is that the historical destruction of the Judaic world circa A.D. 70 followed the same pattern and nature of many Old Testament comings of God, or "days of the Lord," and employed similar apocalyptic language. This historical correlation has been a major part of the methodology and grounding we have presented in this chapter.

In support, theologians Klein, Blomberg, and Hubbard, Jr. confirm that "the historically defensible interpretation has greatest authority. That is, interpreters can have maximum confidence in their understanding of a text when they base that understanding on historically defensible arguments."[42] These scholars further and rightly advise that we "should seek the most likely *time* for the fulfillment of a prophecy in history."[43] Another respected theologian, Moisés Silva, appropriately chimes in that we "must be historical as well as grammatical, and must always seek the meaning intended, not any meaning that can be tortured out of a passage."[44]

The fact is, in every historical instance of Jehovah God's intervention in a coming day of the Lord, his direct and personal presence was evident, but He was never physically seen. And the Jews knew that only Jehovah rode on the clouds (Matt. 26:64-66). Hence, Jesus coming in like manner demonstrated his coming "in the glory of the Father" (Matt. 16:27). Accordingly, Jesus did not appear "in person" circa A.D. 70. Neither did his body appear in the sky to signal this special coming. Yet his bodily presence was there, in keeping with the long-standing day-of-the-Lord motif.

> **But what clearly must be considered beyond contestable is that the historical destruction of the Judaic world circa A.D. 70 followed the same pattern and nature of many Old Testament comings of God, or "days of the Lord," and employed similar apocalyptic language.**

That's why a sign was needed. A sign isn't the reality; a sign points to a reality. A sign is something that is visible and points to something that is currently invisible. The destruction of Jerusalem and the Temple was the physical and visible sign that announced the end of the "last days" of the Jewish age, and not of the Christian or Church age to which there is no end. Those days were the *beginning days* of the Christian age.

Thus, Jesus' predictions of his coming on the clouds and the riding of Revelation's white horse in judgment were fulfilled. The biblical nation of Israel and its Old Covenant system that was birthed nearly 1,500 some years prior was now ended. This is the one and only end the Bible consistently proclaims (see Dan. 12:7). By now, this biblical and historic reality should be perfectly clear, unless we're looking through a futurist veil.[45]

There is no need to explain away anything or do a fancy dance around any scripture. Nor should we be surprised that God chose to send Christ in judgment to destroy Jerusalem circa A.D. 70 in the same way He had come out of heaven many times before in Old Covenant times "with myriads of holy ones" (Deut. 33:2). Jesus, who had come, died, arisen, and gone back to heaven, came down out of heaven to judge the very people upon whom He had spoken seven woes (Matt. 23). The time of grace upon the Jewish nation had elapsed (Matt. 27:25; 2 Thess. 1:7-8; Jude 14; Rom. 11:26; Isa. 59:20-21; 27:9). It's both a fact and a reality of biblical and redemptive history.

In all this, Jesus' prophetic words, the intensifying nearness statements of the New Testament writers, the expectations of the early Church, and even Enoch's "70th generation" prophecy can be plainly understood, in our day, as true.[46] Jesus was a promise keeper. Early Church father Eusebius affirmed it—that Jesus "came" in the fall of Jerusalem.[47] Yet no one except God the Father knew the day or hour (exact time). Nor can we look back in history today and reconstruct or know for certain when the literal "last day" or "last hour" was. The exact day or hour is not important, but the destruction of biblical Judaism is hugely important (see Heb. 9:6-10). It was the culminating event for our "once for all delivered faith" (Jude 3). And it was precisely prophesied and perfectly fulfilled.

To the serious Bible student, the validity of this coming of Jesus should not be a debatable point. If we hold to the authority of Scripture and the divine integrity of Jesus and the New Testament writers, the Bible is quite emphatic that Jesus was to come again, on the clouds, in the glory of the Father, and in judgment in that 1st-century generation. He did not tarry or delay—as many have tried to explain! (see Heb. 10:37; Ezek. 12:21-28; Hab. 2:3). It is simply a matter of honoring the biblical usage of language and applying an historical-grammatical-consistent method of interpretation and understanding.

Thus and appropriately, Foy E. Wallace, Jr. concludes his book, *The Book of Revelation*, with this spot-on assessment:

> The most significant events in all epochs of the world since the creation of mankind are connected with this dispensation marked as the fullness of time (Gal. 4:4). . . . The transition from the old covenant was eventuated by his birth, the cross, the ascension, Pentecost, Patmos, the fall of Jerusalem, and end of Judaism and the expansion of Christianity. . . . —the completion and end of all divine revelation. As it is biblically certain that the God of heaven in times of old descended, in the Old Testament metaphor, on the clouds of heaven to execute judgment on ancient wicked nations and cities (Isaiah 13 and 19), so certainly did the Son of man come in the clouds with his angels of power to execute judgment on the once great city of Jerusalem, guilty of his blood and the blood of his saints and martyrs. This triumphal administration of judgment has been wondrously portrayed in the scenes of the apocalypse.[48]

Knowing and honoring this past-fulfillment truth is part of growing in the knowledge of our Lord and Savior, the greater Jesus Christ. And his cloud-and-horse-riding coming circa A.D. 70 should forever settle the issue as to his being the Messiah. It could also heal a major sickness that has plagued Christianity for nineteen-centuries and counting. The writer of Proverb 13:12 aptly puts it this way, "Hope deferred makes the heart [the Church] sick, but a longing fulfilled is a tree of life."

Lastly, one further point must be mentioned regarding Jesus' coming on the clouds, riding the white horse of the Apocalypse in war, and in age-ending, divine judgment. It may not have been a split-second, one-day, or even a one-year event. His coming and *parousia* presence in this judgment may have stretched over the entire period of the Jewish-Roman War of A.D. 66-70, or further. It is impossible to say or to be anymore exact than that—any more than we can be with similar comings of the Father in the Old Testament. We still don't know nor can we pinpoint the "day or hour."

Today, however, we are living in post-A.D. 70 times. So we need to ask, do we still have a "blessed hope?" Does the greater Jesus still ride that white horse of war and come on the clouds in judgment? Or, after the destruction of Jerusalem and the Temple, did He dismount that steed and hitch it to a post up in heaven never to ride it again? In other words, does Jesus still come in this way, or in any of his other ways, today? We'll address these distinctives in our next chapter.

Knowing and honoring this past-fulfillment truth is part of growing in the knowledge of our Lord and Savior, the greater Jesus Christ. And his cloud-and-horse-riding coming circa A.D. 70 should forever settle the issue as to Him being the Messiah.

Chapter 5

He Still Comes in Many Wondrous Ways

Critical Objection: "The problem with your 'ongoing comings' is that we can't prove any past A.D. 70. The case is really closed right there. Otherwise, it's your word against someone else's denial concerning other 'days of the Lord' past A.D. 70. You yourself have not been able to produce anything other than charismatic prayer comings, etc. 2000 years is a long time to come up with nothing IF your 'ongoing comings' – as in big 'day of the Lord' comings – is true. . . . it would just be your 'claim.' As I said, here is where your endless comings view hits the wall head on."[1]

My Response: Do you know of any spiritual experience you have had in your life—including being born again—that you can prove?

Seriously, do you really believe that Jesus went to all the trouble of lowering Himself, coming down to this earth, being born in human flesh, allowing Himself to be sacrificed on the cross, coming and going many times after his resurrection to demonstrate He was still alive, and then left "Dodge" for two millennia and counting? Or, if He really did come again on the clouds and riding a white horse of war in age-ending judgment circa A.D. 70, do you think that robs us of our "blessed hope" (Titus 2:13)?

What saddens me deeply is the popular idea that Jesus is off somewhere waiting to come back or return when, in fact, He never left, as He said (see again Chapter 1)! Equally troubling, are those who believe that A.D. 70 was his final coming, after which there are no more comings (like my critic above). Please be assured that post A.D. 70 Jesus is still here with us, right now, in our midst, and He still comes in many wondrous ways. His ongoing comings are much more than a single "blessed hope." They are a multifaceted, spirit-realm/physical-realm reality. But billions of Christians and billions more on planet Earth today are totally unaware of this divine and supernatural phenomenon.

To put this ongoing reality in a colloquial vernacular, Jesus is still in the comings business; He is still among his churches in the spirit realm; He is still active and involved with his physical creation (Rev. 1:13, 20). But I am also convinced that not recognizing, teaching, and expecting his many comings is a major reason why most churches and Christians today don't experience Him more fully in everyday life. What a tragedy!

To put this ongoing reality in a colloquial vernacular, Jesus is still in the comings business; He is still among his churches in the spirit realm; He is still active and involved with his physical creation.

It is time for God's people to wake up to the full meaning, power, and reality of Christ's presence with us. Yet some may question if Christ's many comings in and out of the spirit realm is a second-rate option? No! A thousand times, no! The spirit realm is as real as this book you hold in your hands. It may be more real, because it is eternal. And the personal and bodily presence of Jesus Himself in that spirit realm and his comings into and out of the physical realm are still *here and now!* This is precisely what I am suggesting continues to happen, occasionally and/or frequently, from his abiding and omnipresent presence with humankind all around the world. So can I prove it as my critic challenges? Or, are many of my past-fulfillment critics right that heaven now contains Jesus and He no longer comes to, for, or against people on the earth as He has done so many times in the past?

Why All the Comings of Jesus Are a Present and Ongoing Reality

How can we biblically, historically, and pragmatically know that all the comings of Jesus we have been discussing in this book so far are a present and ongoing, spirit-realm and physical-realm reality—and not just some solitary, major news event waiting to happen in the future or only a past and final event that occurred almost two millennia ago?

In the words and advice of one popular but controversial author, "Sometimes people bump into Jesus . . . they drink from the rock, without knowing what or who it was. This happened in the Exodus, and it happens today. The last thing we should do is discourage or disregard an honest, authentic encounter with the living Christ."[2]

Of course, authentic encounters with the living Christ can occur in many ways—from God's Word, in prayer, in dreams, and in visions, etc. And yet none of these encounters can be verified or proven. Why not? It's because they are personal experiences.

Sadly, adequate attention and appreciation has not been given to Christ's many comings throughout the Bible nor to his coming on the clouds and riding Revelation's white horse in judgment and war circa A.D. 70. Once again, this omission is due to the long history and fascination with a futuristic "Second-Coming" and "Return" doctrine and mindset. Thus, many today believe Jesus is still up in heaven where He has been waiting for some two thousand years to come back to earth again someday, perhaps soon. But if you search the Scriptures for what they really say, you will readily see that limiting the coming of Jesus to a single future or past event does not fit the teachings of Jesus or any other scriptures, or the testimony of Scripture.

In this chapter we shall investigate eight key points which should help us rise above and straighten out our misunderstandings over the nature of the Lord's post-A.D. 70 presence with us and his many, countless, and present-day comings. As we shall see, He still is the God Who comes! Maranatha! (1 Cor. 16:22 – Maranatha consists of two Aramean words, *Maran'athah,* meaning, "our Lord comes," or is "coming").

1) Revelation's Timeless and Universal Relevance

A good place to start is with the question we asked at the end of our last chapter. What did Jesus do after He rode his white horse of war in Revelation 19 and in judgment and destruction of Jerusalem and the Temple circa A.D. 70? Did He dismount that steed, hitch it to a post in heaven, and walk away never to ride it again? In other words, is Revelation's value for us today only as a history lesson? Or, does He still ride this horse every now and then, again and again? How can we be sure?

The answer is, as we have seen, fulfillment is not the last word in "the Revelation of Jesus Christ." Revelation's entire prophecy is timelessly relevant and universal in application. This relevancy was the reason why John was instructed to eat the scroll and prophesy "again about many peoples, nations, languages and kings." Thus, the audience relevancy for the whole of Revelation's prophecy has been transformed and broadened beyond its immediate historical fulfillment (Rev. 10:11 – see again Chapter 3, pp. 106-112).

This ongoing aspect might have been part of what Jesus was talking about in Luke 17 when He informed his disciples, "the time is coming when you will long to see one of the days of the Son of Man . . . . '" (Luke 17:22b). As you now know, many comings of the "day of the Lord" are recorded in Old Testament history. Jesus' use of the plural "days" in this verse may have been indicating there would be more than one day of the Son of man.[3]

Certainly, the circa A.D. 70 destruction of Jerusalem and the Temple was a never-to-be-repeated, age-ending, eschatological, and contextualized event that perfectly fit the pattern of an Old Testament "day of the Lord" (Luke 17:30, 31). It also took place over a period of many days. But the "day of the Lord," broadly defined, is any time (not limited to a twenty-four hour day) God the Father or God the Son actively manifests Himself and intervenes in judgment in human affairs, corporately or individually but not visibly. This type of coming is the one most talked about in Scripture. And given its long biblical precedent and consistent pattern of fulfillment, there is no reason for us moderns to arbitrarily limit its occurrence to a final time circa A.D. 70 or to some unscriptural end-of-the-world or end-of-time occurrence.

No doubt, many individuals, groups, churches, institutions, peoples, and nations throughout history have encountered their own particular "day of the Lord"—whether they recognized it as such or not. Moreover, this coming, as well as all of Christ's other comings (past, present, and future), are as a thief in the night. They happen unexpectedly, suddenly, and unannounced (Matt. 24:43; 1 Thess. 5:2-4; 2 Pet. 3:10; Rev. 3:3; 16:15). I'm further suggesting that this promised and consistent characteristic of all his comings still holds true today.

Let's also recall that God prophesied through the mid-exilic prophet Ezekiel that He would "make you [Israel] a ruin and a reproach among the nations around you" as "a warning and an object of horror to the nations around you when I inflict punishment on you in anger and in wrath and with stinging rebuke" (Ezek. 5:14-15). If there are no more judgment comings of this type after circa A.D. 70, then this "warning" is moot and void (also see Dan. 2:21). But please remember, as the Apostle Paul assures us, that all of the many Old Testament comings of Jesus and days of the Lord still serve as examples for us (1 Cor. 10:6-11).

Likewise, let's recall that included as part of the *whole* of Revelation's timeless relevancy and universal applications are the conditional comings promised to individuals in the seven, real, and historic churches to which this prophecy was first addressed (Rev. 1:4, 11). Many over the centuries have understood these seven churches to symbolically represent the entire Church throughout all ages and all over the world.[4] If this is correct, then these other comings of Jesus—which do not correspond with Jesus' coming and destruction of Jerusalem and the Temple and should not be confused with it—are just as real and applicable for us today as they were back then (see Rev. 2 and 3). Some of these comings you don't want to have happen to you, and we should try our best to repent and avoid them. But they may and can happen if we do not repent and change our ways. Why? It's because we serve a present and active Christ, the greater Jesus, Who is still with us and comes in these many and wondrous ways (Rev. 1:7; 22:7, 12, 20; Heb. 12:1, 22-24).

2) *Weaning Ourselves off the Criterion of Visibility*

The ongoing presence of Christ in the judgment events surrounding circa A.D. 70 was real, personal, and bodily. The fact He was also invisible does not make his presence unreal, impersonal or not bodily, or only symbolic or only spiritual. Invisibility does not detract from this ongoing spirit-realm reality, nor lessen its importance or significance.

We materialistic moderns need to see these things through a different set of eyes by following this scriptural admonition to "fix our eyes not on what is seen, but on what is unseen" (2 Cor. 4:18)—and wean ourselves from the idea that the presence of Christ must be a physical optical event.

Once again, a major reason Christ's coming on the clouds (*parousia*) circa A.D. 70 has not been given adequate attention or appreciation is due to the preconceived, widely accepted, and "Second Coming" / "Return" tenet that his coming again must be seeable by the naked eye. The fact that a sign was asked for ["*sign* of your coming (*parousia*)" (Matt. 24:3)] and a "*sign* of the Son of Man in heaven" (Matt. 24:30) was necessary should tip us off that the nature of this type of coming would *not* be a *visible* appearance of Christ.

Of course, many of his other comings are visible. But a coming can be either visible or invisible. That "sign" of his coming on the clouds was not a gigantic, multi-media display of his face or body up in the sky. It was the fall of Jerusalem and destruction of the Temple and the Judaic world. This devastation followed in the same pattern and nature of many Old Testament comings of God called a "day of the Lord" in which God's Presence was directly involved, but never once was He physically/visibly seen. And those comings brought similar destruction upon several nations, cities, peoples, and enemies of God.

Nevertheless, the invisibility of this particular type of coming of Christ has made it hard for most Christians to fathom, let alone believe. But assumptions often blind us to realities. And this is one area to which biblical knowledge, not human speculation, must be applied. Let's recall that at Pentecost there was no visible or physical appearance of the Holy Spirit. Likewise, Jesus said God the Father is "unseen" (Matt. 6:6) and so did John (John 1:18; 1 John 4:12). Nor was the Holy Spirit ever seen (John 14:17). Jesus also said, regarding the nature of the coming of his kingdom, it "does not come visibly" (Luke 17:20b; 2 Cor. 4:18). Then, why must this "coming in his kingdom" (Matt. 16:28) necessarily be visible? Even futuristic rapturists are expecting an invisible coming of Christ to remove them from planet Earth [although falsely].[5] And doesn't our faith consist of being "certain of what we do not see" (Heb. 11:1)?

To top it all off, however, Jesus declared that "the world would not see me anymore?" (John 14:19, also 22). So how long is Jesus' "not . . . anymore," anyway? Do we really trust His words? Do we believe Him? If so, how do we then turn around and preach an unmistakable, universally visible coming to be seen by everyone all over the whole world at the same time someday out in the future?

Something else we need to seriously reconsider is that the insistence on a visible criterion for this type of coming of Jesus is the deception of the elect about which Jesus spoke. Remember, Jesus specifically warned his disciples that there would be "false prophets . . . to deceive even the elect—if that were possible" (Matt. 24:24). If it wasn't possible, why would He have brought it up? Apparently, it was both possible and probable—back then and still today. Jesus continued by saying, "At that time if anyone says to you, 'Look, here is the Christ!' or, 'There he is!' do not believe it . . . So if anyone tells you, 'There he is, out in the desert' do not go out; or, 'Here he is, in the inner rooms,' do not believe it (Matt. 24: 23, 26).

Of course, many of his other comings are visible. But a coming can be either visible or invisible.

No doubt, some of "the elect" (the saints in the Church today, as well as back then) have bought into and succumbed to this deception. Consequently, they also have been falsely prophesying. How so? First, by their misunderstanding of the invisible nature for this type of promised coming. This is why many modern-day saints, if not the majority, are waiting for a physically visible sighting of Jesus in Person, in the sky, in the Israeli desert, in an inner room of a rebuilt temple in Jerusalem, or in some other geographic location to which they can definitely point and in like manner say, "There He is!" Secondly, by their proclaiming that Jesus has not yet come again as and when He promised and as and when He was expected to come under the guidance of Holy Spirit (John 16:13). This supposed "nonoccurrence" is highly problematic to say the least.[6]

We moderns need to wean ourselves from the idea that the presence of Jesus, Who is God, must be visible or somehow materialistic. "For where two or three come together in my name, there am I with them"

(Matt. 18:20). Although unseen, Jesus is truly present with them, personally, even today, isn't He?

Another good example of the reality of invisibility is how Jesus Himself interpreted the Old Testament prophecy of the coming of Elijah (Mal. 4:5-6). This fulfillment preceded the coming and anointing of the Messiah. But it was not fulfilled by a literal reappearance of the Old Testament prophet as the Jews were expecting. Instead, Jesus said, "And if you are willing to accept it . . . ." John the Baptist was the predicted Elijah—the invisible spirit and power of Elijah came into and operated through John the Baptist (see Luke 1:17; Matt. 11:14; 17:10-13). So why did Jesus preface this revelation with the phrase, "And if you are willing to accept it?" Most likely, He knew that many back then and yet today would not and will not accept this invisible spirit-realm reality.

Hence, the most popular objection raised to the Lord's coming on the clouds circa 70 A.D. is this arbitrary requirement of visibility. It's typical of the physical/material mindset that plagues futuristic-termination theology. It's the same kind of physical thinking, erroneous expectation, and spiritual blindness that caused most of the Jewish religious leaders of the 1st century to miss the coming of their Messiah. For some of the same reasons, billions more have missed his coming on the clouds, as well as his many other comings. Consequently, they are forced to wrestle with the so-called "problem of nonoccurrence" and the sickness of a "hope deferred" (Prov. 13:12). In what might be termed the ultimate demotion, Christ is still reckoned to be off somewhere waiting to return, not here, or somehow not here fully. How unnecessary. How erroneous, scripturally. What an admission that we don't really recognize or understand our faith, nor the spirit realm that surrounds us.

Challenge: Find one scripture that says this particular type of coming of Christ (his *parousia*) must be a physically visible appearance.

Caution #1: Jesus' words, "For as the lightning comes from the east and flashes to the west, so will be the coming of the Son of Man" (Matt. 24:27) is an idiomatic expression conveying quickness and effects which are public, but not necessarily demanding a visible appearance.[7] Also, let's recall in Ezekiel's prophecy of Jerusalem's destruction by the Babylonians in the 6th century B.C., thrice the Lord spoke of it as "A sword . . . flashing like lightening!" (Ezek. 21:10, 15, 28).[8] Likewise, we should be hesitant to point to Acts 1:11 for the reasons we covered in Chapter 1, pp – 46-48).

Caution #2: "The Blessed Hope" spoken of in Titus 2:13 is a widely mistranslated verse in most Bibles, "while we wait for the blessed hope – the glorious appearing of our great God and Savior, Jesus Christ . . ." (NIV, KJV). Grammatically, the correct translation (as rendered from the original Greek and in the NAS) is, "looking for the blessed hope and the appearing of the glory of our great God and Savior, Christ Jesus;" Did you catch the difference? The key word here is "glory." It's a noun and not an adjective. Hence, it should not be translated as the adjective "glorious" to modify the noun "appearing." This "glory" is the noun and object that was to appear and not the visible Person.[9] Big difference!

Most notably and appropriately, in every appearance of "the glory of the Lord" throughout the Old Testament, major optical and/or physical manifestations were present (manna and quail dropping out of the sky, a cloud, consuming fire, thunder, a voice, the ground splitting open, a plague, etc.). These were signs of Yahweh / Jehovah God's presence.[10] However, never once was the Person of deity visibly seen. (See for example: Exodus 16:7, 10; 24:16, 17; 40:34, 35, and many more.[11]) Again, the noun "glory" and not the Person was what would appear as "the blessed hope" in Titus 2:13. And it did, as Jesus came "in the glory of the Father" (Matt. 16:27) circa A.D. 70, along with many optical and physical manifestations as we saw in our last chapter.

3) His Continuing Presence Insures Many More Comings

"Men of Galilee, why do you stand here looking into the sky?" the two men (angels) dressed in white who appeared after Jesus' ascension asked of his disciples (Acts 1:11). It's still an appropriate question for today.

The reality of the contemporary Christ and apocalyptic greater Jesus' continuing presence with us has a much broader meaning, scope, and significance than most Christians have hereto considered. Following his localized coming on the clouds in destruction of Jerusalem and the Temple, He still lives and moves in the spirit realm across the whole earth, and not just in Israel. We, therefore, do not need to keep gazing up into the eastern sky. Nor do we need to wait until death brings us to Him. He's in the midst of us and in many of us. He's a living and perpetual presence Who is here to stay.

So what does his universal and omnipresent presence say for the likelihood of many more comings? For one, <u>there is no scriptural justification for a discontinuance of the long biblical and historical pattern of his various comings</u>. Quite to the contrary, his active presence with us, and his omnipresence all over the earth, surely facilitate the likelihood of many more comings—visible and invisible ones, physical and spiritual ones, private and corporate ones. All these are found throughout the Scriptures and, perchance, there are other types of comings not so found, if for no other reason than John tells us Jesus did many others things that were not recorded (see John 20:30; 21:25). But nothing in Scripture (that I know of) precludes the continuance of his many, countless, and wondrous comings in similar fashions for some similar purposes.

As we've seen, the coming of the Lord cannot be lumped into one simplistic event as so many have tried to do. Instead, by taking into account the different meanings of the five main Greek words usually translated as "come" or "coming," by studying their New Testament usage, and by comparing them to the biblical pattern of many different comings, we can readily see: (1) They don't all refer to a single event; (2) Although similar, they can give us greater insight into the multifaceted nature and different senses of Christ's many different types of comings. For He does come in various ways:

- *Parousia,* meaning "presence." As we have seen, his presence never left. And the sign of his presence, asked for and given, for his distinctive coming on the clouds in judgment was literally fulfilled circa 70 A.D. exactly as and when the Lord said it would be fulfilled. And although this sign was a never-to-be-repeated, age-ending event, Christ still rides his white horse and comes on the clouds bringing judgments on other "peoples, nations, languages and kings" (Rev. 10:11). After A.D. 70, Christ's presence continues with us, fully and wholly, and He can manifest Himself to us by this or any of his other multi-repeatable and countless comings, and by other ways as well.

- *Erchomai,* meaning to "come or go" out of the spirit realm into the physical realm and back again into the spirit realm. Is it so hard to believe that Jesus comes in this "like manner" (Acts

1:11)? Angels have this same capability (Heb. 13:2; 1:14; Gen. 18:2; 19:1). Billy Graham concurs that "At times, however, they can assume physical form – and when that happens, they can be seen by us. The Bible indicates this happens only rarely."[12] This coming seems to be the general, overall manner in which most of Jesus' many physical/visible comings occur. So have you ever "longed for his appearing" (*epiphaneia* meaning "a manifestation, advent of Christ, appearing" – 2 Tim. 4:8, 1; 1:10) like this to you? Have you ever experienced one of these comings of the Lord?

- *Emphanizo*, meaning to manifest, exhibit in person, disclose by words, signify, an inward illumination or revelation—but only for those meeting this coming's qualifications (see John 14:21). This promised coming still holds for today. It can and should be the experience of every believer. Today, however, there are only a few who love and look for his appearing to them, individually. Are you one of them? Do you long for the Lord to make Himself real to you by his presence and this type of coming? Let's also note that Jesus can be and often is present without manifesting Himself.

- *Apokalupsis*, meaning to uncover, unveil, appear, come, reveal, manifest or see. As we have seen, the Book of Revelation is not merely the *apokalupsis* of age-ending events, which it was; it's far more than that. Most prominently, it's the unveiling of a Person—the ascended, exalted, glorified, transformed, transfigured, transcendent, apocalyptic, cosmic, crowned, and contemporary Christ of the Apocalypse. And all of this greater Jesus' comings promised and described therein were first "at hand" for 1st-century believers, have been "at hand" for believers ever since, are "at hand" today, and will continue to be "at hand" in the future.

   Revelation's prime focus is in unveiling the unsealed and ongoing reality of the contemporary Christ, the greater Jesus, in all his glory, power and dominion—which lasts "for ever and ever" (Rev. 1:6; 22:10). Scripturally and logically, it then follows that He is not coming from a distance, but is present and in the midst of his churches (Rev. 1:13, 20) and all around us as well (Heb. 12:1, 22-24). Are you also aware that *everything* God wants made known to us has been unveiled and revealed (Matt. 10:26; Luke 17:30; Rom. 8:18; Rev. 1:1)? Sad to say, most traditional interpreters have ignored this truth or re-veil it.

- *Heko*, meaning to arrive, to be present—another type of coming of the plagues promised in the Revelation (Rev. 18:8; also see 2 Pet. 3:10). Don't you desire to avoid these calamities associated with a day of the Lord?

Warning! A temptation exists to call anything and everything a coming of Jesus. This tendency only trivializes the significance of an authentic occurrence. But you never determine the truth of a matter or a doctrine based upon its potential for abuse. The greater and more erroneous tendency has been to limit his comings to only two or three times.

In sum, Jesus is not tied down by a mortal and earthly body anymore, as He was when He was known as Jesus of Nazareth. His *parousia* presence with us, and not absence, insures and facilitates his many, countless, and multifaceted comings all over the world today. He comes and goes. He does not come and stay. These comings of Jesus in everyday life represent both a glorious or threatening kingdom possibility and reality for every individual in every generation and in every nation. His comings (plural) take many different forms. If one of his comings happens to you, it is the ultimate supernatural experience—for good or not so good.

4) *We Need a Fuller Realization of His Presence*

In this author's opinion, the many comings of Jesus is a past, present, and future possibility and reality that Christians should be celebrating, wanting to experience more fully, and exuberantly but cautiously communicating to others. Unfortunately, we're not. For most Christians who fill the pews on Sundays, it is still a someday and singular hope. But like it or not, the degree to which we are or are not conscious of his abiding presence will have a direct bearing on the way each of us leads our individual Christian life, on our confidence and boldness to witness of Him, and/or our lack thereof.

On the other hand, the greater good news is that all Christians have the opportunity to experience a much fuller reality of Christ's presence, in this life, at death, in worship, witnessing, ministry, prayer, baptism, the Lord's Supper, "where two or three come together in my name," and in his many countless comings. He longs to be so discovered. He longs to raise our lives out of our mundane routines to higher levels. He longs for our intimate fellowship. And many of us want to know his presence in a greater way. Yet we have so much difficulty experiencing it.

Today, this greater Jesus still comes, both spiritually and physically, to people. A number of people in recent history, and many alive today, have publicly testified to having direct coming-encounters with this Jesus. Some of these comings have been visual, some audible, some revelational, and some were all three. All are personal, bodily, and intimate visitations. Most are private, but some are public. And some are genuine. But others may not be or are only illusions. Of those that are genuine, they are substantiated by plenty of scriptural precedents and promises.

Popular Christian writer, Dallas Willard, in his book *The Divine Conspiracy* tells this story about one such coming of Jesus to "a well-known Christian teacher, Sundar Singh" in India as he arose early one morning to pray:

> At about a quarter to five in the morning, his room was filled with light. He looked outside, thinking there must be a fire, but he saw none. Continuing to pray, he suddenly saw before him a glorious face filled with love. At first he thought it was Buddha or Krishna or some other deity. But a voice in Hindustani said, "How long will you persecute me? Remember, I died for you; I gave my life for you." Seeing the scars on his body, Sundar Singh recognized Jesus and saw that he was alive, not someone who died centuries ago. He fell at his feet and accepted him as master and worshiped him. Afterward he became a world-famous example of God's life present among human beings.[13]

Willard believes that "God does show himself from time to time in the space of those who seek him, and over time he leaves among his people visible reminders of his constant though invisible presence." He summarizes that "the reason the Judeo-Christian witness regards surrounding space as full of God is that that is where it has from time to time experienced him. That is where he has manifested himself."[14]

Evangelist T.L. Osborn, who has held open-field crusades around the world for the past sixty-some years and preached to millions, vividly remembers the time Jesus came and appeared to him:

> The next morning at 6 o'clock Jesus Christ walked in our room . . . . I saw Him like I see you. He didn't walk on the floor. He walked on the air. I'll never forget it. And I laid there. It was like I was dead. I couldn't move a finger or a toe. I finally laid on my face on the floor until 2 o'clock in the afternoon. It changed my life. I was totally, totally bathed in a new life. That's the best way to describe it.[15]

Former Muslim Naeem Fazal vividly remembers the night Jesus appeared to him in his college dorm room shortly after coming to the U.S. from Kuwait:

> . . . he attended a college-campus Christian event with his brother, who had become a Christian and was praying for Fazal to follow suit. As a Muslim, Fazal wasn't impressed with the idea of a personal relationship with God, but one day during an argument he skeptically asked God, "If you're real, why don't You just show me?"
>
> That night Fazal faced a terrifying encounter in his room. What he calls a demonic presence left him paralyzed with fear in his bed. He describes it as a feeling of death.
>
> When the presence eventually left the room, Fazal's brother told him that Jesus is the only one with authority over angels and demons, so Fazal prayed, "Jesus, I don't know You, but . . . if you would help me I will give You my life."
>
> Later that night he found himself staring at a very different presence. "It looked like a figure made up with light—solid, yet transparent," Fazal says. "It was an experience like no other. The peace I felt from this presence was so powerful, so aggressive . . . and [He] introduced Himself to me and said, 'I'm Jesus; your life is not your own.' The next morning my life changed forever."[16]

Three years ago, a picture and a story on the front page of the business section of *The Indianapolis Star* caught my attention. It featured George Katres, a local restaurateur and immigrant from Greece. The article mostly focused on the growth of his chain of eleven restaurants, his generosity, sense of community, and family success. But it also mentioned one incident that dramatically changed Katres' life. Below is that portion of the newspaper's account of that incident:

> And there was "the miracle," as his Greek-born wife, Helen, puts it.
> The incident that would shape Katres' life occurred after he stepped on a rusty nail at age 11 and it infected his left foot. By the time he saw a doctor, one village away, the infection was so bad the doctor recommended amputation. Instead, on Christmas Eve, his mother bade her son to pray for healing and went off to church.
> That night, alone at home, the boy believed he saw Jesus enter the room, touch him and promise healing. By the next morning, the foot was better.
> "This is God's truth story," Katres says, working on his sandwich and fries. "A lot of people question the, 'Is he telling the truth?' That's the way I remember it. That's why I am a strong believer."[17]

That was the entirety of *Star's* article regarding this miraculous incident. But I suspected there might be more to this story. And knowing that someday I would be writing a book about the many comings of Jesus, I called George Katres and arranged a personal interview. Graciously, he agreed. Below is "the rest of his story" of his seeing Jesus, as he told it to me and in his answers to a few of my questions:

> Actually, I was ten years old at the time. My parents were farmers and I had two sisters (ages six and eighteen). We lived out in the country, in Greece, in a small village, and in a two-story house. Our animals (sheep and horses) were kept on the bottom floor and we lived in a single room above them. Outside was a wooden stairway to our second floor. And we had no electricity. My mother was a strong Christian. My father was not; and he swore a lot.
> Then one day I stepped on a nail. Since it was seventeen kilometers by mule to the nearest doctor, my parents decided not to take me. So my mother wrapped my foot. For two months it was sore, but I could walk. Then an infection set in and grew worse and worse until I couldn't walk. This went on for eight months. Finally, my parents decided to take me to the doctor. He

told them he would have to amputate my leg at the knee. But my parents decided against that and brought me home. My mother told me to pray for Jesus to come and heal me.

Then came Christmas Eve. "Son," my mother told me again before she and the rest of my family left for church services that night, "keep praying for Jesus to show up. Ask him to heal your foot. And keep the fireplace going. Jesus will come to get warm and heal you."

After they left, I was all alone for about two hours. And it was dark outside. But the fire in the fireplace provided warmth and some light. Suddenly, as I lay in my bed wrapped in covers, I heard footsteps coming up the wooden stairway to our second floor. I was scared, closed my eyes, and pulled the covers over my head. Next, without the door opening, the footsteps came inside the house and across the wooden floor over to my bed. Harder and harder I was praying, "Please Jesus come help me! Please! Please!"

I heard a chair being pulled up beside my bed and someone sit down. Then a voice said, "You called me and I'm here. Don't be scared. I'm Jesus." And He touched me.

Still scared, I opened my eyes and saw Him sitting there.

"Son," he told me, "you're going to go to sleep and tomorrow morning when you get up, put on the new boots and start walking."

"Thank you, Jesus. I love you Jesus," I replied. And that was the last thing I remember before falling asleep.

(I asked Mr. Katres – What did Jesus looked like?)

I only remember his face. He looked sort of like a Greek icon but was a plain person with white skin, long hair, a white robe, and very calm.

(How long was He with you? I followed up.)

Not more than five minutes . . . could have been only two.

(Then what happened?)

When I woke up Christmas morning, Jesus was gone. The first thing I remember was feeling no pain in my foot or leg. I jumped out of bed and started screaming "Mom! Mom! Jesus came! I'm okay! My foot is healed! Where are my new boots?"

And since we all slept in the same room, my antics woke everyone up.

Mom didn't answer my question. She started crying and went straight over to the Jesus icon on that wall, got on her knees and started praying. My dad, who unbeknown to me had bought a pair of new boots for me for Christmas, got the boots and gave them to me. I put them on and started jumping around. Remember, I hadn't been able to walk for eight months. My older sister grabbed me and hugged me.

We sat back down on my bed and pulled off the boots and looked at my bare foot. Its appearance had changed. No swelling. The infection was gone. It was all healed up with fresh skin. But still today there is a mark on the bottom of my left foot where the nail went in.

(How did this incident affect your family and you? I further queried.)

My father totally quit swearing and became a strong believer. For me, I reflect back on this incident a lot and everyday. It has made me a better person and a strong believer with a strong desire to share my successes and blessings with other people . . . and to be ready for the "long trip"

(The "long trip?" I repeated.)

The second life.

Lastly, here are two short accounts, which personally resonate with me. The first is a story told by another popular Christian author about a three-year-old girl who . . .

> contracted a serious illness that confined her to bed as death ominously approached. . . . Toward the end, the little girl drifted in and out of a coma. The parents knew they were about to lose her. But just before she died, she smiled with the most peaceful look on her face, and said, "Look, Mommy. Look Daddy. Jesus is saying it's okay to come." She closed her eyes and breathed her final breath.[18]

This last account is about a friend of mine, John Walker. It was relayed by his wife, Kaye. John was a participant in many of our local Bible studies. He died this past year.

As the family was gathered around John, he said "Oh (pause), Hi God." Then he said to me, "Honey, I got to go." This was the last minute of his life. He died in my arms.

The reason these last two accounts personally resonate with me is because several times during my mother's last days on this earth when she was dying of cancer, she would wake up, look up from her pillow to the corner of the ceiling and joyously exclaim, "I see Jesus." But I never saw Him or anything unusual in the room at those times. When I'd ask her to describe what she was seeing and what He looked like, she was always so engrossed in the experience it was as if I wasn't there. And yet no fear was evident in her voice or in her expressions, only a joy and a peace that filled the room. Whatever was or wasn't going on, these times were very special times for my mother, and for me, and sometimes for others who were in the room with us. I will never forget them.

Neither time nor space will permit us to discuss more claims of possible comings and appearings of Jesus to people today, nor all the possible types, or even discuss them in more depth.[19] But I can't resist noting from the Scriptures that one of qualifications of an apostle is having "seen Jesus our Lord" (1 Cor. 9:1; Acts 1:21-22). Paul qualified as an apostle after a special coming and appearance of Jesus to him on the road to Damascus (Acts. 9:3-6). Does this still apply today? Are there still apostles today? Paul writes in one of his epistles, "And in the church God has appointed first of all apostles, second prophets, third teachers . . . ." etc. (1 Cor. 12:28). Well, the Church is still here, isn't it?

You also might be wondering if Jesus has come and visibly appeared or audibly spoken to me. The answer is, no, not yet. But He has to others I know and respect. Perhaps, He has come and appeared to you or someone you know. One thing I've found in talking with people who have had this type of a coming experience with the greater Jesus is most are very guarded and reluctant to talk about it or share it with others—and for good reasons. One reason probably is, they have not had a good biblical basis for explaining and supporting it. But they do now.

Another sobering thing I've noticed from the Scriptures is after a genuine coming and encounter with the Lord takes place, it always produces major changes in the life of the individual who receives Him. Therefore, my opinion is, where no significant change occurs, most likely, no genuine coming of Jesus took place. The evidence of this fruit thus provides a check and balance against counterfeit claims.

On the other hand, the genuine comings of Jesus to some people represent a crucial and glorious spirit-realm/physical-realm reality for every generation. No doubt they are countless, can take many different forms, and produce life-changing results in the individuals who receive them. What's now needed is a fuller realization of this reality and better leadership on how to practice his presence. It's part of the inheritance and privilege we can partake of in his established kingdom and as He comes in his kingdom—to which there is no end.

> **... after a genuine coming and encounter with the Lord takes place, it always produces major changes in the life of the individual who receives Him.**

Have you sensed his presence, experienced Him this way, or beheld his glory? In the words of the great church hymn "Battle Hymn of the Republic" penned in 1861 by Julie W. Howe, "My eyes have seen the glory of the coming of the Lord . . . ." Have your eyes ever seen the greater Jesus and/or his glory? If so, how so?

5) *Jesus Comes When, Where, How, and to Whom He Pleases*

It may come as a shock to some people, but here's a very important aspect regarding Jesus' many comings. The greater Jesus Who comes today is totally beyond human control. He comes when, where, how, and to whom He pleases. Throughout the Bible, He just showed up in many different ways and forms (Mark 16:12): as the angel of the Lord, as theophanies, as an all-pervasive light, as a voice, as an unknown person, as an awesome human-like being with a sword coming out of his mouth, and more.

Of course, we cannot predict when He will come. And there is absolutely nothing we can do in our own strength to bring about one of his comings. We can't pray or meditate Him down from heaven or visualize his coming into reality. He chooses when, where, how, and to whom to manifest Himself. The one exception is his spiritual and inward illumination coming which is a conditional promise (see again John 14:21, 23). But there is one thing we can do, and that is to ask or invite Him to come—"Amen. Come, Lord Jesus" (Rev. 22:20b).

Another most pertinent reality of the greater Jesus, the contemporary Christ, is that He can come and visit us, or come for us, or come against us, personally, at any moment. This possibility should even more undergird our desire to always be ready. Remember, Jesus said, "You also must be ready, because the Son of Man will come at an hour when you do not expect him" (Luke 12:40). Traditionally, this verse has been understood as only referring to one, still future coming that hasn't happened for almost two thousand years. No more.

The witness of Scripture is, He comes and goes, unexpectedly, suddenly, and unannounced—like a thief! Again, this is true of all his comings. The possibility that He might come to you or me at any moment, and in a number of ways, is intended by Jesus to be a most pressing motivation and powerful incentive for righteous living and bold, aggressive ministry—not only for individual Christians, but for the Church and individual churches as well. Surely, this any-moment possibility is more of a motivator than a one-time occurrence that hasn't happened for almost two thousand years and counting.

In this author's opinion, this contemporary and practical realization should make a huge difference in the preaching of every pastor and in the life of every Christian. After all, who would want to miss his or her "day of visitation?" (1 Pet. 2:12). So do you "long for his appearing" to you (2 Tim. 4:8)? According to this scripture, "Everyone who has this hope in him purifies himself, just as he is pure" (1 John 2:3). The best way to prepare for this personal possibility is to never forget Christ's presence in our midst or his many comings and to be "pure in heart, for they will see God" (Matt. 5:8). On the other hand, let's also not forget Jesus' words to Thomas, "Blessed are those who have not seen and yet have believed" (John 20:29).

The present-day comings of Christ in his kingdom are some of the most beautiful but least recognized realities of the kingdom of God. And we've only scratched the surface of all the different types of comings of Jesus, theophanies, and days of the Lord recorded in the Scriptures—not to mention all the things Jesus did which were not written down (John 20:30; 21:25).

Still many of us have an uncanny, human tendency to unduly limit these many comings and box Jesus into a two or three advent box. All of us need to remember that the idea that Jesus is off somewhere waiting to come back at some future time, or limiting the comings of Jesus in any manner is *not* the teaching, terminology, or testimony of the Bible. Nor does "looking for his appearing" mean staring up into the sky. Likewise, we must not arbitrarily qualify, disclaim, or diminish his many comings to only being "spiritual comings," as if that is a lower class of coming. First of all, the Bible does not do this. Secondly, one cannot separate the spiritual aspects of Jesus from his physical aspects. Phraseology that limits his comings in any way has just limited our understanding of and hamstrung our experiences with Him.

6) *A Character and Nature of God Issue*

Conceivably, the best scriptural rationale for the ongoing comings of the greater Jesus is rooted in the revealed character and nature of God. As far back as the pre-Fall garden and throughout redemptive history, both the Father and the Son have chosen to have direct and supernatural involvement with some earthly people. This often-demonstrated attribute is part of what theologians call "immanence" with an "a" (as opposed to "imminence" with an "i," which means near).

Immanence means the pervading presence of God in his creation. This historical immanence and demonstrated direct commune in some lives as well as God's intervention in the history of peoples and nations must be honored and respected. As theologian, George Eldon Ladd affirms, "there is a God in heaven who visits human beings in history."[20] In another book, he adds, "this idea of 'the God who comes' is one of the central characteristics of the Old Testament teaching about God."[21]

When God the Father's and the Son's historical and demonstrated desire to commune and intervene with his creation (people) is coupled with two other revealed aspects of his character and nature—(1) his immutability, "I the Lord do not change" (Mal. 3:6a) and (2) the Father and the Son always being at their work (see John 5:17)—we have a strong scriptural inference for advocating the continuance of divine comings beyond Jesus' circa A.D. 70 coming on the clouds in judgment.[22] In fact, these comings have always been about his presence, his immanence.

Also part of his character and nature are these revealed and intervening facts:

- "for he comes to judge the earth" (1 Chron. 16:33; Psa. 96:13).
- "He changes times and seasons; he sets up kings and deposes them" (Dan. 2:21a).
- "the Most High God is sovereign over the kingdoms of men and sets over them anyone he wishes" (Dan. 5:21b).
- "God reigns over the nations; God is seated on his holy throne" (Psa. 47:8).
- "Surely the nations are like a drop in a bucket; they are regarded as dust on the scales; he weighs the islands as though they were fine dust. . . . Before him all nations are as nothing; they are regarded by him as worthless and less than nothing" (Isa. 40:15, 17).
- "He brings princes to naught and reduces the rulers of this world to nothing. No sooner are they planted, no sooner are they sown, no sooner do they take root in the ground, than he blows on them and they wither, and a whirlwind sweeps them away like chaff" (Isa. 40:23-24).
- "He has brought down rulers from their thrones but has lifted up the humble" (Luke 1:52).
- Also see: Isa. 26:21; 37:16; Jer. 10:7; Psa. 22:28; Prov. 33:10-11.

Isn't this precisely what happened to Babylon, Edom, Egypt, and Nineveh in a coming of God in "day-of-the-Lord" judgment events (see Chapter 2 again, pp-72-74); to Judea in 597-587 B.C. at the fall of Jerusalem, when many Jews were carried away into Babylon captivity; and again in the destruction of Jerusalem and the Temple circa A.D. 70? And since God says "I the Lord do not change" (Mal. 3:6a), upon what basis can we humans contend that these divine interventions, judgment dynamics, and cosmic comings cease in the post A.D. 70 world? Are not all events in history (past, present, and future) at his command? Isn't He still the One who brings judgments upon the earth?

David Chilton believed that in the post A.D. 70 world, the four horsemen of Revelation 6:1-8 still "represent the forces God always uses in breaking disobedient nations." And "all attempts to find peace and safety apart from Jesus Christ are doomed to failure. The nation that will not submit will be crushed by His armies, by the historical forces that are constantly at His absolute disposal."[23]

So what do you believe? Since all judgment has been turned over by the Father to the Son (John 5:22), does Christ still come in the clouds riding a white horse of war and judging individual human beings, groups, and nations today?

Twice in the Book of Revelation we are told that He is the God "who is [present], and who was [past], and is to come [future]" (Rev. 1:4, 8; 4:8). No hint of termination, a deistic departure, or cosmic withdrawal of this divine attribute is presented anywhere. Therefore, and after A.D. 70, this intrinsic and change-not element of his character and nature must remain steadfast. This issue of immanence is absolutely central for understanding how this greater Jesus is present with his people now.

Furthermore, Christ is sovereign and free to utilize whatever means He desires to commune and communicate with us humans and/or intervene in the course of lives and in history. No doubt, Christ's post-A.D. 70, many countless comings are part of his continuing rule in all aspects of his creation and part of his post-redemptive work as He sustains "all things by his powerful word" (Heb. 1:3; also Col. 1:17).

Unfortunately, most of today's Church has fashioned for itself, as one theologian complains, "a Christ who rules in a spiritual remoteness."[24] But if this greater Jesus, the contemporary Christ, is present and active in his creation as not only Creator, Savior, and Ruler, but also as Sustainer, then we must be prepared for both present and future comings—i.e., special manifestations and/or intervention acts of Christ to us personally, as well as corporately (persons, groups, churches, nations). Some of those comings could be for discipline, for judgment, or for commissioning, direction, or blessing. But the prospect of his coming to us, in this life, for whatever reason, must still be considered a highly significant factor for affecting our ethical behavior, teaching, and obedience.

Thus, the popular catch phrase of, "Jesus is coming," is more relevant and more true than most of us have been led to believe. Indeed, He has, is, is, is, is, and still is, and will continue to come, come, come, and come! While we enjoy his abiding presence, we still must always be ready and continue to "keep watch, because you [we] do not know what day [when or how] your Lord will [might/might not] come" [to me or you] (Matt. 24:42-44). This verse now takes on a new and greater meaning, doesn't it? It should! It should also produce a greater level of watchfulness, which must be our constant but renewed watchword as we develop a fuller understanding of the Christian faith, live in obedience to his Word, and prepare ourselves for possible future comings of the greater Jesus.

This heightened attitude of watchfulness, expectation, and motivation for repentance, holy living, and zealous activity contrasts mightily with that of most Christians today. They have been conditioned to wait and watch the sky for a future "Second Coming" and "Return." Notably, however, the teaching of Christ's abiding presence and his ongoing personal and corporate comings (some visible, some invisible) creates a new and greater relevance. This immanence and communal realization can help change our passive under-watchful attitudes. And this spirit-realm reality will preach! Believe me, this will preach!

Thus, theologian Steven C. Roy is correct in noting about God's sovereignty that "God retains the right to intervene unilaterally (and coercively) in human history."[25] Yet he thoughtfully ponders the perplexing question that "if God can intervene sometimes, why not at other times? .... why did God not intervene to stop the Holocaust?"[26] I don't have an answer for these questions. And I don't know of anyone else who factually does, either. Like many before me have realized, this answer must remain one of God's "secret things" (Deut. 29:29). But one thing I do know is, every eye will see Him.

7) How 'Every Eye' Sees Him

> *Look, he is coming with clouds, and every eye will see him, even those who pierced him; and all the peoples of the earth will mourn because of him. So shall it be! Amen.* (Revelation 1:7)

Most people today have been led to believe that "every eye" seeing Jesus only means every eye of those people who happen to be alive on planet Earth at the time of Christ's so-called "Second Coming" and "Return"—as He dramatically hangs suspended in the sky and/or is universally seen via worldwide TV and Internet coverage. But is that really what this phrase means? Is this divine promise and greatly anticipated reality limited to only a future group of people, perhaps future to even us today? Let's look closer.

I submit, this phrase must mean literally and exactly what it says, "every eye will see him." That's *every eye of every person who has ever lived, now lives, or will live on planet Earth.* No exceptions, no exclusions. Especially singled out in the above passage are "those who pierced him" during his crucifixion as the prophet Zechariah had prophesied (Zech. 12:10; 13:1-2, 6-9; also Matt. 24:30; John 19:37; Acts 2:23). Therefore, "every eye" starts with a 1st-century context, i.e., those who physically nailed Christ to the cross, those who instigated it, those who brought false witness, those who convicted Him, and those who called down his blood upon their own heads (Matt. 27:24, 25).

In a similar statement, when Simeon took the eight-day-old baby Jesus in his arms in the Temple courts and was moved by the Holy Spirit, he uttered, "For my eyes have seen your salvation, which you have prepared in the sight of all people" (Luke 2:30-31).

In one possible application, Jesus' Messianic birth, crucifixion, and coming in destruction of Old Covenant Israel and the Judaic system were world-perceived, world-changing, and world-mourning events of that time. They've been persevered and so remembered in every subsequent generation. Thus, in this universal knowledge application, "every eye" *seeing* could mean *realizing* Who He was and is, and cannot be limited to only a single group in either the past or future. You see?

In another, and, I think, more relevant application, and as we covered in Chapter 1, the Book of Revelation's declaration of "Look, he is coming" or "cometh" is explicitly descriptive. In the original Greek language the verb, "is coming," is a present deponent indicative. This verb tense is used to convey either an in-process action or a present and continuous action. In other words, it expresses Jesus as being in the process of getting ready to come and/or the ongoing nature of his many, different, and countless comings. In light of all that has been unveiled and promised in the Book of Revelation itself and what we've covered so far this book, both meanings are supportable.

"Look, he is coming, and coming and coming." He comes in the salvation experience, in witness, in vision, in body, in judgment, in death, in the Eucharist (Catholic belief), in many other ways, and He is to be faced after death. Somehow, in some way or other, at some time or times, in life, in death, and/or after death, "every eye" of every person who has ever lived, lives now, or will ever live, literally *sees* Jesus, at least once. Some may see Him more than once. But not everyone has to see Him at the same time, in the same manner, at the same place, or with the same results. In my opinion, this is the best and broadest explanation of how "every eye" *seeing* Him has been, is now being, and will continue to be realized.

This same universal reality is also true for the biblical expressions of "every knee should bow, in heaven and on earth and under the earth [that would certainly include everyone who ever lived], and every tongue confess that Jesus Christ is Lord [knowingly or unknowingly, willingly or unwillingly], to the glory of God the Father" (Phil. 2:10-11; also see Rom. 14:11; Isa. 45:23; Psa. 22:27-29; Rev. 5:13).

Dare we limit this glorious truth by our unbelief or by our unscriptural two-advent mindset to only those alive at some future time, or to only a heaven/hell, after death experience? Nevertheless, "every eye" *seeing*, "every knee" bowing, and "every tongue" confessing does not mean or necessitate everyone *believing* in Him or being saved, but it could.[27] Somewhere, at some time, at some place, and in some manner all who have ever lived see Jesus, face-to-face, at least once. What a joyous or terrible day that has, is, or will be!

"Look, he is coming, and coming and coming."

What also must be stressed in our biblical unlimiting of the comings of Jesus is, we cannot and should not dogmatically preclude a future, "every-eye-will-see" or "almost-every-eye-will-see" single coming event, which could be physically visible to the world, or most of the world, at large, and even to all at the same time. Will it happen? God is sovereign. So, it could. But, and here is the crucial and distinguishing factor that must be equally emphasized: it doesn't have to happen to fulfill any unfulfilled Bible prophecy. Also, let's not forget Jesus' words, "Before long, the world will not see me anymore" (John 14:19). Again, just how long is Jesus' "not . . . anymore," anyway? If a world-perceiving type of coming does occur someday, as many expect, it will be as one of his many and countless comings in his everlasting kingdom. But it won't end the world, the Church, or his kingdom on earth. According to Scripture, all three of these entities are without end.

8) Is There a Final Coming?

Does this imply that there will be no "final" or "last coming"—after which there will be no more comings? To answer this question, we must continue to submit ourselves to Scripture, and no verse of Scripture uses this language. At best, it's an assumption that's read into the Bible. On the other hand, Scripture states and the Nicene Creed affirms that his kingdom on this earth is "without end" (Isa. 9:7; Dan. 2:44; 7:14; Luke 1:33). Moreover, this world is without end (Eccl. 1:4; Eph. 3:12; and more – see again Chapter 2). Then why should his comings in his kingdom (Matt. 16:28) on this earth have an end, after which there will be no more comings? Regarding his endless kingdom, what's true of the whole is true of its parts. It bears repeating; there is no "final" or "last" coming mentioned in Scripture. Nor is there a "final" grace, "last" judgment, "final" mercy, or "last" love ever mentioned. All these realities are indigenous components of Christ's everlasting kingdom. Get it?[28]

The bottom-line point of this chapter and the last chapter as well, is not so much *how* the greater Jesus comes, but *that* He comes, and mostly to individuals—if we will only break the shackles of traditional teachings and receive Him as He chooses to come. Remember, the idea that this Jesus is off somewhere waiting to come back at some future time or limiting his comings to only two or three times is not the teaching, terminology, or testimony of the Bible.

Why Does It Matter, Anyway?

If you are like most people I meet, it's not easy to shake off the religious conditioning of a lifetime. "This is really great!" some respond. "It certainly makes the Word of God come alive, *but* . . . ."

"It's so unsettling," a student in one of my Bible studies complained. "Why does it matter if you're right?" she asked.

First, it matters because a single "Second Coming" / "Return" doctrine holds people in bondage to an earthly Jesus. The message of the Scriptures, especially in the Revelation, is that we are free from the limitation of just knowing about Jesus in the past (while He was on earth) or about Him sometime out in the future (when He supposedly comes back to earth). We can know and fully experience Him now, in the present, as He *now is—the greater Jesus, the contemporary Christ*. That's because He's not off somewhere waiting to come back, as so many of us have been led to believe. He's here, with us, in the spirit realm! And He can and sometimes does visibly manifest Himself in the physical realm. That's a real coming. At other times, his comings are invisible and spiritual visitations. But both occur in many multifaceted ways. This kingdom reality and revealed truth from the Word of God is greatly compromised when all the coming passages are forced to fit into just one single future-coming event.

Secondly, it matters because much of the Church, in general, doesn't know what is going on in the spirit realm. They are comfortable with a lesser version of the faith that promotes psychological well-being and a distant non-interfering god. Of course, most Christians believe that Christ, or at least the Holy Spirit, comes into them at salvation. But then many tend to deny or ignore the reality of the spirit-realm world around us and rarely venture any deeper to know Christ more intimately. Nor do they look for the possibility of his appearing, individually, to them right where they are.

For centuries, we've been taught to look to the sky for a fleshy Jesus to come down riding on a cumulus cloud. But in another type of coming, Jesus comes and goes, appears and disappears, in and out of the spirit realm and most don't know it. The fact is, Jesus is here, active and involved. He comes in many countless ways, visibly and invisibly—in judgment, in comfort, in revelation, in commissioning, in reward. Most churches, however, don't recognize, let alone teach, his many comings. What a tragedy! They think He tarries, i.e., delays. But He doesn't, as Scripture clearly tells us (Heb. 10:37; Ezek. 12:25, 28; Hab. 2:3). Furthermore, He comes and comes and comes five, ten, twenty, ten thousands times, and maybe more.

Thirdly, it matters because the world of the spirit has authority over the world of the physical. Yet most Christians are so bound up by dumbed-down teachings that the idea of operating in the spirit realm is foreign, if not frightening, to them. That's why you hear confusing statements from preachers saying, "Sure, Christ is in you and He's here but someday He'll return." And, "He's no longer in our world in His body." Well, which is it: Is He here or not? If He's here, is He here as a disembodied Spirit or what? Confusing, isn't it. But it need not be.

We only need to catch a glimpse of just how real the spirit realm is by studying the nature of Jesus' resurrection body during his post-resurrection, pre-ascension appearances (see John 20:19-21:14). It's just as real as human flesh—but it's also different. He walked through closed doors as if they were not there. He suddenly appeared and disappeared. But lest anyone think Him a ghost, He eats bread and fish. The implications are obvious—He is more real than the door or the bread or the fish. We can't think of Him merely as earthly flesh; we have to think of Him in all His spirit-realm reality. The fact is, we shall never be able to operate in the full power God has provided until we can start thinking, believing, and operating in the spirit-realm concepts and realities He has revealed throughout his Word.

The servant of the Old Testament prophet Elisha also experienced the reality of the spirit realm prior to a major battle. In the morning, after the king of Syria had surrounded a city during the night in seeking to kill the prophet, Elisha sent out his servant to reconnoiter. The servant returned visibly frightened. He reported that the king's army with horses and chariots had surrounded the city. With calm assurance, Elisha told his servant not to be afraid because "those who are with us are more than those who are with them." Apparently, the servant wondered, what is Elisha talking about? So Elisha took him back out to the edge of the city and prayed that his servant's eyes would be opened. After which his servant "looked and saw the hills full of horses [of heaven] and chariots of fire [the angelic army] all around Elisha." They would be fighting against the king's forces in defense of Elisha and his men (2 Kings 6:15-17). Is this biblical account just a fairytale or a myth of a bygone era?

As we discussed earlier, this same spirit realm is just as real today as this book you hold in your hands. It may even be more real because it is eternal. Part of that reality is the greater Jesus' many countless comings and goings in his kingdom. They are not a matter of going from one physical location to another, but coming and going in and out of the spirit realm in his ascended and glorified body, in many places at the same time. He is, wholly and totally, in our midst right now and doing just that. Thankfully, we don't have to understand how this works in order to believe and receive it.

<u>Fourthly</u>, it matters because we don't have to live on a hope that Jesus is going to come back someday, snatch us out of this troubled world (the "Rapture") and set us free from the shackles of our flesh. This

is Gnosticism, not Christianity. Moreover, it is not going to happen. As we shall see more fully in Chapter 9, Jesus in his prayer for all believers specifically prayed against this escapist hope. And his prayer is still in effect (see John 17:15, 20).[29]

Let's also recall that Jesus told his original disciples He would "come again and receive you unto myself that *where I am*, there you may be also" (John 14:3, KJV, italics added). This promise does not speak, *per se*, in terms of his coming and taking them to heaven—a la a "Rapture." It speaks of a future coming (at that time) on this earth and some of his disciples still alive being gathered unto Him in the spirit realm in his abiding presence. This is another part of what happened circa A.D. 70 (see Matt. 24:31).

Furthermore, hope is for those who have not received something they desire (Rom. 8:24-25). We today can live in the reality that Christ has already come, that He is coming, right now, and that He will continue to come (Rev. 1:7-8; 4:8; 22:7, 12, 20). And since the greater Jesus is omnipresent, many of these comings can be taking place around the world, simultaneously. But to live in the fullness of that reality, we have to break the shackles of our physical/material mindset, which demands only a single, physical/material "Second Coming" / "Return" and receive his comings as *both* spirit-realm and physical-realm reality, here and now.

When Old or New Testament saints experienced one of Jesus' comings, what a change it made in their lives! What a change recognizing this kingdom reality will make in us, too. Our worship will be transformed as we focus not on an "absent" Lord waiting to return, but rather on a present and active Lord, Who personally inhabits the praises of his people (Psa. 22:3 KJV; 24:7; Exod. 20:24) and casts his judgment on people and nations (Dan. 2:21; John 5:22; Rev. 2-3). Our lives will also be affected by a heightened expectation of his coming and intervening in our lives to bless, enlighten, discipline, curse, or judge. No longer will retreat from our world into passivity and apathy be such an easy option. It is one thing to preach against the New Age movement or the occult for operating in the realm of the supernatural. It is quite another to bring the supernatural into the Church and into Christian lives where it belongs. And a true and personal coming of the greater Jesus Christ—especially one of the good ones—is the ultimate supernatural experience.

The 'Sun of Righteousness' Metaphor

Another supporting component of Scripture is the metaphoric figure of the "sun of righteousness with healing in its wings" from Malachi 4:2. This verse imparts what is termed general revelation. Legitimately, this naturalistic metaphor can be pressed to typify Jesus' many, countless comings throughout human history—past, present, and future. Let's see.

The Bible confirms that God has made known his "invisible qualities, his eternal power and divine nature" by what has been created (see Rom. 1:19-20). This revealing certainly includes the two great lights of the sun and the moon created on the fourth day of creation (Gen. 1:16). In addition to being part of the glory of God, the heavens declare (Psa. 19:1-2), another function of these two great lights was to be "signs to mark seasons and days and years" (Gen. 1:14) and, perhaps, for something else.

The Psalms add credence to the notion of the Lord being symbolized by the shinning sphere of blazing gas at the center of our solar system, which is called the sun: ". . . In the heavens he has pitched a tent for the sun, which is like a bridegroom coming forth from his pavilion . . . ." (Psa. 19:4-5). And Jesus is the bridegroom of the Holy Scriptures, is He not? (Matt. 9:15; 25:1, 5, 6, 10; Rev. 18:23). Even more emphatic is Psalm 84:11's declaration, "For the Lord God is a sun and shield."

Just how appropriate and beautiful this sun figure is will become more evident as we uncover other verses in which God is referred to as "light," or as light emanating from God. What I am suggesting here is this. In some way or ways, the natural sun at the center of our solar system and its radiating light is likened to the Person and nature of both God the Father and the Son (see, for example, 2 Sam. 23:4; Psa. 27:1; 36:9; 43:3; Dan. 2:22; Isa. 60:1-2, 19; 1 John 1:5; John 1:4, 9; 8:12; Matt. 17:2; Rev. 1:14; 21:23; Gen. 1:3-5, 14-19;). Technically, however, scientists tell us this bright-burning ball of fire is a star. Other metaphorical figures, such as "the bright Morning Star" of Revelation (Rev. 2:28; 22:16),[30] as well as, Peter's "day star" which rises in our hearts (1 Pet. 1:19) may also be likened with this sun.

Every person alive knows that each and every day the natural sun arises on the eastern horizon and radiates its light onto this planet and into our lives. One of the great lessons we may be able to learn from this portion of God's physical creation—and one generally missed by those locked into a two-advent mindset—is the sun's many dawnings depict the Lord Jesus Christ's many, countless comings and appearances and illuminations, all over the world and throughout the course of human history. As we have seen, this great lesson of general revelation is fully supported by the special revelation of God's Word. Once this truth is learned and accepted, one will never again be satisfied with the darkness and sickness of only a two-advent faith (see Prov. 13:12).

> **Legitimately, this naturalistic metaphor can be pressed to typify Jesus' many, countless comings throughout human history—past, present, and future.**

Hence, every day the natural sun at the center of our solar system comes forth and proclaims the many countless comings of the greater Jesus, Who is at the center of all creation and comes in many different ways, for different purposes, and at different times. What is it that would now hinder us from grasping this general revelation principle, revealed both in the sky and in God's Word? Should not our hearts cry out, "Come, Lord Jesus?"

He is the "Sun of Righteousness" Who rises and appears (Mal.4:2; also see Rev. 10:1; Luke 1:78; John 1:9; Eph. 5:14; 1 John 1:5; Heb. 12:29; Acts 9:3). He is "the true light" (John 1:9; Isa. 60:1-2, 19; Rev. 21:23). Thus, the sun-rising symbol of the "sun of righteousness" is a fitting figure to proclaim Jesus' many, countless, timeless, and universal comings. And it speaks to us daily.

Let us now expand our proclamation of the greater Jesus, the contemporary Christ, thusly:

> He's arisen! He's arisen, indeed!
> He comes! He comes, indeed!

So I ask you, once again, as the first line of the classic Church hymn, "The Battle Hymn of The Republic," so appropriately states: "Mine eyes have seen [past tense] the glory of the coming of the Lord." Have yours? Perhaps a new day is about to dawn. It could happen any time, even this very day.

"Amen. Come, Lord Jesus!" (Rev. 22:20).

A Simple and Profound Formula

How can you break away from the traditions of men that you've been taught regarding the so-called "Second Coming" or "Return" of Jesus and begin to discover the present realities of his many countless comings? Yes, unlearning is the most difficult part of learning. But the Bible gives us a very simple and profound prescription:

> My son, if you accept my words
> and store up my
> commands within you,
> turning your ear to wisdom
> and applying your heart to
> understanding,
> and if you call out for insight
> and cry aloud for understanding,
> and if you look for it as for silver
> and search for it as for hidden treasure,
> then you will understand the
> fear of the LORD
> and find the knowledge of God.
> For the LORD gives wisdom,
> And from his mouth come
> knowledge and understanding.
> (Proverbs 2:1-6)

Sadly, most people have little or no direct knowledge of the Bible—especially of biblical prophecy. All they know, and what they think is right, is what others have told them. They are like the people to whom Isaiah was sent: "ever hearing, but never understanding . . . ever seeing, but never perceiving" (Isa. 6:9). Here are four ways to discover the reality of Jesus' many countless comings:

1. If you are not already doing it, begin to study your own Bible diligently. Look up the comings Scriptures and study them carefully. Study the whole context of each verse. Use a good

concordance to look up references and see how they relate to all other Scriptures.
2. Recognize that the purpose of Jesus' many countless comings is not to get you out of this world, but to empower you to operate in spirit-realm authority in this world. The way of escape from sin and death and from the evil forces of this world is within the kingdom of God, not off into outer space (see John 17:15, 20).
3. Recognize that, in biblical prophecy, we are talking about spiritual/physical realities, just as we are with terms like *born again, the bread of life, living water,* or *salt and light.* We're also talking about getting beyond Jesus' earthly ministry into the unbridled reality of the greater Jesus, the contemporary Christ—the Jesus of the Apocalypse.
4. And finally, open your spirit and heart to his comings in your own life. One of the most pathetic pictures in the Book of Revelation is of Jesus standing outside the doors of the hearts of churches and believers—trying to get in.

Today, countless people are sitting around in churches, in prophecy conferences, and in front of their televisions and computer screens waiting and asking, "When is Jesus coming back?"

"Here I am!" Jesus calls out. "I stand at the door and knock. If *anyone* hears my voice and opens the door, I will come in and eat with him, and he with me" (Rev. 3:20, italics added). This is one of the many promised, personal, individual, actual comings of Jesus. And it's *only* available for believers who will hear and open their heart's door.

"Yes, I read that," the end-timers say impatiently. "But don't bother me . . . I've just read about another sign in the Middle East . . . I'm trying to figure out—When is Jesus coming back again?"

Don't be like that! He never left! Free yourself up! Stand up in your spirit and go answer the door! Say, like John after he had seen Jesus in all his unveiled glory, "Amen, Come, Lord Jesus" (Rev. 22:20). Jesus has promised He will come in and eat with you. You have his word on it! And you had better be ready!

Speaking of a feast . . . let's next explore another great and available spirit-realm/physical-realm reality and distinctive of knowing the greater Jesus, the contemporary Christ, as He is today.

Chapter 6

He Hosts a Grand Banquet

Imagine that you just received an engraved invitation sent via special messenger to the greatest and most spectacular banquet ever to be staged on planet Earth—greater than any White House dinner, than the most extravagant, celebrity-packed Super Bowl party, and even greater than an evening in a foreign castle dining with a king and queen.

If you are a believer in Jesus Christ, you have already received this invitation. Sadly, most believers will never attend this greatest of all banquets, not even once, nor experience and enjoy the blessings of this supreme privilege on an ongoing basis.

Why not? It's because their invitation has been taken away and concealed from them. By whom? By the same people who limit Jesus' comings to only two or three times and have been sitting around for over 1,900 years waiting for Him to return to earth someday.

Admittedly, the spirit-realm/physical-realm realities revealed in this chapter and the rest of the chapters of this book might aptly be termed part of "God's secret wisdom, a wisdom that has been and that God destined for our glory before time began . . . . the deep things of God" (1 Cor. 2:7-10).

Let's see if you agree.

Welcome to 'the Wedding Supper of the Lamb'

This greatest and grandest of all banquets is called "the wedding (marriage) supper of the Lamb" and "blessed are those who are invited" (Rev. 19:9). This banquet was originated over 1,900 years ago, shortly after these words were penned. Today, as is true of the entirety of the Christian faith, which "was once for all delivered to the saints" back then (Jude 3), this grand banquet is still being served and attended by some.

The mystery of this grand banquet gets right to the heart of the unveiled and revealed greater Jesus in all his spirit-realm reality. William Hendriksen terms it "the climax of that entire process whereby God comes to His people."[1] Rousas John Rushdoony elaborates that "a wedding banquet means rejoicing, dancing, drinking, happiness unbounded. It is a symbol of the fullness of communion."[2] Once you discover the glorious reality the wedding supper of the Lamb entails you'll not only be hungering to attend but be greatly saddened to see how masses of Christians have been prevented from understanding and entering into this supreme privilege and its blessings.

Believe me, covering up this truth and its practical applications has not been an easy chore. For nineteen centuries and counting, most theologians, pastors, and Bible teachers have had to twist and distort the reality of literally scores of Scriptures to pull it off. But because so many Christians don't know what the Bible actually says, and because a future only, up-in-the-sky, one-time, special event called the wedding supper fits so nicely into popular end-times and postponement doctrines, they've been able to trap many people into believing myths and fairytales about it.

In this chapter, we'll examine how most Christians have been robbed of this vital, available, ongoing, earthly, and spirit-realm reality by our own leadership. They are the guilty ones who have futurized and surrounded it with myths and fantasies. We'll also see from the Scriptures what this wedding supper of the Lamb really represents. We'll even check out what's on the menu. And finally, we'll discover how you can sit down to the Lord's banquet table and eat a sumptuous feast with Him and others right now, wherever you are on planet Earth. As we've done and will continue doing throughout this book, we'll stick strictly to the Scriptures and let the Bible interpret itself.

One caveat before proceeding. I confess in advance that this chapter is the one in this book about which I know the least. I admit that I don't have a good enough handle on the reality behind this metaphor to explain it very well to you. In fact, it may be impossible for anyone to understand and explain. The wedding supper of the Lamb must be experienced. And most of us, myself included, may not have ever experienced it or fully experienced it. On the other hand, some of you may have or someday will. If you have and/or do, perhaps you can better explain it to me. However, I shall try to explain some aspects from the Scriptures. I do know that I can explain it much better than those writers who defer it out into the future as something that is not yet available. So given this caveat and your indulgence, let's proceed.

How Myths and Fairytales Keep Millions of Christians Spiritually Starved

Traditional end-times teachers claim the "'wedding (marriage) supper of the Lamb' refers to the future celebration of God and his people in the new heaven and new earth. . . . a future celebration in the consummated kingdom."[3] They paint a scenario something like this. First, the Church, which they call the Bride of Christ, is whisked away into the sky, where millions of Christians sit down at a physical table that stretches to infinity and eat their fill of heavenly hash.

Many say this feast of great joy and gladness only lasts for seven years, while the great tribulation is wreaking havoc on the earth. Then these stuffed saints watch while God destroys the world in the Battle of Armageddon (our next chapter). After that, Satan is bound up in chains and thrown into hell, and all the saints are transported back to earth to reign with Christ for precisely one thousand years. (Just what they will reign over is not exactly clear since all the troublemakers will be gone and even lions will be literally lying down with lambs.) When the one thousand years are over, for some inexplicable reason, Satan will be loosed again to deceive masses of people all over the earth. Eventually, he'll be thrown back into the bottomless pit and the saints will reign and rule with Christ forever—somewhere.

Don't be surprised if that scenario doesn't exactly fit the sequence of events you have been taught. Christians differ wildly over these supposed issues. Some claim this banquet doesn't take place until the so-called and unscriptural "end of time" and it's up "in heaven."[4] Hence, controversy abounds over the details of when, where, and how the wedding supper and all these other events will supposedly take place. Churches—even whole denominations—have split over whether these events happen before, after, or during the Tribulation, or the Millennium; or whether they take place in the sky, in heaven, or back on earth in the New Jerusalem.

The only two points the majority of end-times teachers seem to agree on are: (1) that a literal, physical wedding supper is going to happen someday, somewhere; and (2) that it is not happening now and its main significance is to warn us to be ready.

Why is the idea of the wedding supper of the Lamb as a future-only, up-in-the-sky, one-time, grand event so filled with inconsistencies and doctrinal controversies? It's because making this feast a once-only event and pushing it out into the future is a doctrine of men, not a revelation of God. It is based on the reasoning and imagination of human beings, not on the Word of God.

> **Hence, controversy abounds over the details of when, where, and how the wedding supper and all these other events will supposedly take place.**

Regrettably, this devastating approach contributes to spiritual famine among the very people with whom Jesus longs to eat at the wedding supper, here and now. Another consequence of this deception is, Christians who are suffering from spiritual malnutrition offer little or no resistance to the evil spirit-realm forces and to the worldly beast and prostituting systems they operate through (see Chapter 8).

David Nasser characterizes this famine condition this way:

> You and I are at the banquet table of God's presence and truth, but too often we are so full of junk that we're not hungry. In actuality, spiritually, we are starving to death. We have settled for garbage instead of feasting on the nourishment God richly provides.[5]

What Does the Bible Actually Say?

An amazing number of doctrines have been built up around the wedding supper of the Lamb, especially considering that this particular expression appears only once in the whole Bible—in Revelation 19:9. John simply writes down what the angel told him, "Write: 'Blessed are those who are invited to the wedding supper of the Lamb!' The angel added, 'These are the true words of God.'" That's it! Let's note that in Revelation 19:7 there is a reference to the "wedding (or marriage) of the Lamb," but the word "supper" is not used. Obviously, these two verses refer to the same thing. All other references to a wedding, a table, or eating are implied, but probably and rightfully apply, as we shall see.

This paucity of content, however, does not mean that all the talk about the wedding supper is much ado about nothing. Its spiritual reality signifies the culmination of Old Testament prophecies, expresses the fulfillment of the gospel story, and ushers in the full reality of the new heaven and new earth.[6] It is, therefore, vital that those who are serious about receiving the greater Jesus and his kingdom (Heb. 12:28) both understand and participate fully in this grand banquet.

So what is the wedding supper, and what does it mean? No doubt, volumes could be written to address this question. But basically, it is a symbol in the Book of Revelation describing a particular aspect of the kingdom of God that, nowadays, is as an ongoing spirit-realm/physical-realm reality—and not a one-time, yet-future event. This physical symbol of a spiritual/physical reality is the same type of metaphor Jesus used in describing Himself as the bread of life, which could take away our hunger for anything else (John 6:35), and as the water which could forever quench our spiritual thirst (John 4:10).

Like everything else in the Revelation, it was at hand for 1st-century Christians, it has been at hand ever since, it is at hand for us now and will be at hand in the future. Its full availability and relevance are ongoing following its inception.

What I don't understand is how Christians who readily accept Jesus' statements about the bread and wine (at the Last Supper) as spiritual symbols of his body and blood (Luke 22:19-20) insist on interpreting the wedding supper of the Lamb literally—especially when the latter term is surrounded by symbolic language.

Jesus' Teachings Conflict with the One-Time, Future Event Theory

You have to distort Jesus' teachings considerably to make the wedding supper into a one-time, future event. Let me illustrate. In Jesus' parable of the wedding banquet (Matt. 22:1-14, which is often used to support the doctrine of a future event in heaven), Jesus included these statements:

But when the king came in to see the guests, he noticed a man there who was not wearing wedding clothes. "Friend," he asked, "how did you get in here without wedding clothes?" The man was speechless.
   Then the king told the attendants, "Tie him hand and foot, and throw him outside, into the darkness, where there will be weeping and gnashing of teeth." For many are invited, but few are chosen (Matt. 22:11-14).

How did that guy get in there? Think about it. If this is a one-time, future event that is to take place in heaven *after the Rapture*, how did the man get there? Was he raptured by mistake? Was he the original Rapture-buster? Did he grab hold of some saint's heel and hitch a ride? Was he a stowaway on the good old gospel ship?

Also, think about this: was he thrown back to earth?

No, the wedding banquet symbolizes an ongoing reality of God's kingdom on the earth. It is not a one-shot, physical happening up in the sky or in heaven. Hence, Jesus termed it "the feast in the kingdom of God" (Luke 13:29; 14:15; Matt. 8:11-12). And Jesus was preaching, teaching, and demonstrating the kingdom as a then-and-there, already-present, and earthly reality (see Luke 11:20; Matt. 12:28).

Consider another descriptive kingdom teaching of Jesus which many connect with the wedding supper. Jesus had gathered his disciples into a private room to celebrate his final Passover with them the night before He was crucified.

And he said to them, "I have eagerly desired to eat this Passover with you before I suffer. For I tell you, I will not eat it again until

> *it finds fulfillment in the kingdom of God." After taking the cup, he gave thanks and said, "Take this and divide it among you. For I tell you I will not drink again of the fruit of the vine until the kingdom of God comes." And he took bread, gave thanks and broke it, and gave it to them, saying, "This is my body given for you; do this in remembrance of me"* (Luke 22:15-19).

"Aha!" say the end-times teachers, "that's a prediction of a one-time, future event in the sky." Holy Communion (Lord's Supper, the Eucharist), they further contend is "a foretaste,"[7] an earthly and physical act we do in remembrance of Jesus' crucifixion, and an expression or a partial pledge of our hope for the wedding supper in a still-being-expected kingdom that hasn't arrived yet and only will when Jesus finally comes back someday (1 Cor. 11:26 is also cited).[8] But notice what Jesus said a few verses later in this same discourse. The disciples were arguing among themselves about who would be considered greatest in the kingdom.

> *You are those who have stood by me in my trials. And I confer on you a kingdom, just as my father conferred one on me, so that you may eat and drink at my table in my kingdom and sit on thrones, judging the twelve tribes of Israel.* (Luke 22:28-30).

Jesus said, "I *confer* [not will confer] on you a kingdom" (emphasis added). Does that sound like something yet to come 1,900 and counting years later? No, the kingdom was there, it was then; and it's here, it's now. "Just as my father conferred [past tense] one on me." Also note that Jesus after promising not to eat and drink until his kingdom had come, ate and drank with his disciples on several occasions after his resurrection (Luke 24:30-32, 36-43; John 21:4-14).

This idea of dividing the coming of God's kingdom into two stages—a partial and limited kingdom now and a full and consummated kingdom later—is a doctrine of men, not a truth of God's Word. Nowhere did Jesus teach a two-stage or a partial kingdom, and it is not taught anywhere else in the Bible. Yet, our understanding of the kingdom of God determines our concept of the wedding supper.[9]

So let's take a closer look at what the Scriptures tell us about this vital, spirit-realm/physical-realm reality.

When, Where, and What Is the Wedding Supper of the Lamb?

The idea of a bridegroom, a bride, and feasts and eating did not originate in the New Testament. Old Testament writers make several references to God, or the coming Messiah, as a bridegroom and to Israel as his spouse or bride (see Isa. 62:5; Jer. 2:2, Psa. 19:4-6). However, a problem arose. Israel became an unfaithful wife, played the harlot (Ezek. 16 and 23; Hos. 1:2), and broke covenant, repeatedly (Deut. 31:16-17, 29; Jas. 4:4). Hence, in the 8th century B.C., God gave the northern house of Israel (the ten northern tribes) a "certificate of divorce and sent her away because of all her adulteries." But He remained married to "her unfaithful sister Judah" (the two southern tribes) despite the fact that she "had no fear" and "also went out and committed adultery" (Jer. 3:8f). The Assyrians promptly invaded and carried the ten northern tribes away in dispersion around 722 B.C.

Other Old Testament texts refer to God's preparing a banquet table for his servants (Isa. 25:6-9), and even a table "in the presence of my enemies" (Psa 23:5). The Isaiah 23:6-9 passage is particularly significant stating that some time in the future this feast will be an open feast to "all peoples" and pinpointing when this feast would go into effect, when "he saved us" at "salvation."

Thus, in the Revelation we not only find two cities (Babylon and New Jerusalem); we also have two wives—the harlot, who is proclaimed a "widow" because she had her husband, Jesus, killed (Matt. 21:37-39), but who thinks she is still a "queen" (Rev. 18:7). And, the new and faithful bride as she is about to become fully married (1 Cor. 7:39; Rev. 21:2, 9-10). This contrasting duality represents two covenants and those who are part of them (Gal. 4:21-27).

Israel became an unfaithful wife, played the harlot . . . and broke covenant, repeatedly.

If we had space, we could examine many more of those references in detail and show how they are connected to the kingdom parables of Jesus and the message of the Revelation. I urge you to study them for yourself.

You'll be amazed at how strikingly the Old Testament references resemble the New Testament references to feasts and eating.

Let me illustrate the similarity by citing one of the most vivid descriptions, found in the Old Testament, in Proverbs 9:1-6.

> *Wisdom has built her house. She has hewed out its seven pillars. She has prepared her meat and mixed her wine; she has also set her table. She has sent out her maids, and she calls from the highest point of the city, "Let all who are simple come in here!" She says to those who lack judgment, "Come, eat my food, drink the wine I have mixed. Leave your simple ways, and you will live; walk in the way of understanding.*

This passage describes eating and drinking in the kingdom of God. Remember how in Jesus' parables the servants were always calling people to come in and eat the banquet that had been prepared?

"Wisdom has built here house," the writer says, using a symbol that crops up repeatedly throughout the Bible. It is the house established by the Lord (2 Sam. 7:11), the "house of the Lord" (Psa. 23:6), a "house of prayer for all nations" (Isa. 56:7), a house built on a rock (Matt. 7:24), and the "Father's house" of many rooms (dwelling places) where Jesus went to prepare a place for his disciples (John 14:2)—to mention only a few of the many references to God's house, the house of wisdom.

The Apostle Peter adds a new dimension to the concept of God's house. He speaks of Jesus as the living stone, and says that "you also, like living stones, are being built into a spiritual house (1 Pet. 2:4-5)."

Also, notice the proverb's reference to the seven pillars. That's not there by accident. That numeric language connects it to the Revelation message, where John speaks of seven churches, seven trumpets (messages), seven seals, and seven bowls of wrath. Seven is the prophetic number for completion or perfection.

And what is this wisdom which has set her table? "The fear of the Lord is the beginning of wisdom, and knowledge of the Holy One is understanding," the writer of Proverbs explains a few verses after the above passage (Prov. 9:10).

The wisdom and knowledge referred to here are not human wisdom and knowledge. This is supernatural knowledge and understanding from divine revelation, and it only comes through and from fearing the Lord.

When we recognize the absolute sovereignty of God, He begins to reveal to us his spirit-realm reality. And "knowledge of the Holy One," i.e., especially in our day and time, the greater Jesus—is what the prophecy of the Book of Revelation is all about.

What we're also talking about is the great "mystery" of God, which Paul describes so eloquently in his letter to the Ephesians (Eph. 1:9-10; 3:2-12; also see 1 Cor. 4:1). He says emphatically that this "mystery," which is revealed to us by the Holy Spirit, is none other than Jesus Christ (Eph. 3:4-5).

So the feast table is set in the house of God, which is made up of the lively stones of Jesus Christ and his saints. And, we are invited to partake of the feast. Hence, the feast takes place spiritually—in the spirit realm—within us. It is in us and among us, just as He is. It is part of and within the kingdom of heaven here on earth (Matt. 8:11).

This revelation again confirms that the wedding supper of the Lamb is not a meal that God will someday serve up in the sky, in outer space, or in heaven, by-and-by; it is an ongoing spirit-realm/physical-realm reality that continuously takes place, is available, and relevant within the individual believer. It was at hand in the 1st century, it has been at hand ever since, it is at hand now, and it will be at hand in the future.

Some, I believe, confuse this wedding supper of the Lamb with Jesus' offer to believers in his message to the church of Laodicea wherein He announces that "If anyone hears my voice and opens the door, I will go in and eat (sup) with him, and he with me" (Rev. 3:20). Of course, this language of eating together sounds similar, and I certainly don't want to be dogmatic here. But I believe these two dinings together are different realities and with different blessings. One is strictly individual and in the form of a short common meal. According to Wallace, "the old term *sup* here signifies spiritual communion. . . . he does not force entrance."[10] The other, on the other hand, is a long meal of collective eating, drinking, talking, dancing, and enjoying one another. In one, Jesus comes and eats with you at your house—like He did with the tax collector, Zacchaeus (Luke 19:1-7). And that is special. But the other is much more special because we go to his house and we eat with, fellowship, and enjoy *both Him and one another*.

One of the best descriptions of the wedding supper of the Lamb occurs in Jesus' parable of the wedding feast in Matthew 22:1-10:[11]

He Hosts a Grand Banquet

Jesus spoke to them again in parables, saying: "The kingdom of heaven is like a king who prepared a wedding banquet for his son. He sent his servants to those who had been invited to the banquet to tell them to come, but they refused to come.

Then he sent some more servants and said, "Tell those who have been invited that I have prepared my dinner: my oxen and fattened cattle have been butchered, and everything is ready. Come to the wedding banquet."

But they paid no attention and went off—one to his field, another to his business. The rest seized his servants, mistreated them and killed them. The king was enraged. He sent his army and destroyed those murderers and burned their city.

Then he said to his servants, "The wedding banquet is ready, but those I invited did not deserve to come. Go to the street corners and invite to the banquet anyone you find." So the servants went out into the streets and gathered all the people they could find, both good and bad, and the wedding hall was filled with guests."

In another version of this parable in Luke 14:16-24 the invited guests are too busy to come and make numerous excuses. So how does God feel about their excuses? He instructs his servant to invite others—"the poor, the crippled, the blind, and the lame"—to replace them. Lastly, we are told about those who were initially invited but offered excuses, "not one of those men who were invited will get a taste of my banquet."

Whether these parables were speaking simply of Jewish primacy "first for the Jew, then for the Gentile" (Rom. 1:16b; 2:9-10) at that time or more broadly speaking of all Christians from all nationalities, then and since then, you can make up your own mind. But this one thing is sure. These parables are deeply rooted in the ancient wedding traditions of the Israelites. Part of these traditions was a banquet, much like we hold a reception today. But their wedding banquets were not short, cake-cutting ceremonies, with light refreshments served. Their banquets typically lasted for days—often a week or more—and featured giant smorgasbords of the richest foods and finest of wines freely flowing and on which people gorged themselves, drank, sang, danced, laughed, and played games almost around the clock.

This Israelite wedding celebration and tradition is one of the things to which Jesus likened the kingdom of God. The angel of the Revelation had the same image in mind when he spoke of the wedding supper of the Lamb. And since "the Bible speaks of the marriage covenant as analogous to the covenant between God and His people (2 Cor. 11:2; Eph. 5:22-33; Rev. 19:7-9; 21:9-11),"[12] we would be well-served to better understand the meaning of this sublime metaphor and its possible, perfect, precise, and past fulfillment, and ongoing relevance based upon that 1st-century time context and tradition.[13]

> **These parables are deeply rooted in the ancient wedding traditions of the Israelites. Part of these traditions was a banquet, much like we hold a reception today.**

The fact is, six times in the Old Testament God declares that the way to know Who the one true God truly is, is the fulfillment of prophecy. No other faith, religion, ideology, or philosophy contains this dynamic element of validation and authenticity. These six times are all found in the book of Isaiah: see Isaiah 41:22-29; 42:8-9; 44:6-8; 45:18-24; 46:9-11; and 48:3-6. The seventh occurrence immediately follows "the wedding supper of the Lamb" verse. It reads, "For the testimony of Jesus is the spirit of prophecy" (Rev. 19:10b). I maintain that the meaning of this last verse and from the angel, is identical with the meaning of these six Old Testament statements by God the Father in Isaiah. Furthermore, the timely, perfect, and precise fulfillment of prophecy is the stamp of divinity. Unfortunately, most of Christ's Church over the centuries has ignored, denied, or contradicted the accuracy of the fulfillment of this wedding metaphor, and most all other prophecy as well. But let's see if this divine precision holds true for the fulfillment and ongoing establishment and relevance of "the wedding supper of the Lamb." (For more on divine perfection, see the Introduction in my book *The Perfect Ending for the World,* especially pp-14-18.)

Therefore, let's take a brief review of the Jewish marriage customs of that time.

The Jewish Wedding Customs

A Jewish marriage was not considered to be a single event but consisted of approximately five distinct events or phases. See if you can appreciate these fulfillment parallels:

1) "First comes the **betrothal**. This betrothal period somewhat corresponds to what we today call the engagement period. But it was "considered more binding than our 'engagement'. . . . [because] From this day groom and bride are legally husband and wife (2 Cor. 11:2)."[14] Also, after a marriage contract was arranged between the parents of the bride and the parents of the bridegroom, the bridegroom could pay a dowry to the parents of the bride at this time or later.

   <u>Fulfillment:</u>
   A.D. 30 – Jesus paid the dowry with his blood at the cross. The bride is now betrothed to Christ and considered legally married to Him (Rom. 7:4; 2 Cor. 11:2).

2) "Next comes the **interval of separation** between betrothal and the wedding-feast. During this interval the groom pays the dowry to the father bride if this has not yet been done (Gn. 34:12). Sometimes the dowry is in the form of service rendered (Gn. 29:20)."[15] The groom then leaves his bride at her home and returns to his father's house and remains separate from his bride. During this time the groom prepares a dwelling place in his father's house for his bride, while the bride prepares and adorns herself.

   <u>Fulfillment:</u>
   A.D. 30-66 – Jesus possibly paid another dowry with the sending of the Holy Spirit, while the bride washes and purifies herself by the blood of Jesus and makes herself ready via righteous acts (Rev. 19:7-8; John 14:12; Acts 17:6 KJV; Eph. 5:25-27). Please note that the bride is not the whole Church but the "overcomers," the "sons," within the Church (Rev. 21:2, 7, 9; 2 Cor. 11:2-3;

Jude 24). Meanwhile, Jesus is preparing his house, "I go to prepare a place for you" (John 14:3).

3) "Then comes the **procession** at the close of the interval."[16] The bride must always be ready at a moment's notice. But only when the father of the bridegroom decided all is ready (a year or so later) is the time of separation over. Usually at night, bearing torches, and unexpectedly, the groom, arrayed in his best attire, would assemble his friends and set out for the bride's house. When they got close, someone would shout "Behold the bridegroom comes!" The bride would come out and be received by the bridegroom who would convey her, with a returning procession, back to his home or the home of his parents (Matt. 9:15; also Matt. 23:1ff).

Fulfillment:
A.D. 66 – Josephus records that just before sunset, angelic armies are spotted in the sky running about on the clouds above Jerusalem (Matt. 16:27-28; Luke 21:11).[17]

A.D. 70-73 – Jesus' comes to "take you to be with me that you also may be where I am" (John 14:3), along with the gathering of the rest of the dead (Matt. 24:31; John 6:39, 40, 44, 54; 11:24; 1 Thess. 4:13-17).

4) The **consummation.** Upon their arrival, the two would enter the bridal chamber. After which the bridegroom would come out and announce the consummation of the marriage to the wedding party members waiting outside.

Fulfillment:
A.D. 70-73 – The new marriage is consummated (John 14:1-3). Chilton pictured the judgment and destruction of Jerusalem and the Temple as "the final declaration that God had taken to Himself a new Bride, a faithful, chaste virgin who had successfully resisted the seductive temptations of the Dragon"[18] He further recognizes that "the destruction of the Harlot (apostate Judaism) and the marriage of the Lamb and the Bride –

the divorce and the wedding – *are correlative events* . . . . With the final divorce and destruction of the unfaithful wife in A.D. 70, the marriage . . . was firmly established"[19] (see Hos. 2; Heb. 8:8-13; 9:8; Matt. 21:43-45; 22:1-14; 25:1-13; Rom. 9:25-26; 1 Pet. 2:10). As a quick aside, one of the reasons given for the breaking of the glass at post-A.D. 70 Jewish weddings, and still today, is as a remembrance of the destruction of Jerusalem and the Temple.

5) Finally, comes **the wedding feast**, which includes the marriage supper. The usual festivities last seven, or even more, days. This feasting is the climax of the entire marriage process.

Fulfillment:
Post A.D. 70-73 and forever—the ongoing reality and relevance of "the wedding supper of the Lamb" (Rev. 19:9). Wallace proposes that "this marriage occurs every time one is baptized into Christ, and it is therefore always in process and is continuous. . . . As the marriage itself is continuous, so must be the marriage supper, and it symbolized the continuous fellowship all who are united to Christ; and it is as continuous as the baptism of believers and of the church itself."[20] Hendriksen adds that this feast "is the goal and purpose of that ever-increasing intimacy, union, fellowship, and communion between the Redeemer and the redeemed."[21] But again, and sadly, most Christians, all of whom have been invited, will never attend or participate in this grandest of all banquets.

The Host of the Wedding Feast

The gala wedding feasts of the Jews stood in sharp contrast to the somber ceremonial fasts, concocted from the Mosaic Law, which the religious leaders required the people to observe rigorously. Public fasts were characterized by stark silence, ceremonial cleansings, public offerings, sober reflection, and religious rites. Thus, the fasts of the Pharisees represented all that was superficial and empty in their religiosity, while the wedding feasts represented all that was alive, fresh, and new about the kingdom of God. (Can you think of any parallels here for today? See Chapter 8.)

Early in his ministry, Jesus made his preference quite clear. He performed his first public miracle—turning water into wine—at a wedding banquet (John 2:1-11). Although Jesus apparently fasted personally and privately, He seemed to have little enthusiasm for the ritualistic fasts of the Pharisees. Often He soundly criticized the Scribes and Pharisees for their fasting habits.

His zest for feasting was so pronounced that He was accused of being "a glutton and a drunkard" (Matt. 11:19). Even John the Baptist's loyal disciples questioned Him about his disdain for public fasts. "How is it that we and the Pharisees fast, but your disciples do not fast?" To that, Jesus responded with a question and a statement: "How can the guests of the bridegroom mourn while he is with them? The time will come when the bridegroom is taken from them; then they will fast" (Matt. 9:14-15).

Jesus is obviously implying that the bridegroom's presence makes the difference between fasting and feasting. The bridegroom's presence also makes the difference between dead religious ritual and life-giving reality and vitality.

In the next few verses, Jesus used the parables of the new patch sown on an old garment and the new wine in old skins to indicate that the kingdom of God, then and there present, represented something new and radically different from what had gone before.

What is so different about the new order of the kingdom of God? It is "not a matter of (physical/material) eating and drinking, but of righteousness, peace and joy in the Holy Spirit" (Rom. 14:17). And this new reality is for "anyone who serves Christ in this way" (Rom. 14:18). But who is the Bridegroom?

There can be no doubt that Bridegroom is none other than Jesus Christ. John the Baptist was the first in the New Testament to make reference not only to this marriage imagery but also to Jesus being the bridegroom (John 3:29). And Jesus is the central figure of all the kingdom parables. He is the Good Shepherd who goes out looking for the lost sheep. He is the Good Samaritan who rescues the man who had been beaten and robbed, and He is the Bridegroom who goes out to meet the five wise virgins. He was indeed taken away from his disciples at the crucifixion, and He is still far removed from many people who are caught up in dead religion today.

Therefore, it is not surprising that the writer of the Revelation characterizes the grand banquet as the wedding supper of the Lamb. Jesus Christ invites all people to "come and dine" (John 21:12, KJV). [22] And the greater Jesus will never stop serving the feast. The spirit-realm presence of the Bridegroom in our life determines whether we are fasting or feasting, spiritually.

The Nature of the Wedding Feast

Does all this mean that the historical Jesus really was a glutton and drunkard and that He advocated overeating and drunkenness? Certainly not! This accusation is another good reason not to make the wedding supper a one-time, physical event and shove it out into the future, up into the sky or heaven, and out into the by-and-by. Is God's objective to turn us all into gluttons and drunkards? Even if you go through the linguistic exercise of saying we'll have glorified bodies, the idea of saints gorging themselves on physical food seems more like pagan revelry than righteous worship and celebration. The very idea opposes everything the Bible teaches and stands for.

Jesus often used the symbols of physical food and drink to describe the spirit-realm/physical-realm reality of God's kingdom here on earth. Notice how many of his parables and figures of speech had to do with food and water or wine. And yet on several occasions He miraculously provided physical food for his followers. But He also promised that his heavenly Father would provide food for all who put their trust in Him (Matt. 6:26).

Both Jesus and the Apostle Paul made it abundantly clear that the kingdom does not come through eating and drinking in the physical sense (Matt. 6:31-33; Rom. 14:17). Obviously, Jesus intends these physical symbols to refer to a spirit-realm reality. Why, then, is it so hard for most people to accept the idea that the wedding supper is a physical symbol of a spiritual/physical reality? Much of the answer lies in the fact that most of us have been taught all our lives to expect a literal table, spread with all kinds of goodies, someday, somewhere. But it runs much deeper than doctrinal conditioning.

The Problem Is the Veil

The highlight of the ancient Jewish wedding ceremony was the thrilling moment when the bride removed her veil so she could see and be seen by the bridegroom, face to face, and could eat the wedding banquet. And yes, she and the bridegroom could unite in the ceremonial kiss that publicly sealed their marriage.

Once she removed the veil, she was never to put it back over her face. Never again would it interfere with her union with the bridegroom or with her partaking of all his sumptuous feasts. This act symbolized that the two of them had become one flesh.

The term "the wedding supper of the Lamb" was obviously chosen to describe the full, spirit-realm union of Christ and his bride because this ceremony was so significant. And because it's impossible to enjoy a rich and meaningful relationship without experiencing each other fully, Jesus desires to know us intimately and for us to know Him just as intimately. Consequently, while reading your Bible, going to church, and even praying are important, they are not enough, not all you need, nor all that's available. Experiencing his love, presence, and power happens at the wedding supper of the Lamb. Yes, it's a supernatural encounter with the greater Jesus. To know Him fully we need a healthy balance. All this begins with us removing the veil.

At the moment we remove the veil, we can receive the full revelation of Jesus Christ; and we can begin to eat the wedding supper of the Lamb with Him. What's more, we don't have to wait until we're raptured out of this world to do it. If you think that is exciting, wait until you discover later in this chapter what's on the menu!

But first, before we can see and eat, we have to remove the veil.

What is this veil that keeps us from seeing and knowing and being fully united with Christ? Quite simply, it is our *mental image of Jesus*. "So from now on we regard no one from a worldly (after the flesh – KJV) point of view. Though we once regarded Christ in this way, we do so no longer" (2 Cor. 5:16; also see Heb. 10:20 KJV). As long as we insist on seeing Jesus in just his earthly ministry, flesh-and-bones body and mode, we cannot receive and experience Him in all his present and more glorious, spirit-realm reality—we cannot see Him face to face as He is today and eat the wedding supper with Him.

Why? It's because nowadays He is more than just Jesus of Nazareth; He is the ascended, exalted, glorified, transformed, transfigured, transcended, apocalyptic, crowned, and cosmic Christ, the unveiled and revealed Jesus of the Apocalypse. Many people today, however, remain like the women who went to the tomb looking for Jesus on the morning of his resurrection. The angels asked them, "Why do you look for the living among the dead?" (Luke 24:5). They were looking for Jesus of Nazareth as just a man, but He was now in the spirit realm.

Oddly enough, many would argue with that analogy. "Oh, no!" they'd protest, "We believe in the risen Christ." Yet, if you ask them to tell you where this risen and ascended Christ is, they'll tell you He's off somewhere in space, in heaven, or who knows? But they are expecting Him to come back (return) to earth at any time and set up a material kingdom in a temple rebuilt with human hands in Jerusalem. All that sounds pretty fleshly to me. It's putting us back in history into the Old Covenant economy and its law, which was declared inferior, by inspiration, to what we have now (see Heb. 7:18-19; 9:9; 10:11, 14; Rom. 8:3-4). Without question, this worldly and highly popular belief, in essence, keeps the Jesus of today veiled.

Consequently, most Christians are caught up, mentally and emotionally, in the pre-glorified Christ. That's the Jesus most of us have read, heard about, and studied. So we picture Him as the little baby born in a manger, or as the poor guy in Jerusalem who hung on a cross, etc. Now all that's important, but it is history. *He's not like that anymore.*

In order to eat the wedding supper of the Lamb with the greater Jesus, we have to remove that earthly veil. We have to unearth Jesus by moving beyond just thinking of and picturing Him in terms of his earthly ministry—again, as important as that was and is. We have to progress into worshipping Him in spirit and truth, as He now is and will always be. We have to take that earthly veil off our faces so we won't worship Him after the flesh (2 Cor. 5:16; Heb. 10:20 KJV). That can only happen when we see Him as He is now—in his greater and more glorious form.

When we remove this veil, it will greatly affect the way we think of Jesus, the way we study Him, the way we follow and serve Him, and the way we worship Him. For example, our worship of Him will change from the all-too-common casual approach many of us experience every Sunday to that of the twenty-four elders and the four living creatures and John himself who all "fell down and worshipped" (Rev. 19:4; 1:17).

Chilton poignantly emphasized "the importance of posture, of physical attitude, in our religious activity" and "at the very least" maintains that "our physical position in public, official worship should be one that corresponds to the godly fear and reverence which is appropriate in those who are admitted to an audience with God who sits on the throne."[23]

Once again, if you want the latest, most recent and elaborate description of Jesus, read, visually, Revelation 1:12-18. This passage depicts Him with a sword coming out of his mouth, with fiery eyes, with feet of bronze, and with a voice that sounds like rushing water. Now if you're trying to visualize or literally think about most art which depicts Jesus, you're just not going to be able to grasp that revelation. If you are only focusing on the earthly ministry of Jesus, that veil will prevent you from eating the wedding supper with Him in the spirit realm as He is right now.

In order to eat the wedding supper of the Lamb with the greater Jesus, we have to remove that earthly veil. We have to unearth Jesus by moving beyond just thinking of and picturing Him in terms of his earthly ministry

---

Of course, if you don't remove that veil, you are still saved and bound for heaven. And you can go to church, teach Sunday school, sing in the choir, and go through all the motions, but you will not have this glorious intimacy with Christ that He desires and for which we all long. Why not? It's because you cannot see Him face-to-face as He now is, because you're still looking for a face that doesn't exist anymore. That veil, again, is your mental and emotional attachment to his earthly and historical form. *He's not like that anymore.*

It's helpful to remember that the word *apocalypse* also means to lift a veil, or to remove a shroud or curtain, in order to resolve a mystery. And right here, in the symbolism of the wedding supper of the Lamb, the Apocalypse of Jesus Christ reaches its peak. It's as if everything that precedes Revelation 19:9 is prelude, and everything that follows it is explanation and expansion that marks a new covenantal, not cosmic, creation—"a new heaven and a new earth" (Rev. 21:9; 22:1). And all of this is seen through the metaphor of marriage. If you miss even a portion of this reality and glorious truth, you'll miss the deepest intimacy that Christ longs to share with you right here, right now. But to fully grasp that reality, you must lift the veil.

Honestly, not everyone in the Church will achieve this level of intimacy with Christ because not everyone in Christ's Church is the bride of Christ. According to the Book of Revelation, the bride is not a covenantal union of the whole Church of born-again, saved, heaven-bound believers with Christ at an event at the conclusion of history as we've been told by our leaders from pulpits for centuries. The bride is comprised *only* of the overcomers within the Church (Rev. 21:7-10).[24] However, the great temptation has been and still is to compromise the cost of following Christ and to cheapen this communion experience, i.e., by making it "seeker sensitive" and "friendly." Once again, you must be an overcomer and you must have lifted the veil to be the bride and engage with Him fully, here and now.

Lifting the Veil

The symbolism of the veil runs much deeper than the Jewish wedding tradition. Its roots are also anchored in the worship symbols of God's Old Covenant with the nation Israel. The tabernacle, the symbol of God's presence with his people during their wilderness wanderings (see Exodus 25-40), was divided into two parts: the Holy Place and the Holy of Holies (or Most Holy Place). This was where God promised to visit the people and receive their acts of worship. However, only the high priest, as the intermediary between man and God and only once a year, could go into the Holy of Holies to offer the sacrifices for the people and to commune with God.

A curtain (the *King James Version* of the Bible calls it a veil), reaching from the ceiling to the floor, sealed off the Holy of Holies. This was the curtain, or veil, which was torn asunder (torn in two from top to bottom) at the time of crucifixion of Jesus (Matt. 27:51). The big question here is, what did this tearing in two really signify? Most of us have been told that this tearing signified heaven was now open and every human being now had free access to God. But isn't this an impossible explanation? I think so (see endnote).[25] Rather, I believe it *showed*, physically and visibly, that no one, and no God was in there, and that the Old Covenant system had been made "obsolete; and what is obsolete and aging would soon disappear" (Heb. 8:13) and be left "desolate" (Matt. 23:38; 24:2). It also signified that Jesus Christ had become the eternal High Priest.

Hence, the external regulations about food and drink, the various ceremonial rites, and sacrifices gave way to the new order when Christ came and made a sacrifice for all people of all times (Heb. 9:8-10). The writer of Hebrews further explains how this occurred.

> *When Christ came as high priest of the good things that are already here, he went through the greater and more perfect tabernacle that is not man-made, that is to say, not a part of this creation. He did not enter by means of the blood of goats and calves; but he entered the Most Holy Place once for all by his own blood, having obtained eternal redemption* (Heb. 9:11-12).

So Jesus' crucifixion, resurrection, and ascension transcended and replaced the ritualistic, physical sacrifices offered each year by the Jewish high priest under the old law with the constant, abiding, spirit-realm presence of God through Christ.

Doesn't this explain why we don't have to keep going back through those physical sacrifices year-after-year? Nor do we ever have to keep crucifying Jesus or start sacrificing animals again someday in a rebuilt temple in Jerusalem. Notice the way Hebrews expresses it: "But now he has appeared once for all at the end of the ages to do away with sin by the sacrifice of himself" (Heb. 9:26b). Please observe that this verse does not say he *will appear* . . . at the end of the ages, but that "he *has appeared* once for all at the end of the ages" (emphasis added). It has already happened.

Then after his appearance "a second time" in association with the destruction of Jerusalem and the Temple (Heb. 9:28), we have free and open access to God all day, every day—now! (see again Heb. 9:8-10). Hence, God has torn away the veil that enshrouded the greater Jesus in mystery. In this glorified and ascended Jesus, the mystery is revealed. Jesus is alive in the spirit realm forever—He is part of "the great cloud of witnesses" that surrounds us (see Heb. 12:1, 22-24). All that remains is for us to remove the veil from our own faces so we can see Him as He now is and as clearly as He longs for us to see Him.

Once we remove that veil, we are free to eat the wedding supper of the Lamb with Him, to be married to Him, and to bear offspring (new Christians) as a result of our marital union with Him.

But *we* have to remove the veil; God will not do that for us. We have to move beyond our fleshly ideas of merely the historical Jesus and lay aside our fleshly worship in order to see Him face-to-face as He now is in the spirit realm—if we want to eat the wedding supper with Him.

How do we eat that meal? We'll see shortly. But first let's look at what's on the menu. I believe that once you see what we're going to be feasting upon, your appetite will be so great that you won't want to wait for some future event in the sky, by-and-by. You'll long to dive right in—here and now.

What's on the Menu for the Wedding Supper of the Lamb?

What do we eat at the wedding supper of the Lamb? Some Christians believe "no one knows."[26] But don't take my word for it. Read the menu yourself from God's Word. The one thing you will definitely *not* find being served is milk. If you are a believer and as "mere infants in Christ" are still drinking "milk, not solid food . . . you are still not ready" to attend the wedding supper of the Lamb (see 1 Cor. 3:1-3f; Heb. 6:1-6). The Bible proclaims we *eat the Lamb!* We actually eat Christ. Oh, yes we do!

Eating of the Lamb

During the Exodus, Moses described how flakes of manna appeared on the desert floor for Israel during their forty years of wandering and how the people had enough to eat each day. They couldn't hold it over, however, or it would spoil, except on the seventh day. The Israelites ate manna—real physical food that God provided from the sky—until they reached the border of Canaan (Exod. 16:14-36).

Later on, Moses told about more manna coming down from heaven. But this manna was different. It was like a coriander seed and looked like resin. The people gathered it, ground it in a hand mill, and cooked it into cakes. It tasted like something made with olive oil (Num. 11:7-9). So this second type of manna was better. And manna gets even better as you move through Scripture.

Psalm 78:23-25 reports about God that "He gave a command to the skies above and opened the doors of the heavens; he rained down manna for the people to eat, he gave them the grain of heaven. Men ate the bread of the angels; he sent them all the food they could eat."

Keep in mind that many things in the Old Testament are types of the spiritual truth in and the substance of the New Covenant. This is important because it will help explain what we actually eat at the wedding supper of the Lamb.

Once, Jesus spoke about the Old Testament manna we've been describing. The crowd which thronged around Him asked,

> *What immaculate sign then will you give that we may see it and believe you? What will you do? Our forefathers ate manna in the desert; as it is written: "He gave them bread from the heavens to eat"* (John 6:30-31).

How did Jesus respond? He switched from natural, physical food to spiritual food. "I tell you the truth, it is not Moses who has given you the bread from heaven, but it is my Father who gives you the true bread of heaven. For the bread of God is he who comes down from heaven and gives life to the world" (John 6:32-33).

Once we remove that veil, we are free to eat the wedding supper of the Lamb with Him, to be married to Him, and to bear offspring (new Christians) as a result of our marital union with Him.

But He doesn't stop there. He gets very precise, declaring in the strongest terms exactly what He's talking about: "I am the bread of life. He who comes to me will never go hungry, and he who believes in me will never be thirsty" (John 6:35, 48). A few verses later, He explains, "I am the living bread that came down from heaven. If a man eats of this bread, he will live forever. This bread is my flesh, which I will give for the life of the world. . . . I tell you the truth, unless you eat the flesh of the Son of Man and drink his blood, you have no life in you. . . . For my flesh is real food and my blood is real drink. . . . the one who feeds on me will live because of me. This is the bread that came down from heaven. Our forefathers ate manna and died, but he who feeds on this bread will live forever" (John 6:51-58).

So Jesus' flesh and blood is now the manna, the "angel food." But how can we eat of Him if we are still thinking of Him as an earthly man? *We can't.* We've got to get through this fleshly veil and into the spirit, because we eat and drink of Him as a spiritual/physical reality. It's just as Jesus further said, "the words I have spoken to you are spirit and they are life" (John 6:63b). But upon hearing these words of Jesus many disciples grumbled, "This is hard teaching" and "turned back and no longer followed him" (John 6:60-61, 66).

Of course, observance of communion, the Lord's Supper, which is an act of obedience taken weekly, monthly, or whenever, may be part of this. But in my opinion, we are talking about something far more than a physical sacrament. The greater aspect is the wedding supper of the Lamb, which, as we have seen, is a metaphor or symbol of the intimate relationship and closeness Christ wants to have with each of his followers all the time. To partake, we must stop thinking of this banquet, dining, and fellowship as speaking of physical tables and padded chairs, crystal glasses, expensive china, and gold ware, etc. This ongoing and lavish feast happens in the spirit realm as we dine together with Him and on Him. To this effect, Hendriksen makes special note that "in the East" this dining together "was an indication of special friendship and of covenant relationship. . . . That fellowship begins even in this present life."[27]

More than Showbread

In Hebrews 9, you will discover two different kinds of bread in the Jewish tabernacle and later in the Temple: (1) consecrated bread (the showbread) in the Holy Place, the outer chamber and, (2) the hidden manna contained in a gold jar behind the veil in the inner chamber of the

Most Holy Place (Heb. 9:2-4). These things don't happen by accident. And, yes, I am about to speculate here.

I believe these two breads may typify the two great works of the Messiah, Who is "the bread of life" (John 6:35). They are: the work of salvation and the work of the kingdom. The first is a saving truth; the other is a purifying reality. The manna that fell on the ground would last only for a day, typifying the transitory blessings and nourishment of just a salvation state. Eating of that bread will get you saved.

But the term *hidden manna* indicates a permanent blessedness, a richness in our spiritual lives when we dwell in the Holy of Holies in Him, under the direct operation of the Holy Spirit. I further believe this hidden manna is the manna that is served at the wedding supper of the Lamb. Again, it is available only for those who come through the veil and see Him face to face as He now is, who eat of Him here and now, and live in a marriage relationship with this greater Jesus.

> **So Jesus' flesh and blood is now the manna, the "angel food." But how can we eat of Him if we are still thinking of Him as an earthly man?**

But once again, and sad to say, great masses of nominal churches teach that you cannot have this fullness in Christ until you get to heaven or when the millennium arrives. They say you are not able to eat the wedding supper here and now. Thus, millions of Christians are starving. Yet, eating this hidden manna is what being in Christ (not just having Christ in you) allows (see John 15:4-11; 1 John 2:5-6)—we eat of Him, here and now.

How can we know this for sure? It's not some idea I've concocted. Revelation 2:17, the message to the church in Pergamum, says so: "To him who overcomes, I will give some of the hidden manna." Please keep in mind that at the end of every message to each of the seven churches in Revelation 2 and 3 is the same statement that this message is addressed to the individuals in all the churches (plural – "He who has an ear, let him hear what the Spirit says to the churches"). The hidden manna is one of the promises. It's what we eat at "the wedding supper of the Lamb." It is the spiritual manna that won't melt when the sun comes out and the heat gets turned on. Nor will it spoil or rot because it's the everlasting manna.

We Become What We Eat

An event from the life of Jesus gives us more indication of how wonderful and powerful this spiritual manna is. When Jesus' disciples were disturbed that He had not eaten in some time, they urged Him to eat something. "I have food to eat that you know nothing about," He told them (John 4:32).

Of course, like all today who still hang onto the veil of an earthly, historical Jesus, the disciples thought He was talking about physical food. "Could someone have brought him food?" they further asked (John 4:33).

"My food," Jesus explained, "is to do the will of him who sent me" (John 4:34). Once this earthly veil has been lifted, those who eat of his hidden manna at the wedding supper find that it gives them an overriding compulsion and power to go out and do the same works Jesus had been doing and even greater works (John 14:12). These works then become "the righteous acts of the saints" (Rev. 19:8), which produce the necessary attire—"fine linen, bright and clean"—for continued access and entrance into this grand banquet.

Today, we moderns know, and science has well documented and explained how what we take in through our mouths is transformed within and into our bodies; it then affects our minds and emotions, and energizes our actions. Hence, this image of eating and dining flows throughout the Bible as a "central image of life" with our Creator.[28] We actually become what we eat; we become like Him. Likewise, what goes in through our eyes and ears greatly impacts us as well. If we eat, see, and listen to religious junk food—such as a dumbed-down, diluted, devalued, and depreciated version of Christianity (see Chapter 8 and my book, *Off Target*), we become spiritually anemic and unfit to attend the wedding supper of the Lamb. But if we keep eating the hidden manna and reproducing Jesus' works and greater works, we become spiritually healthy and robust.

So what is this hidden manna? It is the fullness of the Word of God, and Jesus is the Word (John 1:1-4). When we eat of his Word, we eat of Him; we digest Him; we bring Him inside us, we assimilate his character and teachings, and produce Him outside us. We eat what Jesus ate (John 4:32, 34) and do his works and even greater works because we get "in Him" He Who is already in us (1 John 2:5-6; John 15:4-11). Get it?

As we continue to eat of Him, we come more and more into his likeness. We eat of his life, his truth, his attributes, his overcoming power, his mind, his self-control, his health, his perfection, his compassion, his long-suffering, his love, his peace, his joy, his everything. We eat platters and platters of all these things with Him and others at the wedding supper. It's not glorified turkey. It's not heavenly hash. It's Lamb. And we can partake of Him because He is with us and in us. It's spiritual truth and a present-day reality. We eat his fullness and assimilate and regurgitate Him by living Him out through our deeds, here and now.

How Can You Share in the Wedding Supper of the Lamb Right Now?

By now, I hope you are ravenously hungry to begin eating the fullness of Christ at the wedding supper of the Lamb. Below, we're going to practically recap how you can do just that. As with everything else in this book, it is not just a mental exercise or emotional experience. It is an ongoing spiritual/physical reality.

All Is Now Ready

So are you ready to feast? Why not sit down to the Lord's grand banquet table and take in a sumptuous meal, right now! Where? Right where you are! How?

(1) We have to prepare ourselves. The required ticket for getting into the wedding banquet in Jesus' two parables has two dimensions: (1) being clean and having on the right wedding clothes (Matt. 22:1-14). (2) being prepared to receive the Bridegroom (Matt. 25:1-13).

Our preparation begins with purifying our hearts. "Blessed are the pure in heart, for they shall *see God*," Jesus said (Matt. 5:8, emphasis added). That simply means we've got to get sin and corruption out of us.

Jude alludes to this cleansing process as turning away from the self-sufficiency and evil of the flesh, as "hating even the clothing stained by corrupted flesh" (Jude 23; also see Isa. 61:10; Ezek. 16:8-13). As we consistently repent and open and clean our heart, soul, mind, and body to Christ, his blood cleanses us, and we become more and more pure and ready to put on our elaborate wedding clothes—"fine linen, bright and clean." So there can be no doubt as to what this means, John explains in parentheses: "(Fine linen stands for the righteous acts of the saints.)" (Rev. 19:8). Those acts are the works and even greater works of Jesus (John 14:12). Jesus also listed other righteous acts.

> *Then the righteous will ask Him:* "*Lord, when did we see you hungry and feed you, or thirsty and give you something to drink? When did we see you a stranger and invite you in, or needing clothes and clothe you? When did we see you sick or in prison and go to visit you?*" *And the king will reply:* "*I tell you the truth, whatever you did for one of the least of these brothers of mine, you did for me*" (Matt. 25:37-40).

So, preparing ourselves to meet the Bridegroom involves becoming pure in heart (getting our sins forgiven and motives and morals right) and doing righteous acts.

(2) *We have to open ourselves to spirit-realm reality.* Since the wedding supper of the Lamb takes place in the spirit realm, we have to be willing to go there. Why? Because that's were the Bridegroom dwells and where He has spread the table.

How do we do that?

- By being filled with and energized by the Holy Spirit, as symbolized by the oil in the parable of the ten virgins.
- By giving up the dominance of worldly, fleshly thinking, going through the materialistic veil into the spirit realm.
- By regarding "no one from a worldly point of view [or after the flesh]. Though we once regarded Christ in this way, we do so no longer" (2 Cor. 5:16; Heb. 10:20 KJV). We aren't to look at anyone through eyes of the flesh, including Jesus, especially the greater Jesus.

- By readjusting our focus on Jesus beyond his earthly ministry and onto his present-day, glorified reality, i.e., lifting the veil.
- By worshipping in spirit and in truth (John 4:23-24).
- By operating in the spirit realm and into the physical realm (John 14:12).

Yes, this is supernatural phenomena. And God will work with us and share full intimacy with us to the degree that we are willing to behold and enter into the glorified greater Jesus in the reality in which He now exists.

Are you willing to lift the veil, enter in, and eat at the banquet? Notably, John was carried away in the spirit to see these revelations, and so must we. The Holy Spirit will then energize us, empower us, and bring us face to face with the greater Jesus. As we yield our spirits and minds to the Holy Spirit—through praise and worship, prayer, reading, meditation, dwelling, obeying the Word, doing righteous acts, and avoiding unrighteousness—He presents us to the Bridegroom and we enter the wedding feast. But when we don't so yield, we exit this grand banquet. The further good news, however, is, we can reenter through repentance and obedience. Praise God.

(3) We have to stay spiritually ready and alert for the comings of Jesus. Another key issue brought out in the parable of the ten virgins is that we must stay spiritually alert to realize both the presence and comings of the greater Jesus. For Jesus also promised:

> *It will be good for those servants whose master finds them watching when he comes. I tell you the truth, he will dress himself to serve, will have them recline at the table and will come and wait on them. It will be good for those servants whose master finds them ready, even if he comes in the second or third watch of the night. But understand this: If the owner of the house had known at what hour the thief was coming, he would not have let his house be broken into. You also must be ready, because the Son of Man will come at an hour when you do not expect him"* (Luke 12:37-40).

So does Jesus' admonition here incline you to want to follow and serve Him better by serving others all the more, or not? Remember, fruit bearing is always associated with an intimate union with Jesus Christ (John 15:1-8). And once we have tasted of this ultimate union with Him, here and now during this life, we will never be lonely, needing of sympathy, or satisfied with anything less ever again. We shall bear fruit, much fruit, here and now in this life all or much of the time and without being feeble.

And Christ can come to us in countless ways—through some person or people, through circumstances, through the words of Scripture, through enlightened revelation, and through direct and personal appearances. Christ is God, and He can come any way He chooses. He can appear in the physical realm, but we are also to watch for his illuminations in the spiritual realm. He can speak with a physical voice if He so chooses, but He longs for us to stay alert to hear his spiritual voice.

Our task is not to try to figure out how or when He will or might come to us. Our task is to be watching and ready.

What Does It All Mean?

The glorious and climaxing reality of the Revelation is that we don't have to wait for some future, pie-in-the-sky, by-and-by event to occur. We can consummate our marriage to the greater Jesus right now and feast at his wedding supper on a day-to-day basis. The Christian life is meant to transform our individual lives by not only being spiritual but also being experiential, material, communal, and beneficial.

As a child of the Most High God, we were created for great things. But they will not happen automatically. We have to do our part. The greater good news is, the invitation has already been extended to you and me. The wedding supper of the Lamb is part of the package God has made available (see Jude 3). Don't miss out on this opportunity to be treated as royalty by ultimate Royalty, the greater Jesus Himself.

Our task is not to try to figure out how or when He will or might come to us. Our task is to be watching and ready.

Every believer is invited to this "feast in the kingdom of God." Admittedly, the spiritual metaphors we have been exploring in this chapter still constitute a profound mystery that Paul spoke about in Ephesians 5. But this is where and how a Christian moves into the fullness of Christ—not just being saved, but learning how to operate in the spirit realm, here and now. And we can have that kind of relationship with Him, here and now in this life, but only in the spirit.

Within the veil is the place of maximum communion with God, total authority, full life, infinite power—perfect everything. And it's all contained in the greater Jesus.

We don't have to hope for a Rapture or wait until we die and go to heaven to eat the wedding supper of the Lamb with Him and of Him in all its fullness. It is available, here and now. God has brought this aspect of heaven down to earth. But it's only available for overcomers (Rev. 21:1-7 – see Chapter 10). It's in you and among you. And it's been going on for centuries. It's going on today. It will go on tomorrow and forever.

So are you fasting or feasting? Are you on the inside or the outside?

Within the veil is the place of maximum communion with God, total authority, full life, infinite power—perfect everything. And it's all contained in the greater Jesus.

Welcome to the Wedding Supper of the Lamb!

And, yes, in case you are already wondering, attending this grand banquet is almost, if not totally, synonomous with being "caught up with them in the clouds to meet the Lord in the air" (1 Thess. 4:17), the topic of our Chapter 9.

But first we have two chapters of opposition to all we've been presenting to address, i.e., a great battle to fight and a great prostitute to plague.

Warning: Yes, these next two chapters may be intimidating, if not scary. But I ask you, once again, where am I wrong on this, scripturally and historically, on any of this?

Chapter 7

He Fights the 'Battle of Armageddon'

What word best describes the mother of all massive conflicts? Christians and non-Christians, alike, even those who don't read or care about the Bible, know about *Armageddon*.

Most of us have been taught that the infamous Battle of Armageddon is the last, great, and final war of this world in which Satan will deceptively gather the military powers of the world together in the Holy Land to combat the armies of heaven. The battle will rage for some time, ending in the defeat of the forces of evil at the so-called return of Christ. Others "see Armageddon as a symbol of the final conflict between the forces of evil and the forces of God that occurs throughout the earth."[1] Some end-times teachers refer to this cosmic conflict as the proverbial "end of the world."[2]

But on January 13, 2003, the front cover of *Publisher's Weekly* magazine featured this startling headline:

**ARMAGEDDON
UNLEASHING EVERYWHERE APRIL 8, 2003**

An inside-cover headline exclaimed: **'NO ONE WILL ESCAPE ARMAGEDDON.'**

What was happening back in 2003? Were millions being misled?

Fortunately, this alarming headline was not about a real "Battle of Armageddon." It was simply an attention-attracting tactic for announcing the upcoming release of Tim LaHaye and Jerry Jenkins' tenth blockbuster title in their wildly popular *Left Behind* series. Provocatively, it was titled **Armageddon**.

And even though this book was another work of fiction, LaHaye contends that his books are conduits of "God's end-times truths" and contain "prophetic knowledge that God expects His children to have."[3] The sad fact is, the *Left Behind* series has proven to be LaHaye's best vehicle to achieve this goal. Its reported 65 million sold copies (as of 2011) are designed to reach people in a way his "non-fiction" books never will. They are doing just that—literally influencing and convincing multiple millions of the validity of LaHaye's misguided end-time view.

Another best-selling end-times author, who some describe as "Dr. Armageddon" and "Pastor Strangelove," writes in his one-million-plus selling book, *Jerusalem Countdown* (2006), that the United States must join Israel in a preemptive military strike against Iran. Author John Hagee believes this attack will help fulfill God's plan for both Israel and the world and that this all-out mid eastern war is a biblical directive. What is not prominently mentioned by LaHaye, Jenkins, or Hagee as part of their same prophetic scenario, is that two-thirds of those Jews living in Israel at this time will be killed during this final battle. The irony of ironies, however, is this. This "inevitable" consequence comes from authors who see and label themselves as "friends of Israel."

According to one other gloom-n-doom prognosticator, Joel C. Rosenberg, in a 2008 news release titled "War in November," "Iranian TV is running a new anti-Semitic documentary film series entitled, 'The Secret of Armageddon.' Setting the stage for a coming apocalyptic war that will usher in the Islamic Messiah known as the Mahdi or the 'Twelfth Iman,' the series focuses on a series of Bible prophecies that inform Jewish and Christian End Times theology."[4]

On and on we could go. And, admittedly throughout history, bad theology has created many bad wars. No doubt it will continue to do the same.

Oddly enough, however, the idea of a one-time, future Battle of Armageddon—this universal symbol for our world's final conflict—is another doctrine of man and not the truth of Scripture. The fact is, the beliefs and books of the four above authors are based upon an eschatological view that is not held by all Christians, and for good reasons. A quick case in point to illustrate just how far off-target they are, is this. They claim this battle will be fought in a valley. But as we shall soon see, biblically, it was to be fought on a mountain. A mountain is the exact opposite from a valley. Big difference!

What Scripture Actually Says about Armageddon

Below are ten biblical and historical reasons why the theology behind LaHaye, Jenkins, Hagee, and Rosenberg's *Armageddon* story line is *flawed*.[5]

Reason #1 – The expression *Battle of Armageddon* never appears in the Bible. Nor does Scripture ever mention a specific place bearing the name Armageddon. Hence, the name of the battle is *not* "Armageddon" or "the Battle of Armageddon" as the traditions of men have named it. Scripture calls it "the battle on the great day of God Almighty" (Rev. 16:14). Armageddon just happens to be the location of this battle. Big difference, as we shall continue to see!

Also, the name does not appear in ancient geographical or historical writings; neither does such a place appear on either ancient or modern maps. Interestingly, the word "Armageddon" is a composite name formed by two Hebrew words *Har Meggidon*, which we translate as *Armageddon*. But it has no apparent meaning, as names usually did in ancient Hebrew. It does appear in a variety of forms in different ancient New Testament manuscripts, but it does not show up anywhere else in ancient Hebrew literature or in religious or secular writings of the period.

Reason #2 – The location of this battle is *not* in Israel's largest valley, fifty miles north of Jerusalem, as is commonly thought and taught. Yet this twenty-mile long and fourteen-mile wide valley (presently known as the Valley of Jezreel or the Plain of Megiddo) remains one of the popular stops on most Christian tours of Israel.

According to Scripture, the location of this battle in Hebrew is called "Har-Magedon or Har-Megiddo" (Rev. 16:16). But "har" in the ancient Hebrew means mountain—the exact opposite in meaning from a valley.

Once we understand that "the battle on the great day of God Almighty" takes place on a mountain, we shall begin to see how far a field the popular end-time writers truly are. They place it in Israel's largest valley.

Admittedly, however, the ancient town of Megiddo was situated on a small mound adjacent to this valley and on its western side. But it's only about two hundred feet high. I stood on top of it, once. And since in Hebrew the 'h' is silent, the Greek rending became "Armageddon."

Reason #3 – This battle is part of the whole prophecy of the Book of Revelation. According to Revelation itself, and as we have seen, its whole prophecy contains realities and events that *all* "would shortly take place" (Rev. 1:1; 22:6), were "at hand" (Rev. 1:3; 22:10), and were obeyable, heedable, and keepable (Rev. 1:3; 22:7) in the lives of that book's first recipients in that 1st-century time frame.

Hence, a strong case can be made that all the literal and symbolic end-time details portraying Revelation's "Armageddon" prophecy were precisely fulfilled during the events of the Jewish-Roman War circa A.D. 66-70, and in keeping with the time-restricted context that this last book of the Bible imposes upon itself. Consequently, the fulfillment of Armageddon is past not future.

Reason #4 – Revelation's time-context perspective is also why the whole of this prophecy was not to be sealed up (Rev. 22:10). But LaHaye, Jenkins, Hagee, and Rosenberg have, in essence, sealed it up for over nineteen centuries and counting via their postponement interpretation. Now they want to unseal it by claiming that these events will finally and soon occur in our day and time.

Reason #5 – A strong case can be made that the Book of Revelation was written prior to the destruction of Jerusalem and the Temple in A.D. 70 (see again Chapter 3, pp-93-97). This dating allows for its past and 1st-century fulfillment.

Reason #6 – Since the locality and meaning of Armageddon are not specifically spelled out, and since this name appears in a book which abounds in signs and symbols, it is not unreasonable to conclude that it, too, is a sign and a symbolic of a real battle. *Bauer, Arndt, Gingrich and Danker*, the foremost Greek-English lexicon, recognizes that

"Armageddon is a mystic place-name" that "has been identified with Megiddo and Jerusalem." Yet it rightly laments that "its interpretation is beset with difficulties that have not yet been surmounted." Or have they?

Reason #7 – Since Har-Magedon or Har-Megiddo, where this great end-time battle takes place, is a composite name, the most likely case is that Revelation's "Har" is and was Jerusalem. Geographically, Jerusalem sits on top of a mountain. To get there from any direction one must go "up to Jerusalem" (see 2 Sam. 19:34; 1 Ki. 12:28; 2 Ki. 18:17; 2 Chron. 2:16; Ezra 1:3; 7:7; Zech. 14:17; Matt. 20:17, 18; Mark 10:32, 33; Luke 18:31; 19:28; John 2:13; 5:1; Acts 11:2; 15:2; 21:12, 15; 24:11; 25:9; Gal. 1:17, 18). Jerusalem is also called God's "holy mountain" (Psa. 43:3) and the "chief among the mountains" (Isa. 2:2-3; also 14:13; Exod. 15:17; Joel 2:32; 3:16-17).

Reason #8 – Based on other scriptures, one can also make a case for "Magedon" or "Megiddo" pointing to Jerusalem. During the time of Jesus and Revelation's subsequent writing, large crowds of devout Jews would gather three times a year to celebrate their religious feasts in this central city. Other related Hebrew terms supporting this identification are:
- *Har Mo'edh*, the mount of assembly (Isa. 14:13)
- *Ar himdah*, God's city of desire
- *Har migdo*, His fruitful mountain (Mount Zion)
- *Megiddow*, rendezvous – from *gadad*, to crowd, assemble, gather.

Reason #9 – "Magedon" or "Megiddo" may also be comparative imagery. In ancient times a great slaughter once took place in the valley of *Megiddo* (2 Ki. 9:27; Zech. 12:11). Throughout history, this valley was also a favorite corridor for invading armies and the scene of numerous famous battles (Jud. 4-7; 1 Sam. 29-31; 2 Sam. 4; 1 Ki. 9:15; 2 Ki. 9-10; 22; 2 Chron. 35). So much blood was shed in this valley of Jezreel or Megiddo that it became a synonym for slaughter, violence, bloodshed, and a battlefield, as well as a symbol for God's judgment (Hos. 1:4-5). In our day, Armageddon has also become synonymous with and a symbol for the ultimate in warfare and conflict.

In a similar fashion, the name "Waterloo" has garnered a symbolic use. In 1815, this town in Belgium was the battleground for Napoleon's final defeat. Today, we have a saying that some one or some thing has met their "Waterloo." By that we don't mean they have met or visited that city in Europe. We mean, by way of comparative imagery, that they have met a decisive or crushing defeat, or their demise. I suggest Revelation could have employed the word "Magedon" or "Megiddo" in a similar manner.

Reason #10 – History records that a great slaughter took place on a mountain in Palestine within the lifetime of the original recipients of the Book of Revelation. Circa A.D. 70 - 73 the Roman armies of Titus totally destroyed Jerusalem and the Temple. According to Josephus, 1.1 million Jews were killed. Even more perished in the Galilean fighting, died of starvation or disease, and/or were taken into captivity.[6]

This event was certainly a judgment of God. I submit that it was that and more. First, it was a day-of-the-Lord judgment in keeping with Jehovah God's many comings "on the clouds" in day-of-the-Lord judgments in Old Testament times:

- Isaiah 13:10, 13—judgment of Babylon (539 B.C.)
- Isaiah 34:4—judgment of Edom (late 6th century B.C.)
- Ezekiel 32:7—judgment of Egypt (568 B.C.)
- Nahum 1:5—judgment of Nineveh (612 B.C.)
- Joel 2:10—judgment of Judah (586 B.C.)
- Amos 8:9—judgment of the northern kingdom (722 B.C.)

Secondly, since Jesus stated that all judgment has been given by the Father to the Son (John 5:22), I submit that this A.D. 70 coming in judgment was "the great day of God Almighty" (Rev. 16:14). It was also Jesus' coming "on the clouds" (Matt. 24:30; 26:64; Rev. 1:7) and "in the Father's glory" (Matt. 16:27; Mark 8:38; Luke 9:26), exactly as Jehovah God had come many times before in the above-bulleted judgments (see again Chapter 4).

Consequently, in speaking of his coming again, Jesus, who is God, used exactly the same *language* of the prophets (cosmic-darkening and collapsing, earth-shaking words), described it exactly in the same *way* ("on the clouds"), for exactly the same *purpose* (judgment), to accomplish exactly the same *thing* (destruction of a nation), and employed exactly the same *instrumentality* (foreign armies). It all happened within the time frame of the generation in which Jesus said it would happen—his "this generation" (Matt. 23:36; 24:34).

In Sum – The biblical and historical facts seem to indicate that LaHaye, Jenkins, Hagee, and Rosenberg are over nineteen centuries off in their timing and topographically far off-target in their location of this "battle on the great day of God Almighty" (placing it in a valley instead of on a mountain). They, and others of their eschatological persuasion, have also erroneously termed it "the Battle of Armageddon."

In contrast, this decisive battle of the "last days" period, in which they were living back then and there (Heb. 1:2), was totally relevant to, took place during, and was fulfilled within the lifetime of Revelation's original readers. Hence, Revelation's "Armageddon" took place on the mountain of Jerusalem. Historically, this fulfillment is behind us, and not ahead of us. It is past, and not future. According to Drs. Klein, Blomberg, and Hubbard, Jr., "the historically defensible interpretation has greatest authority."[7] And so be it.

The greater Jesus was the Person from the Godhead Who came and fought in this so-called "Battle of Armageddon" back then and there, when He came "on the clouds" riding a "white horse" of war. Therefore, I suggest that it is time for God's people to "wake up, O sleeper . . ." (Eph. 5:14), i.e., those who love biblical truth, and not fiction or fantasy. We must stop abdicating this area of our faith to the likes of LaHaye, Jenkins, Hagee, Rosenberg, and others of their ilk. Everyday, millions are being adversely affected and many more tragically burdened by their biblically flawed view. Perhaps today, as you are reading this book, it is as Jesus said, "then you will know the truth, and the truth will set you free" (John 8:32). First, however, truth must get a hearing. If it doesn't get a good hearing, truth can become what gets left behind.

The two questions we must next address are: (1) Is Armageddon fulfilled, past, and over? (2) Or, and in keeping with the ongoing nature and idealist relevance of Revelation's total prophecy, is this "battle on the great day of God Almighty" still going on somewhere today following its circa A.D. 70 fulfillment (see Chapter 3, pp-106-112)?

What and Where Is Armageddon Today?

Scripture does not tell us Armageddon's location in the New Covenant, post A.D.-70 world, or even what the term means in its new application and ongoing context. It is hard to imagine such an omission as a divine oversight.

But one thing is sure. We don't have to look for a one-time "Battle of Armageddon" to end all battles to be fought in the Middle East at some future date with horses, tanks, soldiers, missiles, airplanes, and maybe even nukes (although many terrible battles have been and will probably continue being fought there). Again, that battle is behind us, not ahead of us.

However, like everything else in the whole prophecy of the Book of Revelation, "the battle on the great day of God Almighty" (Rev. 16:14), was "at hand" when John wrote about it and has been at hand ever since. It is at hand now and will be at hand in the future.

I'm going to suggest that following its A.D. 70 fulfillment, this battle goes on in many places, not just in one. We can support this ongoing and universalized reality, scripturally and historically. It's as easy as answering this question. Where in today's world is the location of God's *Har Mo'edh*, his "mount of assembly" (of his people), his *Ar himdah* "city of desire," his *Har migdo* "fruitful mountain," and his *megiddow* "rendezvous" – from *gadad*, to crowd, assemble, gather . . . located? No longer is Armageddon located singularly in Jerusalem. Over nineteen hundred years ago Jesus foretold of this relocation in saying, "a time is coming when you will worship the Father neither on this mountain nor in Jerusalem" (John 4:21b). That time came when Jerusalem and the Temple were totally destroyed and that Old Covenant system left "desolate" (Matt. 23:38).

Today, there are two different locations where God dwells and meets with his people on this earth in this manner: (1) inside each individual believer and (2) collectively within his churches. Therefore, I am suggesting that these are the two new locations, in the New Covenant and idealist applications (not additional fulfillments), for what is termed "Har-Magedon" or "Har-Megiddo" (Rev. 16:16). If correct, then these two locations are also where "the battle on the great day of God Almighty" (Rev. 16:14) continues to be waged—at this very moment.

How Do We Know These Different and Relocated Venues Are Correct?

Many New Testament scriptures confirm that God has relocated. In the New Covenant era, He no longer dwells in a temple built with hands (Acts 7:48; 17:24). Nowadays, each individual believer is God's temple and in which He dwells (1 Cor. 3:16-17; 6:19-20; 2 Cor. 6:16; Eph. 2:21). But his dwelling and meeting with human beings also has a collective aspect. For instance, "For where two or three come together in my name, there am I with them" (Matt. 18:20). And the Bible's last book confirms this same revelation that Jesus is in the midst of his churches (Rev. 1:13)—is He not?

Let's also look more closely at how all Revelation symbolism ties together and in with so many other scriptures. For instance, Mount Zion, the accepted Old Testament symbol of Israel, was not only referred to as God's "Holy Mountain" (Psa. 43:3) but also "the mountain of your [God's] inheritance – the place, O Lord, you made for your dwelling, the sanctuary, O Lord, your hands established" (Exod. 15:17). Arguably, the New Testament symbolizes the new Israel as being the true Church (Gal. 6:16). That's one reason the writer of Hebrews used Mount Zion like this: "But you have come to Mount Zion, to the heavenly Jerusalem, the city of the living God. . . . to the church of the firstborn" (Heb. 12:22-23: Note also: Rom. 9:33; 11:26; Rev. 14:1).

Consequently and nowadays, the greater Jesus wages this ongoing battle in both of these new "Armageddon" venues—inside believers and within his churches.

Make no mistake about it; evil spirit-realm forces are constantly seeking to thwart God's purposes by waging an ongoing war both within believers and inside churches. Yes, Jesus faced these same evil forces in his conflicts with the temple rulers, and they show up throughout the Book of Acts and the Epistles. As we shall further see, this spiritual warfare also constitutes one of the primary themes of the entire Book of Revelation.

What's more, we believing Christians are called upon to be fellow warriors in this great and ongoing conflict. Certainly, Christ leads us into this battle, just as He always has; but we are his foot soldiers with our boots-on-the-ground and in the trenches, so-to-speak, those who help carry out his battle plan on a day-to-day basis. Once again, and as we have seen, we are "the armies of heaven" riding with Him—are we not (see Rev. 19.14)?

... the greater Jesus wages this ongoing battle in both of these new "Armageddon" venues—inside believers and within his churches.

All sincere Christians need to make sure they are allied with God's forces within the Church and not with his enemies. Armageddon symbolism makes it clear that God deals harshly with the evil forces that constantly seek to seize control, lead his people astray, dumb them down, and draw them off-target in Christ's Church. This was relevant and true in the past. It's still relevant and true today.

Why Is This Prophecy So Distorted?

Arguably, evil spirit-realm forces have successfully deceived masses of Christians into believing an elaborate end-time doctrine that fixes a precise physical location—a valley outside of Jerusalem, near the town of Megiddo—for this supposed and yet-to-be-fought battle. I believe it's part of the deception of the elect Jesus talked about (see Matt. 24:23-26 – see again Chapter 5, p-161).[8] But why would they want to perpetrate such a hoax? What could they possibly hope to gain by misleading people to be looking toward and expecting a final judgment and destruction of this evil world by a righteous God? How could these evil forces hope to gain support for their rebellion by announcing their own ultimate defeat?

This clever deception takes advantage of one basic human flaw—the tendency to procrastinate on decisions and actions that we perceive to have little or no meaning for the present moment, especially when they don't seem to involve us directly. Thus, by depicting this battle as God's war, not ours, and by shoving it out into the future, these spirit-realm forces hope to dupe Christians into believing that the battle on the great day of God Almighty has no direct meaning for their daily lives, here and now. After all, sleeping Christians pose no danger to the enemies of God.

Apparently, their plot is working. Most Christians either ignore Bible prophecy about spirit-realm conflict and how it impacts the physical realm, or they think of conquering evil as something God will do someday out in the future all by Himself. "Let Jesus come back and clean up this mess," they say.

Christians, it is time to wake up! The Revelation is sounding the alarm!

The Time Is *Now!* The Location Is *Here!* The Battle Is *Ours!*

The awesome picture of the greater and present-day Jesus in Revelation 1 with a double-edged sword coming out of his mouth (Rev. 1:12-20) has a definite connection with the warnings issued to and judgments coming upon non-repenting and non-overcoming believers, as well as collectively to each of the seven churches in Revelation 2 and 3.

In the very first verse of Revelation 1, John writes that this prophecy from and of Jesus Christ is addressed to "his servants" (Rev. 1:1), those same people who are also designated "to be a kingdom and priests to serve his God and Father" (Rev. 1:6; also 5:10). Nowhere in this prophetic book is anyone else addressed.

So why is this prophecy addressed only to his servants? Some prophecy teachers say that its only purpose is to comfort the suffering saints by showing them what God will someday do. If so, it is the only book in the Bible written for that purpose. No, John explicitly and repeatedly writes down that God has given his servants the Revelation because He expects them to do something about its message. John writes in the imperative; these things "must soon take place" (Rev. 1:1). Again and again, the Revelation promises blessings to believers who read, hear, and keep or obey its message (Rev. 1:3). The saints are blessed if they wash their robes in his righteousness (Rev. 7:14-17), keep their white garments with them at all times (Rev. 16:15), and keep themselves spotless (Rev. 14:4-5). This is no passive book, written to passive, comfortable, and complacent Christians who are sitting around in a passive state and waiting for God to do something someday out in the future. It is an active book, written for active and, as we shall further see, overcoming Christians, who have a definite mission to achieve in their lifetimes. And if they don't, there will be consequences to pay.

Furthermore, this prophecy is not addressed to an organized and institutional church in a general way. It is addressed to individuals within each church, in very specific ways. Note the frequent use of personal pronouns (he, him, and them) throughout the Revelation. But in Revelation 2 and 3, the judgments contained therein don't fall upon organized religion as a whole or the world; they fall upon individuals within each church as well as that church itself if they fail to repent and overcome what the Lord holds against them.

These judgment warnings and promises are some of the most ominous threats in the Revelation. And these prophetic words to the seven churches are from Jesus Himself (Rev. 2 and 3). He threatens to deal sternly with both individuals and churches like these which cease to act like his Church—those which lose their first love, fail to do the miraculous works of Jesus, and tolerate evil and idolatry.

> **This is no passive book, written to passive, comfortable, and complacent Christians who are sitting around in a passive state and waiting for God to do something someday out in the future.**

Thus, Christ's Church is the ongoing location symbolized by "Armageddon" and relevancy context for "the battle on the great day of God Almighty." Nowadays, this battle describes the ongoing spiritual/physical conflict among and between overcoming and non-overcoming believers *within the Church*—i.e., against those within the Church who oppose the unveiling of the supernatural Christ and his everlasting kingdom. These scriptures create a visual parable of God's kingdom in conflict with the kingdoms of this world, which are not only in the world but also have invaded his churches (Rev. 11:15-19).

Please keep in mind, once again, that this whole prophecy is not about some future, global event that has not yet taken place. Christ is in our midst, not off somewhere waiting to come back. He is alive and active in the spirit realm; He is involved in the physical realm. In our day and time, this is a timeless, ongoing battle with countless applications. And his admonitions to each and every individual in these churches is to both repent and overcome the failings and/or abuses He holds against not just their church, but in all the churches as well (plural – "He who has an ear, let him hear what the Spirit says to the churches").

Consider these specific judgment threats that the greater Jesus issued to individuals in each of the seven churches mentioned and, idealistically, still issues today to each Christian and his or her church:

- To the church at Ephesus (Rev. 2:1-7): "I will *come* to you and remove your lampstand from its place," Jesus says. In simple words, "You will cease to be a church." Any church that loses its first love and fails to do the supernatural works of Jesus that it did at first will no longer be the Church of Jesus Christ (see John 14:12).
- To the church at Smyrna (Rev. 2:8-11): Jesus only warns them about those in their church who "are of the synagogue of Satan" and the persecution they are about to suffer.
- To the church at Pergamum (Rev. 2:12-17): Jesus' promises to come and "fight against them with the sword of my mouth." Let's face it. This is a declaration of war by Jesus against people in that church who harbor and don't repent of their false teachings and doctrines.
- To the church at Thyatira (Rev. 2:18-29): "I will cast her on a bed of suffering, and I will make those who commit adultery with her suffer intensely, unless they repent of her ways. I will strike her children dead. Then all the churches will know that I am he who searches hearts and minds, and I will repay each of you according to your deeds." What were her deeds? It was tolerating their teacher Jezebel and her teachings by which "she misleads my servants."
- To the church at Sardis (Rev. 3:1-6): "But if you do not wake up, I will come like a thief, and you will not know at what time I will come to you." Sardis had a reputation for being alive but was actually dead. It may have had a thriving program, strong organization, and many members, but it was spiritually dead to the reality of Christ, the greater Jesus. The bottom line is, it did

not meet God's standards to be *a Church*. Those in Sardis (and all the other churches) who would not repent of these ways would come under the judgment of this type of promised coming of Jesus (one you do not want to have happen to you).

- To the church at Philadelphia (Rev. 3:7-13): only praise and encouragement to "hold on to what you have, so that no one will take your crown." Who might have taken their crown? "Those who are of the synagogue of Satan" who might come into their church with their false teachings and idolatrous practices.
- To the church at Laodicea (Rev. 3:14-22): "I know your deeds, that you are neither cold nor hot. I wish you were either one or the other! So, because you are lukewarm—neither hot nor cold—I am about to spit you out of my mouth." This last church of Laodicea is perhaps the most vivid picture of a castaway church. That's why Jesus threatens to spit them out of his mouth because of their lukewarmness. The King James Version's "spew you out of my mouth" more accurately captures the revulsion Jesus feels toward this rebellious church. It implies a sudden, violent expulsion of something that is sickening to the taste, i.e., vomiting. Nothing in Scripture seems so repulsive to God as people who have a form of godliness but deny his power (2 Tim. 3:5; Jer. 6:20). And, "no man, having put his hand to the plough, and looking back, is fit for the kingdom of God," Jesus said (Luke 9:62 KJV).

QUESTION: How would you and your church hold up today under this level of scrutiny from the greater Jesus Himself? Many theologians maintain that these seven churches symbolically represent Jesus' Church as a whole throughout the world at that time and from that time on, i.e., "the whole Church in every age."[9] If this is correct, it means all the above admonitions, rewards, and judgment consequences therein stated and threatened are totally relevant for us, individually and collectively, in our churches, today—does it not?

And make no mistake; this is a real battle. That's why I maintain that both the individual believer and churches are the location today of "Armageddon" and "the battle on the great day of God Almighty" (Rev. 16:14).

The good news for those believers who repent and overcome is they do not suffer the terrible fates the non-repenters and non-overcomers are promised. For those who hear his knock and open the door, He promises: "I will come in and eat with him, and he with me" (Rev. 3:20). He promises that overcomers will "eat from the tree of life" (Rev. 2:7), "not be hurt at all by the second death" (Rev. 2:11), will be made "a pillar in the temple of my God. . . . will write on him the name of my God and the name of the city of my God, the new Jerusalem" (Rev. 3:12), be given "some hidden manna" and "a white stone with a new name written on it, known only to him who receives it" (Rev. 2:17). They will be given "authority over the nations" and will receive "the morning star" (Rev. 2:26, 28). They will be "dressed in white" and not have their names erased from the book of life (Rev. 3:5), and they will receive the "right to sit with me [Jesus] on my [his] throne" (Rev. 3:21). These seven letters and messages in Revelation 2 and 3 clearly imply that those who don't hear his knock, repent, and overcome, do not receive any of those promises, blessings, and privileges. Even worse, He fights against them. And all this is in the Church and here and now. Once again, this place of assembly is, most likely, the modern-day location and ongoing reality of "Armageddon" and "the battle on the great day of God Almighty."

This identification means these promised judgments apply today. Like Ananias and Sapphira in the Book of Acts, who want to be identified with their fellowship but "lied to the Holy Spirit" (Acts 5:1-11). Sure, they were going through all the motions publicly, but they were not willing to pay the price, to yield themselves totally to God. That deceptive couple became subject to the wrath of God and paid the ultimate price.

The good news for those believers who repent and overcome is they do not suffer the terrible fates the non-repenters and non-overcomers are promised.

One of Jesus' first actions at the opening of his public ministry was to cleanse the Temple (John 2:13-17). Guess what? Many of his temples today still need cleansing and He's still in the cleansing and purifying mode. And God's judgments always start with his people (1 Pet. 4:17). Nowadays, his people are the Church and, more specifically, individuals within the churches (see Rev. 11:1-2; Heb. 12:5-6). Why is this still so? It's because only purified and spiritually alive Christians can advance the kingdom of God against the kingdoms of this world in both the Church and in the world (Rev. 11:15b).

The bottom line of all these judgment threats is, those people in God's Church who refuse to repent and overcome those things Christ's has against them lose their identity as the people of God and suffer these judgments.

God's Battle Plan

The Revelation makes it clear that this battle rages on (Rev. 10:10-11). If you don't believe it yet, look around at some of the believers in your church, former believers, or some churches you know about. Furthermore, this prophecy outlines a battle plan for fighting and winning. Christians are not merely to repent and overcome and then sit idly by as spectators and watch the conflict; they are to engage and overcome the enemy within themselves, within their church, and out in the world. These are our marching orders if we desire to be considered by Christ as an overcomer.

In order to fight and win this ongoing battle, we believers shall need the same supernatural and spirit-dimension power exhibited in the book of Acts and by those in Thessalonica (1 Thess. 1:4-8). We shall have to be dressed in white robes of righteousness (Rev. 19:8) and do "the works of Jesus" and "even greater works" (John 14:12; Rev. 2:26 KJV). We shall have to overcome much opposition, human and superhuman, "by the blood of the Lamb and by the word or their testimony," and by not loving "their lives so much as to shrink from death" (Rev. 12:11). Yes, this is a real battle. And according to the greater Jesus, Christians and their churches are its primary and first-and-foremost battleground.

To prove this, start doing the works of Jesus in your church and see what happens. Why? It's because that's where the battle line is drawn—in the boundary between the material realm and the spirit realm. This battle line was drawn there in the Gospel era (John 10:31-32), during the period of Acts and the Epistles (Acts 4:7; 1 Cor. 12:1ff), and it is drawn there today. It is drawn between those who are lukewarm for God and those who are red hot, between those who walk in the flesh and those walking in the spirit (Rom. 8:1, i.e., "who do not live according to the sinful nature but according to the Spirit"—this later phrase is a manuscript discrepancy left out of some Bible translations).

But the good news is, we can be more than conquerors! So let the trials, scourging, chastising, and woes come! The desolating sword of the Warrior-King cuts off those in his churches that will not serve Him as He requires. Yes, the sweet little baby Jesus is all grown up, ascended, and transformed into the greater Jesus. And it was He who said, "Do not suppose that I have come to bring peace to the earth. I did not come to bring peace, but a sword" (Matt. 10:34; also see Rev. 1:16).

Therefore, and as Hendriksen rightly maintains, "for this cause, Har-Magedon is the symbol of every battle in which, when the need is greatest and believers are oppressed, the Lord suddenly reveals His power in the interest of His distressed people and defeats the enemy."[10]

Spirit-realm Anatomy of This Ongoing Battle

End-time pundits love to terrify people with their talk about the beastly creatures of the Apocalypse. And who of us has not heard spine-tingling tales describing awesome physical displays of God's wrath? Countless sermons, books, movies, and dramas have played on such vivid, literalistic themes as:

- The ruthless "four horsemen of the Apocalypse."
- Giant locusts with stingers in their tails.
- A great red dragon chasing an expectant mother.
- Multi-headed beasts, one inflicting his dreaded mark on unsuspecting humans.
- The seductive, but deadly, Harlot—the great prostitute.
- The fiery-tailed dragon being cast down to earth.

What do all these things mean? Are they God's ways of showing us how vindictive He can be when He doesn't get his way? Were they written to give us a countdown to a future doomsday?

The answer is both: yes and no. Yes, all these fearful descriptions were applicable to Revelation's fulfillment in the events circa A.D. 70 in

Jerusalem. But they are also equally applicable to Revelation's ongoing relevance as the greater Jesus continues to confront these ongoing and spirit-realm/physical-realm entities and realities. In both regards, these fear-producing descriptions are visual parables about the spirit-realm activities behind the material world. To reduce them to single physical events and push them exclusively out into the future or back into the past is to miss their vital message for individuals and for Christ's Church today. It's a message about which most Christians are ignorant, to their detriment.

Whole books could be and have been written about each of the subjects listed above. Obviously, we cannot explain in the remainder of this chapter all the mysteries behind apocalyptic imagery—mysteries which have confounded theologians for two millennia. (I shall systematically address these and strip away more of the mythology surrounding these creatures and events of the Revelation and clarify, from the Scriptures, the spiritual and material significance of such symbols in my future book and commentary on Revelation tentatively titled, *The Scene Behind the Seen*).

. . . these fear-producing descriptions are visual parables about the spirit-realm activities behind the material world. . . . It's a message about which most Christians are ignorant, and to their detriment.

Nonetheless, and in concluding this chapter, let's take a brief behind-the-scene look at what the Bible further says about this so-called "Battle of Armageddon." We shall focus on two passages: Revelation 16:12-21 and 19:11-21. Please be forewarned, however, a proper understanding of these visions and images does not come simply through explanation, but by revelation (Eph. 1:17). And even though I can show you how the fallacy of reducing all the symbols to physical and material creatures and events serves only to limit ones understanding of the spiritual realities God has revealed through them, only the Holy Spirit can make them come alive for you.

Of course, there have always been battles. But if you really want to get a grasp of the expansiveness of this so-called "Battle of

Armageddon," let me suggest that you read Revelation chapters 16-19 in its entirety before reading the remainder of this chapter and our next chapter as well.

Remember, we have to think both spiritually and physically, not just one to the exclusion of the other.

Revelation 16:12-16

Verse 12: "The sixth angel poured out his bowl. . . ." *Angel* is more correctly translated *messenger*, and could refer to either an angel or a human saint. I favor the former understanding. Earlier, these bowls are called *the bowls of God's wrath*, (Rev. 16:1), and they represent the judgment of God in all its awesome fury. When God's messages are repeatedly ignored, the unrepentant face terrible consequences (Luke 10:12).

Verse 12: ". . . on the great river *Euphrates*. . . ." In the context, a literal reading of "Euphrates" makes no sense. Obviously, this is a spiritual symbol. It was recognized as the eastern boundary line of the Garden of Eden (Gen. 2:14) and of the Promised Land (Gen. 15:18; Deut. 11:24; 1 Chron. 5:9). Today I believe it represents the boundary line between the kingdom of God and the kingdoms of this world. That's because the kingdom of God is the inheritance of his New Covenant people (Matt. 25:34; Gal. 5:21; Jas. 2:5) and the anti-type (fulfillment) of the Promised Land (type) of the Old Covenant economy (Num. 26:53; 33:53; 34:29; Deut. 1:8, 38; 4:38). This river also represents the supernatural power source that sustains and energizes Babylon, the great prostitute, as we shall see in our next chapter. It contains demonic beings and forces that empower false doctrines, compromised beliefs, religious politics, human egos, and many other unsavory things. The Euphrates River stands in sharp contrast to the crystal clear "river of the water of life . . . flowing from the throne of God and of the Lamb" through the Holy City, the New Jerusalem (Rev. 22:1-2).

Verse 12: ". . . and its water was dried up. . . ." With modern technology—tanks, troops, and artillery parachuted from airplanes, and missiles traveling thousand of miles—drying up a physical river would be a totally unnecessary step in preparation for a battle. The statement implies that God has to dry up Babylon's polluted power source before a successful onslaught against his enemies can take place.

Verse 12: ". . . to prepare the way. . . ." The dried-up river bed represents the boundary line between the material and the supernatural, where the battle rages. Further, this is something God does. Satan cannot launch a successful attack against Christ's true Church or against the saints who have overcome and are living inside the boundary.

Verse 12: ". . . for the kings from the East." These may or may not be literal, earthly rulers. More likely, these kings are overcoming saints who have been purified by the letters, seals, and trumpets, given white robes of righteousness, and stamped with the seal of God. These saints go out to engage the enemy and lay hold of the kingdom of God by force (Matt. 11:12; Luke 16:16). The fact that these kings come from the East symbolizes that they come from God. In prophetic writings, God always comes from the East—from the direction of the rising sun (see for instance, Matt. 24:27).

Verse 13: "Then I saw three evil spirits that looked like frogs. . . ." These are demonic, spirit-realm beings (and/or forces) stationed by Satan in the boundary line to ward off all attacks against his domain, i.e., the beast system and the great prostitute. They represent the same spirit-realm reality Jesus encountered when He dealt with the demons and evil spirits in people of the Gospel era. It's the dark side of Revelation—evil spirit realm beings deceiving, controlling, and energizing human beings and their institutions (including churches)—in order to persecute and kill the blood-washed saints who dare exhibit the testimony of Jesus.

Verse 13: ". . . they came out of the mouth of the dragon, out of the mouth of the beast and out of the mouth of the false prophet." The blasphemous words of the unholy trio—Satan, the beast system, and the great prostitute—release the evil spirits (and fight against the true Church and those in it). Since Satan and his cohorts are spirits, they have to work through physical beings and material systems (Matt.8:30-31). And arguably, the human action that most effectively releases demonic power is the spoken word.

Verse 14: "They are spirits of demons performing miraculous signs. . . ." These might be human actions (good works) that are so great they seem miraculous. The term *miraculous signs*, however, implies that they are supernatural feats performed by superhuman forces working through boundary dwellers (people who are close but won't cross on over into the kingdom of God). Make no mistake about it, the Bible contains many indications that evil spirits can perform miracles (Acts 16:16-19; Eph. 6:12). It is the way they gain credibility for their agents—the boundary dwellers. Challenge their human agents and these demons become formidable enemies (Acts 16:19).

Verse 14: ". . . and they go out to the kings of the whole world. . . ." These boundary dwellers, operating in evil spirit-realm power, become Satan's messengers to warn that an invasion is coming (just as the overcomers, symbolized as trumpets and angels, become God's messengers by proclaiming the Word of God and doing the works of Jesus). "The kings of the whole world" may symbolize masses of people, and not just their rulers.

Verse 14: ". . . to gather them for that battle. . . ." No negotiated peace treaty will result from this war. Any effort by Jesus to invade the beastly world system or the idolatrous great prostitute is sure to meet with strong resistance—both human and demonic (John 9:1-34).

Verse 14: ". . . on the great day of God Almighty." As we have seen, the day of the Lord is a prophetic symbol for the ongoing comings of the greater Jesus to an individual, a group, a nation, or a church. The context and wording of this phrase implies that Jesus comes to judge the individuals in churches as well as a church itself.

Verse 15: "Behold I come like a thief!'" He comes suddenly and without warning. He comes to fight against evildoers who accept the mark of ownership (the name or number) of the beast system. He comes to pour out his wrath on those in the Church who have refused to heed warnings of the letters, the seals, and the trumpets (messages).

Verse 15: "Blessed is he who stays awake and keeps his clothes with him, so that he many not go naked and be shamefully exposed." He also comes to bless those who have his seal and are clothed in white garments—the righteous acts of the saints. "Stays awake and keeps his clothes with him" serves as a solemn reminder of two things: (1) that it is very easy to get lulled to sleep spiritually and lose your righteous clothing to the beast system and the great prostitute (Matt. 26:35-45); and (2) that the real danger of slipping into unrighteousness is being caught spiritually naked before God (Gen. 3:8-10). In Genesis, the consequence of being shamefully exposed was exile from Eden. But in the Revelation the consequence is being cut down by the sword of Jesus.

Verse 16: "Then they [the demon-empowered boundary dwellers] gathered the kings together to the place that in Hebrew is called Armageddon." Again, the ongoing (Idealist) application of the term *Armageddon* is a spiritual reference signifying where the battle takes place—within the individual believers and in churches.

The verses which follow (vv. 17–21) give a vivid, symbolic description of the terrible devastation that Christ and his warriors inflict upon the unfaithful and idolatrous, prostitute, Babylon the Great. Using spiritual symbols like history's worst earthquake, fierce thunderstorms, and giant hailstones, John says that God gives Babylon "the cup filled with the wine of the fury of his wrath." This is no slap on the wrist; it is open warfare and total defeat.

So complete is this devastation that we'll devote our next chapter to the fall of "Mystery Babylon the Great the Mother of Prostitutes and of the Abominations of the Earth" (Rev. 17:5).

Personal Dimensions of Armageddon

21st-century Christians make a big deal of the Church as an organized structure, but the historical Jesus said very little about it. In fact, He mentioned the church only twice in all four Gospels. Both times He was talking to and about individuals.

His first statement about the Church came in response to Peter's receiving a personal revelation that Jesus was "the Christ, the Son of the living God" (Matt. 16:16). He told Peter that it was upon the "rock" of this truth—personal revelation of Jesus' lordship—that He would "build my church" (Matt. 16:18). He went on to give Peter (and all who receive this personal revelation) the "keys of the kingdom of heaven," which includes the power to bind and loose spirit-realm forces (Matt. 16:19).

In his only other reference, Jesus talked about one individual sinning against another, and ordered that the offender be taken to the church only as a last resort. "If he refuses to listen even to the church, treat him as you would a pagan or a tax collector," He commanded (Matt. 18:17). In other words, consider him a part of Satan's kingdom (the world), whose mark he bears, and not a part of God's kingdom (with the seal of God upon him).

Again, He went on to talk about binding and loosing spirit-realm forces on the earth. Then, He made his famous promise, "For where two or three come together in my name, *there I am with them*" (Matt. 18:20, emphasis added). So Jesus was promising to come in his spirit-realm reality and, as the greater Jesus, whenever and wherever two or more people gather in his name.

21st-century Christians make a big deal of the Church as an organized structure, but the historical Jesus said very little about it.

All this doesn't mean that Jesus feels the Church is insignificant. Such a view would be inconsistent with other New Testament Scriptures. But it does mean that Jesus thinks of his Church, not as a merely human organization, but as a vital part of Himself—a spiritual organism of which He is the head. This collection of individuals is to be the earthly instrument of his heavenly kingdom. His kingdom and his true Church are all parts of the same spirit-realm/physical-realm reality, "the body of Christ" (1 Cor. 12:27).[11]

That's why the Revelation is addressed to each person within the Church. Hence, and once again, the battle for the kingdom wages, first and foremost, within individual believers and within the Church. And his comings bring blessings and rewards or precipitate "the battle on the great day of God Almighty." Christ Himself, the greater Jesus, comes and fights against those in his churches who hold to false doctrines, unrighteousness, and idolatry, and submit to evil spirit-realm forces operating within and through individuals in that church.

Only a remnant of Christians—those who repent and overcome—will cross over the boundary line and enter into the kingdom of God (see Acts 14:22 for instance). That remnant of overcomers will be protected from and become a part of God's ongoing judgment of that particular church as well as the world.

Of course, human words and logic alone cannot explain this ongoing spirit-realm/physical realm dynamic and reality; as far as I'm concerned, much of this still is in the arena of mystery. But a greater understanding only comes through a personal revelation of and a personal relationship with the greater Jesus as He is today, as well as from personal experience in fighting this battle, as I'm sure some of you can so attest. Bystanders, however, don't have a clue about the depth and breadth of this conflict, some or much of which they may be experiencing but do not know or understand what is happening.

The Rider on the White Horse Rides Again: Revelation 19:11-16

The symbolism of Revelation 1 has a definite connection with the pouring out of the sixth and seventh bowls of wrath. Most end-times teachers correctly identify this as the beginning of the so-called Battle of Armageddon.

But let's look more closely at Revelation 19:11-16. As we discovered in Chapter 4, no one else in history has ever been like the rider on the white horse. The names and descriptions of the rider make it clear that He is Jesus Christ. The rider is called "Faithful and true" (Rev. 19:11), and "his name is the Word of God" (see John 1:1). He even has a name that "no one but he himself knows," signifying that certain aspects of his spirit-realm reality are beyond human comprehension. "He judges and makes war" (Rev. 19:11); "His eyes are like blazing fire" (Rev. 19:12); "He is dressed in a robe dipped in blood" (Rev. 19:13); "the armies of heaven were following him" (Rev. 19:14); and "Out of his mouth comes a sharp sword with which to strike down the nations" (Rev. 19:15). There can be no doubt that this is the greater Jesus Christ in all his present, ascended, exalted, glorified, transformed, transfigured, transcendent, apocalyptic, crowned, cosmic form, and spirit-realm reality. This is the Jesus who comes in many wondrous ways still today.

But in verse 12, a very interesting set of symbols begins to emerge, suggesting that there may be even more to this rider's identity. Remember, these are physical symbols of ongoing, spirit-realm/physical-realm realities.

First, John says of the rider on the white horse that "on his head are *many crowns*" (emphasis added). Earlier, we were told that Jesus had only one crown on his head (Rev. 14:14); now He has many. What has happened?

In Chapter 4 we stated that the "many crowns on his head" may symbolize, as McKenzie suggests, the "many realms in his universal kingship"[12] as the "Supreme Ruler."[13] But now let's add this perspective. Following "the wedding supper of the Lamb" (Rev. 19:6-10), the bride of Christ (the righteous saints) has lifted her veil and has been united with Him. Christ and his true Church have become one (see Gen. 2:24; John 17:20-21). Therefore, what was represented by one crown may now be represented by many crowns as overcoming saints are conjoined with Him.

Second, in verse 16 we are told that "on his robe and on his thigh he has this name written: KING OF KINGS AND LORD OF LORDS." We can understand why He might have a monogram on his robe of righteousness. But why would He engrave the name on his thigh? As we saw in Chapter 4, one possibility is that, in the thick of a battle, foot soldiers might confuse the identity of a rider on a horse. The name on his thigh would be at eye level—easily recognizable by anyone. But another possibility is it may symbolize that the righteous saints have become bone of his bones and flesh of his flesh (Gen. 2:23). Thus, his identity with them is complete. The saints are actually riding with Him in the battle and share in his triumph. In other words, He has "made us to be a kingdom and priests," to reign, rule, and serve with Him (Rev. 1:6; 5:10).

Third, verse 14 states that "the armies of heaven were following him, riding on white horses and dressed in fine linen, white and clean." Note that the armies are *of* heaven, not *from* heaven. Nowhere does it say that this army comes down from heaven. Jesus used this same terminology to describe his disciples as *in* the world but not *of* the world, even as He was not *of* the world (John 17:16). If this understanding is correct, it means that the blood-washed saints on earth today belong to the armies of heaven. This is part of our enthronement as his people together with Him (More on this in Chapters 9 and 10). In other words, as Chilton acknowledged, this is the greater Jesus coming as the Lord and Judge over history and humankind "not to save, not to heal, but to destroy"[14]

Therefore, what was represented by one crown may now be represented by many crowns as we are conjoined with Him.

Notably, many Christians today would deny that "their" God or "their" Jesus would bring such calamities upon individual believers or upon even one of his churches. They claim "their" Jesus is the Good Shepherd and the God of mercy and reluctant to exercise his wrath because He loves his people. Hence, Christ, too, is designated as the one who only loves us. But how does this view hold up when conjoined with the violent apocalyptic imagery in the Revelation and elsewhere in the Bible? Consider a few of the many judgments God placed upon his people in the past who were unfaithful, disobedient, and idolatrous according to the Law. And remember that these and other judgments are "examples" for us that the Apostle Paul cited "to keep us from setting our hearts on evil things as they did" (1 Cor. 10:6):

> *If she has defiled herself and been unfaithful to her husband, then when she is made to drink the water that brings a curse, it will go into her and cause bitter suffering; her abdomen will swell and her thigh waste away, and she will become accursed among her people* (Num. 5:27).

> *So the Lord plagued the people because of what they did with the calf which Aaron made* (Exod. 32:35).

> *But if you will not listen to me and carry out all these commands, and if you reject my decrees and abhor my laws and fail to carry out all my commands and so violate my covenant, then I will do this to you: I will bring upon you sudden terror, wasting diseases and fever that will destroy your sight and drain away your life. You will plant seed in vain, because your enemies will eat it. I*

will set my face against you so that you will be defeated by your enemies; those who hate you will rule over you, and you will flee even when no one is pursuing you.

If after all this you will not listen to me, I will punish you for your sins seven times over. I will break down your stubborn pride and make the sky above you like iron and the ground beneath you like bronze. Your strength will be spent in vain, because your soil will not yield its crops, not will the trees of the land yield their fruit.

If you remain hostile toward me and refuse to listen to me, I will multiply your afflictions seven times over, as your sins deserve" (Lev. 26:13-21).

The Old Testament contains many more passages that speak of God pouring out his wrath on his unfaithful and disobedient people. There is no doubt the Church has been reluctant time and again to communicate, even to acknowledge, this aspect of the Godhead and his divine judgment. But please especially note this relevancy factor. Leviticus in the Old Testament speaks of four sevenfold judgments (Lev. 26:18, 21, 23-24, 27-28). The Revelation in the New Testament also speaks of four sevenfold judgments (Rev. 6:1-2; 8:6; 10:4; 15:1). This corollary or correspondence is not coincidental because, "I the Lord do not change" (Mal. 3:6a). What has changed in the New Covenant economy is the greater Jesus is now the Person of the Godhead Who implements these divine judgments against God's unfaithful, disobedient, and idolatrous people (John 5:22).

Hence, in the New Testament we find this statement regarding the ongoing reality of these types of divine judgment in association with taking the communion (the Lord's Supper) "in an unworthy manner" . . .

Therefore, whoever eats the bread or drinks the cup of the Lord in an unworthy manner will be guilty of sinning against the body and blood of the Lord. A man ought to examine himself before he eats of the bread and drinks of the cup. For anyone who eats and drinks without recognizing the body of the Lord eats and drinks judgment on himself. That is why many among you are weak and sick, and a number of you have fallen asleep. But if we judged ourselves, we would not come under judgment. When we are judged by the Lord, we are being disciplined so that we will not be condemned with the world (1 Cor. 11:27-32).

Likewise, for adding or subtracting from "words of the prophecy this book" [the Revelation]:

If anyone adds anything to them, God will add to him the plagues described in this book. And if anyone takes words away from this book of prophecy, God will take away from him his share in the tree of life and in the holy city, which are described in this book (Rev. 22:18-19; also Deut. 4:2).

These are not idle threats! They are totally relevant today. And many believers, in my opinion, have been guilty of either this adding or subtracting and/or both (see again my story in Chapter 2, pp-75-76).

What we Christians must better and more fully realize is, we are in a battle—a spirit-realm/physical-realm battle—whether we like it or not. And there is no demilitarized or neutral zone. Part of this battle goes on inside us and inside our own churches and is based upon our faithfulness and obedience (or lack thereof) for believing and doing what Jesus has commanded us to believe and do—things most of us are falling far short of. And the Revelation is telling us that there are consequences to pay.[15]

Armageddon Now and Forever

Face it! The so-called Battle of Armageddon—actually "the battle on the great day of God Almighty"—has been going on for a long time and is going on right now! It takes place both within you and within the Church. It was at hand in the 1st century; it has been at hand ever since; it is at hand now; it will be at hand in the future. This is no time to hang out around the boundary line between the kingdom(s) of this world and the kingdom of God. You can get eaten alive by the evil forces and human counterparts stationed there.

So, what should we do? We must bind up the evil spirit-realm forces that seek to control our lives and compromise Christ's Church and come into the full realities and truths of the greater Jesus. We must overcome the evil within ourselves, and then engage and overcome Christ's enemies within his Church and throughout the world. As we shall continue to see, that is the duty and responsibility for everyone who professes the name of Christ. Anything less is less. And anything less is irresponsible and comes with consequences—huge consequences.

This means:

> We are to hear his knock and open the door to our hearts so the unveiled Christ can come into us and eat with us.
> We are to enter into his supernatural reality though praise, worship, and righteous acts (including warfare).
> We are to allow the Lamb to break all the seals and open every aspect of our lives to the judgment of God, conquering all the unrighteousness within us so that we can overcome.
> We are to hear and respond to his messages (trumpets) calling us into the battle which rages both within the Church and in the world.
> We are to act as kings and priests of his kingdom, sounding the trumpets and pouring out bowls of his wrath by proclaiming his Word and doing the works and greater works of Jesus upon those boundary-dwelling believers who refuse to hear, repent, and come into the kingdom.
> We are to bind up and rule over evil spirits that are fighting against God's kingdom within his Church and in the world.

In short, you and I are part of the Body of Christ, and we are to join with the greater Jesus to co-fight in and co-win "the battle of the great day of Almighty God" within us, within the Church, and in the world. If we do, we have his promise that He will place his name and seal upon us, so that we cannot be touched by the second death (Rev. 2:11). Instead, we will receive "the crown of life" (Rev. 2:10), so that we can rule and reign with Him forever and someday hear the words "Well done, good and faithful servant" (Matt. 25:21, 23).

Face it! The so-called battle of Armageddon—actually "the battle on the great day of God Almighty" —has been going on for a long time and is going on right now!

How can we do all that? We can do it only if we ride a white horse with Him and live daily in the supernatural power of the unveiled and revealed greater Jesus. That becomes possible when we are eating "the wedding supper of the Lamb" with Him and of Him.

But, as we shall discover in our next chapter, there will be more major opposition from a source and people we know and love—and all because of prostitution—major prostitution.

Chapter 8

He Plagues the Great Prostitute

Warning: This chapter may be the most provocative, challenging, and controversial of this book or any chapter I have ever written. You may be shocked. Others will be amazed. A few of you may become so upset you throw this book across the room. Some will not be surprised at all. Many may object and say it's too harsh. A few will complain it's not harsh enough. But please know that I, too, am as guilty as anyone in some of this. I only pray that in all this God will get the glory, eyes and hearts will be opened, and his will done more increasingly "on earth as it is in heaven" (Matt. 6:10b).

That said, what do all these entities have in common: Rome, New York City, every city of the world, the world's system (empire), secular government, the United Nations, the Roman Catholic Church, the World Council of Churches, a New World Order, and a One-World Government?

The answer is: each has been dubbed by some interpreter of the Book of Revelation and at various times in human history as the identity of "Mystery Babylon the Great the Mother of Prostitutes and of the Abominations of the Earth" (Rev. 17:5). No doubt, the immense power, influence, and entitlements in the world, as well as the self-indulged, arrogant, boastful, prideful, abusive, and idolatrous practices of each of these above entities account for this negative notoriety.

But in my opinion another worldwide institution in today's world better fits Revelation's portrayal of this great prostitute.

First and foremost, let's recall from Chapter 3, pp-95-96, that a strong case can be made that this "Babylon" in Revelation's "what-must-soon-take-place" fulfillment (Rev. 1:1b; 22:6b) was 1st-century Jerusalem and its apostate Judaism. At that time and previously, Israel (actually, only Judah, the two southern tribes) was not only God's people and the carrier of his will (the Old Covenant system), she was also God's wife and expected to be faithful to her covenant with God. Instead, she played the harlot (Deut. 31:16-18; Isa. 1:21; Jer. 2:20; Ezek. 16:14-15; Hos. 9:1). Consequently, this Babylon became the unfaithful wife and greatest enemy of God's emerging new people—his new bride (Rev. 21:2, 9-10) and the new carrier of his will (the New Covenant system – Matt. 21:43; Heb. 8:13; 9:9-10; 1 Pet. 2:9; Rev. 1:6: 5:9-10). (See again Chapter 6, p-196.)

This first Babylon utilized the power of the pagan Roman Empire (Revelation's beast – Rev. 13:1)[1] to try and stamp out Christianity until her divorce, destruction, and desolation circa A.D. 70. In this chapter, we shall not be discussing this first Babylon, since our focus here is more on the greater Jesus, what He is like and doing today. But please be assured, everything covered in this chapter totally and fully applies to that Babylon back then and there—as Israel (both the northern and southern tribes) had been playing the harlot, God's unfaithful wife, for centuries and ultimately rejected its Messiah, which was the last straw.[2] The two questions we will address herein are: (1) Who is this great prostitute today? (2) What is her contemporary significance?

As we shall see, the identity of this Babylon in Revelation's ongoing applications and relevance is a different story, matter, and entity. Notably, this second entity was also at hand in that same 1st century time period, has been at hand in each succeeding century, and is certainly at hand for us today. Hence, this great prostitute has proven to be "a durable metaphor"[3] with "expansive potential."[4]

So, what modern-day and worldwide institution best fits the descriptions given throughout Revelation 17 and 18? Who is this great prostitute, this great enemy of God's rule on our planet after biblical Judaism's complete destruction and desolation circa A.D. 70? As you will see, there are significant parallels between and equivalencies with the Jewish Pharisees and Sadducess back then and with the people of this second Babylon entity. Surprisingly, for some, these largely follow in the same behavioral pattern of unfaithfulness, disobedience, and idolatry.

When John saw who she was in his day and time, he wrote, "I was greatly astonished" (Rev. 17:6b). I think you will be greatly astonished when you see who she is today. I was. Why? It's because she is clothed in garments of respectability and enjoys much social approval. She is also greatly revered by many and yet feared and hated by the kings and peoples of many nations who endow her with great power and wealth.

> **... the identity of this Babylon in Revelation's ongoing applications and relevance is a different story, matter, and entity.**

So who is this seductive woman the world both loves and hates?

To determine her present-day identity, let's take a highlighted tour of Revelation chapters 17 and 18. We shall explore fourteen textual clues (there are more) along with my comments and the comments of others. No doubt, some of you could add your own comments from your experiences with this great prostitute. But others of you may not be particularly persuaded or may dispute some of my specifics. I certainly don't claim to have a corner on the market or on all truth on this. But if I have only a part of it right, it deserves our attention. Thus, I suggest we use this verse as our plumb line: "by their fruits you will recognize them." / "You will know them by their fruits" (Matt. 7:20 NIV / NAS). And, to reuse but rephrase a popular saying from a few years ago, "If the fruits/clues fit, we must convict."[5] Agreed?

I invite you, as Revelation 17 and 18 invite its reader, to confront this Mystery Babylon today with an informed, prophetic, and apocalyptic edge versus capitulating and selling out to her, knowingly or unknowingly. The inspired scriptures we shall be looking at recognize and warn that we are all susceptible and vulnerable to being seduced into committing fornication with this great prostitute. But Scripture also warns that being joined to a prostitute is always dangerous and leads to trouble and demise (see Prov. 5:1-5; 7:1-27). Involvement with her can also be compared to the so-called (but arguable) illustration of a frog being placed in a pot of water and slowly boiled to death. This great prostitute can slowly seduce you and draw you in before you know what's happening. Again, I have been involved with her, and in many different forms, since I was a child. So beware.

Before we begin, I recommend that you read Revelation 17, 18, and 19:1-3 for yourself.

Fourteen Textual Clues

Clue #1 – "who sits on many waters. . . . The waters you saw, where the prostitute sits, are peoples, multitudes, nations, and languages" (Rev. 17:1, 15). These two verses immediately let us know that this prostitute is a worldwide institution. To sit on means to hold down and control. When my four-year-younger brother and I were growing up, we'd sometimes have tussles and I would end up sitting on him—holding him down and controlling him. He didn't like it one bit. But there was nothing he could do about it, until Mom came along. Then, guess who got punished.

Next, let's recognize that similar language is employed in Revelation 5:9 for those purchased by Jesus' blood, i.e., "from every tribe and language and people and nation." It is also used in Revelation 10:11 regarding those John was commanded to "prophesy again about." (for three other uses see: Rev. 7:9; 13:7; 14:6). If this language is consistently employed throughout Revelation (I believe it is), there can be little doubt what or who this worldwide institution has to be in Revelation's ongoing application and Idealist relevancy. As we shall continue to explore, I believe, at the least, it describes some of today's institutional churches. But it may be more pervasive than that. The New Testament Church is supposed to be God's new bride and his faithful wife. But some in the today's Church seem, once again, to be playing the harlot and seeking conformity and control by sitting on their people instead of allowing freedom and encouraging life.

If my tentative identification herein is correct, then this great prostitute is also the modern-day location of God's *Har Mo'edh*, his "mount of assembly" (of his people), his *Ar himdah* "city of desire," his *Har migdo* "fruitful mountain," and his *megiddow* "rendezvous" – from *gadad*, to crowd, assemble, gather, i.e., "Armageddon." That means it is also where "the battle on the great day of God Almighty" (Rev. 16:14) is currently being fought (see again Chapter 7, p-225).

Let's see if this tentative identification holds up or breaks down throughout our remaining thirteen textual clues.

Clue #2 – "With her the kings of the earth committed adultery and the inhabitants of the earth were intoxicated with the wine of her adulteries" (Rev. 17:2). How did this woman, personified as the great prostitute, become a harlot? As was true with apostate biblical Judaism in Bible times, it began with the apostasy of her leaders for the purpose of forming religious-political alliances with heathen nations (the Roman Empire) around her in order to do commerce. Instead of turning to and trusting God for help, these leaders led the people astray and turned to and trusted in the "kings of the earth" (the rulers) who "gather together against the Lord and against his Anointed One" (Psa. 2:2). How could they do this, you ask? They, too, were intoxicated and seduced and could not and did not think straight or right.

The adultery spoken of here does not, however, refer to sexual activity. It's a metaphor for corruption and idolatry. Howard-Brook and Gwyther appropriately elaborate that this adultery conveys "the image of . . . infidelity to one's covenant partner—that is, YHWH. It also suggests the cause of such infidelity [is]: seduction."[6] Furthermore, this adultery results in "the selling out of the radical message of YHWH to the practices of the people who lived around them."[7] These authors further emphasize that "people usually do not enter rationally and deliberately into a situation of evil; rather, they are seduced into it."[8] Indeed, the attractions of Babylon today are powerful, intoxicating, and seductive. Like what?

For starters, how about some Christians worshipping idols like a preoccupation with their church building, their celebrity pastor, their church's music, their denomination's particular version of the faith, or their own social fellowship? Of course, these focal points are not necessarily wrong or evil in and of themselves. But they can become idols that we slavishly follow, adore, and allow to usurp the place of the greater Jesus, his kingdom, and the practice of the genuine Christian faith. When this happens it produces what we might call "church people" who do not take Christianity seriously but, instead, practice a much lesser, partial, and shallow version of our authentic faith. In actuality, it's a diminished, civilized, and sanitized version we might term "churchianity." It produces masses of casual Christians (including me and most Christians I have known, sad to say) who are not doing a very good job of following in the footstep of Jesus and our 1st-century ancestors.

Additionally revealing is how some churches today go to extremes to create an artificial atmosphere and experience of spirituality. I call it synthetic spirituality. During worship services (productions or performances) they utilize special devices and stage effects such as lighting, darkness, smoke or fog, hi-tech screens and enhanced audio systems to accentuate their music and messages. Of course, these hi-tech devices and effects are not wrong or evil in and of themselves. They do become deceptive and wrong, in my opinion, when we become comfortable in substituting the synthetic for authentic, i.e., while serving up a watered-down, diluted, devalued, diminished, depreciated, and degraded message and practicing a lesser version of the Christian faith than what we see modeled, preached, and practiced in the New Testament. Hence, this hyped-up but degraded departure from original and genuine Christianity can only be called for what it is: seduction, prostitution, and adultery that produces a temporary intoxication. Where am I wrong on this?

In a recent *Wall Street Journal* article, Naomi Schaefer Riley cites a Barna Group statistic that "church engagement falls by as much as 43% between the ages of 18 and 29." Next, she highlights the methodology by which "40 or so area churches" in Charlotte, N.C. are "trying to reach this demographic." She reports:

> In order even to get them in the door . . . churches have to offer "the wow factor." But the wow factor—expensive bands, charismatic preachers, elaborate social events—doesn't come cheap. What's more, many religious leaders worry that offering that kind of experience only encourages young people to think about "the attractional church," the kind of place you go for entertainment but not for any long-term commitment.

She further cites these two "downsides" that "the leaders try to steer clear of controversial issues (religious and political) that might divide their sponsoring churches" and that this competitive approach—"hipper music or a better social scene" is considered "sheep-stealing" by some other churches.[9]

Thomas E. Bergler is more pointed in a recent article in *Christianity Today* titled, "When Are We Going to Grow Up?" and subtitled, "The juvenilization of American Christianity." Bluntly, he writes:

It began with the praiseworthy goal of adapting the faith to appeal to the young . . . . but it has sometimes ended with both youth and adults embracing immature versions of the faith. . . . Today many Americans of all ages not only accept a Christianized version of adolescent narcissism, they often celebrate it as authentic spirituality. God, faith, and the church all exist to help me with my problems. . . . we must conclude that juvenilization has revitalized American Christianity at the cost of leaving many individuals mired in spiritual immaturity.[10]

A friend of mine, who is a former praise and worship leader in his small charismatic church but who became disillusioned and left the Church entirely, lamented to me in a recent email about this supposed prostituting trend: "the altar rails are all gone now to make way for the instruments and amps and keyboards and drum sets and video screens covering our platforms and making them look like every OTHER rock show in town. We sing to each other, God is nowhere. . . . We know more 'about' God than ever before and have no clue what it means to walk into church Sunday morning and come face to face with Him. How can we? He ain't there!!!!!!"

Clue #3 – **"woman sitting on a scarlet beast that was covered with blasphemous names . . ." (Rev. 17:3).** I believe that this "sitting" depicts a mutual alliance, collusion, and dependency. So let's explore one major manifestation of this blasphemous dependency here in America, i.e., how this prostituting woman fornicates with the increasingly secular and anti-Christian government in a way that moves her further away from her faithful calling and the Lordship of Christ.[11]

(NOTE TO READER: I am indebted to the Alliance Defense Fund for much of the following content. For more, see ADF's website: www.alliancedefensefund.org).

To set the stage, the ADF notes on its "Religious Freedom" page:

Throughout our history, America has been a land defined by religious faith and freedom. Religious freedom is our first and most fundamental, God-given right deemed so precious that our Founding Fathers enshrined it in the U.S. Constitution.

So why is religious freedom under attack in America today?

For decades, the American Civil Liberties Union (ACLU) and other radical anti-Christian groups have been on a mission to eliminate public expression of our nation's faith and heritage. By influencing the government, filing lawsuits, and spreading the myth of the so-called 'separation of church and state,' the opposition has been successful at forcing its leftist agenda on Americans.

Their targeted attacks on religious freedom are more serious and widespread than you may realize. In courtrooms and schoolrooms, offices and shops, public buildings and even churches . . . those who believe in God are increasingly threatened, punished, and silenced.

History documents that the main reason America's forefathers came to this country was for religious freedom. Since they arrived on America's shores, pastors have been free to preach whatever they want, i.e., on any cultural, political, societal, or moral issue, and for or against any laws and political candidates, and the consequences thereof. Nothing was off limits. Every aspect of the society that needed addressed from a biblical perspective could be directly and boldly confronted without fear . . . until 1954. That's when this freedom was largely lost. That's also, I'm suggesting, when most of America's churches decided to sit on the scarlet beast (the U.S. government) and become dependent upon and controlled by it. Consequently, that prostituting alliance turned the name of their church into a blasphemous name. How so?

In 1954, then-Senator Lyndon Johnson sponsored and the U.S. Congress amended the U.S. tax code (501c3 organizations) to prohibit any speech supporting a political candidate by any tax-exempt charitable organization. That amendment specified that non-profit, tax-exempt entities of any type (including all churches) could not "participate in, or intervene in (including the publishing or distribution of statements), any political campaign on behalf of or in opposition to any candidate for public office."

Since this government intrusion into the affairs of the Church, the courts have upheld it and the IRS has steadfastly maintained that *any* speech by pastors about candidates for government office as well as upon a wide variety of moral, social, and political issues of the day can result in a loss of tax exemption and tax deductibility for that church.

Of course, ADF believes this blatant incursion to religious freedom was and is unconstitutional, censorship, and a violation of the so-called "separation of church and state." It also violates the First Amendment, which states that: "Congress shall make no law respecting an establishment of religion, or prohibiting the free exercise thereof, or abridging the freedom of speech, or of the press; or the right of the people to assemble, and to petition the Government for a redress of grievances."

> **Nothing was off limits. Every aspect of the society that needed addressed from a biblical perspective could be directly and boldly confronted without fear . . . until 1954.**

Regardless, the IRS has steadfastly interpreted this restriction to apply to a pastor's sermon from the pulpit—what he or she basically can and cannot say. And all churches must abide and comply whether they are or are not a 501c3 corporation, or risk losing their tax-exempt, tax-deductible status.

In other words, the Johnson Amendment trumped the First Amendment by requiring the government to monitor churches, to discriminate against speech, and to hamper the free exercise of religion—and all under the threat of losing tax exemption and deductibility status. Even worse, if possible, no Congress since Johnson's time has sought to repeal this unconstitutional and infringing amendment. Rather, they strengthened it in 1987 to clarify that the prohibition also applies to statements opposing candidates.

To top it all off, and according to the IRS itself,

> Each election cycle, the IRS reminds 501(c)(3) exempt organizations to be aware of the ban on political campaign activity. The IRS published its most recent reminder in a public news release which you can read here. [see endnote][12]

Once again, we must reemphasize, that prior to this 1954 amendment and since America's founding, churches and pastors have freely spoken for and against political candidates, as well as upon a wide variety of moral, social, and political issues of the day. But today, and armed with this 501c3 regulation and threatening ban, some anti-Christian groups are reportedly sending "spies" into churches to gather information and report infractions.

To their credit, ADF is trying to challenge these restrictions by either getting this amendment repealed by Congress and/or declared unconstitutional by the courts. Sadly, they report that prospects do not appear promising. And why not?

It seems most of America's churches today are content with the status quo and comfortable with keeping this ban in place. They would be uncomfortable challenging and changing it. As a rule, most of them are not inclined to support or oppose political candidates or get involved in partisan issues for fear of creating conflict and division within their own congregation and losing some members or even costing church leaders their jobs. Nor is it likely that enough support can be garnered in Congress for a repeal of the Johnson Amendment. The anti-Christian and secular forces supporting this ban are well-financed, well-organized, extremely aggressive, and increasingly hostile, all things most of today's institutional churches and most Christians are not.

The net effect of the Johnson tax-reform Amendment has been to intimidate and self-silence pastors and church leaders for fear of losing financial support. Nowadays, they fear IRS investigations (audits) and the possible loss of their church's tax-exempt, tax-deductibility status, as well as the threat of lawsuits from anti-Christian groups like Americans United, Americans for Separation of Church and State, and the American Civil Liberties Union. Some critics have termed this capitulation to government intervention as "hush money" or being "gagged."

ADF summarizes America's current situation this way:

> Churches have too long feared the loss of tax-exempt status. Rather than risk confrontation, pastors have self-censored their speech, ignoring blatant immorality in government and foregoing the opportunities to praise moral government leaders. Pastors who long to be relevant to society, to preach the Gospel in a way that has meaning in modern America, often studiously ignore much that goes on in politics lest they draw the attention of the IRS."[13]

The bottom line is: Sen. Johnson and Congress, beginning in 1954, throttled a once-powerful voice. As a result, we Christians here in America have now returned to what our forefathers in the faith left—being told what we can or cannot say and do in our churches. It is also, of course, just this sort of compromise with government authorities (the

Beast) that Jesus lambasted in his messages to the seven churches in Asia Minor (Rev. 2 and 3).

I agree with ADF that we American Christians need to wake up and take a stand against this blasphemous affiliation and our profane complacency with it. As these blatantly unconstitutional devices have browbeaten and driven most pastors and churches out of the public square, we have become increasingly less willing and able to speak the full truth of God's Word into our society. Hence, America's heritage of religious liberty has been and is steadily continuing to be stripped away to allow for a more anti-Christian, secular, and "tolerant" society. This is an example of the conversion process going the wrong way. Unfortunately, it also seems that most, if not all, American churches have been seduced and intoxicated into a spiritual stupor by and a political fornication with this governmental beast.

In my opinion, any church that has and/or is allowing this loss of religious freedom to occur because of this unscriptural accommodation with the "kings of the earth" (U.S. the federal government) is "sitting on a scarlet beast" and becoming a "blasphemous name," as warned about in Revelation 17 and 18. Giving up our God-given right of religious freedom, compromising our faithful calling and duty to be salt and light in the world, and succumbing to government intimidation to limit free and bold speech in an increasingly hostile culture must be called for what it is: seduction, prostitution, and adultery. And as quoted in Clue #2, it's once again "the selling out of the radical message of YHWH to the practices of the people who lived around them."[14]

Consequently, this sin of accommodation must make any church's name a name of blasphemy. In essence, they have made a deal with a blasphemous entity by agreeing not to criticize the almighty government, politicians, or anything political. Voluntarily, they have surrendered their First Amendment rights instead of fighting for them. And, once again, these churches, as well as the individuals in them, are the location of "Armageddon" today. They are the ones the greater Jesus has promised to come against, to fight, and to judge (Rev. 2 and 3).

If this insight into this clue is correct, to see a listing of these blasphemous names, open the Yellow Pages of your city's phone book to the C's and look under "Churches." Again, the names in and of themselves are not blasphemous. What makes them blasphemous is their accommodation with a blasphemous entity and resulting reductionistic and self-censored ministry. But there is much more to this blasphemy as we shall continue to see.

In other countries, we must mention, churches have undertaken similar and blasphemous accommodations. One only has to recall Nazi Germany and the capitulation of the Christian churches in that day and time. Despite this adulterous and hostile relationship, many governments court the church's favor for helping them keep the peace and to preserve their time and power in office. But eventually this fornication becomes a source of corruption, apostasy, and hate. More often than not, however, the Church has become infatuated with the pleasures and treasures of the world, resulting in a hardening of themselves against God and a compromising of the true faith—how it is preached, practiced, and perceived.

Clue #4 – "**the woman was dressed in purple and scarlet, and was glittering with gold, precious stones and pearls**" **(Rev. 17:4a).** Purple is the color of royalty and nobility (John 19:2, 5; Acts 16:14). Scarlet is the color of sins (see Isa. 1:18). Have you noticed some of the flamboyant ceremonial dress (ornate robes, capes, sashes, etc.) or $1,000 suits that some church leaders wear? Have you ever wondered why some further adorn themselves with ostentatious jewelry and/or with various other ceremonial paraphernalia (scepters, staffs, etc.) and parade around in a rather religious yet pompous display of formality, splendor, and ritual in front of the laity? Does this type of worship really glorify God or who? In my opinion, these audacious trappings are the symbols of office. They only glorify the office holder, distinguishing his or her high position and separating them from and setting them above the laity, i.e., the clergy/laity divide. What's more, it's another example of creating an atmosphere of synthetic spirituality.

Likewise, have you ever visited some of the grand cathedrals of Europe, which are now mostly museums? Or have you visited some of the impressive and lavishly adorned mega-churches in America and been wowed with their ornate structures and expensive furnishings?

Long ago, the Roman Catholic Church, as well as the Church of England, discovered that the physical building is the structure of power and control to hold people in subjection. Without a building, the clergy system could not hold sway. This system of clergy/laity separation, which was totally foreign to the vocabulary and life of Jesus' first followers and the early Church for its first three centuries, is what we have come to know today as the "institutional church system."

According to the Revelation, the great prostitute adorns herself to the hilt in order to call attention to herself and seduce "many waters" (people)—rather than to simply and humbly present herself as a follower of the Christ she claims to represent. To pay for these extravagances, many churches pound the tithing message (to be given to their church *only*). A few even engage in "name it and claim it" schemes, i.e. God will return the money you give to them back to you with an increase of 30, 60 or 100 fold, citing Matthew 13:8 and Mark 4:20. So what happens to the monies that are given?

. . . these audacious trappings are the symbols of office. They only glorify the office holder, distinguish his or her high position, and separate them from and set them above the laity, i.e., the clergy/laity divide.

According to the latest survey in *The State of Church Giving through 2009*, the average breakdown of all contributions received by churches in America in 2009 was: 85% spent on internal operations and 15% given to external missions and benevolences, with approximately a 2% portion of the latter going to overseas missions. This is a significant and downward change from 74% and 24%, respectively, in 1968.[15] The budgetary split at the mega-church I currently attend is 93% and 7%.

How do these latest church stewardship percentages strike you— between primarily being used for a church's own internal needs and much less going to the needs of others outside their congregations— pretty good, not bad, pretty poor, disturbing, pathetic, or "these statistics are deceiving and do not reflect the influence money spent internally can and does have externally?"[16]

In summarizing this survey report, the authors commented rather matter-of-factly that "for over 40 years, there has been a pronounced trend to turn inward on the part of congregations[17]. . . . particularly that portion spent beyond the local congregation, has been declining over four decades."[18] Others, on the other hand, who are quoted in Table 47 of this survey report and titled "Church Leaders Comment on the Lukewarm Church in the U.S.," are highly critical. Here's a sampling:[19]

> "I quickly found that the American church is a difficult place to fit in if you want to live out New Testament Christianity." (Francis Chan).

> "Look in the mirror. The Church, the bride of Christ, has been unfaithful. WE are at fault. We-collectively and individually-have chased after every idol the world has to offer. We have tried so hard to be relevant that we've become almost completely irrelevant. . . . there is nothing distinctive about us." (Chuck Colson)

> "What it clearly says to us is that no matter how much our people profess that they love Jesus, they love their money more." (Bryant Wright, president of the Southern Baptist Convention, commenting on the level of giving to missions).

This survey report concludes by citing "a 2010 Gallup poll [that] found seven in ten Americans felt that 'religion as a whole is losing its influence on American life'"[20] and that since "Jesus took the disciples' attachment to himself and transferred it to the 'least' [Matt. 25:31-46]. The church in the U.S. has a choice about the degree to which the least will become our increased priority."[21]

John A.T. Robinson is perhaps even more introspective. He believes that the "real problem" is a product of the church having "become heavily institutionalized, with a crushing investment in maintenance. . . . It is saddled with a plant and a programme (sic) beyond its means, so that it is absorbed in problems of supply and preoccupied with survival."[22] In other words, American religion—especially Christianity—has become big business.

Diane Butler Bass further elaborates in her book, *Christianity After Religion*, that "denominations offered religion as the product . . . . [and] church executives became too distanced from the regular folks . . . . [and] the business of the church replaced the mission of the church." What has been the result of this shift? Bass states, "Slowly, then more quickly, customers became disgruntled."[23] In other words, many churches have become inner-directed and more interested in their own agenda than in making a real difference in their community and in the world. After all, just follow the money trail, it's argued.

Mega-church pastor, Tony Evans, captures this disparity situation this way:

> Let me put the problem to you in the form of a question. How can we have all these churches on all these street corners, filled with all these members, led by all these preachers, elders, and deacons . . . and yet still have all this mess in America? Something is wrong somewhere![24]

So what does all this religious appearance produce? It has produced an institution that mostly and basically compromises and/or denies the supernatural reality of the greater Jesus in favor of their watered down, diluted, devalued, and diminished versions. Most of these versions are pale in comparison to the genuine version of Christianity Jesus presented, modeled, and conferred. And yet she lures people into her chambers via her various seductions. Am I being overly critical here?

In support of my accusations, J. Lee Grady in an article titled, "The Devil Is Religious" insists that "the devil's primary target is the church." And although Satan is not behind every problem, he and his cohorts are active within many churches deceiving "even the elect—if that were possible" (Matt. 24:24). Grady makes his overall case like this:

> Today, many believers act as if the Harry Potter books are hell's primary tools to infiltrate our families with witchcraft. I don't buy that. Satan is much more subtle. . .
>
> He comes "as an angel of light" (2 Cor. 11:14, NASB) and is an imposter who claims to speak for God. He can mimic piety. He's OK with choir robes, clerical collars and the whole Sunday morning routine. He knows how to dress to fit in.
>
> He detests genuine praise music that exalts God, but he's fine when he can turn worship into dead formality or manipulate it in a fleshly way to glorify the performer. He hates the Bible (because he must bow to its authority), but he has impressive knowledge of the Scriptures and can twist them to create false doctrines.
>
> He despises preachers, but if he can tempt them to embrace greed or arrogance (or lure them into denominational politics), he can use them like puppets on a string. He hates it when Christians love each

other, so he uses every trick in his bag to trigger jealousy, strife, divorce and painful church splits

The apostle Paul didn't seem too concerned about the devil's influence in pagan culture. He was much more alarmed that Satan infiltrated the church without anyone's knowing it.

"Who has bewitched you?" he asked the Galatians (Gal. 3:1). He told the Corinthians: "I am afraid that, as the serpent deceived Eve by his craftiness, your minds will be led astray from the simplicity and purity of devotion to Christ" (2 Cor. 11:3).

Has the American church given the devil a place to hide? Satan thrives on religious hypocrisy. He also loves backbiting, pride, greed, selfish ambition and hidden perversion. As long as we tolerate such things, we create an atmosphere of spiritual compromise that attracts the enemy and gives him a safe haven.

Religious people don't even realize they are part of this evil plot.[25]

On the other side of the proverbial coin, Bass admits that "I frequently meet clergy who either publicly or privately confess to discontent, anger, and doubt with the organization they serve . . . .the constant bickering over meaningless garbage, evening meetings and working every weekend. . . . Disillusionment, discouragement, and discontent are driving even leaders away from institutional religion."[26]

Obviously, some, if not many, Christians and church leaders might question or even doubt that Satan and his cohorts really are at work today in churches and influencing their behaviors. But the Bible does not call believers to "test the spirits" (1 John 4:1) and mention "discerning of spirits" as one of the gifts of the Holy Spirit (1 Cor. 12:10) for nothing. No, not everything amiss is directly from the devil or his cohorts. But this spiritual/physical battle within the Church is real. Jesus knew it (see Rev. 2 and 3). And the admonition that we must refuse to "give place to the devil" (Eph. 4:26-27) in our midst is not given without purpose and cause, as we shall continue to see.

<u>Clue #5</u> – "She held a golden cup in her hand, filled with abominable things and the filth of her adulteries" (Rev. 17:4b). This scripture also presents figurative language that represents a real reality. When you attend a prostituting church (I have attended a few), you are given this golden cup and expected to take it, drink it, and swallow these abominable things without question. I believe these abominations are this church's unscriptural teachings, doctrines, and practices that are presented weekly to the saints and offered up as holy and true. They are a part of her ritualistic observances. But in reality many of them (not all) are unclean and defiled from within by her omission and commission abominations. Factually speaking, a jarring distinction exists between what most churches teach, proclaim, and practice versus what we see proclaimed and modeled in the New Testament, especially in the Gospels and Acts.

Like what? You have many different ideas and opinions about the faithfulness of today's various churches. And you may be able to make your own list. But here are a few major and widely practiced abominations that I believe defame the Christian faith and distort or contradict God's Word. Consequently and significantly, they have led God's people astray, dumbed them down, and drawn them "off target." You may or may not agree with me. And I may or may not be right about some of them. But for me, this great prostitute can further be identified by any of these characteristics (perhaps but not necessarily listed in rank order). And some churches may be guiltier than others.

In my opinion, churches that are not proving faithful (1 Cor. 4:1-2) are those that . . .

- Deny the deity of Christ and the authority of the Bible.[27]
- Teach a re-Judaization of Christianity, i.e., a future reinstitution of Old Covenant animal sacrifices in a rebuilt Temple in Jerusalem—thus denying the sufficiency of Christ's "once for all" sacrifice (Heb. 9:26; 10:10; 1 Pet. 3:18). Arguably, this may be the greatest heresy in the evangelical church today.[28]
- Tell us that the everlasting form of the kingdom of God is not here anymore, or not here fully—only initiated/inaugurated but not established. For them, the central teaching of Jesus is no longer their central teaching. But Jesus, presented and taught the kingdom of God as an at-hand, there-and-then, here-and-now, and a fully present and operative reality (see Isa. 9:6-7; Luke 1:33).[29]
- Reduce the gospel to only being the death, burial, and resurrection of Jesus, i.e., eliminate the kingdom from the gospel message (see Mark 1:14-15; Matt. 24:14).[30]

- Condone a mostly passive Christian lifestyle while awaiting one's reward of salvation in heaven after death.[31]
- Argue that the Bible needs to be interpreted with the aid of tradition and/or a learned clergyman as a guide to lessen the excesses and errors of those less knowledgeable and less mature in the faith.
- Have concocted and subscribed to an unscriptural "delay theory" (see Hab. 2:3; Heb. 10:37) to explain why all the things Jesus said would happen supposedly didn't happen exactly as and when He said they would and every New Testament writer and the early Church expected to happen within their lifetime—as they were guided into all truth and told about the things to come by the Holy Spirit (John 16:13).[32]
- Are literally *not* contending for "the faith that was once for all delivered to the saints" (Jude 3). Instead, they contend for a faith that has only been "partially delivered," to date, and are holding "the end" out over everyone's heads like a giant guillotine blade poised to drop and cut off our future.[33]
- Teach an absentee Jesus Who someday will come back or return.[34]
- Limit the comings of Jesus to only two or three times.
- Deny, ignore, or oppose the supernatural and here-and-now reality of the greater Jesus, the contemporary Christ.
- Further paralyze their parishioners by proclaiming we are now living in the "last days," when the Bible clearly states otherwise—they are behind us (Heb. 1:2).[35]
- Contradict Jesus' prayer for all believers by teaching a soon-coming "rapture" removal from planet Earth of all/some believers (see John 17:15, 22; also Heb. 9:27).
- Undermine our Lord's Prayer that "your kingdom come, your will be done on earth as it is in heaven" by disclaiming that "we're never going to see this culmination perfectly fulfilled, of course, until Christ returns in full glory, when he will bring a highly visible end to the rebellion of the world's system. But until that time, our rescued condition . . . compels us . . . . [to] sharing and showing the good news of Jesus."[36]

- Deny, doctrinally and/or functionally, the continuance and relevance of spiritual gifts.[37]
- Do not preach, teach, model, practice, nor exhort their attendees to do the supernatural works of Jesus and even greater works. Or reduce them to being the provision of humanistic services or church work. <u>Question</u>: Why shouldn't these churches and individuals within them be considered within the ranks of the unbeliever? After all, Jesus plainly stated, "He that believeth on me, the works that I do shall he do also; and greater works than these shall he do;" (John 14:12).[38]

Chances are, if you cannot provide a biblical defense for what you believe, then you likely have been seduced by the great prostitute and taken into captivity by what Jesus termed the "traditions of men," which "nullify the word of God" (Mark 7:8, 13; also Matt. 15:6). For more, see my books, *Off Target: 18 bull's-eye exposés* as well as *The Perfect Ending for the World*, and perhaps even *Hell Yes / Hell No*.

As a result of these many different beliefs (and more) about what the Christian faith is and is not, Robison and Richards lament that "there are now some 42,000 denominations worldwide. We seem to be better at splitting than working together. . . . Christians have been so ineffective . . . . We don't even have one big alternative Christian network where we can pool our resources and reinforce our efforts. We have all sorts of separate, non-overlapping, even hostile Christian institutions and networks. It hardly matters if 80 percent of the population is Christian if we're so riddled with divisions that we work at cross purposes. Secularists are much more functionally unified than believers. . . . It is no surprise that we have not shaped our culture like we should have."[39]

<u>Clue #6</u> – "This title was written on her forehead: MYSTERY BABLYON THE GREAT THE MOTHER OF PROSTITUTES AND OF THE ABOMINATIONS OF THE EARTH" (Rev. 17:5). The root word for the mystic name of Babylon is Babel, which "sounds like the Hebrew word for *confused*."[40] It was at Babel that rebellious men attempted to build a tower that would "reach to the heavens" and defend them from the judgments of God. But God came "down and confused their language so they" could "not understand each other," and "scattered them over the face of the whole earth" (Gen. 11:1-9). Later, Babylon became the prophetic name of a nation whose rulers defiantly enslaved God's people, enshrined idols in the temple of God, and used the temple vessels for sensuous feasts in celebration of false gods (see Dan. 1:1-2; 5:1-4).

Hence, the prostituting church is called Babylon as a parabolic name and symbol for confusion. But this confusion implies much more than just the chaos of conflicting ideas and doctrines; it represents idolatrous confusion. Today, both conflicting and idolatrous confusions run rampant in most Christian churches in America. A 2009 nationwide survey of adults conducted by The Barna Group validates this state of confusion. It summarizes "that Americans who consider themselves to be Christian have a diverse set of beliefs – but many of those beliefs are contradictory or, at least, inconsistent." Below are a few significant and extracted examples from this survey:

> Only 78% see God as the "all-powerful, all-knowing Creator of the universe who rules the world today." The others "chose other descriptions of God . . . that are not consistent with biblical teaching."
> 40% strongly agree "that Satan 'is not a living being but is a symbol of evil' . . . 19% said they 'agree somewhat'. . . 8% were not sure."
> 22% strongly agreed and 17% agreed somewhat "that Jesus Christ sinned when He lived on earth." And 6% did not have an opinion.
> 38% strongly agreed and 20% agreed somewhat "that the Holy Spirit is 'a symbol of God's power or presence but is not a living entity." 9% were not sure.
> Only 55% strongly agreed and 18% agreed somewhat "that the Bible is accurate in all of the principles it teaches." 5% were not sure what to believe.

Based on these results, George Barna concludes that "Americans are struggling to make sense of their faith . . . . [and] of biblical teachings."[41] But who can blame them, with all the different denominations and flavors of the faith with which we have to deal. The one word that best describes this maze of differences over core beliefs is Babylon, i.e., "confusion." In essence, we have devised all sorts of different

Christianities, all of which fall far short of the faith preached, practiced, and perceived in the 1st century and documented in the New Testament.

Clue #7 – **"the woman was drunk with the blood of the saints, the blood of those who bore testimony to Jesus" (Rev. 17:6).** This is another clear and concise textual clue that this drunken woman could be none other than some parts of the institutional church. Not only is she beautiful, alluring, impressive, and seductive, she is also spiritually intoxicated by her own success, richness, and power over God's people, the saints.

This drunkenness is none other than the biblical sin of pride. Hence, the primary focus of many of those in leadership in these prostituting, unfaithful, disobedient, and idolatrous churches is on themselves and their institution. Their major, if not only, interest is themselves. They see themselves as better than those who attend. Not surprisingly, when these leaders' expectations are not met, they become angry, rigid, and headstrong. Rarely are they genuinely concerned about the welfare of their attendees or others in their community. Not surprisingly, when questioned or criticized, they become defensive, intimidating, and blame-shifting. Obviously, they are too busy listening to themselves than to be able to fully listen to God, or love God, or truly love the saints and others. This drunken pride siphoned from the blood of the saints undermines everything. And many people in their pews see this drunkenness manifested in various ways. But most have been conditioned to live with it because that is the way it has always been and how they were raised.

Notably, the Bible teaches that "life . . . is in the blood" (Lev. 17:14a). And these prostituting, unfaithful, disobedient, and idolatrous churches derive their success, richness, and power from the lives of the saints who submit to her. But as a prostitute, she only "loves" people for money. It's a pretend love that actually draws people away from God. But to be successful, these churches must attract, love, and keep people and their money, i.e., "nickels and noses" is their primary focus.

If you doubt this is true, all you have to do is attend a church growth conference or seminar sometime. They teach "easy and proven ways" for making churches more "seeker friendly," "lovable," and "bigger." Sadly, seduction is what they are all about. After all, these are the comparative markers many pastors and church leaders use, brag or moan about—how many people attend their church and the size of their budget. And they all want to learn the latest "easy way" to imitate successful churches and their celebrity leaders. Most, however, will never attain the numerical "success" they covet regardless of how many "proven" success techniques they try to employ.

The unfortunate by-product of this competitiveness is the saints are, more and more, thought of and treated as numbers to be gained and pawns to be manipulated into more giving. All the while, these churches parade their lesser and dumbed-down versions of Christianity as the "true" faith. The church-growth thinking is that to make things better the system only needs to be tweaked or tinkered with. But what's wrong is much more fundamental than that. Once again, what they do and don't do doesn't come close to matching what we see preached, practiced, and modeled in the New Testament Church.

If you doubt this is true, all you have to do is attend a church growth conference or seminar some time.

And there is this one other "little" thing with which some of you may also identify. If you complain to a prostitute about how you are or are not being "loved" by her or question or challenge anything she is doing or not doing, she will stop loving you, drop you like a hot potato, and tell you quite bluntly, "to go take a hike" (go somewhere else). And, if I am right about my identification of this great prostitute today, there are plenty of other prostitutes willing to take you in—as long as you behave according to their parameters. Make no mistake; the prostituting, unfaithful, disobedient, and idolatrous church's number one priority is self-preservation (maintaining the institution—you cannot grow if you don't first maintain). Thus, they must eliminate anything or anyone that presents a threat. Yes, because of all this and more, some, perhaps many, churches have become a culture unto themselves and are increasingly being viewed as irrelevant by growing numbers of former attendees, disengaged young people, and unimpressed and non-attending neighbors.

Not surprisingly, as Bass claims, "American Christianity is in a mess. . . . Some 42 percent of churchgoers confess they are only moderately satisfied or dissatisfied with their churches." She blames "all three of America's great Christian traditions—Catholic, mainline

Protestant, and evangelical" as having "bungled the faith pretty badly in the last decade."[42] In actuality, this decline has been going on for longer than that. But you be the judge.

Clue #8 – "**The beast and the ten horns will hate the prostitute. They will bring her to ruin and leave her naked; they will eat her flesh and burn her with fire**" **(Rev. 17:16).** Rome (the beast) hated 1st-century Jerusalem and its apostate Judaism (Babylon), turned against her, and destroyed her. Today's beasts (antichristian governments), likewise, hate the Church and are lying in wait for the right time and place to do the same thing.

Many examples could be cited throughout history to illustrate how the secular state tries to control, weaken, and/or destroy the Church. In American today, the state's primary and destructive devices are legislation, taxation, bureaucratic regulations, and the courts. Make no mistake; this is a negative and adversarial relationship that demands a disastrous accommodation. The beast wants to silence God talk, purge the Church's influence from all of society, and take over the void—thus, becoming god.

Deceptively, however, the official position between the beast and the great prostitute is one of tolerance. As long as the church "stays in its place" and doesn't criticize or preach against the governmental system, its leaders, policies, and/or actions (separation of church and state), this unholy alliance stays in place. But the moment a church steps out of line into "where it doesn't belong" and dares to challenge the other (which has become increasingly rarer nowadays) the beast rears its ugly head, bares its fangs, and, if necessary, bites down hard.

John W. Chalfant in his book, *America a Call to Greatness* (formerly titled, *Abandonment Theology*) characterizes the result of this intimidation as a great retreat:

> . . . much of the clergy, along with their millions of victimized American Christians following their pastors' lead, have retreated from the battlefront to the social, non-confrontational, noncontroversial reservation [i.e., their church]. They say that Christians should confine their religious activities to politically noncontroversial roles and keep their Bibles out of the political process.[43]

Clue #9 – "**The woman you saw is the great city that rules over the kings of the earth**" **(Rev. 17:18).** This is another clear clue that this woman could be none other than some or a significant part of the worldwide institutional church. As we have seen, the Book of Revelation is written only to believers. And, as we shall see in Chapter 10, it can be appropriately characterized as a "Tale of Two Cities"—Babylon and "the Holy City, the New Jerusalem, coming down out of heaven from God" (Rev. 21:2). The latter city is also God's new "bride, the wife of the Lamb" (Rev. 21:2, 9-10) who "must prove faithful" (1 Cor. 4:1-2). So this Babylon the "great prostitute" is set in stark contrast with "the bride, the wife of the Lamb." Therefore, as Babylon is a city, God's unfaithful wife, and a prostitute, the New Jerusalem is a city, the new bride, and "nothing impure will ever enter it" (Rev. 21:27a).

The fact is, Babylon is the relentless enemy of God and, according to Chilton, the product of a "demon-inspired rebellion against God."[44]

Clue #10 – "**Fallen! Fallen! Is Babylon the Great! She has become a home for demons and a haunt for every evil (unclean) spirit, a haunt for every unclean and detestable bird**" **(Rev. 18:2).** Hendriksen is right on-target when he warns Christians today of the ongoing relevancy of this verse's proclamation: "Here Babylon's fall is announced as if it had already occurred; so certain is its fall. Let this serve as a warning for all!"[45] Howard-Brook and Gwyther expound that this certainty is because of its "bearing the seeds of its own physical demise."[46]

The question that must be raised here is, do we have prophetic and apocalyptically keen enough eyes to see this same truth about today's prostituting, unfaithful, disobedient, and idolatrous churches? Richard Bauckman factually answers that "the fall of Babylon, which occupies so much of Revelation, is what human opposition to God must come to. . . . so that the New Jerusalem may replace her," and so that we "may be won from the deceitful charms of Babylon to the genuine attractions of the New Jerusalem."[47]

As we have seen, a significant part of today's churches pragmatically preach and practice much lesser versions of the Christian faith than what we see portrayed in the Gospels and in Acts. Another reductionistic factor helping to produce this malaise is, as Bass relays, "much of contemporary church is the same" because their lesser versions of the faith are largely mass-marketed and purchased programs. She writes:

> Successful churches have also become products—bigger-is-better buildings with slick programs that cater to an expanding religious market. Yet spiritual commercialization creates a culture of sameness. . . . Want your church to grow? Attend the latest pastor's conference offered by a celebrity minister. Offer an extensive array of programming. Put on a dazzling Christmas spectacular. Buy Vacation Bible School in a can. . . . any number of church programs . . . programs on how to pray, how to read the Bible, how to evangelize . . ."[48]

Refreshingly, Bass further recounts that when leaders of the highly successful Willow Creek Church "sensed that something was amiss," they "embarked on an intensive self-study. . . . The study revealed that church programs had little to do with spiritual depth, maturity, or character." It seems that "at Willow Creek, programs *about* Christianity had actually replaced *practicing* Christianity as a way of life. The result? A big building with lots of people, but little spiritual depth."[49]

Unfortunately, Bass summarizes that today the "first impulse" of many churches is to transform spiritual practices "into a program that will attract more members to a church and increase the number of pledges. . . . but as soon as institutional religion turns spiritual practices into programs, the life-giving energy of practice drains away."[50]

Today, the great need for those of us who call ourselves God's people, followers of Jesus Christ, and fellow workers in his kingdom is, we must have the faith and courage to see past this seductive delusion and soon-to-fall counterfeit. In the 1st century, this fallen proclamation was literally a life-and-death concern for those who claimed to be Christians (see Matt. 24:15-16; Luke 21:20-22). It's still critical for us today. If this Babylon of our day and time has already "fallen" from God's perspective, what does that mean for us if we continue residing in her and supporting her?

Of course, we must allow for a sense of ambiguity and complexity about this Babylon. But the reality is the eventual demise of these churches and the individuals in them if they don't repent and overcome (Rev. 2 and 3). For instance, look at what has happened to most of the great cathedrals in Western Europe, or to many churches in the

Northeastern U.S., or maybe even to Robert H. Schuller's Crystal Cathedral in California. Are these possible examples? The Bible's prophetic tradition asserts that all churches are answerable to God and are never to stand autonomous. And when a church refuses to be answerable, faithful, and obedient to its high calling, dreadful things are promised, may and can happen, and demise ensues.

<u>Clue #11</u> – **"For all nations have drunk the maddening wine of her adulteries. The kings of the earth committed adultery with her, and the merchants of the earth grew rich from her excessive luxuries" (Rev. 18:3).** How have the merchants grown rich? In order to substantiate this clue for further identifying this worldwide prostituting institution, we only have to mention two annual and highly commercialized rituals by which all these groups are substantially attached together. Christmas and Easter. Add to these two commercial feed-fests the year-long supplying of other "luxuries," products, goods, and services. All of which the merchants of the earth are more than happy to supply in abundance or overabundance.

As I began the writing of this chapter, the pagan-named but Christian holiday of Easter is only two weeks away. Yesterday I discovered that the Methodist church one mile from my home is advertising on their front billboard a "Community Easter Egg Hunt." Why do you think they resort to this un-Christian attraction? Clearly, it's to draw parents into bring their toddlers, preschoolers, and elementary-aged children to their church with the hope that some of these families will start attending and perhaps even join their church and contribute to its budgetary needs, is it not?

**... we only have to mention two annual and highly commercialized rituals by which all these groups are substantially attached together.
Christmas and Easter.**

Also advertised is the Easter Bunny himself "will be on site to sign autographs!" So they used the Easter Bunny and Easter eggs (filled with candy) to seduce small children and attract the parents. Hey, everyone, come and see the Easter Bunny and get his autograph and some candy too. Later, they will tell them about how to believe in Jesus. Unfortunately, you cannot see Jesus or get his autograph at their church. Do you see any kind of problem with this mixed but associated message? Or am I being overly critical, once again?

So I decided to Google "Indianapolis Easter Egg Hunts." What do you think I found? It was not just this Methodist church who was involved. Many different types of organizations (Christian and otherwise) were advertising these ritualistic hunts along with special appearances by the Easter Bunny. They included: the First Baptist Church (sponsored by Kiwanis Club), New Bethel Baptist Church, Southwood Assembly, Northminster Presbyterian, Southport United Methodist, St. John Lutheran Church, Messiah Lutheran Church, and Park Place Church of God in Anderson, IN. Also competing against them, according to *The Indianapolis Star*, are hunts at the Indianapolis Motor Speedway in Turn 2 and at the Plainfield Aquatics Center for an underwater Easter egg hunt.[51]

Even more tellingly, if possible, I received an emailed article from Zionica News announcing the cancellation of this year's annual Easter egg hunt, which had been held for several years in a park in a historic area of Colorado Springs, CO. The reported reasons were "helicopter parents" and "the behavior of aggressive parents who swarmed into the tiny park last year, determined that their kids get an egg." Apparently, at last year's debacle several parents jumped "over the rope to help their kids . . . . the hunt was over in seconds, to the consternation of egg-less tots and their own parents."[52]

But Easter-egg hunts aren't prostitution, some will argue. They're just harmless fun. For example, Lori Walbury in her illustrated Christian children's book titled, "The Legend of the Easter Egg," maintains that the Easter egg is "an ancient symbol of new life" and "for Christians has become a symbol of the resurrection."[53] Oh, really? I didn't know that. Or can we be that easily seduced? Or am I being overly critical, once again?

Those of you who have prophetic and apocalyptic eyes to see know that believing in Jesus and believing in the Easter Bunny are not compatible. Sad to say, for many Churchgoers today, there is not much difference, only indifference. But in my opinion, this Easter ritual is not only emblematic; it is also the tip-of-the-iceberg of the derogations and diluting associations we've perpetrated upon our faith, and at great expense. But what do you think?

Clue #12 – "**cargoes of gold, silver, precious stones and pearls; fine linen, purple, silk and scarlet cloth; every sort of citron wood, and articles of every kind made of ivory, costly wood, bronze, iron and marble; cargoes of cinnamon and spice, of incense, myrrh and frankincense, of wine and olive oil, of fine flour and wheat; cattle and sheep; horses and carriages; and bodies and souls of men" (Rev. 18:12-13).** This long list of cargoes or goods is idolized by many as emblematic of material prosperity but lacking in eternal value—until we come to its final commodity. All secular cities and many institutions on this planet today deal with this long list of goods—with one exception— "bodies and souls of men." For the great prostitute, however, that makes little difference. People, too, become a mere commodity (nickels and noses, attendance numbers, and pawns to manipulate).

McKenzie points out that in the 1st century this merchandise and materials were "used in the Temple buildings and garments of the high priest . . . . [and] in the sacrifices and offerings." Furthermore, "those familiar with the Temple would have seen connections here[54] . . . . The Temple was big business; it had needs similar to those of a city."[55] He characterizes this Jerusalem as "one of the most lucrative markets in the ancient world.[56] . . . . The Jerusalem Temple was the epitome of luxury. . . . Josephus describes the Temple as 'the most wonderful edifice ever seen or spoken of. . . .'"[57]

But today there is only one worldwide institution whose most basic trade is in the "bodies and souls of men." That's the Church in all its various forms. And yet, as we have already seen, a significant part of it has and is prostituting herself and leading her "cargo" of the "bodies and souls of men" astray into lesser versions of the faith. Consequently and over time, these lesser versions have ceased to be the comprehensive, world-changing faith we see manifested throughout the pages of the New Testament. Oh, these lesser Christianities may get you into heaven after you die, but much of the rest of what they present (or don't present) is prostitution and dilution, which brings about severe consequences— bondage, oppression, impotency, and plagues (Rev. 18:4-8).

Interestingly, Bass ponders "if pews are misleading in churches." She wonders if pews "trick people into thinking that Christians learn best by sitting quietly in rows, listening to lectures, and memorizing ideas about the faith." In contrast, Bass believes that "churches should not be lecture halls." In fact, for Christianity's first three hundred years, Christians never met in lecture-hall-type settings. They met in houses.

A recent article in *The Indianapolis Star* titled, "Moving beyond lectures," sheds more light on this issue. It declares that "the lecture hall is under attack," even at "many universities" who are "worried that it's driving students away." Educators "say the lecture is a turn-off, high education at its most passive, leading to frustration and bad grades . . . . Just because teachers say something at the front of the room doesn't mean that students learn."[58] Perhaps, the Church should learn something from these universities. But this passive-pew structure for preaching and worship services is well established and ingrained.

George Barna in his book, *Pagan Christianity*, echoes similar skeptical sentiments. He discusses in some detail why the largest room in most church buildings, the sanctuary with its rows of pews, "is perhaps the greatest inhibitor of face-to-face fellowship" and "a symbol of lethargy and passivity."[59] It's in that room where the sermon is "central, and the people are passive and not permitted to minister."[60] He claims that "contemporary church architecture" provides a structural element purposely designed that "separates the clergy from the laity. . . . Its structure implicitly suggests that the choir (or worship team) performs for the congregation to stimulate their worship or entertain them."[61] He adds that "despite . . . variations, all Protestant architecture produces the same sterile effects" since it encourages "the congregation to assume a spectator role . . . . toward passivity."[62]

> **. . . a significant part of it has and is prostituting herself and leading her "cargo" of the "bodies and souls of men" astray into lesser versions of the faith and into some severe consequences . . . .**

He suggests that "perhaps the only sure way to thaw out God's frozen people is to make a dramatic break with the Sunday morning ritual"[63] and for "every member" to have "both the right and the privilege to minister in a church meeting,"[64] which is exactly how the early

Church operated. Of course, most churches today would find Barna's remedy unacceptable. But why? Barna concludes that it is because "We have abandoned those church practices that were acceptable and normative in the New Testament."[65]

Revelation's next verse lays out the consequence of treating "the bodies and souls of men" as commodities—"the fruit you longed for is gone from you" (Rev. 18:14; also see Matt.21:43). No longer is this great prostitute a faithful and courageous witness. Her fruit is gone. Nor will the light of God shine in her again, or out into the world.

Clue #13 – **"The light of a lamp will never shine in you again. The voice of bridegroom and bride will never be heard in you again. Your merchants were the world's great men. By your magic spell all nations were led astray" (Rev. 18:23).** These solemn words represent the final result of unfaithfulness, the derogation of the authority of God's Word, and the dilution of the faith. They also represent the loss of discernment and wisdom in how his Word is to be presented and taught to those in her congregation and to those in the world—many or most of whom have been led astray by those called to be salt and light. (Again, see my book, *Off Target: 18 bull's-eye exposés*, which asks, on its front cover, this appropriate question: "Have we Christians been led astray, dumbed down, and drawn off target by our own leaders?" Indeed, many of us have.)

Regarding these "merchants," "great men," and "all nations" that "were led astray," Hendriksen sees them as being "the men of influence of the earth" who "have committed whoredom with this harlot . . . in other words, they have yielded to her temptations and have enjoyed her luxuries."[66] Equally sad, this great prostitute has miserably failed them as well by failing her high calling and duty to lead all who come across her path into the salvation and kingdom of God.

Clue #14 – **"In her was found the blood of prophets and of the saints" (Rev. 18:24a).** Certainly, and once again, this language was true of 1st-century Jerusalem and its apostate Judaism, for only they killed the prophets of old (Matt. 23:34-37; Luke 13:33; 11:47-51; 1 Thess. 2:15-16) (see again Chapter 3, p-95). But in the ongoing reality of Revelation's prophecy, this killing is still going on in almost if not every city in the world.

In the Jewish prophetic tradition, the prophets of old continually chastised the leaders and people of Israel for not living up to their covenant with God. But Israel did not want to hear it. Therefore, they physically killed their prophets.

Today, this great prostitute does not want to hear that they are not living up to covenant. She is quite comfortable with her lesser versions, brands, or flavors of Christianity. Of course, those in bed with her will not agree with the contents of this chapter and my identification of this great prostitute. And if you don't believe this blasphemous religious system will put you to death (at least figuratively by shunning and/or casting you out), just start questioning some of their beliefs cited in Clue #5 above, or deviating from some of their approved practices, or try doing the same miraculous works that Jesus did during his earthly ministry through the power of the Holy Spirit in their midst and see what happens to you.

If intimidation and threats don't bring you back in line, they will "kill" you. They always have. They still do. They are comfortable with their lesser versions of Christianity. Some of them even believe their version constitutes the true faith. Therefore, any challenge is viewed as ungodly or demonic, and its troublemakers need to be stomped out. Yes, if you'd like to know, I've been "killed" several times, face to face, but many more times, behind my back—thereby greatly increasing my reward in heaven (Matt. 5:11-12). How about you?

What Can We Learn from These Clues?

No longer is this harlot woman 1st-century Jerusalem and its apostate biblical Judaism. At that time she was the foremost enemy of the Church. That religious institution was left totally "desolate" exactly as and when Jesus said it would be (Matt. 23:36, 38: 24:3, 34).

But properly identifying this great prostitute today still "calls for a mind with wisdom" (Rev. 17:9). In all honesty, I see no way this woman could be Rome, New York City, every city of the world, the world's system (empire), secular government, the United Nations, the Roman Catholic Church, the World Council of Churches, a New World Order, or a One-World Government. Nor could she be commercialism in general, anti-God educational systems, the entertainment industry, the secular media, or even other religions. That only leaves one other viable and worldwide candidate.

> **If intimidation and threats don't bring you back in line, they will "kill" you. They always have. They still do. They are comfortable with their lesser versions of Christianity.**

In keeping with the durable and expansive metaphor of Babylon, this city and woman is supposed to be God's faithful people, who instead have decided to play the harlot. And remember our agreement at the start of this chapter—"if the fruits/clues fit, we must convict." In other words and today, the foremost enemy of Christ's Church is the prostitute church—promoting heresy, committing idolatry, compromising the true "once-for-all-delivered faith" (Jude 3). As Chilton appropriately recognized, the "common Biblical metaphors for covenant-breaking are fornication and adultery."[67] Thus, "Christ condemns churches that are ineffective . . . . Since God's will is to be performed on earth as it is in heaven."[68]

The bottom line for most of us is this. We have become "children of a lesser faith." Since we were raised in a church or in several churches that preached and practiced lesser versions of Christianity, we feel comfortable with our lesser Christianities—even though they greatly pale in comparison and are far removed from what we see presented in the Gospels and in Acts and that turned the world of that day and time "upside down" (Acts 17:6 KJV).

But let's give ourselves a little slack. We were seduced. We were led astray into thinking our lesser version was/is okay and perhaps even the genuine faith. In reality, however, it's a watered-down, diluted, devalued, diminished, and degraded product of an institution calling itself God's people when in fact she is playing the unfaithful harlot. No, it's not just the Catholics, or the Baptists, or the Presbyterians, or the Methodists, or the charismatics, or the Calvinists, or the Liberals, or whoever has defiled the faith and compromised the glorious message and ministry of Christ and the Bible. But since beliefs have consequences, this prostitution may be more widespread than we'd like to think.[69] And it's not new in our day and time.

A classic case in point, and one that most Christians readily admit was wrong, was what happened during the Crusades of the 11th-13th centuries. Those times are an obvious example of distorted Christian thinking and teaching. Ultimately, they accomplished nothing while doing major damage as Christians slaughtered many innocent people, raped women, and burned cities. And all this was done in the name of our Lord Jesus Christ. But much more good fruit of Christianity has also been squandered and is still being fouled up by this great prostitute. Sad to say, prostitution is big business—far bigger than most of us realize!

I believe that's why we today are finding growing numbers of believers tired of "playing church," putting up with "churchianity," and even being called "church people." They are also fed up with losing our youth (6-7 out of every 10 by age 23) and seeing society in general deteriorate.[70] How about you?

How Many Churches Are Involved?

I admit, I don't know how many churches around the world may or may not be sitting on their people as the great prostitute. Therefore, I don't know how many Christians have been or are being seduced. But if Jesus' threatening and "I-have-this-against-you" messages to 5 of the 7 churches in Revelation 2 and 3 are any indication and proportional, it's 5 out of every 7 churches.

> **Sad to say, prostitution is big business—far bigger than most of us realize!**

On the other hand, if his admonitions to each individual in each of those seven churches is applicable in this regard ("He who has an ear, let him hear what the Spirit says to the churches" – note the plural "churches" in each message), it may be more pervasive and pronounced than we'd like to think. In other words, even those churches that Christ commends, He calls them to be mindful, careful, and watchful to heed all the messages to all these churches. Why so? I believe it's because all church leaders may have this prostituting tendency and all Christians may be vulnerable to being seduced by this harlot into becoming unfaithful, disobedient, and idolatrous. If so, we all need to be on guard against and repent of these sins, do we not?

According to the late Chuck Colson we do. In an online article titled, "A Sign for the Times: Repent!" Colson elaborated rather stingingly about the pervasiveness of this great prostituting tendency and seduction vulnerability:

> I want to be walking up and down the aisles of every American church, carrying a simple message: Repent! . . . So many Christians these days I talk to are positively wringing their hands over the state of our nation. . . . Whose fault is that? . . . Look in the mirror. The Church, the bride of Christ, has been unfaithful. WE are at fault. We-collectively and individually-have chased after every idol the world has to offer. We have tried so hard to be relevant that we've become almost completely irrelevant. We offer no other way, there is nothing distinctive about us. We have not been what Jesus called us to be: Salt and light. We have blended in with the world so well that we are practically invisible . . . .
>
> Enough of self-absorption. Enough of going to church for self-validation-because it makes us feel good; enough of buying into the 'Jesus and me' brand of Christianity that we evangelicals are especially susceptible to. Enough of living exactly like our non-believing neighbors, glued to electronics, engaging in promiscuity and infidelity, spending beyond our means. Enough of ignoring the suffering of the poor. Enough of being ashamed of the truth claims of the Gospel. It's time to repent. . . . to become, the bride of Christ. Pure.[71]

The Biblical Instruction

So what are believers to do if they feel or find themselves involved with a prostituting, unfaithful, disobedient, and idolatrous church? The scriptural instruction is pure, plain, and clear:

Come out of her, my people, so that you will not share in her sins, so that you will not receive any of her plagues; for her sins are piled up to heaven, and God has remembered her crimes.

Give back to her as she has given; pay her back double for what she has done. Mix her a double portion from her own cup. Give her as much torture and grief as the glory and luxury she gave herself. In her heart she boasts, 'I sit as queen; I am not a widow, and I will never mourn.' Therefore, in one day her plagues will overtake her; death, mourning and famine. She will be consumed by fire, for mighty is the Lord God who judges her (Rev. 18:4-8).

Throughout the whole prophecy, the Book of Revelation warns believers against assimilation and compromise with ungodly influences, forces, and institutions. But there is only one worldwide institution in which God's people are resident and called to "come out of her, my people." I believe the fourteen textual clues we have addressed above are more than obvious. That institution is some, much, most, or all of the institutional church. Then what does this instruction mean to "Come out of her, my people?" Does it mean to physically leave a church, abandon her to her fate, and discontinue attending any church anywhere ever again?

In its 1st-century fulfillment context it meant exactly that and nothing less. It was a life and death matter—a physical and geographical separation out of the city of Jerusalem (Matt. 24:15-21; Luke 21:20-24). But the seven churches in Asia Minor to whom Revelation was originally addressed were not in Jerusalem. Therefore, what did this instruction mean to them? I believe it meant for them to come out of biblical Judaism—to make a final break with temple-system, feast-oriented, law-based, and economic-driven Judaism. McKenzie agrees and contributes, "while Babylon was centered in Jerusalem (in the Temple), it represents all of the old covenant community that rejected Jesus, not just the city of Jerusalem."[72]

Please be assured, God's judgment upon disobedient Israel can happen to us today as well. But in its ongoing relevancy this instruction may or may not mean a physical departure in any or every situation. Of course, finding a non-prostituting church may not be easy. This one thing, however, is certain. If you stay, it means, in my opinion, to definitely come out from being under bondage, submission, dependency, and seduction—spiritually, emotionally, socially, educationally, and financially. In plain language, it means to become "un-prostituted."

But there is only one worldwide institution in which God's people are resident and called to "come out of her, my people."

Yes, you can still attend, participate in some things, and give money if you are so led by the Holy Spirit. I still do. But long ago I became increasingly frustrated by the partially true substance I was being fed and the shallow and superficial practice of the faith I was observing and experiencing at various churches I attended. I soon realized I was being seduced into accepting a depreciated and denigrated brand of Christianity—because of the non- and unbiblical things being added and the biblical things being subtracted. I figured I had three choices: (1) accept it and keep quiet; (2) leave the Church altogether; (3) stay and change my expectations and commitments. I decided upon the latter and began viewing the Church and churches as a mission field rather than a submission field. After all, didn't Jesus minister to prostitutes, I kept reminding myself (Luke 7:36-50; Matt. 21:31-32)? Then why shouldn't I?

But each of us, who desires to follow both the historic Jesus and the greater Jesus, needs to carefully pray through this decision and not join ourselves to a "harlot," lest we receive her plagues and judgment from this Jesus (Rev. 18:4-8; also 19:1-3; 22:18-19). Don't kid yourself. This association is serious stuff. I assure you, based on the authority of God's own Word, Jesus takes it seriously. And make no mistake; it's the greater Jesus Who sends these plagues (John 5:22).

In this regard, Hendriksen offers two helpful and relevant insights, although he, like many others, identifies Babylon as being "the world."

1) "The admonition to leave Babylon is addressed to God's people in all ages."
2) "To depart from Babylon means not to have fellowship with her sins and not to be ensnared by her allurements and enticements."[73]

After all, didn't Jesus minister to prostitutes, I kept reminding myself? . . . Then why shouldn't I?

In a similar manner, Howard-Brook and Gwyther state that coming out "does not mean physically to leave. . . . Rather it is a call . . . to discern the true character of where they were and how to distance themselves from the . . . seduction of their time and place . . . . the idea is to resist, to refuse to participate, to create alternatives."[74] For me, I see this coming out as like being *in* the world but not *of* the world (John 15:19; 17:14, 16; 18:36; Rom. 12:2; 1 John 2:15).

Lastly, and once again, I believe the scriptural evidence strongly points to these prostituting churches as being the modern-day location of "Armageddon"—the mountain of assembly where Jesus fights against them in "the battle on the great day of God Almighty." (See again Chapter 7). Not only do these churches teach some doctrines and practices that are patently and scripturally false and/or watered-down and dumbed-down, they preach, present, and practice lesser versions of the Christian faith. Many are also rife with politics, human egos, demonic forces, and many other unsavory things. Those destructive dynamics may be part of "her plagues." Notably, recent newspaper and magazine articles documenting the two- to four-year-or-so demise of the Crystal Cathedral are ripe with reports of just such internal battling and family divisions. Not good fruit!

Arguably, if "Come out of her, my people!" was a relevant and correct response for Christians associated with apostate biblical Judaism in the 1st century, it is still a relevant and correct response for God's people in our day and time.

On the other hand, we'd be well advised to contemplate, if not heed, these wise words of caution and admonition usually attributed to Augustine:

"The Church is a whore, but she's still my mother."[75]

How about You?

Who would want to reside in this Babylon today? The painful answer may just be that most of us already do. We just didn't know it. Make no mistake; Mystery Babylon is still a "great city." But it's time for us Christians to get out of Babylon and into the greater city into which you and I have been beckoned.

Like me, maybe you, too, long for a better sort of Christianity and a different kind of church—one like we see in pages of the New Testament, with robust fellowship, vibrant community, full engagement with God, and out and about and highly effective in the world. But institutions of all types resist corrective messages and are slow to change. They are guarded and protective of their power, wealth, and influence. When Jesus came and prophetically challenged and preached a message of substantial transformation of biblical Judaism, look what the religious leaders did to Him and his followers.

What we've addressed in this chapter is the possibility that some, much, most, or all of us in today's Church have become like them—a prostituting and/or seduced institution—at least in some degrees and aspects. I'm also suggesting that this past and present reality is part of what Jesus referred to as the deception of the elect (Matt. 24:23-26).[76] The good news is, we are still the elect. Yes, as I stated in the first paragraph of this chapter, I, too, am as guilty as anyone in some or much of this. But ideas do have consequences.

Who would want to reside in this Babylon today? The painful answer might just be that most of us already do.

Consequently, as Bass reports, "many Americans are articulating their discontent with organized religion and their hope that somehow 'religion' might regain its true bearings in the spirit."[77] Moreover, "People intuit that the modern conceptualization of religion as an ideology or institution is bankrupt and has already, in some significant ways, failed. . . . People are searching for something new."[78]

The greater good news is fallen Babylon prepares the way for the vision of the New Jerusalem, the Holy City, the greater city, and ultimate reality here on earth. This is the city in which you and I and all Christians should and can earnestly desire to dwell. At best, Babylon is a counterfeit of this ultimate, authentic, and here-and-now reality. Today, young people, especially, want authenticity. This other city will be the focus of our last chapter.

But first we must re-explore how you and I can get "caught up with them in the clouds to meet the Lord in the air," right now.

Chapter 9

He 'Raptures' a Remnant

"Caught up with them in the clouds to meet the Lord in the air" (1 Thess. 4:17). What does it really mean?[1] Does it make any biblical or rational sense?

In this chapter, we shall address how this catching up to meet the greater Jesus in the air *could* happen to you and/or me, *right now*—and without our feet leaving the ground!

But first, and according to a front-page story in the *New York Times*, to multiple millions of Christians being "Raptured" means "in an instant, millions of people disappear from the face of the earth, shedding their clothing, shoes, eyeglasses and jewelry."[2] And all this is going to happen some time in the near future.

It's a near-frantic preoccupation with the idea of Christians mysteriously and physically being levitated off the surface of planet Earth, alive, and whisked away, en masse, on a gigantic flight though outer space to heaven.

You can read it on bumper stickers:
- "In case of Rapture, this car will be unmanned!"
- "Rapture: The only way to fly!"
- "He's coming to take me away! Ha! Ha!"
- "Get right, or get left behind!"

You can see it in print:
- Books: *88 Reasons Why the Rapture Will Be in 1988*

- The "Left Behind" series—"the hottest trend in apocalyptic literature since Hal Lindsey's The Late Great Planet Earth."[3]
- Fundraising Letters: "We don't want to delay the Rapture—We need your financial support, NOW!"
- Tracts: "We're in the RAPTURE Generation!"

You can see, hear, and read it in the media:
- On Television: "Folks, this could be our last broadcast! The Rapture is *that* close!"
- On Radio: "This program is recorded, so I may already be in heaven by the time you hear it! We're talking Rapture, people! We're talking any day . . . a minute! Are you *reeaaddyy?*"
- In Newspaper Headlines: "Harold Camping – May 21, 2011 bust."

You can hear it in the gospel songs:
- "I want to hear that trumpet sound,
  I want to feel my feet leave the ground!"
- "Some glad morning, when this life is o'er,
  I'll fly away!"
- "Oh, I'm gonna' take a trip,
  In the good old gospel ship!"

As we saw in Chapter 2, you can also hear how it adversely affects some people:

> "When I was a little boy, I used to go to church and hear preachers telling hair-raising tales about how the Second Coming could happen that very night. They'd show all these charts about the Millennium and frightening pictures of beasts and swarms of locusts. I'd go down to the altar and cry my eyes out and confess every sin I'd ever thought of committing, but it never seemed to help. I'd still get up and go home scared half to death and lie awake until I saw the morning sun peeping through the windows. All night long, I'd keep tiptoeing into my mother's room to see if she was

still there . . . I figured that if anybody was going to get raptured it would be her. Eventually, I just dismissed the whole business as superstition born of ignorance. Now I don't think you can be certain about anything. But, at least I don't go to bed with goose bumps all over me anymore."

You can hear how it's argued about:
- Whether it will be pre-trib, mid-trib, or post-trib.
- Who will or won't go, and who will be left behind.

From the ridiculous to the sublime, it's not just a small lunatic fringe promoting the idea of the "Rapture." You'll hear sermons, read books, and see movies about how automobiles driven by Christians will suddenly be driverless; airplanes piloted by Christians will be pilotless; doctors operating on Christians will be patientless. What's more, the physically decayed bodies of dead saints will come out of their graves and join those alive believers in a flight up through the sky. You'll hear this rapture message in some of the biggest churches in the world. It's a most popular teaching taught in many major seminaries and appearing in the literature of some of the largest denominations.

A Touchy Subject

The idea of a one-time, physical, corporate Rapture is a touchy doctrine to question. Oh, it's all right to argue about *when* it will occur. If you're a post-tribber, you might get shouted down by an audience of pre-tribbers, or vice versa. But they won't call you a heretic—they'll just say you're ignorant about the Bible.

But for millions of people the "Rapture" is their "blessed hope" (Titus 2:13). They want out of this world, its problems and responsibilities, and before the Antichrist and the big 7-year Tribulation. And, they want out without dying. Others, however, are questioning all this Rapture mania, while the masses are simply confused. Their heads say it must be true because they've been conditioned all their lives to believe it. But they have this nagging feeling that something doesn't quite fit, especially since so many predictions have failed. It's just like the Proverb says, "Hope deferred makes the heart sick" (Prov. 13:12).

What Did God Mean by It?

Certainly God could speak a few specks of dust out of earthly graves and off this earthly mass, which He originally spoke into existence, at any time He wished. But He hasn't. And, of course, removing a group of dead saints and living believers through a Rapture is a possibility. But this has not happened throughout Church history to the best of our knowledge.[4] So *what else* might God have had in mind when his Holy Spirit inspired the Apostle Paul to pen these perplexing words nearly twenty centuries ago: "caught up with them in the clouds to meet the Lord in the air" (1 Thess. 4:17)?

I believe He had something in mind far more pertinent and glorious than snatching his Church out of the world before He wreaked havoc upon it. After all, where's the victory in a great escape? No, I believe that God has something far more wonderful and exciting in mind. Think about the Bible as a whole, not just as a few isolated statements.

Scripture emphasizes a triumphant God who enables his people to triumph as well. Never do God's people run away or get rescued out of their troubles. The book of Exodus, for example, tells much more than the story of Moses rescuing God's people from bondage in Egypt. Rather, it emphasizes God's efforts to purify his people and create godly character within them while leading them to the Promised Land, which they would go into, take, and win by his power. Jesus conquered death by dying, not by climbing down from the cross or calling angels to rescue Him. He conquered sin by facing temptation head on and refusing to give in, and by taking sin's awful guilt upon his shoulders.

After all, where's the victory in a great escape? No, I believe that God has something far more wonderful and exciting in mind.

That's the spirit of the Scriptures—facing up to sin, death, troubles, and evil in this world—and conquering them. This courageous living out of one's faith is exactly what the early Church did (Acts 17:6; Rev. 12:11). And overcoming in this world, then and there and here and now, is the overarching theme of the Book of Revelation.

An Idea of Man or Truth of God?

Before one too readily subscribes to the Rapture theory, it is important to put this doctrinal teaching into perspective. When, where, and by whom was it introduced in Church history? Does it reflect traditional Christian thinking? Most people who have grown up in the last half-century or so, at least here in America, have never heard any other teaching, and they assume that it has always been taught in the Church. It has not. Here are three things the Rapture is not.

First, the word 'rapture' is not a scriptural word. It does not appear anywhere in Scripture and is not a proper translation of any Hebrew or Greek word found therein. Hence, it never came from the Word of God, but from the mind of man. It's derived from the Latin word "raptizo" which means "caught up." Biblically, the words "caught up" (1 Thess. 4:17) or "gather[ed]" (Matt. 24:31; 2 Thess. 2:1) are preferable. The word "trinity" is also not a scriptural word.[5] So the question becomes, is a rapture-removal of all or some living believers and the corpses of dead saints from the earth a correct scriptural event and concept?

Second, rapture-removal is not the historic teaching of the Church. One of the more astonishing facts in the history of eschatological thought, and one that most Christians are unaware of, is that the idea of a secret pre-tribulation, Rapture-removal from the earth of the Church is a fairly recent theory in Church history. In theological circles, it's a "Johnny come lately" and departed dramatically from the historic position of the Church, which had never considered the hope of a bodily removal prior to this introduction. Even the historic creeds, conspicuously, don't mention it. In fact, it was relatively unheard of and never taught until the early 19th century, and it didn't become widespread until the 20th century. Since then, it has spread like wildfire. But the many failed predictions of its coming have made it an embarrassment.

So how did it all start?

The first known reference may have appeared in two obscure but contestable sentences from a 4th century A.D., 1,500-word sermon written in Latin by someone called "Pseudo-Ephraem."[6] If so, this idea went essentially unknown and undeveloped for fourteen centuries. According to most researchers, the idea of a Rapture-removal from planet Earth prior to a "great tribulation" period began to surface in the late 18th and early 19th centuries. Possible but only slight and vague mention of it may have been published in the writings of a famous Calvinist theologian, Dr. John Gill (1748); an early American Baptist pastor, Morgan Edwards (1788); a Jesuit priest Emmanuel Lacunza (1812); and Edward Irving, who translated Lucunza's book (1826).

Most scholars, however, agree that the secret Rapture theory was launched into prominence around 1830 by a group of people in Scotland who had become known as the Plymouth Brethren. Under the direction of John Nelson Darby (1800-1882) and others, they began to hold Prophetic Conferences. Supposedly, during one of those conferences, or from a sickbed during one of them, a charismatic utterance came forth as a prophetic message from the Lord through a young, fifteen-year-old Scottish girl named Margaret Macdonald. While in a trance, she received a private vision and revelation that only a select group of believers would be removed from the earth before the days of the Antichrist. But she also saw other believers enduring the tribulation—something most rapturists nowadays do not teach.

Soon thereafter, Darby coupled this highly questionable vision of a secret, pre-tribulation Rapture with another idea originated by the Jesuit priest Francisco Ribera. In 1585 A.D., Ribera was the first to introduce the idea of interrupting Daniel's 70-week, end-time prophecy and inserting a "gap" between the 69th and 70th weeks. This was done to deflect apocalyptic heat from the Reformers who were fueling reformation fervor by claiming that the Pope was the Antichrist and the Catholic Church the beast of Revelation. Ribera surmised that the first 69 weeks (483 years) concluded at the baptism of Jesus in 27 A.D., but God had extended the 70th week into the future.[7] Therefore, the Pope and the Catholic Church could not be so accused. Darby grabbed hold of Ribera's severance idea, connected his "Rapture" to the beginning of that final week, and changed the nature of that week from a 7-year period of covenantal confirmation to one of tribulation—big difference! (Notably, the Bible never mentions a future 7-year period of tribulation.)[8] He then introduced this now fully developed, pre-tribulation Rapture view (theory) in Europe and later in America. It was popularized in America by its inclusion in the notes of the *Scofield Reference Bible* in 1917 and by elaborate End Time event charts published in Clarence Larkin's *Dispensational Truth* in 1918.

Conspicuously, one of the consulting editors of the *Scofield Reference Bible*, W.J. Eerdman, who served and accepted Darby's view, subsequently refuted it. In a tract entitled *A Theory Reviewed*, he wrote, "Better the disappointment of truth than the fair but false promise of error."

Of course, the relative newness of the "Rapture" theory in Church history (180 some years ago) neither proves nor disproves its biblical correctness. But it certainly shouldn't be blindly accepted or excluded from being questioned and tested (1 Thess. 5:21). Ultimately, the truth can only be found in the Scriptures. But what began as a result of one woman's private vision and charismatic utterance became widely taught, accepted as the truth, and popularized in the thinking of millions. It has become so deeply entrenched that many pastors and Christian leaders assume it is an essential teaching of Church history extending back to apostolic times. It is not. What's more, it is not believed by the majority in the Church today, for many more good reasons.

At present, this Rapture scheme, though popular in recent years, is collapsing under the weight of criticism from Bible-believing seekers of truth. So *what else* might God have had in mind when He inspired Paul to write, "Caught up with them in the clouds to meet the Lord in the air?" Let's take a closer look.

Third, here are ten Reasons why being "caught up" is not a removal of a group of alive believers from the surface of planet Earth. "The Rapture" is a new and seductive teaching about futuristic, end-time events and an escapism gospel that's looked to by so many believers as their "blessed hope." They don't expect to die. They don't expect to go through any tribulation. Instead, they eagerly await a secret return of the Lord to rescue them out of this world and all its troubles. Some warn that only a select portion of Christians—those who are "ready and looking for it," or those who are among the "true saints of God"—are going up in the air. All the rest will remain on planet Earth and suffer the horrors, plagues, and the Antichrist rule in the 7-year tribulation—the worst troubles the world has ever known—as God supposedly resumes and concludes his 70-week program for Israel and Jerusalem. Then, these high-flying saints will return to earth in a universally visible public coming of Jesus and reign and rule the world with Him for a thousand years. But over what will they rule, since all wrongs will have been righted and all evil destroyed, according to their scenario?

During the 20th Century, the "pre-tribulation rapture" of the Church became a, if not the, dominant eschatological view. Its central passages of Scripture are 1 Thessalonians 4:13-18 and 1 Corinthians 15:51-58; along with a heavy use of inferences, deductive reasoning, and a highly complex array of other "supporting" scriptures. Prior to Darby, however, the Church always viewed these "rapture" scriptures as resurrection passages.

Regrettably, most proponents are so emotionally bound up by the Rapture's escapist appeal, that inside their fellowships you cannot question this doctrine. If you do question the meaning and fulfillment of these famous words "caught up together with them in the clouds, to meet the Lord in the air," you are liable to incur the "left foot of fellowship" coming against you. Yet, sharp differences of opinion on what these words mean abound within the body of Christ. The facts are, the "rapture view" has not been received by the majority in the Church and by a large number of conservative scholars. They dismiss it as an imaginary creation of some fanatical fundamentalists, and for some good reasons.

Here are ten more good reasons to reject it. Let's look at them, honestly and humbly. Our purpose here is not to mock or embarrass, but rather to discover biblical truth:

1. Jesus prayed we would not be removed. "My prayer is not that you take them out of the world but that you protect them from the evil one" (John 17:15).

In this, Jesus' prayer for all believers (John 17:20), Jesus was sending forth his disciples, and us today, into the world to be a light (John 17:23; Matt 5:14). His prayer is still in effect. And most of us believe Jesus' prayers were and are still answered. Furthermore, He told us that "in the world ye shall have tribulation" (John 16:33).

How sad today to see so many of God's people making so much of "the rapture" as a means of escaping tribulation, and hoping, trusting, and pleading for God to take them out of this world just when they are most needed. Yet the modern doctrine of the "Rapture" and its withdrawal mentality is in consistent opposition to Christ's prayer and teachings as well. Jesus prayed for God to keep his people in the world to carry on his work, not take them out of it. He wants us here working to expand his kingdom and to think long-term about the future of human existence on this planet. But a longing for escape thwarts this purpose and produces too many lazy and apathetic Christians, who too easily retreat from society and passively wait for Jesus to come back and finish the job. They have no hope of things ever getting better until things get much worse and they are removed. In essence, they have given up on this world, abandoned their calling, and drawn away from involvement. They reason, "Why bother?" because this world is about to end and the Rapture is very near. Like it or not, it's a prevailing rapture mentality, and it's a natural response. Also, as we've seen, it's a relatively new theory in Church history.

> **His prayer is still in effect. And most of us believe Jesus' prayers were and are still answered.**

Let's call this new theory of a Rapture for what it truly is, an affront to Jesus' prayer that we would not be removed (John 17:15, 20). It's also a disgrace to the great God and his Christ whom we claim to follow. Rapturists have bought into a highly fabricated and severely flawed system of interpretation. Its abuses and mishandling of Scripture to support this scenario can be only partially covered in this chapter, but are further addressed in other of my writings.[9] The responsibility, however, of rightly teaching God's Word is an awesome responsibility. Therefore, just to discredit this new teaching by scripturally refuting what it's *not* is not enough. We must also rediscover what this "rapture" truly *was* and prove what it *is* for us today and in the future.

2. Die once and face judgment. Rapturists think they are going to defy the death rate—which to date is 100 percent—and get out of this world without going through the grave. The Bible, on the other hand, teaches that it's "appointed unto men once to die, but after this the judgment" (Heb 9:27). A Rapture-removal would, at best, be an exception to this, or an outright contradiction. Also, an escape from planet Earth is not the subject of any Old Testament resurrection prophecy or promise to be fulfilled by the coming Messiah.

Since there is no direct or explicit teaching to support Christ coming *for* the Church and taking it to heaven, the Rapture-removal doctrine grows out of deductive reasoning (inference) and goes something like this. Since sin and death exist in the material world, God must snatch his saints out of it, destroy it, then create a new and sinless world. Forget about God loving the world enough to give his only begotten Son for it (John 3:16-17). Forget about Jesus' prayer for God to keep his people in the world to carry on his work, and not to take them out of it (John 17:15, 20). Those Scriptures, according to the Rapture doctrine, are *not* to be taken literally; but the ones about a catching up and snatching away *are* to be taken literally.

3. Paul's "we" was them. Paul wasn't writing to some far-distant generation of people 1,900-plus-years away from his day. He clearly expected that he and some of his hearers would survive and still be alive and included in that "caught-up" event. Hence, Paul speaks personally and contemporarily, not editorially or rhetorically, about a future "those" group, when he says "we" and "you" multiple times (meaning Paul and his readers) ". . . we who are still alive, who are left till the coming of the Lord . . ." (1 Thess. 4:15; also see 4:17; 5:1-11; 1 Cor 15:51-52). He told them "this day should not surprise *you*" and to "be alert!" (1 Thess. 5:4, 6). By using these personal pronouns and the strength of this imminency language, Paul was more than implying that the Lord would come for this purpose and in this way *during their lifetime*. He was assuring *them* that some of them would not all die before this event (1 Cor 15:51). Was he mistaken? Were his followers misled? In opposition, futurist Leon Morris, who believes this event has not happened yet, cautions that "we should not read too much into Paul's 'we who are alive.'"[10]

But before answering too quickly, remember, the Holy Spirit had been given to guide, first and foremost, Paul and his "you" group into all truth and to show them, specifically, the end-time things that were yet to come (John 16:13). This language of imminency is the same as we find used throughout the New Testament. If you were living back then and read these words from Paul, what would you have understood their timing to mean? Scholars confirm that Paul and his contemporaries expected all this to happen within their lifetime. Apparently, they understood this language very personally and as urgently significant. Once again, if history has proved that these inspired words of Paul and his and his readers' expectations were wrong on such a monumental issue as this, how can we trust them to have conveyed other aspects of the faith along to us correctly?

4. "According to the Lord's own word." Paul wasn't the first to teach this idea. He both referred and deferred to "the Lord's own word" (1 Thess 4:15) on this subject. But where did Jesus speak on it? In his most famous end-time prophecy, Jesus spoke of sending his angels to "gather his elect from the four winds, from one end of the heavens to the other" (Matt. 24:31; also John 14:1-3) and ". . . from the ends of the earth . . ." (Mark 13:27). Paul's "caught up" and Jesus' "gather" describe the same event, as we shall see later. But notice that Jesus also time-limited this event when He said, "This generation [the one physically and literally standing before Him] will certainly not pass away until all these things have happened" (Matt. 24:34). Consistently, throughout the New Testament the word construction "this generation," which is used twenty times, always refers to that same contemporary group of people alive, there and then. There are no exceptions. So, if Jesus was inspired, if He said what He meant and meant what He said, and if He used the plain and naturally understood language of his day, then "all these things," including this gathering, happened *as* and *when* He said they would and *as* and *when* Paul and his readers expected. As we shall see, they surely did.

5. An argument from silence. Most rapturists teach that the events in chapters 4 through 18, in the Bible's last Book of Revelation, transpire after the removal of the Church from planet Earth. They infer this since the word "church" never appears in these chapters. Not only is this deductive assertion an argument from silence, but it fragments the structural integrity and unity of the book. It also violates what this book says about itself in both the first and last chapter regarding the whole of "the words of this prophecy":

- "things which must shortly come to pass." (Rev 1:1; 22:6 KJV)

- "Blessed is he that readeth, and they that hear
    the words of this prophecy, and keep those things
        which are written therein: for the time is at hand."
                                        (Rev 1:3; 22:7 KJV)

- "Seal not the sayings of the prophecy of this book:
    for the time is at hand."   (Rev 22:10 KJV)

Of course, the absence of a word does not guarantee the absence of the reality related to that word. At best, it's questionable to make a case for or against anything from a position of silence. Someone once said, "Silence is consistent with everything and proves nothing." To the contrary, the two words most often used in the New Testament to describe God's people are "church" and "saints." But the word "saints" appears eleven times in Revelation chapters 4-18, and they are clearly on earth, not in heaven. Furthermore, in the middle of Revelation, John records this warning to the same "saints": "He who has an ear, let him hear" (Rev 13:9),[11] a phrase repeated seven times after each of the seven letters to the churches in chapters 2 and 3.

In another argument from silence, rapturists equate John's experience of being commanded to "come up here" (Rev 4:1) with a rapture-removal of the Church. Again, it's a major deduction and not directly justifiable, nor inductive. Likewise, the two phrases "after this" in this same verse are often taken by rapturists to mean after passage of the so-called Church age. Yet a natural reading of the context makes it clear that the first "after this" means next in the vision, and the second "after this" means after opening the door to the spirit realm. The opening of this door demonstrates a spiritual enlightenment or vision for John, not a physical removal out of the world for the Church.

6. Two different "air" locations. An Italian proverb proclaims, *Traduttori traditori*, "translators are traitors." And there is some truth in it. No translation can do full justice to the original since no two languages fully correspond in their various meanings and nuances. The New Testament was written in Greek, which is a more elaborate and descriptive language than English. A notable example is the Greek word translated "air" in Paul's often-quoted "caught up . . . in the air" statement. Consequently, a better understanding of the Greek meaning can help us better grasp what Paul was talking about and the reality he was expressing to his 1st-century readers.

According to Strong's Exhaustive Concordance of the Bible, two different Greek words are translated as "air" in the New Testament. One is *ouranos*. It refers to the air where birds fly and higher: above the mountain tops, in the atmosphere, outer space or heaven itself. The other word is *aer*. This is the one Paul uses in his 1 Thessalonians passage. This "air" is the location into which living saints are "caught up." As we shall further explore later in this chapter, its primary meaning is the internal breathing air (inside us) and air within our immediate proximity (as exhaled), i.e. within approximately ten feet above the earth's surface—and not the sky or atmosphere air.

This technical but important distinction makes a huge difference. Essentially, it renders the popular "rapture" concept of a flight through the sky up into the atmosphere and onto heaven as suspect and difficult to support.[12] In short, one's feet don't have to leave the ground to get "caught up" in this air (*aer*) with the Lord.

... its primary meaning is the internal breathing air (inside us) and air within our immediate proximity (as exhaled) ...

To this point, McKenzie also recognizes that the word "meet" in "meet the Lord in the air" (1 Thess. 4:17; also used in Matt. 25:6 when the virgins go out to "meet" the bridegroom – Greek *apantēsis*) "draws from the ancient practice of the citizens of a city going out to meet an important dignitary at his coming (parousia) to their territory . . . . and escorting him back to their city." He concludes that "the idea of believers being transported to heaven in a physical rapture is not found in this image."[13] Again, more on this "air" later.

7. The symbolic usage of clouds. Paul's two passages are filled with symbolic language, so it's not unreasonable to think that his usage of clouds is also symbolic. If correct, then to interpret the clouds into which we are caught up to meet Jesus as literal, visible clouds of physical water vapor floating around in the sky above our literal earth would be a materialistic misinterpretation. What if Jesus came in this way on literally a cloudless day in your section of the world? Would you then be left behind? Surely, this isn't what God had in mind. In prophetic/apocalyptic usage, clouds often symbolize humans, spirit-realm beings, and those who have died in the Lord, not atmospheric clouds (see Heb 12:1; 22-24; Jude 12). And as we saw in Chapter 1, in the Old Testament, God came against nations "in" or "on clouds," i.e., through the actions of human armies. Jesus promised to do the same (Matt 24:30).

Let's also note that this interpretation and understanding of these clouds is fully consistent with the location of the air (*aer*) into which the saints are caught up.

8. *Plural usage of "times and dates."* Why did Paul immediately follow his famous "catching up" passage by saying, "Now, brothers, about times and dates . . ." (1 Thess. 5:1)? Notice the plural usage. If this happening is only a one-time occurrence, why didn't he use the singular "time and date?" His words are no mere slip of the pen. The simple, straightforward answer is (as we shall see): there is more than one "catching up." It's a fulfilled, countless, ongoing, and multifaceted reality and part of our "faith that was once for all delivered to the saints" (Jude 3).

The fact is, for 17 centuries of Church history, Paul's words in 1 Thessalonians 4:13-18 were accepted as resurrection verses, not as verses describing a single-event rapture of the Church or an escape of a few believers from the earth to heaven. Many interpreters feel there are multiple resurrections, both spiritual and physical, spoken of in the Bible—some which have happened already and some which are yet to come. For example, John in the Book of Revelation described a "first resurrection" (Rev 20:5b). Doesn't that imply a second and maybe more? Jesus mentioned at least two: "a time is coming and has now come when the dead will hear the voice of the Son of God and those who hear will live . . . a time is coming when all who are in their graves will hear his voice and come out . . ." (John 5:25, 28a). Matthew records that after Jesus' resurrection, "the tombs broke open and the bodies of many holy people who had died were raised to life. They came out of the tombs . . . they went into the holy city [Jerusalem] and appeared to many people" (Matt. 27:52-53). How many resurrections do these passages account for? How do you count or discount them?

9. *Various meanings of "caught up."* The Greek verb *harpazo*, translated as "caught up" or "snatched away," is variously used in three other places in the New Testament:[14] In 2 Corinthians 12:2 and 4, Paul uses it to describe a temporary and apparent spiritual experience of a man he knew who was "caught up to the third heaven." Yet Paul was not sure of the nature of this event. "Whether it was in the body or out of the body I do not know—God knows." Thus, "caught up" does not necessarily mean the physical body was lifted off the ground. But in Acts 8:39 it is used to describe the Spirit's physical snatching away of Philip after he had witnessed to the Ethiopian. It's used in Revelation 12:5 to describe the man child's (Jesus) being snatched up to God. Perhaps it also describes John's experience, "then the angel carried me away in the Spirit into a desert" (Rev 17:3).

What reasonable conclusions may we draw? Coupling together the New Testament's meaning of the Greek word *aer* with the Bible's symbolic usage of clouds and its various examples of being "caught up" or "snatched away" should serve notice not to limit these fulfillments or applications to a single event. Look at it this way, "caught up with them in the clouds to meet the Lord in the air" is like "circumcision," "born again," and "bread of life." It's a biblical metaphor for a valid experience(s). But that experience(s) is not a physical removal of dead corpses from graves or alive bodies from the surface of planet Earth, as we shall continue to see.

10. Confusion prevails. In spite of the above cited scriptural problems, Rapture teachers passionately affirm that the Lord's coming back to take away his Church is the *next event* on God's prophecy calendar. Yet they claim no signs are required before this happens. Then why do they spend so much time preaching and teaching on current events as "signs of the times" leading up to this "any-moment, sign-less" event? Seems totally inconsistent, doesn't it? Adding to this confusion, rapturists must infer the exact timing of this great escape event in relation to their proposed 7-year tribulation period. But no such timing or period is mentioned in the Bible. It seems that deductive reasoning is notoriously perilous (see especially 1 Pet 3:15-16).

To top it off, rapturists are forced into thinking that we are now somehow separated from the Lord. Only after our removal from planet Earth will we "be with the Lord forever" (1 Thess. 4:17b). Doesn't this mean we are now serving an absentee Lord—absent the entire length of the Church age? Apparently so. In a *Christianity Today* magazine article titled "The Day We Were Left Behind," Barbara Brown Taylor lays out her defective belief this way:

. . . we baffle ourselves, proclaiming the good news when the news is so bad, trusting the light when the sky is so dark, continuing to wait on the Savior in our midst when all the evidence suggests that he packed up and left a long, long time ago. To be theologically correct, we have been waiting on the Savior ever since the first Ascension Day... Ascension Day is the day the present Lord became absent . . . . We go to church to worship, to acknowledge the Lord's absence and to seek the Lord's presence . . . and to be filled . . . with the abiding presence of the absent Lord until he comes again.[15]

To top it off, rapturists are forced into thinking that we are now somehow separated from the Lord. Only after our removal from planet Earth will we "be with the Lord forever" (1 Thess. 4:17b).

Are you confused? Which is it? Absent or present? What it really is, is flawed theology. As we have seen throughout this book, we can confidently confirm the greater Jesus Christ is here with us! And He didn't have to return because He never left, just as He said. Not only is He with us, He is also in many of us, totally, personally, and bodily. He is not absent from us in any way. We do not serve an absentee Lord. What's more, there is no record or hint that 1st-century Christians were expecting to leave the earth en masse, or did, in order to be with the Lord.

What Else Might God Have Had in Mind?

Have you ever wondered why so many Christians risk so much on their novel idea of a rapture-removal from planet Earth—versus staying here, living, reigning and overcoming with Christ as we've been commanded to do? Count on it! Anything that gets your mind and heart off what God wants to do in you, with your life, and through you into the lives of others—thus, furthering his kingdom—is a deception.

Flesh Wants an Easy Way Out

It's easy to see why the idea of a great escape is so believable and appealing to the flesh in us. I believe there are two strong reasons people grasp at any hope of avoiding a trip through a dirt grave to reach heaven.

First, the high emotionalism associated with the Rapture grows out of a very human desire—a compelling drive to survive. Most Christians are afraid of dying. Oh, we'll talk about going to a better place and say we long to see Jesus face to face. But let us get a sharp pain in the chest and we'll spend more money trying to stay alive than we'd ever give to the Lord.

Couple the survival instinct with a deep belief that this world is an evil place that is beating us up, and the idea of a Rapture offers the easiest of all possible alternatives—a way to get out of this evil world as soon as possible, without dying.

Second, the physical and corporate aspects of the Rapture idea appeal to us because we have grown up with a Western worldview. We live in the Western Hemisphere, and that has influenced the way we view the world and our role in it.

Our Western worldview tends to be materialistic and scientific, and we do live in the era of space flight. It operates on a basic assumption that there is a scientific framework which assumes order, control, and material existence as reality. What we can see, feel, and test is real; what we can't is not real. Thus, we've been conditioned by our culture to think of everything as literal, physical, and scientific—versus figurative, spiritual, and faith-centered. Yet, the Bible is written with a Middle Eastern worldview—looking at reality spiritually, poetically, or symbolically.

The problem all this creates is that we tend to view spiritual reality as *inferior* to physical and material reality. "If you start spiritualizing this and that from the Bible," one Rapture teacher warned me, "pretty soon you have nothing left!"

But I didn't start it—God did. He breathed his own life into human nostrils, and man became a living being (Gen. 2:7). Until then, man was nothing but a dead lump of clay. Life itself is spirit—the very Spirit of God Himself.

The bottom line is this: we will never be able to grasp the glorious truth of being "caught up with them in the clouds to meet the Lord in the air" (1 Thess. 4:17) until we throw out the notion that saving our flesh is what matters most to us and to God. This is why God's Word gives example after example and promise after promise, not of "rapturing" his people out of their tribulation, but to see them through it.

Many have further wondered why God would be prophetically obliged to rescue a "Church" from the world's mess that the Church's neglect and impotency is largely responsible for allowing. Within the past century, the Church in America has lost much of its long-range vision and its unique position, moral influence, and leadership in our society. Pessimism and fatalism now prevail in many of its ranks. While we have been awaiting the "Rapture," Satan and his cohorts have been stealing our children, our schools, and our whole culture.[16]

Christians, wake up! The idea of a one-time, future, physical removal of believers is a major factor in this decline. It's also a new theory in Church history and does not reflect the terminology, teachings, or tone of the Bible. It's a false hope and a destructive teaching. God has chosen to leave his people and his Church in the world, and for good reasons. But, to recap, it's easy to see why the idea of a great escape is so deceptively appealing:

1) Many Christians are afraid of dying and will grasp at any hope of avoiding a trip through a dirt grave to reach heaven. We'll spend more money trying to stay alive than we've ever given to the Lord.
2) This world is an evil place that is beating up on us, and the idea of a Rapture offers the easiest and quickest way out.
3) It offers a most-convenient excuse to avoid our scripturally mandated responsibilities here on earth in this life and to soothe our guilty conscious.

In this chapter our objective will not be to conclusively define what "caught up" is, but to illustrate why we can't limit its reality to a single, yet-unrealized occurrence and stick it on a futuristic timeline. We've started out by showing that it's highly doubtful that a physical removal of a group of believers from planet Earth was ever meant.

Rather, it is a flawed doctrine of man that's based on a pick-and-choose approach to interpreting isolated Bible passages. It is not a reality of God that reflects the terminology, teachings, and testimony of the Bible. Throughout history, God has chosen to leave his people in the world. He has not and will not take them out of it, although He could.

So *what else* might God have had in mind? As we'll see, it was something far different and more glorious.

A Multifaceted Reality

The scriptural passages that speak of being caught up speak of a multifaceted, totally fulfilled, eternally established, ongoing, and fully available, spirit-realm/physical realm reality that is far more in tune with the spirit, teachings, and documentations of Scripture than the idea of a physical, corporate, one-time removal of the Church from the world. These passages speak of resurrection, not of rapture-removal. Like everything else, they were timely and precisely fulfilled and are ongoing in relevance. We'll address two of those facets:

1) **Bodily Resurrection of the Dead Ones (Plural)**
2) **How You Can Be 'Raptured' Right Now, Alive**

Bodily Resurrection of the Dead Ones (Plural)

All the passages used by popular "Rapture" writers and teachers were actually fulfilled by real and bodily resurrections. What's more, they all occurred within the time frame Jesus specified (Matt. 24:34), and every New Testament writer and the 1st-century Church expected as they were guided into all truth by the Holy Spirit (John 16:13). Unfortunately, these occurrences are some of the most ignored, distorted, confused, and misunderstood realities and concepts in Christianity. No more!

Key passages are: 1 Thessalonians 4:13-18 and 1 Corinthians 15. In the 1 Corinthians passage we find an ordering, or sequencing, for these resurrection occurrences is revealed:

> *But Christ has indeed been raised from the dead, the firstfruits of those who have fallen asleep. For since death came through a man, the resurrection of the dead comes also through a man. For as in Adam all die, so in Christ all will be made alive.* **But each [every man] in his own turn [order]:** *Christ, the firstfruits; then, when he comes [at his coming], those who belong to him. Then the end will come* . . . . (1 Cor. 15:20-24a *NIV*, [*KJV*] bold emphasis is mine).

The Greek word translated "turn" or "order" is *tagma*. This is the only place in the New Testament where it's used. *Tagma* is a military term that means "a series or succession." The thought is of soldiers marching or of a parade in which others follow along individually. This "ordering" beautifully harmonizes with what happened back then in the 1st century and with all the other fulfillments we've been presenting in this book.

If, however, it is true, as the "Left Behind" people tell us, that for over nineteen centuries and counting these inspired words of Paul have not been fulfilled, then the nonoccurrence of this event presents a highly problematic dilemma:

- Paul's words of encouragement turned out to be a cruel misrepresentation in the lives of his original readers.
- 1st-century believers actually ended up deceiving each other with these words rather than encouraging each other (1 Thess. 4:13, 18). And they died "in vain" not having received what they expected in their lifetime (1 Cor. 15:14).
- If Paul's Holy-Spirit-guided imminency expectations proved false, how can we trust him to have conveyed other aspects of the faith along to us correctly (John 16:13)?

Let's see if we can arrive at a better understanding, from a *sola Scriptura* standpoint, of the order and time of fulfillment in four successive resurrection stages. Most of the rest of this section on these four stages is an excerpt from my book, *Off Target*:[17] For an amplified version of these four stages as well as more descriptions of the nature of these bodily resurrections: please listen to podcasts on PRI's website (www.prophecyrefi.org) for the "Unraveling the End" MPC series or on (www.unravelingtheend.com) and listen to Lessons #12 and 13a. This series is also scheduled for release in an expanded book form at the end of 2012.

Stage #1 – Jesus' resurrection.

The bodily resurrection of Jesus Christ is one of the most well-attested and well-known facts of human history. No other event has such overwhelming weight of evidence and left such an impact on the world. But even though Jesus' resurrection is basically uncontested in conservative evangelical circles, *how* and *when* an individual believer participates in Christ's resurrection, here and now and upon physical death, has been one of the most distorted, confused, and misunderstood concepts in the Christian faith.

What is also not well-known is that this event marked the beginning of the "last days"/eschatological resurrection of the dead ones (plural). Why so? It's because other resurrections "out of the graves" also occurred in that 1st century. Therefore, Jesus' resurrection was not an isolated event separated by centuries of time from a yet-future resurrection. But He was the "firstborn from the dead" (Col. 1:18), the "firstfruits" (1 Cor. 15:20, 23), and actually the "first of the firstfruits" (Exod. 23:19; 34:26; Ezek. 44:30 KJV).

Stage #2 – More bodily resurrections.

Using harvest imagery and the metaphor of the "firstfruits," more resurrections took place as the bodies of many (not all) Old Testament saints came out of their graves and paraded through the streets of Jerusalem:

> *And behold, the veil of the temple was torn in two from top to bottom, and the earth shook; and the rocks split, and the tombs were opened; and **many bodies** of the saints who had fallen asleep were **raised**; and coming out of the tombs (graves), and **after** his* [Jesus'] *resurrection they entered the holy city* [Jerusalem] *and appeared to many (Matt. 27:51-53 – bold emphasis is mine).*[18]

Obviously, some kind of literal and bodily (*soma*) resurrection took place *after* Jesus' death and resurrection. Not surprisingly, many interpreters have tried to sidestep, downplay, or ignore this biblically recorded and collective event.[19]

But this one thing is for sure. This event confirms that they were living in the eschatological and biblical "last days," back then and there, because the general resurrection of the dead was now underway (see Isa. 26:19; Dan. 12:2; John 5:28-29). No doubt, this was why the Apostle Paul, during his defense before King Agrippa remarked, "Why should any of you consider it incredible that God raises the dead?" (Acts 26:8). The Greek word translated "dead" here is actually in the plural, i.e., "dead ones" or "dead persons." This is the proper translation. For more plural usages see: Acts 17:32; 23:6; 24:21; 26:23; 1 Cor. 15:12, 13, 15, and 16. But resurrection for the rest of the dead ones (the harvest) was still being anticipated as the New Testament was being penned.

Stage #3 – Resurrection day for the rest of the dead ones.

Thirty years after the above two resurrection events, the Apostle Paul wrote:

> . . . *I believe everything that agrees with the Law and that is written in the Prophets, and I have the same hope in God as these men, that there **will be** [to be about to be] a resurrection of both the righteous and the wicked* (Acts 24:15, bold emphasis is mine).

Two of Paul's key words in this passage are *mellein esesthai*. Traditionally, they have been translated as "will be" or "shall be." In the literal Greek, however, they are: "to be about to be." This double-intensified force of imminency is missed in nearly all major English translations of the Bible. But the dye was already cast. The resurrection harvest had already begun. All that awaited was the "last day" (singular – John 6:39, 40, 44, 54; 11:24) of the "last days" (plural – Heb. 1:2), because "the harvest is the end of the age" (Matt. 13:39), i.e., the Jewish age (Matt. 24:3, 34 in fulfillment of Dan. 12:4, 7b).

Please note that the Christian age (the age to come, the kingdom age, the Messianic age, and even for the world) has no end and, therefore, no "last day" upon which to place a resurrection of this harvest (see Isa. 9:6-7; Dan. 2:44; 7:13-14; 12:2, 4, 7; Luke 1:32-35; Eph. 3:20f; Heb. 12:28; Rev. 11:16f). So what else is there in Scripture or logic to justify postponing this resurrection of the rest of the dead ones from Hades?

That day came! At some point in the late summer or early fall of A.D. 70, or perhaps two or three years later in A.D. 72 or 73—when the last stone was removed (Matt. 24:2), the field plowed over (Mic. 3:12; Jer. 26:18), and the prophesied point of "desolation" reached (Matt. 23:38)—the rest of the dead were raised. But unlike before, and in keeping with the applied harvest metaphor, no resurrection bodies were seen rising out of graves or parading around Jerusalem. Rather, their souls were taken out of the hadean realm, that spirit-realm holding place of the dead, taken to heaven (bypassing earth), and given their judgment and "spiritual" resurrection bodies (1 Cor. 15:44). This end is history. It all took place within the spirit realm and within the time span of Jesus' "this generation" (Matt. 24:34). Moreover, this fulfillment is in perfect harmony with the imminency expectations of every New Testament writer and the early Christian community (John 16:13). This often-prophesied and imminently expected end was covenantal, and not cosmic. Once again, it occurred within history, and not at history's end—for which there is no end and, therefore, no "last day" upon which to have a resurrection.

Stage #4 – Post end (telos) – the ongoing reality—"each" or "every man in his own turn/order."

From that time of the end of the age on, the next saint to physically die, never again went to Hades, that temporary, spirit-realm holding place of the dead, to await resurrection and judgment. Jesus, who holds "the keys to death and Hades" (Rev. 1:18; 20:13-14), had emptied it out and locked it up, forever. Therefore, after Resurrection Day on the "last day," it's straight to heaven upon physical death for believers to receive their judgment and a new, "spiritual body" (1 Cor. 15:44), which God "gives" (1 Cor. 15:38). Heaven's door is now open wide. This fulfilled reality is in contrast to no one being in heaven prior to, during, and for some time after Jesus' earthly ministry (see John 3:13; 13:33, 36).

Thus, the "last enemy" of "death" was destroyed (1 Cor. 15:26) and "swallowed up in victory" (1 Cor. 15:54; Isa. 25:8). That last enemy was not death itself. Living and dying still continue and always will (Heb. 9:27). What was terminated was the temporary holding place of the dead, Hades or Sheol. No more would it prevail (Matt. 16:18). Yes, this end-time fulfillment has been largely misunderstood, ignored, and/or denied, to our detriment. From then on, it's only one step from this life to the judgment and resurrection state in heaven. Thus was fulfilled Revelation's proclamation, "Blessed are the dead who die in the Lord from now on" (Rev. 14:13). It's all a done deal and part of "the faith that was once for all delivered to the saints" (Jude 3)!

"Therefore, encourage each other with these words" (1 Thess. 4:18).

'Bones-are-still-in-the-graves' objection.

Critical Objection: Not so, insist the vast majority of Christian scholars. Go to any graveyard, dig up a grave, they insist, and we can prove that this "last day" resurrection has not yet taken place. Why not? It's because the "bones are still in the graves." And one day, "at the end of this present age, God will reunite our souls with our bodies."[20]

This objection is simply a misunderstanding of the nature of bodily resurrection. It's assumed that since Jesus' self-same earthly and physical body arose from the grave, so will our old dead, decayed, and perhaps decomposed bodies. But is this assumption biblically accurate? Here are three reasons why it is not:

1) Jesus' body was the only one promised not to see decay (Acts 2:25, 27, 31; 13:35 from Psa. 16:10; 49:9). This promise was made only to the Messiah and to no one else. The rest of us are told "for dust you are and to dust you will return" (Gen. 2:7; 3:19; 1 Ki. 2:2; Psa. 90:3).
2) God does not need our old and perhaps scattered atoms and molecules from our previous physical body to give us a new "spiritual body" (1 Cor. 15: 38, 44).
3) In Paul's seed analogy in 1 Corinthians 15:37, the outer shell of a seed is left behind, stays in the ground, and decomposes. It does not become part of the new plant. The seed holds the germ of the new body, which is something greater. So our physical earthly body holds the germ (the Spirit of the Godhead) of something greater (the "spiritual body"). What

could be any clearer than this? Scripture never speaks of us receiving a resurrected and rejuvenated, old, decayed, decomposed, earthly, and physical body. In accordance with Paul's seed analogy, we shed that shell at death. Big difference!

Consequently, the Bible never mentions a "resurrection of the body," "resurrection of the flesh," resurrected body," or physical resurrection." Instead, the Bible uses two inspired phrases: "the resurrection of the dead" and "dead ones" (Matt. 22:31; Acts 17:32; 23:6; 24:15, 21; 1 Cor. 15:12, 13, 21, 42; Heb. 6:2) and "resurrection from the dead" (Luke 20:35; Acts 4:2; Rom. 1:4; Phil 3:11). Again, big difference!

This objection is simply a misunderstanding of the nature of bodily resurrection. It's assumed that since Jesus' self-same earthly and physical body arose from the grave, so will our old dead, decayed, and perhaps decomposed bodies.

So what will our new "spiritual body" be like? All we are told is, it "will be like his [Jesus'] glorious body" (Phil. 3:21). Consequently, this resurrection body may be both material and immaterial, physical and spirit. As Boa and Bowman further admit, "the Bible offers no formal definition of 'death' and no detailed exposition of what happens to people when they die." Therefore, they further explain, "we must infer our understanding of death [and resurrection] from a whole range of biblical statements pertaining to the subject."[21]

But one other thing is also for sure. None of these resurrection verses promised a future Rapture-removal of a group of alive believers and dead corpses off the surface of planet Earth.

(Again, for more on resurrection fulfillment and ongoing reality: listen to podcasts on PRI's website (www.prophecyrefi.org) for the "Unraveling the End" MPC series or on (www.unravelingtheend.com) and listen to Lessons #12 and 13a. This series is also scheduled for release in an expanded book form at the end of 2012.)

How You Can Be 'Raptured' Right Now, Alive

The so-called "Rapture" passages that speak of being caught up *do not* just describe the bodily resurrection of the dead ones. But since resurrection is a multifaceted reality, they also speak of an ongoing, spiritual/physical experience of some living believers being caught up, in the Sprit, in Christ. This other aspect of resurrection reality is most relevant for those believers who attain the fullness of Christ in their individual lives here on planet Earth.

Yet, if the truth be known, most of us know very little today about being in the Spirit. Satan and his spirit-realm and physical-realm cohorts have taken this truth right out of the Church at large by leading us instead to believe a fairytale—something about a giant space trip!

Yet, you can find believers throughout the history of the Church who knew what is meant to be gathered, or raptured, into the presence of the Lord. No, this experience is not something ordinary; but it can and should be part of any believer's growth in Christ. Each of us should desire to experience it while our feet are still firmly planted on the ground. Desiring anything less just leads to slothfulness.

Our present society and most of the Church as well, however, do not understand or accept the idea of getting caught up into the spirit realm—being raised up into the great cloud of angels in joyful assembly, the church of the firstborn, God, the spirits of righteous men made perfect, and the greater Jesus (Heb. 12:1, 22-24).

But we don't get into this spirit realm experience by getting out of ourselves and going someplace. Rather, and as we'll see in a moment, we get there via the spiritual dimension inside us. And yet, this spirit-realm reality does not deny a life after death for Christians. On the contrary, it means that, for the overcomers, life after death simply continues the resurrected life of ruling and reigning with Christ, which we can enter into here and now. This available experience could have been what John called the first resurrection (Rev. 20:4-5). It certainly was not a one-time event, but a spirit-realm/physical-realm reality—obeyable, heedable, and keepable for all who would partake. After all, didn't Jesus say, "I am the resurrection and the life?" The resurrection is a Person, not just a single historic event.

With this in mind, let's look more closely at this key "Rapture" passage, 1 Thessalonians 4:13-18. Again, it's the one most commonly used to support the physical-removal Rapture idea.

1 Thessalonians 4:13-18

> *Brothers, we do not want you to be ignorant about those who fall asleep, or to grieve like the rest of men, who have no hope. We believe that Jesus died and rose again and so we believe that God will bring with Jesus those who have fallen asleep in him. According to the Lord's own word, we tell you that we who are still alive, who are left till the coming of the Lord, will certainly not precede those who have fallen asleep. For the Lord himself will come down from heaven, with a loud command, with the voice of the archangel and with the trumpet call of God, and the dead in Christ will rise first. After that, we who are still alive and are left will be caught up with them in the clouds to meet the Lord in the air. And so we will be with the Lord forever. Therefore encourage each other with these words.*

Let's start off my noting that it is quite possible Paul, even though anointed by the Holy Spirit, wrote down the things he didn't fully understand, if for no other reason than the Book of Revelation had not been given at the time of this writing. That's not to take away any of the validity of Paul's message any more than it is to say that the Old Testament prophets did not understand all they wrote down about the coming of the Messiah.

There are many examples throughout Scripture in which writers described coming events for which they had no frame of reference or basis for understanding. For instance, Isaiah, Ezekiel, and Daniel all spoke of Jesus from the limited Old Testament perspective. They had not had the privilege of reading the Gospel narratives, as we have today.

Our real problem, however, in grasping scriptural truths and realities seldom stems from the limited historical perspective of its writers. Our problems most often stem from the modern-day biases and limiting doctrines that influence the way we interpret specific passages. The Gospels give many accounts of Temple leaders who, having read the Scriptures, attacked Jesus because they had drawn diametrically opposed conclusions to his (see Matt. 3:7; 15:1; 16:6; 19:3; 22:23; 23:2; Luke 7:30).

Let's look at some of the key concepts in 1 Thessalonians 4:13-18. As we examine their meanings and some of the original language, we can readily see how this passage has been largely distorted.

"Not want you to be ignorant..." As we have already seen, millions of Christians have fallen for a new and seductive teaching. Sadly, it is the predominant view in conservative, evangelical Christianity. It has become even more entrenched and well-known since the phenomenal success of the *Left Behind* series. However, only in the timely and precise fulfillment explanations that we are providing in this chapter is the "ignorant" removed and replaced with a knowable, multifaceted, fulfilled, and ongoing and totally relevant, resurrection reality.

"Caught up ... in the air." We are caught up, yes, but to where? Are we caught up in an atmospheric ring around the world, some of us going up and others down (Northern and Southern Hemispheres)? How confusing? Also notice that we are not gathered up around the throne in heaven, but in this air on earth.

Once again, the key to this expression's meaning is found in the Greek word used here and translated as *air*. Fortunately, its etymology is not difficult to trace. And, as we also mentioned earlier, in the Greek language words convey much more accurate and detailed meanings than do our English translations. The New Testament translates two Greek words as *air*. The first on is *ouranos*, or atmospheric air (see Matt. 6:26; 8:20; 13:32), where the birds fly (or higher). This is *not* the word Paul uses in the so-called "Rapture" passage. Paul uses the other Greek noun, *aer*. According to *Strong's* (#109), it comes from the Greek root verb *aemi* meaning "to breathe unconsciously, i.e., respire; by analogy to blow); 'air (as naturally circumambient: – air.)" In the Greek language, nouns are often derived from verbs. Hence, and in contrast to *ouranos, aer* means the internal breathing air within you and that within our immediate proximity.

1st-century Christians would have immediately known what Paul meant by his use of the word *aer*. Further, notably, the Greeks viewed breath and the spirit as synonymous. In the Bible the Hebrew word *rauch* and corresponding Greek word *pneuma* are variously translated as "breath," "wind," and "spirit." Hence, Paul used this same word *aer* in Ephesians 2:2 to symbolize the spirit realm—"the *kingdom of the air.*"

Revelation uses the same word to describe the air into which the seventh vial is poured out (Rev. 16:17 – for more uses and critical objections to this understanding, see "An Academic Excursus on *Aer*" at the end of this chapter).

But where is the spirit realm? It's both inside us and surrounds us (see. Heb. 12:1, 22-24). Once again, it's like the air we breathe; it's not only inside us, but also surrounding us. This is not the same air where birds fly, and it is not what most people think about when they contemplate a flyaway "Rapture" up through the sky into outer space and onto heaven. Rather, as Paul expresses in the 1 Thessalonians passage, we are to be caught up into the spirit realm with the greater Jesus, and not into our lungs nor physically removed from the earth. Thus, being "caught up . . . in the air" is an inner spiritual/physical reality that does not require our feet leaving the ground.

Paul's usage of *aer* also suggests something else quite significant in my opinion. As you have been reading this chapter, you have been breathing so naturally that you have not thought about it—you have just been doing it. That's what "to breathe unconsciously" means. Conversely, when you are "caught up with the Lord in the air," you just unconsciously do things with Him, and that pleases Him. In other words, you don't have to consciously discipline yourself to do them. You delight in doing them so much that you don't even have to think about it. This is the highest level of involvement in the practicing of spiritual disciplines. Some term this progression the "3D's:" (1) Desire; (2) Discipline; and (3) Delight.

Like learning a new skill, such as playing the piano or some other musical instrument, driving a car, riding a bicycle, ice skating, or something, you first must *desire* to do it. But then it requires mental and conscious effort, physical energy, and focus. Each movement involves intentional choice and repetitive *discipline*. But as one continues and practices over time, gradually more and more becomes subliminal, i.e., taken care of below the threshold of consciousness. In other words, it becomes inscribed into our unconscious so that we automatically respond the way we've been conditioned. We are now able to *delight* in this activity without have to consciously think about it. Get it?

When most people become Christians, we start out at Level 1 – we desire to please Jesus by practicing spiritual disciplines such as prayer, Bible reading and study, worship, etc., etc. But we find that we have to discipline ourselves, consciously, to do them – that's Level 2. And this can be tough to keep going. But when a Christian breaks through to Level 3, you find yourself delighting in doing things with Him, for Him, and that please Him, without having to think about them. You just want to do them. That's what being "caught up" with Him in this unconscious breathing "air" is all about. It's a this-world, here-and-now opportunity, experience, and realizable reality.

But where is the spirit realm? It's both inside us and surrounds us (see. Heb. 12:1, 22-24). Once again, it's like the air we breathe; it's not only inside us, but also surrounds us.

The Bible also likens it to being "in Christ" or "in Him," the One who is both the resurrection and the life. Please be advised, as most Christians are not, that Christ in you and you in Him are two different things. Check out Jesus' discussion of this dichotomy for yourself in John 15:1-8. And it's all for this purpose: "This is to my Father's glory, that you bear much fruit, showing yourselves to be my disciples" (John 15:8; also see 2 Cor. 13:5).

So how do we know if Christ is in us? According to Paul, if you "have been crucified with Christ . . . Christ lives in" you (Gal. 2:20; also 3:27).

How do we know if we are "in Him" or not? The Bible tell us, "This is how we know we are in him: Whoever claims to live in him must walk as Jesus did" (1 John 2:5b-6; also see 3:23-34). "Walk as Jesus did" is a Greek idiom. It means to do what Jesus did. He is our model. It includes his relationship with the Father, his inner life, his outer life, his compassion, his ministry to others, and his miraculous works. This is also exactly what Jesus was talking about when He proclaimed that "Verily, verily, I say unto you, He that believeth on me, the works that I do shall he do also; and greater works than these shall he do; because I go unto my Father (John 14:12, KJV).

In Scripture, reaching the heights of being "in Christ" is also described as a five-step positional reality that begins when He comes "in you." It's also a progressive, dynamic, and conditional reception and application of what He has done as you get "in Him." It requires a keen sense of spiritual discernment (1 Cor 2:14) and affects the whole person—spirit, soul, and body. I call them the "Co's." This process starts by reckoning oneself to be a co-heir with Christ (Rom. 8:17; Gal.3:29; 4:1-7) and advances by participating with Him in a progression of spiritual identifications and applications. Therefore, being "in Christ" requires being:

1) *Co-crucified* (Rom 6:5-6; Gal 2:20). A sacrificial surrender of oneself to Christ for the forgiveness of sins.

2) *Co-buried* (Rom 6:4; Col 2:12). Dying to sin, buried with Him in baptism, and repentance.

3) *Co-resurrected* (Rom 6:4-5; Col 2:12-13; Eph 2:1-5; Rom 11:15). Born again by the Spirit of God, raised out of baptism alive in one's spirit in the Presence of God, and walking in newness of life with the miraculous and great power of resurrection inside us.[22]

4) *Co-ascended* (Eph 2:6; Col 3:1). Trusting in Him to lead one's life, being obedient to his Word and seeking those things that are above—his kingdom, his righteousness (Matt. 6:33).

5) *Co-seated* (Eph 2:6-7; 1:18-23; Col 3:1-3; Rev 3:21; 2:26-27). The high level of being co-seated on his throne and demonstrated by reigning and ruling with Him, here and now, on this earth (Rev. 5:9-10). By this co-seating, God is involving you and me in the process of setting this world right—advancing and extending his will, reign, and rule in this world.

These five steps produce the fullness of resurrection life. They enable us to live the co-heir life with the greater Jesus on this earth, here and now, to be "in Him," and to be caught up with Him in the "air." They are not strictly successive steps or stages in Christian growth and living. Rather, they are dynamic and go and grow together. Hence, all five "Co's" involve an almost, if not, daily identification and application. But this process is only one facet of the multifaceted resurrection life and reality. It does not stop here. Francis J. Crosby in the Refrain for the famous church hymn "Near the Cross" (pub. 1869) recognized this ongoing and multifaceted nature of resurrection reality with these lyrics:

> In the cross, in the cross,
> Be my glory ever;
> Till my ***raptured*** soul shall find
> Rest beyond the river. (bold emphasis mine)

As we have seen, resurrection reality continues after death when we receive our new "spiritual body" that God gives (1 Cor. 15:38, 44), and there is more.[23]

Truly, truly, and here and now, the Christian life is a "high calling" (Phil. 3:14; 2 Thess.1:11; Heb 3:1; 2 Pet 1:10; Eph 4:1, 4) and an example to be set (Titus 2:7). To "walk as Jesus did" requires unwavering belief, total trust, and a yielded spirit. It produces godly character that results in proper conduct glorifying to God. Such a life is realizable on this earth and in this human body. Jesus did it, Paul did it. They are our models of the Christian life (1 Cor 11:1; 2 Cor 10:3-6), as well as many Thessalonians (1 Thess. 1:4-9). Dare we make any less of it as so many have?

Sadly, my observation has been that the far too many professing Christians stop their progression somewhere between steps 1 and 2, with being co-crucified and co-buried with Christ. They then become conditioned to a nominal, sedentary, and casual Christian lifestyle and, therefore stay in the position of being co-dead with Christ. But this is not where you or I want to pull over and park. Jesus didn't stop at the cross. Please don't misunderstand. As important as the cross was and is, it's not the final word, nor the victorious event. Being co-crucified and co-buried are only stepping stones to the greater victory. The greater victory is attained through the next three steps, co-resurrected, co-ascended, and co-seated, just as it was for Jesus. But only a remnant, at least in this life, attains and sustains this height of being "raptured" with Christ, i.e., being "in Christ" (1 John 2:5-6). The Apostle Paul knew this when he wrote this admonishment to *believers* (not unbelievers), "the saints in Ephesus, the faithful in Christ Jesus" (Eph. 1:1) . . . . "Wake up, O sleeper, rise from the dead, and Christ will shine on you" (Eph 5:14).

This five-step identification with Christ should be a Christian's continual life experience. Yes, it's the ideal. But it's also what having Christ formed in us and having "the mind of Christ" (1 Cor 2:16) is all about! We commune with Him (Rev 19:7-9; 22:1-5, 14). We reign with Him both in the spiritual and material worlds (Gen. 1:28; Rom. 5:17; Rev. 5:10; 22:5)! This is the goal of Christian conversion in this life, here and now. It's far different from sitting, soaking, and soaring in a church pew waiting for Jesus to return and rescue you from a doomed, sin-cursed planet. Dare we subtract from this available spiritual reality today (Rev. 22:18-19)? Sadly, many have and do.

Being co-seated is also what "caught up with them in the clouds to meet the Lord in the air" is all about (1 Thess. 4:17). And it all takes place "in the air," i.e. in the realm of the *aer* inside you and around you. That's the true meaning and understanding of this Greek word. Once again, in Hebrew and Greek thought this "air" was synonymous with the spirit dimension (see Gen. 2:7; Job 33:4; 34:14; John 20:22). And the spirit realm is where the greater Jesus is resides. Just as we can breathe either consciously or unconsciously, so too we can walk out our Christian life. When we are "caught up with the Lord" in this unconscious breathing air, we unconsciously abide in his Presence and do the things that please Him without ever having to think about doing them or forcing ourselves. He becomes our reality. Isn't this spiritual "caught-up" more scripturally honoring and Christ glorifying than the new theory of a flight of escape through outer space?

All of this is also part of the abundant life that Jesus came to give us (John 10:10). It's the most exciting life anyone can live on this earth. It's the victorious life that's to be experienced before physical death. The apostle Paul said it well, "I want to know Christ and the power of his resurrection . . . and so, somehow, to attain to the resurrection from the dead" (Phil. 3:10-11). If Paul was talking about a physical resurrection from physical death, it would have been senseless to write that he had not already attained it, or partially attained it (Phil. 3:16). Spiritually, this is the essence of what the normative Christian life should be. That which Paul longed for, is now available. After the completion of resurrection fulfillment, and post-A.D. 70, Christians can have it all in its fullness. "Therefore, encourage each other with these words" (1 Thess. 4:18).

"With them in the clouds . . ." As we've seen, in prophecy, clouds symbolize humans, spirit-realm beings, and those who have died in the

Lord—not atmospheric clouds. For instance, Hebrews 12:1 speaks of our being "surrounded by . . . a great cloud of witnesses." To see who is in this cloud read verses 22-24. Jude 4 and 12 also describe "godless men, who changed the grace of our God into a license for immortality and deny Jesus Christ" as "clouds without rain." Once again, Paul's message here is that, as we are caught up in the spirit realm, we become a part of that great cloud of witnesses.

"To meet the Lord . . ." Our feet never have to leave the ground for us to meet the Lord. In the Spirit, we meet (literally, have *a friendly encounter with*) the greater Jesus and are transformed into the fullness of his reality. As we are caught up in the spirit realm, where He is, we unconsciously do the things of the Lord (that please Him) without ever having to think about doing them. He becomes our new reality.

"Asleep in him . . ." Acts 7:60 says that Stephen fell asleep. He physically died in Christ (also see 1 Cor. 15:6). The *asleep* (a euphemism) are the physically dead who have died in Christ. Paul comforts his hearers by assuring them of what happens to believers who have died physically. But there *is more*.

"The dead in Christ . . ." This could be those described above who were asleep, or it could refer to another group. Jesus said in John 5:25, "A time is coming and *has now come* when the dead will hear the voice of the Son of God, and those who hear will live" (emphasis added). Proverbs 21:16 says, "A man who strays from wisdom comes to rest with the dead." Also, as we have seen above, "Wake up, O sleeper, rise from the dead, and Christ will shine on you" (Eph 5:14). This last verse refers to those believers who are physically alive but spiritually co-dead with Christ. They are not reigning and ruling with Him, nor "in Him," nor caught up with Him. Of course, they are saved and heaven-bound. But other than that, they are only co-crucified and co-buried with Him.

"We who are still alive . . ." These are the people who are physically alive and have come alive in Christ.

"And so we will be with the Lord forever . . ." Being "with the Lord forever" can start now as we are caught up with Him and in that "so great a cloud of witnesses!" (Heb. 12:1, 22-24).

"Encourage one another . . ." Being caught up in the Spirit is not simply a gleeful escape from physical/material reality. The Spirit changes, equips, and empowers us for ministry and for spiritual warfare. It does not make us disappear. Disappearance is *not* where the power is.

Anything Jesus did in his earthly ministry, we can do now and even greater things. And we receive levels of authority, blessings, and power to the degree that we are caught up with Him. 1st-century believers expected this kind of empowerment in their lives. Were they mistaken? Misled? Under a delusion? If it didn't happen then or hasn't happened for over nineteen hundred years, could they also have been wrong about other aspects of their faith? Of course not!

Please note, once again, that the next verse (1 Thessalonians 5:1) refers to times (plural) and dates (plural). There have been, are, and continue to be many occurrences of this available reality and opportunity addressed in this important passage. This "caught-up" experience has occurred, and I believe still is occurring, in the lives of individual believers throughout the history of the Church. Are you a part of this marvelous resurrection truth and fantastic promise? Maybe, now that you have seen a greater application, reality, and opportunity than you previously saw, you soon will be. Unfortunately, I think and feel that only a remnant, a small portion of those claiming to be Christians ever attain this level of being "caught up" with the greater Jesus, here and now, in this life, and on planet Earth.

1 Corinthians 15:51-57

> *Listen, I tell you a mystery: We will not all sleep, but we will all be changed—in a flash, in the twinkling of any eye, at the last trumpet. For the trumpet will sound, the dead will be raised imperishable, and we will be changed. For the perishable must clothe itself with the imperishable, and the mortal with immortality. . . .*
>
> *Then the saying that is written will come true: "Death has been swallowed up in victory. Where, O death, is your victory? Where, O death, is your sting?"*
>
> *The sting of death is sin, and the power of sin is the law. But thanks be to God! He gives us the victory through our Lord Jesus Christ.*

"We will all be changed . . ." Paul was talking about a coming reality in everyone's life. Please note, he does not say *removed*, but *changed*—transformed into the likeness of Christ. This change is miraculous; it is affected by the greater Jesus Christ, and it can occur "in a flash, in a twinkling of an eye," instantaneously. When the revelation of the unveiled and revealed greater Jesus hits us and we respond (remember, each in his own turn or order), it is like a spiritual lightning bolt. Suddenly, the Bible becomes a new book and the world of the spirit opens up to us.

"At the last trumpet . . ." When was all this to occur? Let's locate the last trumpet in Scripture. It's the seventh trumpet in Revelation 10 and 11. In prophetic symbolism, an angel sounding a trumpet represents a voice, or message, from God. And that's exactly what the last trumpet is! It is the message from the heavenly host proclaiming, "the kingdom of the world has become the kingdom of our Lord and of his Christ, and he will reign for ever and ever" (Rev. 11:15).

The last trumpet has already sounded in human history, many times, but not everyone has heard or received it. It continues to sound for individuals as they personally receive the revelation of the greater Jesus. The sounding of the last trumpet does not summon people to leave, but to reign on this earth in this life. "And you *have made them* to be a kingdom and priests to serve God, and they will reign on earth" (Rev. 5:10 – emphasis added). This is the same trumpet Jesus referred to when He said, "And He will send forth his angels with a *great trumpet and they will gather* his elect from the four winds, from one end of the heavens to the other" (Matt. 24:31, italics added; also see Zeph. 3:20).

When we receive and appropriate the unveiling and revealing of the greater Jesus, we are changed instantaneously into kings and priests to rule and reign in the kingdom of God. Quit trying to put this all off into the future. This is a powerful spiritual/physical reality, available then and here and here and now.

"The dead will be raised imperishable . . ." Who are these dead? In the facet of resurrection reality we are exploring here, they are those who are physically alive, but not reigning and ruling with Christ. As Paul said, "I want to know Christ and the power of his resurrection . . . and so, somehow, to attain to the resurrection of the dead" (Phil. 3:10-11). When? In his earthly life. Once again, that is why he also admonished believers to "Wake up, O sleeper, rise from the dead, and Christ will shine on you" (Eph. 5:14).

Earlier, Paul had written, "Flesh and blood cannot inherit the kingdom of God, nor does perishable inherit imperishable" (1 Cor. 15:50). We keep trying to drag the flesh into the kingdom; but the flesh is what holds us back from inheriting the kingdom. Our flesh is perishable, but our spirit is imperishable. It is eternal. "For you have been born again, not of perishable seed, but of the *imperishable*, through the living and enduring word of God" (1 Pet. 1:23 – emphasis added).

When we fully receive the revelation of the last trumpet, we are changed, i.e., transformed, not removed. We suddenly realize that we are *eternal*. Our bodies even change as we offer them to God as instruments of righteousness (Rom. 6:13) and living sacrifices (Rom. 12:1). Of course, our physical bodies die, stay on earth, and return to dust. This human eventuality and divinely determined destiny does not change (Heb. 9:27). But our spirits live forever, and postmortem, in new "spiritual bodies" that "God gives" (1 Cor. 15:38, 44).

The reality of the last trumpet revelation is that if we have been made alive in Christ, we *are immortal* (2 Cor. 5:4; Prov. 12:28). And when we fully realize our immortality, we are changed. We look at everything differently; we don't get all worried about earthly things; we think and operate on a different plane. We are "caught up with them in the clouds to meet the Lord in the air" (1 Thess. 4:17).

"Death has been swallowed up in victory . . ." Christ, by his resurrection, has destroyed death as a universal fact. It's a done deal (2 Tim. 1:10; Rom. 8:2; Rev. 21:4, 6). Therefore, when we are co-resurrected in and with Him, individually, death is destroyed for us (John 8:51). We no longer live after the flesh, but after the spirit. The reason most Christians are scared of physical death is that they have so little experience with the spirit dimension. It's actually a fear of the unknown. But when you get caught up in the Spirit and live in the Spirit with the greater Jesus, death loses its sting. It's no longer a big deal. But, if you haven't so been "caught up," death still holds its sting for you.

"The sting of death is sin . . ." Adam was afraid of meeting God and he hid from Him (Gen. 3:10). Why? It's because he had sinned. The result of his sin was death. Paul said, "For as in Adam all die, so in Christ all will be made alive" (1 Cor. 15:22). When we are dead in sin, all we know is the flesh. The idea of losing that flesh is frightening, because we feel it is all there is of us. So we hang on to it. We try to make our flesh safe, secure, happy, and comfortable—because we think it's all we have. But, when we are made alive spiritually and caught up in the air in Christ, we discover that our flesh is no longer our problem, or our treasure. We crucify it so we can be raised even higher spiritually in Christ and in the power of the resurrection. When that power takes over, the power of sin over us is gone. We can let the flesh go and live the resurrected life of Christ. We can walk supernaturally, unconsciously in the Spirit, now, in this life, and on this earth.

"The power of sin is the law . . ." Many of us keep trying to earn immortality by doing things, by obeying the law. We've got this image from the Dark Ages of Saint Peter standing at the gates, weighing our good deeds against our bad deeds. If getting into heaven through our good works of the flesh were possible, Christ's death on the cross would have been unnecessary. New Testament reality is that the power of sin—the flesh's inability to fulfill the law—is broken by the *fact* of Christ's death and resurrection, and it is broken *in us* by our co-resurrection in Christ. We are freed from doing the works of the flesh so that we can do the works of Jesus and even greater works by the power of his spirit.

"But thanks be to God! He gives us the victory through our Lord Jesus Christ." He gives—present tense—not will someday give. It is a great victory, here and now, not a great escape someday, by-and-by.

Please note, again, this major difference in human priorities and God's priorities. Human beings think mostly in terms of surviving and staying physically healthy, prospering materially, being emotionally happy, and perhaps being morally good. God's priorities are that we worship Him in spirit and truth, develop godly character (purity of heart), and that we reign and rule, spiritually and physically, with the greater Jesus in his kingdom on this earth, here and now. Oddly, enough, when we order our lives after God's priorities, we get more than we ever dreamed. We don't just survive, we thrive; we don't just prosper materially, we gain the riches of Christ. We don't just have happiness, which can be destroyed by circumstances; we have his joy, which cannot be touched by circumstances—even by our own physical death, which will certainly happen someday (Heb. 9:27). At that time we shall enter heaven, receive our new "spiritual body," and start enjoying our eternal rewards and/or suffering eternal loss.[24] In the meantime, we are not just good; we are empowered to do the works of Jesus and even greater works. That's a very, very good trade.

> **It is a great victory, here and now,
> not a great escape someday, by-and-by.**

And it's all about being "caught up with them to meet the Lord in the air" (1 Thess. 4:17).

How You Can Live in Raptured Reality—Now

As we have seen, the essence of being caught up in the air to meet the Lord and being changed in the twinkling of an eye is this: one must be *in Christ*—i.e., the greater Jesus. How do you know when you are in Christ? You will walk as Jesus did (1 John 2:6)—i.e., you will be doing the works that He did and even greater works (John 14:12).

But it goes deeper than that place of the internal breathing air—the place of the spirit. "Christ *in you,*" said Paul, is "the *hope* of glory" (Col. 1:27 – emphasis added). However, one hopes for something that one does not have (Rom. 8:24-25). As long as this hope remains a hope, you don't possess the fullness of Christ. For you "in Christ" is glory, here and now (2 Thess. 1:12; also Rom. 8:18; 9:23; 15:17). When we are caught up in the spirit in Christ, and He shows Himself to us as He is today, we are transformed into his likeness and are equipped to live victoriously and to minister in his power. In that dwelling place, we can live in such fellowship with Him that we don't have to consciously think about what we are doing or not doing. His presence becomes as natural to us as the air we breathe. And his glory is revealed in and through us.

Is it hard to enter into that kind of raptured relationship? Well, yes and no. It is hard because the flesh does not die easily or willingly. All we have to do is read Paul's laments in Romans 7 to see how our flesh struggles to keep from being crucified. It's also difficult to shake off the teachings of man (unlearning)—as good and sincerely motivated as they may have been—and respond to God's Word, illuminated by his Spirit.

But it is also easy because it is what the greater Jesus wants most to happen, and it is something He participates with us in doing, individually. Our part is to yield ourselves completely to Him in love and receive his revelation. "If anyone loves me," Jesus said, "he will obey my teaching. My Father will love him, and we will come to make our home with him" (John 14:23).

The hour of temptation, however, is that point in time when we are about to go into the spirit realm—to operate in the Holy Spirit, to learn, and to minister in the Spirit—but our flesh pulls us back. Likewise, we may still desire to get out of this world. Psychologically, all this appeals to our flesh. We want to get out of our problems and let Jesus come back to take care of the mess. But his desire and plan is for us to become an integral part of his kingdom, to co-reign and co-rule with Him as kings and priests, and play a vital role in changing the world.

Jesus is the resurrection and life. When we are in Him, we co-reign and co-rule with Him and we have life to the fullest. Anything less is less, much less. This is the reality of what being "caught up with them in the clouds to meet the Lord in the air" is all about. We can choose to partake or not partake—*right now!* So, how about you? How will you choose?

An Academic Excursus on *Aer*

Critical Objection:

Since I first wrote on the topic of this chapter in my now out-of-print books, *The Apocalypse Conspiracy* (1991) and *Shattering the 'Left Behind' Delusion* (2000), several charges have been leveled against me, especially my view regarding the meaning of the Greek word *aer* and the resulting location of Paul's catching up (1 Thess. 4:17). One such case was by someone who considers himself to be proficient in the Greek language used in the New Testament. His major charges are contained in this excursus, anonymously but principally and in quotes below, along with my response to him. Not surprisingly, no response came back.

Caution: The material in the excursus is written in an academic style and may be too tedious or technical for some. If so, skip this excursus and go to the next chapter. Others of you, however, may find it quite insightful and further supportive of my position re: *aer*. For easy and quickness of review and in keeping with academic style, I've placed reference footnotes at the bottom of the page instead of at the end of the book as I've done with all other endnotes:

- "*Strong's* does not assign the meaning of the related word 'aemi' to the word 'aer.' It merely says that 'aer' came from a word (aemi) which had a different (but related) meaning."
- "Very few of the lexical authorities even listed this related word 'aemi' or gave its definition."
- "There is no lexical basis whatsoever for the suggestion by some that the definition of the related word "aemi" is the meaning we should assign to the word "aer.""
- ""Aer" means the "air" in the atmosphere or sky above, not the air in our lungs or a euphemism for 'spiritually inside us.' All the other lexicons agree. Anyone asserting otherwise is going up against all the lexical authorities in the world."
- "... have erroneously taken *Strong's* definition for 'aemi' and applied it to 'aer' .... have not provided any other lexical support beyond *Strong's*."
- "In view of the usage of the word '*aer*' in the above passages, how could anyone make a statement such as the following: 'The word '*aer*' is never used in the sense of the sky above, where the clouds are and the birds fly.'"
- "The standard lexical authorities we quoted above confirm this 'atmosphere above the earth' meaning of 'air.'"
- "And the passages which use the word 'aer' define it just like the Greek lexicons do."
- "The lexicons do not restrict the meaning of 'aer' to just twelve feet above ground."
- "[This] contrary view . . . requires setting aside the standard lexical definitions and all seven of its New Testament uses."
- "The absurdity of this definition of "aer" becomes easily apparent when we plug it back into the context and see its implications."

My Response:

William Barclay's comments certainly apply here: "On the meaning of words everything depends. No one can build up a theology without a clear definition of the terms which are to be used in it."[1]

First, my interlocutor admits that "the actual connotative meaning of a Greek word cannot be obtained merely from its lexical definition, but is best derived from its general usage throughout the New Testament." He further states that "it is a common error of first year Greek students to assume that the root definition must be applied in every usage." He cites "context" and not "lexicons" as "the final determining factor."

Klein, Blomberg, and Hubbard recommend that "students should feel free to question the lexicons. That is, students will not always agree with the category of meaning in which the 'experts' have located a specific text. Because of the complexity of word meanings, the interpreter should seek to discover all the information about a word that may help in determining its meaning in a specific passage."[2]

Likewise, Barber agrees that "lexicons are indispensable reference tools" but clarifies that "sooner or later, however, some expertise in biblical languages becomes a necessity."[3] He actually warns that "even the finest of lexicons may be misleading." Hence, "a new generation of Bible students [must] be able to modify and advance the work of those who have preceded them."[4] Of course, that is my intention in this case.

Secondly, my interlocutor also admits that "in the air" is "that realm . . . all around us" and "the spiritual realm is all around us." To this I agree. Yet this "air" is not "the air where the clouds are," as he later claims. There is a clear distinction in the Greek, which brings me to my next point.

Thirdly, in the New Testament two words are translated as "air"—*aer* and *ouranos*. But he never mentions this other word. And while it is

---

[1] William Barclay, *More New Testament Words* (New York, NY.: Harper, 1958), 9.
[2] William W. Klein, Craig L. Blomberg, and Robert L. Hubbard, Jr., *Introduction to Biblical Interpretation* (Dallas, TX.: Word, 1993), 199.
[3] Cyril J. Barber, *Introduction to Theological Research* (Newburgh, IN.: Trinity Press, 1982), 101.
[4] Ibid., 114.

true "not all Greek language resources recognize this distinction" and that both can be considered as air between earth and heaven, many resources do recognize a significant difference.

Louw and Nida, in their section titled "Regions Above the Earth" contrast the meaning of these two Greek words thusly: *Ouranos* as "the vault arching high over the earth from one horizon to another, as well as the sun, moon, and stars – sky."[5] *Aer* is "the space immediately above the earth's surface, and not including the dome arching over the earth – air . . . 'for you will be talking into the air 1 Cor. 14:9.'"[6]

Robinson agrees that *aer* is "the lower vapoury atmosphere" as "opp. (opposed to) the higher purer region."[7] Abbot-Smith draws the same contrast for *aer* as "the lower air which surrounds the earth, as opp. To the purer . . . of the higher regions."[8] Thayer's makes the same distinction.[9]

Friberg and Friberg concur with this distinction that *aer* is "the space immediately above the earth"[10] and *ouranos* is "(1) as the atmosphere directly above the earth, *sky, air firmament* (MT 6:26; LU 17:24); (2) as the starry heaven *firmament, sky* (MT 24:29a)."[11]

Arndt, Gingrich, and Danker cite "the atmosphere immediately about the earth's surface" as their first meaning and "the space above the earth, *sky, space, air*" as their second and broader meaning of *aer*.[12]

---

[5] Johannes P. Louw and Eugene A. Nida, eds., *Greek-English Lexicon of the New Testament based on Sematic Domains*, Vol. 1, (New York, NY.: United Bible Societies, 1988), 1.5, 2.
[6] Ibid., 3.
[7] Edward Robinson, *Greek and English Lexicon* (New York, NY.: Harper, 1855), 15.
[8] G. Abbott-Smith, *A Manual Greek Lexicon of the New Testament* (Edinburgh: T & T Clark, 1921), 11.
[9] Joseph Henry Thayer, *A Greek-English Lexicon of the New Testament* (New York, NY.: Harper, 1898), 13, 464.
[10] Timothy Friberg and Barbara Friberg, *Analytical Lexicon of the Greek New Testament* (Grand Rapids, MI.: Baker Books, 2000), 36.
[11] Ibid., 288.
[12] W.F. Arndt, F.W. Gingrich, and F.W. Danker, *A Greek-English Lexicon of the New Testament and Other Early Christian Literature*, 3rd ed. (Chicago, IL.: University of Chicago Press, 2000), 23.

Fourthly, the question next becomes, how low is the lower air? This is where etymology becomes most helpful. Etymology is "the study of the original form and meaning of words."[13] Robinson insists "on the importance of the student's seeing the original form and import of each word and suffix or prefix." He admits that "this is not all that is needed by any means, but it is a beginning, and the right beginning."[14] In his section on "roots" he says that "they represent the original stock from which other words as a rule come." He estimates that "of the 90,000 words in a Greek lexicon only 40,000 are what are termed classic words" and that "the new words . . . are usually made from one of the old roots by various combinations, or . . . after the analogy of the old words."[15] Curtius views "this [etymological] process" as "the oldest method of word-formation."[16]

Barber emphasizes that "the study of Greek terms must also be in accordance with the root of the word." Yet he cautions the student that "some Greek terms have an obscure origin, and the root may be hard to trace."[17]

Fortunately, the etymology of the Greek word *aer* is not difficult to trace. In addition to *Strong's* recognition of the derivative relationship of *aer* with its root verb *aemi* – meaning "to breathe unconsciously, i.e., respire; by analogy, to blow); 'air' (as naturally circumambient): – air," we have others.

Liddell and Scott, for instance, indicate that *aemi* is etymologically related to *ao*, which means "blow."[18] Pickering relates *aer* as derived from *ao*.[19] Thus, we have a continuous flow of meaning that brings us full circle. Hence, Liddell and Scott in their meanings for *aemi* give

---

[13] A.T. Robinson, *A Grammar of the Greek New Testament in the Light of Historical Research* (New York, NY.: Hodder & Stoughton, 1919), 143.
[14] ibid.
[15] Ibid., 144.
[16] Georg Curtius, translated by Augustus S. Wilkins and Edwin B. England, *Principles of Greek Etymology*, Vol. 1, 5th ed., (London: John Murray, 1886), 24.
[17] Barber, *Introduction to Theological Research*, 113.
[18] Henry George Liddell and Robert Scott, *A Greek-English Lexicon* (Oxford: Clarendon Press, 1968), 299.
[19] John Pickering, *A Comprehensive Lexicon of the Greek Language* (Boston, MA.: Wilkins, Carter, and Co., 1848), 21.

"breathe hard" and "blow." For their meanings of *aer*, they cite the "lower air" and compare it with a "mist, haze." This is in opposition to *aither*, which is "the pure upper air." They also mention "exhalations."[20] Hence, *aer* is the air that is close by and we breathe.

Likewise, Greenlee's lexicon ties *aer* back to *aemi*,[21] as does the *The Word Study Concordance* with *aemi* meaning "to breathe."[22]

Lastly, and in light of the above lexical and etymological insights, let's review the seven uses of *aer* in the New Testament with an interest in identifying the location of this "lower air":

Verse (KJV)	Location of air
Acts 22:23 – "tossing dust into the air"	Immediate proximity
1 Cor. 9:26 – "I box in such a way, as not beating the air"	Immediate proximity
1 Cor. 14:9 – "speaking into the air"	Inside a person and Immediate proximity
Eph. 2:2 – "prince of the power of the air, of the spirit that is now now working in the sons of disobedience"	Inside a person and immediate proximity
1 Thess. 4:17 – "to meet the Lord in the air"	?
Rev. 9:2 – "the sun and the air were darkened"	Inconclusive
Rev. 16:17 – "poured out his bowl upon the air"	Inconclusive

---

[20] Liddell and Scott, *A Greek-English Lexicon*, 30, 37.
[21] J. Harold Greenlee, *A New Testament Greek Morpheme Lexicon* (Grand Rapids, MI.: Zondervan, 1983), 4.
[22] George V. Wigram and Ralph D. Winter, *The Word Study Concordance* (Wheaton, IL.: Tyndale, 1978), 15.

Four of these seven usages under consideration above certainly signify a location within the immediate proximity and/or inside a person. The latter two usages are most likely symbolic and inconclusive as to location. So our question is, where is the "air" in 1 Thessalonians 4:17 located?

I must conclude that a legitimate lexical, etymological, and usage case can be made for the location of *aer* as being within a person and in the immediate proximity. For other reasons that I have further outlined in this chapter, I believe Paul's use of this *aer* in 1 Thessalonians 4:17 is synonymous with the spirit and the spirit realm. Surely, it is not the air in the sense of the sky above, where the clouds are located, the birds fly, the stars and planets revolve, or heaven itself. That air is clearly distinguished in the Greek as the *ouranos* air.

At my request, Dr. Ronald J. Allen, a Greek scholar and Associate Professor at Christian Theological Seminary in Indianapolis, Indiana, has reviewed all the arguments and correspondence between me and my interlocutor on the possible meaning of this word *aer*. He writes:

> "Noē has established a plausible, though not provable, interpretation of the connection between *aer* with *aemi*. While it may be true that a derivative may not always directly echo its root in meaning, it is nonetheless true that derivatives can do so. Conversely, there is no reason to assume that a derivative and a root are disconnected. In addition, it must be acknowledged that people who write lexicons are driven by theological viewpoints. They may not be prepared to find Noē's meaning. But Noē has established a high degree of possibility and that is all a scholar can do."

In conclusion, Paul's "catching up" was both an eschatological event for the dead in Christ and a real, literal, and spiritual experience for alive believers back, then and there. For the alive, it did not necessitate their feet leaving the ground or their being removed from planet Earth. I further believe that this catching up has been an ongoing and available reality, opportunity, and experience ever since. Unfortunately few Christians are aware of it or seek it out.[23]

In this regard, Ladd has noted that the meaning of "the expression 'in Christ'. . . has been vigorously debated." He states that some have emphasized "its 'mystical' dimension." But in harmony with what I have presented in this chapter and excursus, he contends that "it is analogous to the air. As we are in the air and the air is in us, so we are in Christ and Christ is in us."[24] Of course, this dualism of Christ in you and you in Christ is presented by Jesus in John 15:1-7. Yet many have assumed that both of these phrases are speaking singularly of salvation. Certainly, Christ in you is part of the salvation experience and an ongoing reality. I maintain the you-in-Christ portion is something else, i.e., part of the catching up experience (see 1 John 2:5-6; 3:6, 24; John 14:12).

> **"They may not be prepared to find Noē's meaning. But Noē has established a high degree of possibility and that is all a scholar can do."**

---

[23] For more on this see: John Noē, *Shattering the 'Left Behind' Delusion* (Bradford, PA.: International Preterist Association, 2000), 23-25, 32, 102-105, 110, 117-118 – Out of Print.

[24] George Eldon Ladd, *A Theology of the New Testament* (Grand Rapids, MI.: Eerdmans, 1974), 523.

Chapter 10

He Wants You to Live in the City

A city coming down to earth from heaven! Entering through pearly gates! Walking on streets of gold! Eating fruit from the tree of life! Drinking water from the river of life! No more death or mourning or crying or pain! Perfect everything! What could possibly be wrong with such visions, such divine promises?

Absolutely, nothing! Revelation 21 and 22 promised all those things and more. These last two chapters of the Bible unveil and reveal the climax, the grand finale, the peak, the pinnacle, the culmination of God's plan of progressive revelation and the fulfillment of his plan of redemption.

> *"Come, I will show you the bride, the wife of the Lamb." And he carried me away in the Spirit to a mountain great and high, and showed me the Holy City, Jerusalem, coming down out of heaven from God.* (Rev. 21:10).

What does this climactic verse really show us and mean? Once again, and like with the Wedding Supper of the Lamb in Chapter 6, I cannot adequately explain this reality (though I shall try). It must be experienced.

A Tale of Two Cities

Instead of "The Revelation of Jesus Christ," another title the Book of Revelation could have employed is, "A Tale of Two Cities"[1]—i.e., Babylon and New Jerusalem. Together they comprise over four of Revelation's twenty-two chapters. And as we have already seen with Babylon (Chapter 8), the proper identification of the who, where, and when of these two prophetic cities is critical to the proper understanding of and for the obedience with the whole of its prophecy.

Howard-Brook and Gwyther set the stage for this two-city comparative in noting that "the vision of Babylon as fallen prepares the way for the vision of New Jerusalem. . . . In the vision, New Jerusalem is the ultimate reality, while Babylon is a gross counterfeit of that reality."[2] Therefore, who would want to live in Babylon? The sad answer, sad to say, and as we shall continue to see is that most of us already do.

Confusing and obscuring the proper identification of this New Jerusalem has been the evolution of five major views over the course of Church history:

1) Eusebius, a 4th-century Christian leader and writer, who is often called "the father of Church history," mused that "Constantine's buildings in Jerusalem might be the new Jerusalem of prophecy (Eusebius *Life* 3.33)."[3]
2) It's heaven itself—"the final destination of God' people, the heavenly city, where they will experience the presence of God for eternity."[4]
3) It's "the creation of new heavens and a New Earth, a resurrected universe inhabited by resurrected people living with the resurrected Jesus (Revelation 21:1-4),"[5] a "cosmic resurrection and regeneration,"[6] "God's victorious transformation of the whole cosmos."[7]
4) It's a restored "final Garden of Eden" in which "the curse of the fall is reversed and God's plan to live among his people is fully realized" and "where God will fulfill all human needs."[8] It's "a beautiful connection between the first book of the Bible and the last. . . . a paradise which was lost. . . . a paradise restored. . . . the same heaven and earth but gloriously rejuvenated, with no weeds, thorns, or thistles, and so on."[9]

5) A literal, cube-shaped, and future space city or mother-ship space station hovering in air over earth – "1,400 miles" wide, 1,400 miles long, and 1,400 miles high.[10]

What Really Is the New Jerusalem?

Something is dreadfully wrong with what the end-time traditionalists keep telling us about the glorious realities of "the Holy City, Jerusalem, coming down out of heaven from God" (Rev. 21:10).

First, they tell us that, as wonderful as all those realities are, we can't have them now. They want us to believe that God's most exciting promises are all out in the future somewhere awaiting fulfillment someday.

But, and once again, chapters 21 and 22 are part of the whole prophecy of Revelation, which was all declared to unveil and reveal things that *all* "must soon (shortly) take place" (Rev. 1:1; 22:6b), were "at hand" (Rev. 1:3; 22:10b), were obeyable, heedable, and keepable (Rev. 1:3; 22:7), and were not to be sealed up (Rev. 22:10a), back then and there for Revelation's original readers and have been just as relevant, just as "at hand," for us ever since that time (Rev. 10:11)! The fact is, Jesus kept his word—He was and is a promise keeper—and did come "soon" riding a white horse, on the clouds, and in age-ending judgment (Rev. 22:7, 12, 20 – see again Chapter 4). He also brought into being this Holy City.

Second, they tell us that these realities of the New Jerusalem are all literal, physical, material objects. They want us to believe that God's highest ideal for humankind is a physical, material paradise—a space city or space craft.

But, as we shall see, those are man's ideas, not God's. In the Revelation, much of the language is parabolic and figurative, not literal and physical. As we have seen, it uses physical symbols we understand to convey spiritual/physical truths and realities that we don't understand. Also, numbers have spiritual significance, not mathematical meanings.

Third, they tell us that it's a new or renewed planet and a new or renewed cosmos and heaven after God has destroyed this present material world, its atmosphere, as well as the heaven that now exists.

But in many places the Bible states that our present cosmos (planet and universe) are "without end" and have been "eternally established."

What's more, nowhere does the Bible prophesy of another heaven taking the place of the one now existing.[11]

Fourth, they tell us that it's a restored, sinless, evil-less, pure and pristine Garden of Eden where "someday all the evil and injustice of this world will be destroyed."[12]

But the biblical and historical facts are that the original, pre-fall, and God-characterized "very good" Garden of Eden contained both evil and sin (Gen. 1:31). They were put there by God Himself; first, in the form of the tree of the knowledge of good and evil (Gen. 2:9, 17) and, secondly, via the tempting serpent, Satan (Gen. 3:1), whom God cast down to this earth and into this garden (Isa. 14:12; Ezek. 28:13-19).[13]

Indeed, something is dreadfully wrong.

Why Such Deceptions?

Why would Satan and his superhuman cohorts go to such elaborate lengths to get us to believe a bunch of half-truths and fantasies about God's ultimate plan for humankind? I can think of three very good reasons:

1) They know that human beings don't feel nearly the sense of urgency about future hopes and fantasies that they feel about the pressing concerns of their day-to-day lives.
2) They know that once we grasp and tap into the full reality of what God has promised, they can never again use the weaknesses of our flesh to intimidate us and keep us from reaching our full potential in Christ, here and now.
3) They know that once people enter the present reality of the Holy City, they lose all control over them, allowing them to pose a major threat to their strongholds in the world.

Think about it. These deceivers are smart enough to know that they cannot get Christians to abandon the idea of the kingdom of God. Jesus had too much to say about it. And they know that Christians long for a better day, in a better world.

So what do they do? They take God's truths and twist them just enough to make their distortions sound plausible and attractive. With Eve, Satan said in effect, "You can beat this death rap God is holding over your head. Besides, God knows that knowing good and evil will make you your own god, and you'll no longer need Him or be subject to his commands." What did Eve do? She said, "That sounds good to me. . . . Give me a bite. . . . Adam, you've gotta' taste this forbidden fruit!" But she and Adam did not immediately drop dead, physically. It took a while before they began to realize just how much they'd lost, both physically and spiritually. Many people still don't understand or so realize this loss.

But now, in the promise of the Holy City, God has announced the restoration of everything that was lost in the Garden of Eden. So, what do Satan and his demonic cohorts do? They say, "Sure, there's going to be a New Jerusalem, and you can live with God in it if that's what you want . . . but that's all out in the future. . . . Right now, you have more important things to think about."

They take God's truths and twist them just enough to make their distortions sound plausible and attractive.

Does this deception work? Just look around at the fruit it is producing through the distorted teachings and prostituted preaching of religious Babylon. Masses of Christians today are squabbling with each other over when it will all take place and whether a literal city—where they will live in perfect harmony with everybody—will come down out of the sky some day, or whether they'll be caught up ("raptured") to it. Millions of Christians, who talk endlessly about the future dawning of a better day, drag out of bed each morning and go out to lead defeated lives in the day that faces them. People who can't even control their own lives talk about reigning and ruling over the whole universe someday.

Ridiculous, you say? Exactly!

In this final chapter, let's see what the Scriptures actually say about the reality and nature of the New Jerusalem, what we'll be doing there, and why you don't have to die to go and live in this glorious city. Next, we'll see how other scriptures interpret the various symbols of this city. Then, as we've done in each of the preceding chapters, we'll examine what these biblical truths mean for us Christians in our daily lives, here and now.

A Present Spirit-Realm/Physical-Realm Reality

As we have seen, Christianity today, and in general, has become a pale shadow of the faith and kingdom its Founder announced, taught, modeled, conferred, delivered, and intended. Nowhere is this disparity more obvious than in Revelation 21 and 22, where Jesus described the normal state of those who are "forcing his way into it" (the kingdom of God – Luke 16:16; Matt. 11:12). As you read the rest of this chapter, compare Jesus' description here to the prostituted, watered-down, and diluted doctrines and practices that are being taught, modeled, and experienced in most churches today. Let me explain.

In his Gospel teachings, Jesus spoke of the kingdom of God as a present, ongoing, spirit-realm reality that powerfully impacts both the spiritual and physical realms. In Revelation 21 and 22, He presents his bride as a Holy City, the New Jerusalem, which is made up of overcomers—and *only* overcomers—people who are being refined through great tribulation, people who are standing firm against the beast systems of the world, and people coming out of submission to the great prostitute. These are those who hold to his testimony by doing his kingdom works and even greater works. Hence, these are those who continuously clothe themselves in the robes of his righteousness.

Yet religious Babylon (the great prostitute, antithesis, and constant opponent of the New Jerusalem) falsely announces herself to be the bride of Christ. She proclaims the judgment of God and the New Jerusalem to be literal and future events and holds them like a sword to the throats of all who dare to live in their reality in this present world. She uses the symbols of judgment and rewards to make idols of the law and of her rituals and programs, and she extracts great sacrifices and material wealth from all who get caught up in her bondage of self-fulfillment and faithless works. For every promise of life in the Apocalypse of Jesus Christ, Babylon offers a deadly counterfeit that can only be discerned by the eyes and ears of the spirit (see again Chapter 8).

During Jesus' earthly ministry, most Jews were so busy looking for a political messiah to come and liberate physical Israel that they crucified the real Messiah when He appeared. Likewise, the religious Babylon of our day is so busy looking for an earthly Jesus to come back and set up a material kingdom on this earth and centered in a rebuilt temple in

Jerusalem that they, in essence, are crucifying the unveiled, spirit-realm, and greater Jesus who lives and operates in and among us now.

This isn't something new I've dreamed up. The Apostle Paul knew all this. That's why he used the expression *the present city of Jerusalem* to represent what John called Babylon and characterized it as "slavery (bondage)." "But the Jerusalem that is above is free, and she is our mother"—not someday "will be" but "is," back then and there (see Gal. 4-5, esp. 4:25-26). Furthermore, Jesus prophesied of the coming destruction of that present city of Jerusalem and its Temple, but never of its rebuilding or the reestablishment of animal sacrifices—nor did any New Testament writer. This re-Judaization-of-Christianity notion is, arguably, the greatest heresy in the Church today.

Another View

I believe that what we shall be laying out in this chapter is the most pertinent, relevant, and life-giving understanding, fulfillment, and ongoing relevancy for the new heavens and new earth and its city the New Jerusalem. It is my sincere hope that Christians reading this explanation will open their hearts to let God give them his "spirit of wisdom and revelation" (Eph. 1:17) about the present-day truths and realities of this vital portion of Scripture.

But first let me offer this suggestion that can help you receive the glorious spirit-realm/physical realm realities of this climactic destruction and restoration vision.

Quit Putting This Out into the Future or Back into the Past

The first step toward achieving the intended and proper understanding of Revelation 21 and 22's prophecy is to quit putting all of its significance out into the future or back into the past (the preterist view). For far too long, most Christian churches have emphasized coping with life in the physical and material world, while getting ready for future cataclysmic events and going to heaven. Consequently, Jesus has been depicted as a cosmic buddy who looks out for us, gives us whatever we want, and will someday zap all our enemies and wipe out this evil planet. Meanwhile, heaven has often been presented as little more than an ethereal place Christians go to when they die.

Yet that's not the message of the Revelation. I believe it's time for a renewed sense of judgment and fear of the Lord in the body of Christ. We Christians are deceived if we think we are not going to be judged for our cowardly, unbelieving approach to serving God. Many are being judged right now. That's why so many Christians are leading troubled and defeated lives. Likewise, many churches are being judged right now and are caught up in a great turmoil and confusion because of their prostitution of and disobedience to the Word of God (Chapter 8).

It's time to abandon our preoccupation with the end of the world; Israel, and a millennial utopian paradise. Those "last days" are behind us, not ahead of us.[14] Our business is hearing, heeding, and acting upon what is at hand and most relevant. Our task is to overcome—here and now—and inherit all that God has provided.

The Holy City, the New Jerusalem, is the climax. It is not a future physical city that's going to drop down out of the sky into the Middle East someday or be suspended in space and hover above American soil. It is the present, ongoing reality of the greater Jesus and his blood-washed, kingdom-advancing saints living in perfect union in God the Father, the Son, and the Holy Spirit. Here is the text for this present-day revelation and reality: Revelation 21:1-7:

> *Then I saw a new heaven and a new earth, for the first heaven and the first earth had passed away, and there was no longer any sea. I saw the Holy City, the New Jerusalem, coming down out of heaven from God, prepared as a bride beautifully dressed for her husband. And I heard a loud voice from the throne saying, "Now the dwelling of God is with men, and he will live with them. They will be his people, and God himself will be with them and be their God. He will wipe every tear from their eyes. There will be no more death or mourning or crying or pain, for the old order of things has passed away."*
>
> *He who was seated on the throne said, "I am making everything new!" Then he said, "Write this down, for these words are trustworthy and true."*
>
> *He said to me: "It is done. I am the Alpha and the Omega, the Beginning and the End. To him who is thirsty I will give to drink without cost from the spring of the water of life. He who*

overcomes will inherit all this, and I will be his God and he will be my son.

John's Last Vision – What Does It Mean, How Was It Fulfilled?

From this, John's last and lengthiest vision, we will highlight and address key portions of this poignant passage of prophecy and explain what it means by utilizing other Scriptures. Thus, our methodology will employ, once again, the basic hermeneutical principle of "letting Scripture interpret Scripture."

"Then I saw a new heaven and a new earth, for the first heaven and the first earth had passed away." Some six hundred years before Christ, God first promised through the prophet Isaiah, "Behold, I will create new heavens and a new earth. The former things will not be remembered . . . . I will create Jerusalem to be a delight and its people a joy. . . . the sound of weeping and of crying will be heard in it no more" (Isa. 65:17-19; 66:22). Also, "the Lord is coming with fire . . . he will bring down his anger with fury, and his rebuke with flames of fire. . . the Lord will execute his judgment upon all men (Isa. 66:15-16). These Old Testament verses clearly foretold the prophecies of Revelation 21 and 22.

As we saw in Chapter 2, pp-61-62, something most Bible readers *do not know* is—*three different entities* in the Bible are called "heaven and earth." One of those entities would never pass away. Another had already passed away at the time of Jesus. A third would soon pass away and be made new.

Since I have written extensively about these three different "heaven-and-earth" entities in my book *The Perfect Ending for the World* and, scripturally and historically, demonstrated them to be: the physical creation, Babylon in the 6th century, and Old Covenant biblical Judaism, respectively, I shall not go into these details or duplicate that material here.[15] Also, as I documented therein in a chapter titled, "The New Heaven and New Earth—Are They Really a Sequel?" and supported with quotations from the Jewish-Roman and only eyewitness historian,

Josephus, 1st-century Jews viewed their Temple as if it were a "heaven and earth."

McKenzie adds this tidbit to this understanding:

> . . . the Jews saw the Temple (being God's abode) as a microcosm of the universe. Just as heaven was God's throne and earth this footstool (Acts 7:44-50), so the Temple mirrored the created order (cf. Heb. 8:5). . . . Josephus understood the tripartite structure of the tabernacle to signify 'the earth [= outer court] and the sea [= inner court], since these . . . are accessible to all, but the third portion [the holy of holies] he reserved for God alone, because heaven is inaccessible to men (*Ant.* 3.181; cf 3.123)."[16]

That Old Covenant, Temple system was the old heaven and earth that Jesus said would "pass away" or "disappear" (Matt. 24:35; 5:18). It did, exactly as and when Jesus specified (Matt. 24:1-34; Luke 21:20-22, 32 – see again Chapter 4).

Thus, the Bible's new heaven and new earth was not and will not be a re-creation of the physical universe. Also, it is not heaven—there are evil and sinners in it, as we shall see. Rather, it was the complete arrival of the new covenantal order on planet Earth upon the destruction and desolation of that old order (see Matt. 23: 36-38; Heb. 8:13; 9:8-10). Likewise, the Holy City, the New Jerusalem, which is located in that new heaven and new earth, is also determined by this completed change in God's covenants and does not await a future change of cosmos—contrary to most popular views.

"And there was no longer any sea." Some end-timers insist this statement means someday the oceans (if not all waters) that form the natural divisions of this earth will be gone and our world, which today is mostly covered by water, will be one big land mass. We won't need water, they maintain, because our new resurrected bodies will not require it (unlike our present bodies whose blood is approximately ninety percent water). Other interpreters take a more figurative approach saying it means someday there will no longer be a distinction between God's people and all others, because the great "sea of humanity," which had separated Israel from non-Israelites (Gentiles), or among the people of the earth in general, has been removed. Some others say it refers to a future and placid state of society that is no longer tossed about like the sea because there are no longer any evil powers, evil people, or sin.

But if you were a 1st-century Jewish person hearing or reading these words your mind would have immediately gone to that "heaven-and-earth" Temple. Why? It's because a literal "bronze Sea" was located in the southeast corner of the Temple and used for purification washings. Second Kings 25:13 tells us so, and how the Babylonians broke it into pieces and carried the metal back to Babylon.

Two other accounts of this Sea discuss its construction in 1 Kings 7:23-44 and 2 Chronicles 4:2-5. Its size was "ten cubits (7 1/2 feet) from rim to rim and five cubits high" (also see Jer. 52:17, 20-23). It is estimated that this Sea held up to 20,000 gallons of water. No doubt, that is why it was referred to as a "Sea." So when the "Sea" was taken from the Temple during the Babylonnian exile and again by the Romans following the Jewish-Roman War of A.D. 66-70, it was obvious that God was in the midst of judging his people. Hence, when John in Revelation writes "there was no longer any sea," 1st-century Jewish thought would have immediately gone to the Temple and its soon-coming destruction by the Roman armies, exactly as prophesied by Christ. This "Sea," along with many other valuable items, were taken away from the Temple and back to Rome for the Triumph parade and spoils for the soldiers.

"No more sea" could further have meant that there was no longer any need to travel to the Temple to be cleansed, for the sea had been transformed into a mighty river of grace and life flowing throughout the world from the heavenly temple (see Ezek. 47:1-9).

"I saw the Holy City, the New Jerusalem coming down out of heaven from God, prepared as a bride beautifully dressed for her husband." Twice, and clearly and succinctly, John the revelator states that "the Bride is not just *in* the City; the Bride *is* the City:"[17]

> *One of the seven angels who had the seven bowls full of the seven last plaques came and said to me, "Come, I will show you* **the bride,** *the wife of the Lamb." And he carried me away in the spirit to a mountain great and high, and showed me the* **Holy City, Jerusalem,** *coming down out of heaven from God* (Rev. 21:9-10 – bold emphasis added).

Notice that you don't go up to this city—it comes down to you! And it's not heaven, but comes down from heaven. Heaven is its origin. It came down in John's day, and it keeps on coming down. The fact that this New Jerusalem constantly keeps coming down out of (*from*) heaven is further proof that it is not heaven itself.[18]

And who is the bride? We've met her before. She, too, is the product of the change of covenants and not a change of cosmos. She is the bride who has made herself ready for the wedding supper of the Lamb, who is dressed in "fine linen, bright and clean [which stands for the righteous acts of the saints]," and who lifts her veil (the mental image of the historical Jesus and his earthly ministry) in order to eat the marriage supper and become one with the Bridegroom (Rev. 19:7-9; see again Chapter 6). Before that, John had described her as the 144,000 (symbolizing a very large number) who bore the name of the Father on their foreheads (a symbol of ownership, in sharp contrast with those who have the mark or number of the beast) (see Rev. 7:3-8; Rev. 13:16-18), and as a multitude who were singing a new song that only they knew, who did not defile themselves but kept themselves pure, who follow the Lamb wherever He goes, who were purchased by the Lamb and offered to God and the Lamb as first-fruits, and in whose mouths no lie was found (Rev. 14:1-5).

Now again we meet the bride as the Holy City, the New Jerusalem. Notice that most of the same symbols characterize her in this description as well. She looks like a bride beautifully dressed for her husband; the glory of God shines on her like the brilliance of a fine jewel; she is built on twelve foundations (Rev. 21:14 – the teachings of the apostles), has twelve gates (Rev. 21:12 – for the twelve tribes of Israel); she has intimate relations with the Lamb, and nothing impure is ever to enter into her (Rev. 21:1-22:5; compare with Eph. 2:20).[19]

The fact that this New Jerusalem constantly keeps coming down out of (*from*) heaven is further proof that it is not heaven itself

---

The bride is definitely not the faithless Israel whom God gave a "certificate of divorce and sent her away because of all her adulteries" (Jer. 3:6-11). Nor is she her unfaithful sister Judah. Nor is the bride the adulterous wife, the great prostitute who today calls herself, the Church, who is also cast out (Rev. 19:1-3). Rather, she is the greater Jesus' faithful and "pure virgin" bride (Rev. 19:7; 2 Cor. 11:2). The bride consists of only "those who [continuously] wash their robes [via righteous acts], that they may have the right to the tree of life and may go through the gates into the city" (Rev. 22:14; Isa. 61:10). Hendriksen elaborates that "every person carries about with him a robe. He is always weaving it, for his every thought, word, and deed enters into to it. That robe is splashed, dirty, and altogether filthy. . . . In the entire world . . . there is no power that can clean it. . . . all earthly detergents are useless. . . . That robe is your character."[20]

"And I heard a loud voice from the throne saying, 'Now the dwelling [the tabernacle] of God is with men and he will live with them. They will be his people, and God Himself will be with them and be their God.'" God didn't always dwell inside people. Once He dwelt on Mount Sinai and gave Moses the Ten Commandments. Then He had the Hebrew people build a tabernacle, or a tent, for Him to dwell in. Later He had Solomon build a more permanent temple for his dwelling place. But "now," i.e., back then and onward and based upon the work of the Messiah, Jesus, in that 1st century, God has again relocated. He has also cleared away Christianity's greatest obstacle in its path—biblical Judaism.[21] "Now" He dwells inside Christians (*in new heavens, and He wants to make them new earth*, as we shall shortly see.) Nowadays, we Christians are God's tabernacle, his dwelling place, and the "living stones" of his temple "built into a spiritual house to be a holy priesthood, offering spiritual sacrifices acceptable to God through Jesus Christ" (1 Pet. 2:5; Eph. 2:20-22; John 14:23).

Hence, no temple or "special place of God's presence," is needed (Rev. 21:22) for "the city itself becomes a temple."[22] The fellowship of the inhabitants "with their God is direct and immediate."[23] We are "now" "his people" (1 Pet. 2:9-10) and "constantly in [can be] His immediate and loving and abiding presence."[24] Hence, these "citizens joyfully obey God's will. His will is their desire. They see his face; they enjoy His favour. . . . They worship Him. . . His name is on their foreheads, for He openly acknowledges them as His very own, and they joyfully confess Him as their Lord. Thus, they reign for ever and ever."[25] All this joyful reality is more evidence that this new and available reality is covenantal and not cosmic, having been determined by the change of covenants and not a still-future change of cosmos.

"He will wipe every tear from their eyes. There will be no more death or mourning or crying or pain, for the old order of things has passed away." This definitely has not happened yet, masses of Christians are still being told today. To prove it, all you have to do is look around—death, tears, mourning, crying, and pain still exist. Therefore, this verse could not possibly have been fulfilled reason most Christians.

But long before the birth, life, death, resurrection, and age-ending judgment of Jesus the prophet Isaiah utilized these same words in speaking of this coming time of covenantal change and the salvation to be brought by the Messiah:

> *On this mountain he will destroy the **shroud [sin]** that enfolds all peoples, the **sheet [Old Covenant system]** that covers all nations; he will **swallow up death [via resurrection]** forever. The Sovereign Lord will **wipe away the tears from all faces**; he will remove the **disgrace [sin]** of his people from all the earth. The Lord has spoken.*
>
> *In that day they will say, "Surely this is our God; we trusted in him, and he **saved us**. This is the Lord, we trusted in him; let us rejoice and be glad in his **salvation*** (Isa. 25:7-9; also see 2:2; 35:4-10; 65:17-19 – bold emphasis mine).

Jesus fulfilled these very prophecies exactly as and when He said He would—within the generation of his contemporaries via the completed change of covenants:

- His "once-for-all" sacrifice took/put away sin (Heb. 9:28; Rom. 6:21-23).
- He destroyed/abolished death via resurrection (2 Tim. 1:10; John 8:51-52; 11:26; Rom. 6:7-9).
- He wipes "away every tear from their eyes" (Rev. 7:17).
- He destroyed the works of the devil (1 John 3:8; 5:18-20).
- He delivered salvation completely (Luke 21:28; 1 Pet. 1:5; Jude 3).

- His coming on the clouds in age-ending judgment desolated the Old Covenant system (John 5:22; Matt. 23:36-38; 24:1-34).

And He accomplished it all by the time "the old order of things" passed away. What old order? It's the old order as contrasted with the "new order" and described thusly by the writer of Hebrews:

*They are only a matter of food and drink and various ceremonial washing—external regulations applying until the time of the **new order**. When Christ came as high priest of the good things that are already here, he went through the greater and more perfect tabernacle that is not man-made, that is to say, not a part of this creation* (Heb. 9:10-11; 8:13 – bold emphasis mine).

The destruction of the old order, the old heaven and earth, was the destruction of Jerusalem and the Temple circa A.D. 70. It all happened, exactly and precisely, as and when Jesus said, "I tell you the truth, this generation will certainly not pass away until all these things have happened. Heaven and earth will pass away, but my words will never pass away" (Matt. 24:34-35; 5:17-18). That old order of heaven and earth did pass away, and the only thing that remains, post A.D. 70, from that whole Old Covenant system is God's Word, both the Old and New Testaments, precisely as Jesus said above. *Perfect fulfillment!*

But in spite of the above scriptural affirmations, many Christians are still being told and believe that "someday he [Jesus] will return to destroy all evil and establish his kingdom."[26] Or that the fulfillment and realization of this verse only takes place "in heaven."[27]

But Church history documents how so many early Christians were so convinced of these glorious, then-and-there-present, and "no-more" realities that they eagerly confessed themselves Christians, volunteered, and joyously went to their physical deaths for the cause of Christ, as a witness to Him, and to share in his sufferings—rather than deny the Lord or surrender their faith. They were not the least bit afraid of dreadful torture or some of the most horrendous and cruel forms of death. Rather, they had a passion for and found fulfillment in martyrdom, the worse the form of death the better. They termed it receiving their crown of martyrdom. History records many of them being tortured, beheaded, butchered with the sword, lit on fire, thrown into the sea from boats, becoming food for wild beasts, or crucified. Remarkably, they remained cheerful, praising and confessing Christ, and singing hymns to their last breath.

You can read the accounts of some of these heroic martyrs in Eusebius, *The Church History*. He summarizes the impact of their ultimate sacrifices like this:

> In all these trials the magnificent martyrs of Christ were so distinguished throughout the world that eyewitnesses of their courage were astounded. They provided in themselves clear proof that the power of our Savior is divine and ineffable indeed. To mention each by name would be a long if not impossible task.[28]

Bauckham cogently remarks that the reason the martyrs' witness was so effective was "because their faith in Christ's victory over death was so convincingly evident in the way they faced death and died."[29]

Astounding, isn't it, the outrageous agonies joyously endured with divine enthusiasm by the Christian martyrs in comparison to low degrees of commitment many Christians today express and manifest, or don't express or manifest, with regards to their level of faith?

But let's honestly and sincerely ask ourselves, if Christ is in us and we are in Him and we are overcomers, what possible negative event could happen to us or to any of our loved ones that could harm us or cause us to lose this level of joy? Perhaps, it's "our watered-down, diluted, heaven-only-focused, gospel of death" that's too small, i.e., Jesus died so that when you die you can go to heaven?[30] "Wake up, O sleeper, rise from the dead, and Christ will shine on you" (Eph. 5:14). Surely, it's time to wake up, come truly alive, and live all of life at this high and available level by being raised to life in the New Jerusalem!

Inspiring Words from Two City Dwellers

<u>Dietrich Bonhoeffer (hanged in prison):</u>
"In his last letters from prison, Bonhoeffer reveals how his Christian faith gave him the resources to give up everything for the sake of others. . . . Bonhoeffer . . . had a joy and hope in God that made it possible for him to do what he did:"

It is not religious act that makes the Christian, but participation in the sufferings of God in the secular life. That is metanoia [repentance]: not in the first place thinking about one's own needs, problems, sins, and fears, but allowing oneself to be caught up into the way of Jesus Christ. . . . Pain is a holy angel. . . . Through him men have become greater than through all the joys of the world. . . . The pain of longing, which often can be felt physically, must be there, and we shall not and need not talk it away. But it needs to be overcome every time, and thus there is an even holier angel than the one of pain, that is the one of joy in God.[31]

A Ninety-Year-Old Grandmother:
Years ago, I heard this powerful story and have shared it many times with different groups. It almost always brings a tear to my eye. Unfortunately, I do not have a source reference. It's about a ninety-year-old grandmother on her death bed with only a few days to live. She calls in her entire family (children, spouses, grandchildren, and great-grandchildren). They arrive and encircle her hospital bed for one last time, while she is still lucid. With a weakening voice, here is what she told them, "For ninety years I have been modeling for you how to live the Christian life. Now, I'm going to model for you how to die like one."

"He who was seated on the throne said, 'I am making everything new!'" Make no mistake; this is the greater Jesus speaking out.

But what's wrong with this world is not the physical earth, its atmosphere, or the universe. It's not this material planet that needs to be wiped out and replaced with a new one. Certainly, it's somewhat polluted, but that's not really the problem.

The problem with this earth is the people who live on it (you, me, and others). We are what need made new, here and now. The Greek word for *new* means to be rejuvenated, a perfecting experience. And since God's Word refers to people as "heavens" and "earth" (see Deut. 32:1 Isa. 1:2-3),[32] *I believe God wants each of us to come alive, in a personal application, as a new heaven and new earth.* I further believe that Revelation's new creation prophecy can be so applied individually, contemporaneously, and with the focal point of ethical and moral living. After all, the Revelation repeatedly addresses individuals within the churches. And it continually reminds us, "Let *him* who hears," and "let *him* come," and "*whoever* wishes, let *him* take of the free gift" (emphasis added). There's a constant emphasis on the individual.

So how might we, individually, become transformed into this new creation of a new heaven and new earth?

A New Heaven

God calls people "heavens" and "earth." Hence, the Song of Moses in the book of Deuteronomy begins with this exhortation, "Listen, O heavens . . . Hear, O earth" (Deut. 32:1). Isaiah started his Old Testament book with the same words, "Hear, O heavens! Listen, O earth" (Isa. 1:2a). To what or to whom were these two prophets directing their messages? Did they expect the actual physical stars and planets to hear, and the global Earth to listen and take note? Of course not. Isaiah tells us that "O heavens" and "O earth" are simply other names for God's "children," or "my people" of Israel (see Isa. 1:2b-3). They were the ones who could and were to hear and listen.[33]

In accordance, therefore, the first (or former) heaven represents the born-again believer's old natural spirit, which was dead to and at enmity with God. The new heaven represents the new spirit God gives a person at salvation (See Ezek. 36:26-27). It is made new by God's Spirit and becomes the dwelling place (tabernacle, temple, heaven) of God inside the believer (1 Cor. 3:16; Eph. 2:21-22). After all, heaven is located wherever God is, right?

As a new heaven, you no longer need be caught up in sin, in old religious forms, or prostituting practices. You are now enabled to live in a vital, glorious relationship with the Father, the greater Jesus, and the Holy Spirit in a spirit realm reality that's inside you and all around you as well (Heb. 12:1, 22-24).

A New Earth

Being a new heaven is truly a beautiful spiritual reality. The problem is, "We have this treasure in earthen vessels" (2 Cor. 4:7 KJV). As believers, our biggest problem is our own flesh. It holds many of us in bondage. That's where we need to get the further victory. That's why we need to be *both* a new heaven and a new earth. We need to quit being terrified of the so-called "end times" scenarios and start being transformed in our time.

So even though our spirit is made new or renewed, we still have an old mind and body (earth). They, too, need to be made new or renewed. But they only become so when we are in Christ. "Therefore, if anyone is in Christ, he is a new creation, the old has gone, the new has come" (2 Cor. 5:17). The key is being *in Christ* (see again Chapter 9, pp-320-323). Christ being in you brings your flesh before his throne of judgment (Rev. 20:11). But you being *in Christ* produces restoration. I believe this is the personal application and at least part of what these words of Christ mean, "I am making *everything* new" (emphasis added). It's not just renewal of our spirit, but also the renewal of our old earth.

Our old (or former) earth, also termed our flesh, consists of our unregenerate physical bodies, minds, and emotions (Psa. 103:14; 2 Cor. 4:7). When Paul used the word *flesh* (the Greek word is *sarx*) in his letters, he was describing human nature with all its passions, lusts, self-reliance, and carnality. It often includes conformity to the values and morals of this world. When used collectively about all humanity, it represents the realms of sin, of religious tradition, and of death. Becoming a new earth is an ongoing process by which God, with our consent and cooperation, breaks the power of our bodies, minds, and emotions (our flesh). Our lives are no longer dominated by them but increasingly controlled by the power of God's Spirit through our renewed spirits (Rom. 12:1-2; 2 Cor. 5:17). Paul summed up this ongoing process like this in his letter to the Romans:

> *Therefore, I urge you, brothers, in view of God's mercy, to offer your bodies as living sacrifices, holy and pleasing to God—which is your spiritual worship. Do not be conformed to this world, but be transformed by the renewing of your mind, that you may prove what the will of God is, that which is good and acceptable and perfect* (Rom. 12:1-2; also see Eph. 4:22-24).

Since the body is controlled by the mind, this transformation process starts with changing our mental focus from the flesh realm to the spirit realm. Through it, we can come into Christ, overcome the flesh, and live by the Spirit. As we increasingly do that, we can live here and now in victory and authority as kings and priests. Then, after death, we can face the judgment with "no condemnation." "Therefore, there is now no condemnation for those who are in Christ Jesus, *who do not live according to the sinful nature but according to the spirit* (Rom. 8:1 – emphasis mine). Unfortunately, this latter and italicized portion is also a manuscript discrepancy and relegated to footnote status in some Bibles. But when do you want to face up to the judgment and walk in newness of life—now while you can do something about it or later when you cannot? I find it helpful to pray like this, "Your kingdom come [in me], your will be done on earth [in my earth] as it is in heaven" (Matt. 6:10).

Thus, the new earth symbolizes your flesh (body, mind, and emotions) that has been crucified, redeemed, and transfigured with Christ. And when your body, mind, and emotions are thusly transformed, you are *both* a new heaven and a new earth, *a totally new creation.*

As the new temple (dwelling place) of God, here and now, Christians can either believe it and act like it or not believe it and not act like it. If we don't, we can go ahead and struggle and hope for something better some day out in the future—which will include divine judgment. This struggle between our old person, the flesh (our old earth), and our new spirit (our new heaven) continues until we die. After physical death, our struggle with the flesh is over because we have been separated from it, glorified, and completely purified. But why not move to or, at least, toward living out this fully operative, available, and new-creation reality, here and now, as the Psalmist writes:

> *Who may ascend the hill of the Lord?*
> *Who may stand in his holy place?*
> *He who has clean hands and a pure heart,*
> *Who does not lift up his soul to an idol*
> *or swear by what is false.*
> *He will receive blessings from the Lord*
> *and vindication from God his Savior.*
> *Such is the generation of those who seek him,*
> *who seek your face, O God of Jacob.*
> *Lift up your heads, O you gates;*
> *be lifted up, you ancient doors,*
> *that the King of glory may come in.*
> (Psa. 24:3-7)

Stop Futurizing

So, once again, quit pushing the fulfillment of this beautiful prophecy out into the future and thinking it does not presently apply to you and me. It applies to all believers whether we seek to grasp it, heed it, and obey it—or not.

This above realization is why I believe these material-realm symbols of heaven and earth are not only *covenantal*; they are also *individual and internal*. Inside believers is where they are brought together. It's the same dual reality Paul explained this way: "The first man [Adam] was of the dust of the earth, the second man [Jesus] from heaven. As was the earthly man, so also are those who are of the earth; and as is the man from heaven, so are those who are of heaven. And just as we have borne the likeness of the earth man, so shall we bear the likeness of the man from heaven" (1 Cor. 15:47-49; also Eph. 4:22-24).

That's why I say the first step is to quit thinking of the new heaven and new earth as something that's going to happen someday out in the future to our planet and the cosmos. Accept the fact that it's happening inside you right now. If you're always thinking about God coming back and jerking you off this planet and melting planet Earth, you aren't really going to be motivated to change and become this Christ-like, are you? This future-oriented stargazing has been the devil's tool and stumbling block for too many for too long. It keeps us from tapping into the spiritual power and supernatural authority that we have to reign and rule with the greater Jesus. It keeps us from experiencing the fullness of God.

To Reign and Rule

We can reign and rule with the greater Jesus only to the degree that our old earth (our flesh) is made new. This is God's desire and goal for each of us—to destroy the sin and self-reliance of our flesh so that He can share intimate personal relationships with purified, reigning, and ruling saints. Sadly, many Christians are far from being co-seated on the throne with the greater Jesus. Rather, they are standing in front of it and under his feet. Hence, they are not reigning and ruling with Him; they are under his judgment.

This available reality of reigning and ruling with the greater Jesus was at hand back in the 1st century, and the saints of that day and time turned the world upside down with it (Acts 17:6). It's at hand now. So how are we moderns doing? Not too well, sad to say.

The great and climactic message of the Revelation is we are to overcome the beast, the dragon, the great prostitute, and the flesh—everything that keeps us from reigning and ruling with the greater Jesus, here and now. To do that we must cross over and span the boundary line between the physical realm and the spirit realm and seize the God-given opportunity to function as kings and priests in the kingdom of God (which is why most Christians most likely will not enter into this available reality). But why is this reality true, available, and relevant today? It's because of this next verse.

"He said to me, 'It is done. I am the Alpha and the Omega, the Beginning and the End.'" What do you think *it is done* means? Notice, it is written in the past tense—"It is done!" Certainly, not everything was "finished" at the cross as some believe (John 19:30), or even with Jesus' resurrection and ascension. Much more remained to be done and fulfilled.

First, I believe Jesus was referring to the deliverance of all this new heaven, new earth, and New Jerusalem reality being put in place and made fully available, universally. The event that marks this fulfillment of the covenantal-changing process was "when the power of the Holy people has been [was] finally broken, all these things will be completed" (Dan. 12:7b; also Luke 21:28; 1 Pet. 1:5). Can I prove this? Yes, I can. Jesus told his 1st-century disciples, "When you see Jerusalem surrounded by armies, you will know its desolation is near. . . . flee . . . . For this is the time of punishment in fulfillment of all that has been written" (Luke 21:20-22). "All that has been written," i.e., the Old Testament scrolls, would have included Isaiah's prophecies of the coming of the "new heavens and a new earth" (Isa. 65:17; 66:22).

But in an application sense, it is not "done" within each individual believer until we individually come into Christ and thereby enter into this reality (1 John 5:5-6). Or it happens when we die, shed our flesh, and go through our own divine judgment (Heb. 9:27). In other words, it is the difference between the announcement and fulfillment of a universal and timeless reality and individuals coming into the reality, "but each in his own turn (order)" (1 Cor. 15:23)—just like salvation and resurrection. And we have a vital role to play in this realization of this reality and way of living, here and now. It's as the Scripture says, "flesh and blood cannot inherit the kingdom of God, nor does the perishable inherit the imperishable" (1 Cor. 15:50). But redeemed and renewed flesh and blood certainly can and do enter the kingdom (Acts 14:22).

Physical death, on the other hand, is a process of complete physical change for believers who cannot, or will not, change themselves into new earth in this life. Yes, we will all die (Heb. 9:27). But many, if not most of us, won't let much of our flesh, the old earth, pass away while we are still walking around on this physical planet. We have to go through the grave to finally get rid of it all, our old earth.

Does this application of the new-creation reality make sense to you? Or, is it too spiritual or esoteric to grasp? Or, do you find it spot-on? Do you want to do this, some of this, most of this, now or wait until later after you die physically? Becoming a new heaven and a new earth by faith and obedience, here and now, is a beautiful, spiritual, practical, available, and relevant reality in the New Covenant economy.

"To him who is thirsty I will give to drink without cost from the spring of the water of life." The symbols of flowing rivers, streams, and springs of water run throughout the Bible. The historical Jesus of Nazareth answered the Samaritan women at the well with these words, "If you knew the gift of God and who it is that asks you for a drink, you would have asked him and he would have given you living water. . . whoever drinks the water I give him will never thirst. Indeed, the water I give him will become in him a spring of water welling up to eternal life" (John 4:10, 14).

Later, Jesus said and John explained, "'If a man is thirsty, let him come to me and drink. Whoever believes in me, as the Scripture has said, streams of living water will flow from within him.' By this he meant the Spirit, whom those who believed in him were later to receive" (John 7:37b-39a; see Isa. 35:6; 44:3; 55:1; 58:11; Psa. 46:4).

Most Christians today believe this living water of life is a New Covenant reality, is present and accessible, and they can drink freely of and from it. But this water is located in the New Jerusalem (Rev. 22:1, 17). It is simply not logical to think that these promises are fulfilled spiritual realities in the New Covenant era, and then postpone the arrival of the city in which these waters are located to sometime in the future. Let's prove these statements using a simple syllogism:

> **Major premise:** Most Christians believe they can drink freely of the "water of life" (John 4:10, 14; 7:37-39; Rev. 21:6; 22:17). On this we agree.
>
> **Minor premise:** The "water of life" is located in the New Jerusalem (Rev. 22:1).
>
> **Conclusion:** The New Jerusalem is a present reality.

You cannot have it both ways. They both go together. A similar syllogism exists for access to the "tree of life" (Rev. 2:7; 22:2, 14).

> **Major premise:** Most Christians believe they can now eat of the "tree of life" (Rev. 2:7; 22:14). On this we agree.
>
> **Minor premise:** The "tree of life" is located in the New Jerusalem (Rev. 22:2).
>
> **Conclusion:** The New Jerusalem is a present reality.

If we are "in Christ," we already can enjoy a part of heaven here on earth now. It's the covenant-determined New Jerusalem that came and comes *down* from heaven (Rev. 21:2). Thus, we can drink from its "water of life" and partake of its "tree of life." But not so if this Holy City is a future space city, a renovated planet, or heaven itself, as so many have misconstrued. It is a city that exists here on this earth and we can live in it now. Any other view is purely fantasy Christianity.

"He who overcomes will inherit all this," i.e., inherit the new heaven and earth, and the realities of its Holy City, the New Jerusalem. The bad news for most Christians, however, is that not all of them or all the Church will inherit, enter, or partake of these realities. Only the overcomers will.

In *Strong's Exhaustive Concordance of the Bible,* the verb "overcome" (Greek #3528: *nikaō*) means to "conquer, overcome, prevail, get the victory." And Jesus challenges all the believers in the seven churches, and us today, to overcome several definite and ungodly tendencies—loss of their first love, persecution, false teaching, sexual immorality, resisting idolatry, suffering, and even death (see Rev. 2 and 3). Moreover, He rewards those who do overcome (Rev. 21:1-7). What it means to overcome is also clearly and best summarized in Revelation 12:11: "They overcame him by the blood of the Lamb and by the word of their testimony; they did not love their lives so much as to shrink from death."

Since the inheritance of dwelling in the New Jerusalem is only promised to overcoming believers in the Church, "it should be apparent to anyone who has been around Christian circles that not every Christian is living a life worthy of ruling the world with Christ as humble servants."[34] Again, only the overcomers, and them alone . . . .

- Have the "right to eat from the tree of life," which is located in this Holy City (Rev. 2:7), and may enter by the gates into the city.
- Are given "a white stone with a new name written on it, known only to him who receives it" (Rev. 2:17).
- Are given "authority over the nations" and "the morning star" (Rev. 2:27-28).
- "Are worthy" and dressed "in white" and never have their names erased "from the book of life" (Rev. 3:4-5).
- Are given "the right to sit with me [the greater Jesus] on my throne" (Rev. 3:21).
- Are "a kingdom and priest to serve our God, and . . . reign on the earth" (Rev. 5:19).
- Have "come out of her [Babylon, the great prostitute], my people" (Rev. 18:4).
- Are "invited to the wedding supper of the Lamb" (Rev. 19:9).
- Ride "on white horses" and are "dressed in fine linen, white and clean" (Rev. 19:14).
- Are "in Christ" (to see what this means, see again 1 John 2:5-6; John 15:1-8).
- Have lifted the earthly veil off their faces so they don't worship Jesus after the flesh—"Though we once regarded Christ in this way, we do so no longer" (2 Cor. 5:16).
- Are "caught up with them in the clouds to meet the Lord in the air" (1 Thess. 4:17).

When we are born again, Jesus gives us the right, the authority, and the opportunity to do and be involved in all the above bulleted realities. Remember, this is not something off in the future or back in the past. It was at hand in the 1st century and is at hand now. But even though we have this accessibility, the choice to be an overcomer and a victorious Christian in this life is up to each of us. It is always our choice.

But what happens to non-overcoming believers? Not only are they excluded from all these things and relegated to being outside the city with unbelievers, a number of other Scriptures in both the Old and New Testaments indicate that non-overcomers are subject to God's judgment, perhaps both in this life and in the afterlife in heaven. Consider, for example:

"Woe to you who are complacent in Zion" (Amos 6:1). In Amos' time, Zion was God's holy mountain. But, as we have seen, today Zion is his Church and those in it.

"A curse on him who is lax in doing the Lord's work. A curse on him who keeps his sword from bloodshed" (Jer. 48:10). That doesn't sound like unbelievers to me, does it to you?

"Let no one deceive you with empty words, for because of such things God's wrath comes on those who are disobedient. Therefore, do not be partners with them. For you were once darkness, but now you are light in the Lord. Live as children of light. For the fruit of light consists in all goodness, righteousness, and truth, and find out what pleases the Lord. Have nothing to do with the fruitless deeds of darkness, but rather expose them. For it is shameful even to mention what the disobedient do in secret. . . . This is why it is said: 'Wake up, O sleeper, rise from the dead, and Christ will shine on you!" (Eph. 5:6-14). Here, Paul is writing to believers who are physically alive, isn't he? And yet he is telling them to rise up from the dead. Why? It's because this being "dead" has to do with one's relationship with and obedience to God. In fact, if a believer in Christ is not reigning and ruling with Christ (in the manner He prescribes), God considers him or her dead in Christ (see again the "Co's" in Chapter 9, pp-321f).

Similarly, Paul warned Timothy to beware of people *"having a form of godliness but denying its power"* (2 Tim. 3:5). This would include many prostituting churches and those in them, would it not?

And Jesus had much to say about his servants having the form of religion but denying the power of God, such as: *"The servant who knows his master's will and does not get ready or does not do what his master wants will be beaten with many blows. But the one who does not know and does things deserving punishment will be beaten with few blows. From everyone who has been given much, much will be demanded; and from the one who has been entrusted with much, much more will be asked"* (Luke 12:47-48). These servants could not possibly be nonbelievers, could they?[35]

One of the most emphasized ideas of the New Testament is that not all who are dead are in the graveyard. This is the clear implication of Jesus' statement "Follow me, and let the dead bury their own dead" (Matt. 8:22). He further emphasized this theme when He quoted the father of the returned prodigal, "For this son of mine was dead and is alive . . . ." (Luke 15:24) and when He characterized the Pharisees as "whitewashed tombs . . . full of dead men's bones and everything unclean" (Matt. 23:27b).

In Paul's writings, believers can be either dead to sin and alive to Christ, or alive to sin and dead to Christ. For those who are not "in Christ," they are spiritually dead even though they may have Christ in them and be heaven-bound upon their physical death (see Rom. 6-8 – especially note 6:11-13). Additionally, according to Paul, the most vital signs that tell whether a believer is alive or dead with Christ is if they are offering the parts of their bodies to Him as instruments of righteousness and renewing their minds (Rom. 12:1-2). That's being a new earth!

If we want to become a new heaven and a new earth and reign and rule with the greater Jesus, here and now, in his Holy City, we have to overcome and enter via faith and obedience. He or she who overcomes then becomes a son (daughter) of God. The sons of God are no longer just children of God. Big difference and our next topic!

"I will be his God and he will be my son." Notice, the emphasis is on being a "son" of God. Something else most Christians do not know and are not told is, there is a difference between being a son of God (gender is not a factor here – see 2 Cor. 6:18) and being a child of God. Most have been told or assume that they are synonymous. But another of the glorious benefits of being an overcomer in the manner the Revelation presents is in being a full-fledged son of the King—God Himself—and being able to enjoy this highest and fullest level of communion with God, here and now, in this life, while on this earth. Be assured, heaven itself will be even greater—but especially so for the overcomers.

A simple straightforward and comparative word study of the Greek words used for child and son and some of the key verses contrasting their characteristics will demonstrate this biblical differentiation:

Is there a difference between a child of God and a son of God?

Child/Children of God (*teknon* = "little child, birthed")

- *"Yet to all who received him, to those who believed in his name, he gave the right to become **children** of God"* (John 1:12 – KJV mistranslates this word[36]). Every human being is made in the "image" and "likeness" of God (Gen. 1:26). But only those who receive and believe on Jesus Christ are children of God.
- *"The Spirit himself testifies with our spirit that we are God's **children**. Now if we are **children**, then we are heirs—heirs of God and co-heirs with Christ, if indeed we share in his suffering in order that we may also share in his glory"* (Rom. 6:16-17). As we shall see, sharing in this glory is the privilege of the sons.
- *"that the creation itself will be liberated from its bondage to decay and brought into the glorious freedom of the **children** of God"* (Rom. 8:21). Please stop ascribing this verse to the creation of a new planet Earth. We're talking about the new creation of people, there and then, here and now, on this planet.
- *"How great is the love the Father has lavished on us, that we should be called **children** of God! And that is what we are! . . . Dear friends, now we are **children** of God, and what we will be has not yet been made know"* (1 John 3:1-2). Yes, the children of

God go to heaven when they physically die. But there is something more being expected herein.

Child/Children/Infants of God (*nepios* = "babe without full power of speech, childish")

- *"Brothers, I could not address you as spiritual but as worldly – mere **infants** in Christ"* (1 Cor. 3:1). Paul's talking to and about believers here.
- *"What I am saying is that as long as the heir is a **child**, he is no different from a slave, although he owns the whole estate. He is subject to guardians and trustees until the time set by his father"* (Gal. 4:1-2). In this verse and the next, Paul equates a child with being a slave under the rule of others. This could include those saints being sat upon by the great prostitute (Rev. 17:1, 15).
- *"So also, when we were **children**, we were in slavery under the basic principles of the world"* (Gal. 4:3). Here's a possible change-of-covenants context.
- *"until we all reach unity in the faith and in the knowledge of the Son of God and become mature, attaining to the whole measure of the fullness of Christ. Then we will no longer be **infants**, tossed back and forth by the waves, and blown here and there by every wind of teaching and by the cunning and craftiness of men in their deceitful scheming. Instead, speaking the truth in love, we will in all things grow up into him who is the Head, that is, Christ"* (Eph. 4:13-15). Maturity is the goal and criterion expressed here for one's growing out of infancy and coming out of bondage to the great prostitute.
- *"We have much to say about this, but it is hard to explain because you are slow to learn. In fact, though by this time you ought to be teachers, you need someone to teach you the elementary truths of God's word all over again. You need milk, not solid food. Anyone who lives on milk, being still an **infant**, is not acquainted with the teaching about righteousness"* (Heb. 5:11-13). Sadly, this admonishment is applicable to and describes most Christians in most churches today. They are not sons of God but mere infants and are staying that way.

Next, note the huge differences as we explore the "son" verses.

Son of God (*huios/huiothesia* = "son" and "adoption of sons")

- *"Blessed are the peacemakers, for they will be called **sons** of God"* (Matt. 5:9). Are all believers in Jesus Christ peacemakers?
- *"But I tell you: Love your enemies and pray for those who persecute you, that you may be **sons** of your Father in heaven."* (Matt. 5:44-45a). Are all believers in Jesus Christ loving their enemies and being persecuted?
- *"because those who are led by the Spirit of God are **sons** of God"* (Rom. 8:14). Are all believers in Jesus Christ being led by the Spirit of God?
- *"For you did not receive a spirit that makes you a slave again to fear, but you received the Spirit of **sonship** . . ."* (Rom. 8:15). Another slavery comparative.
- *"The creation waits in eager expectation for the **sons** of God to be revealed"* (Rom. 8:19). Again, please stop thinking about a new planet. We're talking about the new creation of believers into being new earths.
- *"Not only so, but we ourselves, who have the firstfruits of the Spirit, groan inwardly as we wait eagerly for our adoption as **sons**, the redemption of our bodies"* (Rom. 8:23). Again, please stop putting this out into the future. Think in terms of your becoming a "new earth." The redemption of your body is not something that happens after physical death—then God gives you a new "spiritual body." Your body can be and is to be redeemed right now. How so? See again our last chapter and especially Romans 12:1-2.
- *"You are all **sons** of God through faith in Christ Jesus"* (Gal. 3:26). Prophetically and/or proleptically, no doubt, Paul terms all those present as sons. Yet note how he continues.
- *"But when the time had fully come, God sent his Son, born of a woman, born under the law, to redeem those under law, that we might receive the full rights of **sons**. Because you are **sons**, God*

sent the Spirit of his Son into our hearts, the Spirit who calls out, 'Abba, Father.' So you are no longer a slave, but a **son**; and since you are a **son**, God has made you also an heir" (Gal 4:5-7). Remember, a child is considered to be a slave.
- "he predestined us to be adopted as his **sons** through Jesus Christ, in accordance with his pleasure and will" (Eph. 1:5). This verse cannot be used to teach predestination to become only a child of God, nor can Roman 8:29-30. It only speaks of a sonship predestination.
- "In bringing many **sons** to glory, it was fitting that God, for whom and through whom everything exists, should make the author of their salvation perfect through suffering" (Heb. 2:10). Sonship brings glory to God through your works and witness.
- "And you have forgotten that word of encouragement that addresses you as **sons**: 'My **son**, do not make light of the Lord's discipline, and do not lose heart when he rebukes you, because the Lord disciplines those he loves, and he punishes everyone he accepts as a **son**.' Endure hardship as discipline; God is treating you as **sons**. For what **son** is not disciplined by his father? If you are not disciplined (and everyone undergoes discipline), then you are illegitimate **children (bastards** in KJV) and not true **sons**" (Heb. 12:5-8). Tough words, but they only apply to the sons. The children of God have other problems in this life (see again Gal. 4:13-15 above).
- "He who overcomes will inherit all this, and I will be his God and he will be my **son**" (Rev. 21:7). Once again, only the overcomers are the sons. They alone, out of all believers and the Church, inherit all this and enjoy the blessings and privileges of the Holy City, the New Jerusalem, here and now, in this life.

This same biblical dichotomy is also foreshadowed in the Old Testament and seen elsewhere in the New Testament, though not specifically termed as sonship. Here are two example passages:

*"'Ah, Sovereign Lord,' I said, 'I do not know how to speak; I am only a **child**.' But the Lord said to me, 'Do not say, 'I am only a **child**.' You must go to everyone I send you to and say whatever I command you. Do not be afraid of them, for I am with you and*

will rescue you,' declares the Lord. Then the Lord reached out his hand and touched by mouth and said to me, 'Now, I have put my words in your mouth. See, today I appoint you over nations and kingdoms to uproot and tear down, to destroy and overthrow, to build and to plant. . . . for I am watching to see that my word is fulfilled.'" (Jer. 1:6-10, 12). This commission is what the sons do. How many Christians do you know who are doing these things? Well, God is still watching today, isn't He?

"For this very reason, make every effort to add to your faith goodness; and to goodness, knowledge; and to knowledge, self-control; and to self-control, perseverance; and to perseverance, godliness; and to godliness, brotherly kindness; and to brotherly kindness, love. For if you possess these qualities in increasing measure, they will keep you from being ineffective and unproductive in your knowledge of our Lord Jesus Christ. But if anyone does not have them, he is nearsighted and blind, and has forgotten that he has been cleansed from his past sins" (2 Pet. 1:5-9). Especially note the phase "in increasing measure." Growth into sonship is a process, a this-life process.

This differentiation between being a son of God verses only being a child of God is in perfect harmony, consistency, and correllary with Christ in you and you in Him (see again John 15:1-8; 1 John 2:5-6), with being an overcomer, and with being "caught up with them in the clouds to meet the Lord in the air" (1 Thess. 4:17), with taking "your inheritance, the kingdom prepared for you since the creation of the world" (Matt. 25:34; Jas. 5:2; but also see Gal. 5:19-21), and with forcefully advancing the kingdom of God (Matt. 11:12; Luke 16:16). Anything less is less.

In concluding, here are a few supportive comments of other writers:

"Everything changes when we understand that we are sons and daughters of God. . . . Satan's greatest fear is that sons and daughters of God will know who they are and walk in their authority, but it's the Father's greatest longing for them to do so. . . . possessing and using *all* the full rights of that privilege."[37]

(Ché Ahn)

"In the ancient world a son . . . was adopted at maturity. The child was tutored by an educated slave until the child understood and demonstrated maturity gleaned from that education. At that time the father would 'adopt' his son, which meant that the son was now in a position to participate in the responsibilities of the father."[38] (DeVern Fromke)

"God wants us to open our eyes to see the wonders of who we truly are—His children—and reach out to claim all this is ours by right of sonship. It all comes down to a decision that each of us alone must make: whether we will live as sons and daughters in the Kingdom of God, or as subjects in the kingdom of the world."[39] (Myles Munroe)

"So a man who calls himself a Christian, attends church, and has some hope of heaven when he dies has *not* received the lion's share of what God intended him to receive through the work of Christ. He will find himself living still very much alone, stuck in his journey, wondering why he cannot become the man he longs to be. He has not come into sonship."[40] (John Eldredge)

Eldredge further and accurately notes that "None but a child could become a son: the idea is a spiritual coming of age; *only when the child is a man is he really and fully a son.*[41] Later, he discusses "thoughts on what God is after in raising his sons to full sonship" and defines this as being "a man so *yielded* to him, so completely surrendered, that his heart is easily moved by the Spirit of God to the purposes of God."[42]

So, do these above comments describe you? If not, why not? And if not, why are you settling for anything less than sonship?

Alas, Rousas John Rushdoony retorts that "most men today are sons of the church, and, more often, sons of the state, and both institutions make eunuchs out of their sons, and therefore slaves, because they are jealous of their power and authority. The purpose of God, however, is to restore His sons into power and dominion."[43]

Amen?

In a Nutshell

As simply as I can put it, the New Jerusalem is not a literal city, or a cube-shaped space city, or a new Garden of Eden. Nor is it heaven itself, the totality of God's people, or all the Church.

The New Jerusalem is: <u>the earthly, universal, and New-Covenant-determined community of overcoming saints</u>—the bride of Christ. Only these overcoming saints manifest the kingdom of God internally in their lives and externally advance it to make a positive difference in this world. They do so in behalf of and in service to the poor, sick, the enslaved, and the oppressed through selfless acts of love, persuasion, and seeking justice and mercy (see again Gal. 4:24-31; Heb. 11:16; 12:1, 22-24; 13:14). Not only are they overcomers, they are world changers.

The arrival and consummation of this Holy City in human and redemptive history coincided with the obsolescence and desolation of the old earthly city of Jerusalem and its Temple circa A.D. 30-70. The New Jerusalem is the positive "flipside" of that divine judgment and timely destruction. It is part of the "faith that was once for all delivered to the saints" (Jude 3). Since then, its inhabitants only include those who have overcome the hindrances and oppositions mentioned in the Book of Revelation, are caught up with the greater Jesus in the clouds in the air (*aer*), and are reigning and ruling with Him, here and now on this earth (Rev. 5:9-10). Sadly, this community does not contain or describe most Christians today. It does, however, and, most likely, describe many, if not most, Christians in the 1st century who were accused of turning the world of their day upside down (Acts 17:6 KJV)—a world that was much more hostile than what we Americans face in our country today.

In this ultimate, earthly, and Holy City is the most intimate relationship with the Lord God and the Lamb. They are its temple, its light source, its throne, and its river of living water (Rev. 21:22-22:2). This concluding and climactic passage of Scripture symbolizes the ultimate fulfillment of what Jesus declared the night before He was crucified: "On that day you will realize that I am in my Father, and you are in me, and I am in you" (John 14:20). But this perfection of union comes only from lifting the veil to behold the greater Jesus, dining at his wedding supper, and doing his works and even greater works.

Another factor we need to re-mention is, this city of God has twelve foundations "on them are the names of the twelve apostles of the Lamb"

(Rev. 21:14) and twelve gates, on them "were written the names of the twelve tribes of Israel" (Rev. 21:12). McKenize believes these twelve foundations and twelve gates symbolize that "the New (covenant) Jerusalem consists of the faithful of both the new and old covenants."[44] Literally, these twelve gates are *from* the east, *from* the north, *from* the south, and *from* west—possibly depicting people and nations coming into this city *from* the four points of the compass (Rev. 21:12-14). These gates not only provide entrance through faith and obedience. They also provide exit through lack of faith and disobedience. Consequently, we don't just enter and take up residence forever; entering is not a once-and-done deal. It's an ongoing commitment and continuing involvement.

The New Jerusalem is: the earthly, universal, and New-Covenant-determined community of overcoming saints—the bride of Christ.

What's more, you might be surprised by whom you'll meet when you enter this city. In fact, throughout the writing of this book I've had the strongest feeling that some who will be reading it may already be experiencing some, if not all, of the glorious realities we've been talking about. Of course, you may not express these realities in the same terms I have. But if you are one of them, I hope this book has enabled you to better define and express what you've been experiencing.

If you are not one of them yet, I hope this book has awakened within you a hunger for the deeper, greater, and higher things of God that are available on this earth, in this life, and here and now via the greater Jesus.

What's the Purpose of This Holy City?

One thing you won't spend your time doing in the New Jerusalem is flitting about on the clouds on angel wings and playing cherubic melodies on a golden harp—as depicted in most celestial art—or sitting on the bank watching a lazy river flow by. This glorious city of the Revelation is not a Christian retirement village, theme park, or fantasy land. Its citizens are far too busy reigning and ruling over their own lives and in their spheres of influence.

Moreover, this city has a definite and defined purpose as the vision of the New Jerusalem continues:

> *Then the angel showed me the river of the water of life, as clear as crystal, flowing from the throne of God and of the Lamb down the middle of the great street of the city. On each side of the river stood the tree of life, bearing twelve crops of fruit, yielding its fruit every month. And* **the leaves of the tree are for the healing of the nations**. *No longer will there be any curse. The throne of God and of the Lamb will be in the city, and his* **servants will serve him**. *They will see his face, and his name will be on their foreheads. There will be no more night. They will not need the light of a lamp or the light of the sun, for the Lord God will give them light. And they will reign for ever and ever* (Rev. 22:1-5).

Once again, this symbolic description is not of heaven. There are no nations, sicknesses, curses, or imperfections in heaven in need of healing. Likewise, why would the nations need healing if sin and evil no longer existed outside the city in the new heaven and new earth?

Interestingly, similar language was used by Isaiah to describe Israel's return from Babylonian exile (see Isa. 60:19-20). Therefore, this scenario is earthly and touches our lives and the lives of many, if not all others, in very tangible, spirit-realm and physical-realm ways, here and now. Hence, its truths and realities are graspable, heedable, and obeyable, and not veiled in secrecy. Everything we need to know has been made known and available, forever and ever, here and now. We don't have to wait for some future "millennium" or a remade planet and cosmos. The question next becomes, can we appreciate and grasp these full spirit-realm/physical-realm truths and realities as relevant and present for us today?

In this regard, Chilton specially points out that "the word Tree is *xulon*, often used with reference to the Cross (cf. Acts 5:30; 10:39; 13:29; 1 Pet. 2:24); in fact, it is likely that Christ was crucified on a living tree." He surmises that "the cross of Christ, the wood of suffering and death, is for Christians a tree of life."[45] Hendriksen, adds that the reason for the water being "crystal clear" is because "sin shall not mar our fellowship with Christ."[46] Wallace contributes that seeing "his face" means "to bask under the smile of his approval . . . . the love and the favor of God (see Psa. 31:16)."[47]

Please also know that the application of this prophecy, as we have been presenting throughout this book, does not make divine judgment any less awesome or restoration any less glorious. Indeed not! It makes divine judgment a far more pressing concern and restoration an exciting, present reality. Spiritual reality is just as real as physical reality, if not more so. Neither can be effectively separated or compartmentalized from the other.

But who in these nations needs this healing? It's those outside this earth-bound city. "Outside are the dogs, those who practice magic arts, the sexually immoral, the murderers, the idolaters and everyone who loves and practices falsehood" (Rev. 22:15). Who are those people? Don't make the mistake of limiting them to only being non-Christians. They also include the great prostitute (Babylon) and the "many waters" of non-overcomers on whom she sits and who have not "come out of her, my people" (Rev. 17-18).

If this identification is not clear enough and you would like more contrast in comparison with the people who make up the Holy City (the bride), then consider this similar but other list in Revelation 21: "But the cowardly, the unbelieving, the vile, the murderers, the sexually immoral, those who practice magic arts, the idolaters and all liars—their place will be in the fiery lake of burning sulfur. This is the second death" (Rev. 21:8).

Stop for a moment and think of this list in terms of some inside the Church. Notice what heads up this list—the cowardly. If you're ashamed of the Son of Man in front of other people or knuckling under to the flesh, isn't that cowardly? If you are not obeying any portion of God's Word (you only believe what you obey), isn't that unbelieving? If you speak ill of those trying to do the works of Jesus or the greater works, isn't that being vile? If you persecute other Christians by your ad hominem comments and/or actions, isn't that an assassination? If you condone homosexuality, adultery, or pornography, isn't that sexually immoral? Likewise, I'm sure some of you can come up with examples of those who practice magic arts, idolaters, and liars.[48]

But one thing, at least, I hope we can now agree on is: these two lists of the type of people residing outside the earthly gates of the New Jerusalem make the notion of a future time of universal peace and/or an evil-less, sinless existence on this planet a mere fantasy, and not the promise of any biblical text. Would you agree? Where am I wrong on this?

Why then is it so hard to get people to accept this fulfilled, at-hand, and totally relevant message and reality? It's because *having* requires taking responsibility, which seems to have fallen into major disfavor lately.

For one, as Eldridge explains, many have "lost both a noble view of the earth and how God uses it to disciple us." How did they lose it? It's "the old Gnostic heresy, the division of the sacred and the profane."[49] All their lives they've been told by people they trust and love that "someday all the evil and injustice of this world will be destroyed."[50] But the existence of those outside the gates of this earthly New Jerusalem—on the last page of the Bible—should put that piece of fantasy Christianity to rest. Would you now agree?

Instead of *having*, most Christians have been conditioned into *hoping*. But hoping is not God's best. At best, hoping is God's second best. Why? It's because one hopes for something one does not have. What you are hoping for is that when you do finally have it you'll be better off (see Rom. 8:24-25). Once again, Christ in you is *"the hope* of glory." But you in Christ *is glory* (see again Chapter 9, p-329). Having also demands taking responsibility and seizing what is at hand, graspable, heedable, and obeyable. This is what the sons of God do.

If we are Christians and not reigning and ruling with Christ, here and now, on this earth, God sees us as dead in Christ. And dead, non-overcoming folks do not have access to the Holy City. It's that clear in Scripture, is it not?

For far too long much of the Church has been in retreat. We've become apathetic and have given up major amounts of God's territory to the beast system, to the dragon and his human and superhuman cohorts, and to the great prostitute. In the prophecy of the New Jerusalem (and elsewhere in Scripture as well) God is calling his overcoming saints to be instruments of healing for the nations of their sin-racked sicknesses.

Unfortunately, too many churches have been seduced by false prophets and teachers into idolatrous self-fulfillment, godless worship, and prostitution of God's Word. Many have withdrawn into their private reservations. Consequently, atheistic humanists have seized control of our nation's political, governmental, judicial, educational, communicative, commercial, and even ecclesiastical systems and institutions. It's time for us Christians to quit retreating, resting, and waiting for Jesus to return someday. It's time we start reigning and ruling with the greater Jesus Who is here with us today! Can I get an Amen on this?

The pessimistic outlook of gloom-and-doom and destruction of God's world brought on by catastrophic and flawed end-times doctrines has led far too many to take a short-term view of their tasks and responsibilities in this present world. After all, they reason, why bother with making disciples of all nations when they're all going to be burned up some day anyway, by Christ Himself, to make way for the new heaven and new earth and New Jerusalem? Let's be honest, how can you view the world with a long-term perspective or be willing to invest in future generations when you think you are part of the terminal generation?[51]

If we are Christians and not reigning and ruling with Christ, here and now, on this earth, God sees us as dead in Christ.

To the contrary, the Revelation proclaims that God has not given up on the human race, and He has not given us permission to give up on it either. Isaiah prophesied of Jesus, "For to us a child is born, to us a son is given, and the government will be on his shoulders.... Of the increase of his government and peace there will be no end. He will reign on David's throne and over his kingdom, establishing and upholding it with justice and righteousness from that time on and forever" (Isa. 9:6-7). From what time on and forever? "For to us a child is born." That event happened over twenty centuries ago. What's more, this Messianic prophecy does not sound as if God has given up on the world? No way!

Even more incredible, if not beyond human comprehension in my opinion, is the fact that God has entrusted to the likes of you and me the task of co-reigning and co-ruling with the greater Jesus for the healing of the nations of this world, here and now. He who said, "*I am* the light of the world" (John 8:12) also said, *"You are* the light of the world, *a city on a hill cannot be hidden"* (Matt. 5:14 – emphasis added). How and why did we get to be God's light? *"I have made you a light* for the Gentiles, that you may bring salvation to the ends of the earth," God says (Acts 13:47 – emphasis added). Jesus also said, *"You are* the salt of the earth" (Matt. 5:13 – emphasis added). But He never said He was the salt of the earth. Salt is totally us. And what does salt do? Several things. It flavors, it preserves, it stings, and it heals.

You see, the Great Commission (Matt. 28:18-20; Mark 16:15; Luke 24:47) is far greater than most of us have been led to believe. In it, Jesus speaks of being given *"all* authority in *heaven and earth."* He then confers all this authority on us and commands us to go into *"all* the world" and to *"all creation,"* to "make disciples of *all nations,* and to "teach them to obey *everything I have commanded you"* (emphasis added).

Jesus also conveyed that "I am the vine, you are the branches" (John 15:1-8). Do you know what branches do? They produce leaves. Do you know what leaves do? Waving these "leaves" enables us to praise God. Laying these leaves on lives, laws, institutions, and relationships enables us to do Christ's works and greater works, thereby healing the nations. These leaves enable us to be like Jesus and "like a tree planted by streams of water, which yields its fruit in season and whose leaf does not wither" (Psa. 1:3).

Likewise, Jesus also admonished us to be fruit-bearing trees: "Every tree that does not produce good fruit will be cut down" (Matt. 3:10). And notice that John speaks of the tree of life producing "twelve crops of fruit" and "yielding its fruit every month" (Rev. 22:2b; also Ezek. 47:12). That means this fruit-bearing is never-ending for the overcomers. People should be able to receive and eat this fruit from us at all times. God's plan is for his overcoming sons (and daughters) who live in his Holy City to become a forest of trees of life walking in this truth and bringing this healing reality to all the nations of the earth.

Certainly, Christ is the "King of kings and Lord of lords" (Rev. 19:16b). But He has also given us "the keys of the kingdom" (Matt. 16:19), commanded us to seek it "first" (Matt. 6:33), and conferred upon us a "just as" kingdom—"just as the Father conferred one on me" (Luke 22:29-30). In addition, He has given us specific instructions on how we are to reign and rule in it and to advance his kingdom with Him, here and now. Get it?

How Are We To Reign and Rule?

Since the greater Jesus has given us his all-inclusive authority in heaven and on earth to carry on the work of his kingdom, and since He does not give out tasks without empowering them, and since He has given us the keys to his kingdom so that we can bind and loose anything or any force that hinders our reigning and ruling with Him (Matt. 16:17-19; 18:18), and since He has given us his Great Commission to execute it all, the bottom line is this. How do we carry it out? Here are four crops of fruit I believe we Christians are to produce in our world for the healing of the nations.

(1) We have to measure up to God's standards. "The angel who talked with me had a measuring rod of gold to measure the city, its gates and its walls" (Rev. 21:15; also 11:1). First, we have to measure up. Note that this angel was only measuring the bride, the overcomers; all others were outside and not measured.

To measure is to ascertain size or stature by a fixed standard. We must measure up in fullness in Christ (Eph. 4:7), in our spiritual maturity (Eph. 4:13), in our faith (Rom. 12:3), in our obedience to God's Word (Rev. 22:7), and in the degree to which we have the Holy Spirit within us (2 Cor. 10:7-15; also Matt. 6:22).

> **... the Great Commission ... is far greater than most of us have been led to believe.**

How are we measured? The passage does not specifically say, but another obvious way is by how we fit in. In Solomon's temple, and as a possible type, every stone was chiseled, honed, shaped, and polished in the quarry. Then, it was measured against a precise standard. When it measured up perfectly, it could then be fitted into place without sound. Typically, the trials and tribulations we go through shape us up and prepare us to fit smoothly into the walls of this city as "living stones" (1 Pet. 2:5).

Why is all this necessary? It's because, as God told Jeremiah, "'Today I have made you a **fortified city**, an iron **pillar** and a bronze **wall** to stand against the whole land – against the kings of Judah, its officials, its priests, and the people of the land. They will fight against you but will not overcome you, for I am with you and will rescue you,' declares the Lord." (Jer. 1:18-19 – bold emphasis mine). But in the New Covenant economy all this has been universalized and greatly expanded and enhanced.

(2) We are to do the works of Jesus. The launching pad for all effective ministry is doing the works that Jesus did and commands believers in Him to do (John 14:12). People must see evidence of God's presence in you before they will listen to anything you have to say about what it can do for them. This is the way Jesus said that you can tell the true prophets from false ones—by the fruits they produce (Matt. 7:15-23). Doing his works is the continuation of his witness by his faithful and overcoming followers. Christians being sat on by the great prostitute will not do these works. Nor will they like hearing this message or the messages in the next two sections, or this entire book.

Since I have written extensively elsewhere on this and the next topic, I shall only make a few concluding comments here.[52]

Certainly, doing the works of Jesus means exhibiting the fruit of the Spirit: love, joy, peace, patience, meekness, and so forth (Gal. 5:22-26). That is basic. But the works of Jesus also include all the natural and miraculous works He did in his earthly ministry. "I tell you the truth," Jesus said, "anyone who has faith in me will do what I have been doing" (John 14:12a). And what did He do? He proclaimed the gospel of the kingdom, healed the sick, cast out evil spirits, fed the multitudes, raised the dead, and performed many other miracles, did He not?

Am I saying that we are to be doing those same things? Hey, I'm just reporting what Jesus said! And, "the testimony of Jesus" is the very "spirit of prophecy" (Rev. 19:10). That word *testimony* means *evidence given*.

Meanwhile today, many sat-upon Christians and prostituting churches are downplaying the existence of the spirit realm as evil spiritual forces are wreaking havoc in individual lives and throughout our country as well. It's time for us Christians to wake up to the powers of the spirit realm and get on with doing the supernatural works of Jesus, as well as all the other things we're supposed to be doing.

(3) We are to do even greater works. Jesus further promised, "He who has faith in me . . . will do even greater things than these, because I am going to the Father (John 14:12b).

What did He mean by that statement? It's not hard to figure out. It's spelled out throughout the Scriptures.[53]

In short and first, we are to do all the things He did (including the supernatural), then to do "the greater works." Here's my working definition for those "greater works:" <u>"The works Jesus did not do during his earthly ministry, but works God's people have been instructed to do throughout Scripture—from the beginning of the Bible in the Old Testament to the end in the New Testament.</u>

For example:[54]

- Jesus did not take on Rome or try to take it back for God, but we are to (?)
- He didn't make disciples of all nations, i.e., change not only lives, but also laws, institutions, and relationships. But we're commanded to do all of that (?)
- Jesus was "only sent to the lost sheep of the house of Israel" (Matt. 15:24). But we are to leave Judea and Samaria and go into "all the world" (Acts 1:8).
- He didn't take back all the territory Satan (and his forces – human and superhuman) had seized, but we're instructed to do it (?)
- He didn't reign and rule over governments, peoples, and nations, but we are to do it (?)
- He did not engage in politics, take on political powers and structures, nor attempt to fix, steer, or assault the tyranny of the Roman government. Rather, He allowed Himself to be crucified by them. . . .
- Jesus did not set out to reform society, but we are to do that (?)
- He did not work to build a government or take a stretch of land, but Israel did and we are to, sometimes (?)
- He refused to use the means of this world – either the clash of arms or the processes of politics to further his ends. (Are we?)
- He refused to be made "King;" but we were made to be "kings and priests" (Rev. 1:6; 5:10).
- He did not exert this kind of open power, but we are to (?)

To most of the world of his day, Jesus was anything but victorious. He was a cultural failure, despised, rejected, spat upon, beaten, and put to death like a common criminal. Clearly, his victory was not cultural, but the victory of the Cross—yielding and submission to the powers that be. And yet, there are these "greater works"—something Jesus either did not do at all or not do much of . . . that his followers are called to do. Perhaps, Jesus' "greater works" are some or all of the above. But I think there might be even more to them. And that something more may not be something new but something old. Again, this message is presented throughout the Bible from Genesis to Revelation and follows naturally, logically, and directly from the *Lordship* of Christ.

Before we go there, however, let's specially note that Jesus did not change the world. What He did do was to provide the means for his followers to change the world by doing the works He did and even greater works. Remember that Jesus came into human history to establish two great messianic works. Those of:

        1) The everlasting kingdom.
        2) Salvation.

These two messianic works were both announced and accomplished in that order. And all this took place in a small postage-stamp-sized patch of land in the Middle East during a short 74-some-year period of time—4 B.C. – circa A.D. 70. Since then and today, we believers in Him are to continue his mission and witness by doing his works and greater works. And we know what his works were. He modeled them for us. His "greater works"—in my opinion—can further be characterized in this manner. We are to <u>implement</u> / <u>advance</u> / <u>expand</u> / <u>extend</u> / <u>promote</u> / <u>put into practice</u> these two great works of the victory of God through Christ in and throughout the whole world. That means we are not only to transform human lives and activities but to transform all of society as well—lives, laws, institutions, and relationships.

- In essence, societal transformations are the "greater works" and part of our grand destiny as believers in and followers of the historical and greater Jesus Christ.

- This duty is also the strength of the historic postmillennial view—its advancement of the kingdom of God throughout the world and into all areas of society.
- This is how all Christians are biblically called to live out the radical difference in our lives that Jesus has made available.
- Jesus is going to do this all right. Be assured, He is present, active, and involved. But He also does it through his Holy-Spirit empowered, co-reigning people.
- Yes, it's about activism vs. pietism and not "reclaiming for Christ" but "transforming through Christ."

In other words as Chilton elaborated and emphasized, "Christianity applies to every area of life; it renovates the world."[55] And that renovation starts with us as individuals. We have to be able to reign and rule over our own lives before we can reign and rule in and over the world—in every aspect and area of our earthly existence. That means having our flesh and our minds under the control of the Spirit, reaching our full potential in Christ, and being the best we can be at whatever God has directed us to do. Sadly, most believers shrink from living at this level of responsibility, influence, power, and blessings. They are quite ready to leave all behind for the so-called Antichrist and Beast to occupy.

> **Jesus did not change the world. What He did do was to provide the means for his followers to change the world by doing the works He did and even greater works.**

Will this theology go against the grain and traditions of many Christians? Absolutely! Therefore, not everyone will agree with me, initially, at least. But there is an abundance of support throughout Scripture for all this. In a future book, I will go further into the Bible and make a case for this above understanding of the "greater works."[56]

Remember that "the leaves of the trees [us] are for the healing of the nations" (Rev. 22:2b). And what is the sickness of the nations that needs healed? In essence, it is the delusion that the nations can come together and solve all the world's problems without God. Healing this sickness sometimes involves pouring in the balm of kindness; but, in cases of serious illness (deception), it often means radical surgery.

The bottom line of the Revelation, and of the whole Bible, is that we are to take dominion over God's creation—to reign and rule over everything. And, yes, we have the numbers to do it. The problem is that at the present time we don't have the will. Why don't we? Whose fault is that? May I suggest, it's because of the great prostitute who "sits on many waters" (Rev. 17:1). She is to blame. Where am I wrong on this?

(4) We are to defeat the enemies of God and to expand his kingdom. The battle for control of this world starts in the spirit realm, where evil powers run rampant. That's why the Apostle Paul wrote, "Our struggle is not against flesh and blood, but against the rulers, against the authorities, against the powers of this dark world and against the spiritual forces of evil in the heavenly realms" (Eph. 6:12). Could anything be any clearer?

I believe the biggest reason the Church here in America and in our generation has given up so much ground is that it has failed to take into account (and in many cases has even denied the existence of) the supernatural enemies of God behind the physical and visible human agents. Jesus recognized and did battle with them. So did the 1st-century Church. But how can we expect to reign and rule the world with and for Christ when we don't even acknowledge or understand how to deal with the powers and beings that control much, if not most of it, now?

By the way, you don't have to worry about finding these spirit-realm and physical-realm enemies to engage them. If you start doing the works of and even greater works than Jesus, they'll find you. Can we conquer them? Again, Paul explains the weapons we have at our disposal. "The weapons we fight with are not the weapons of the world. On the contrary, they have divine power to demolish strongholds" (2 Cor. 10:4). In the Word of God, as revealed to us by the Spirit of God, we have all that we need for complete victory in every sphere of our lives and ministries throughout the entire world. Amen? Or, is this prophetic message and divine mandate too much for you, and you're out of here?

Why Is This Present Reality So Controversial and Repulsive?

Why is the idea that the Holy City exists as a present reality, inside us and among us, so hard for most Christians today to swallow? Why are these most significant events in all of human history since the creation of the world and marked as the fullness of time so ignored and denied? Why the urgency of Revelation's commands to keep, obey, or heed "the words of the prophecy of this book" (Rev. 1:3; 22:7), that the whole of its prophecy was and is "at hand" (Rev. 1:3; 22:10), and to "not seal up" (Rev. 22:10), if these events and realities were nineteen-centuries-and-counting removed and remote from their original audience, as well as still future for us today, and as most Christians have been told? Wallace rightly acknowledges the major ramification of this omission. It "would amount to convicting the inspired apostles of contradictions and of teaching error."[57]

Once again, we must keep reminding ourselves that many, if not most, Christians are dealing with a prostitute. And this prostitute has seduced them into believing lesser versions of the faith—different Christianities (a better term may be different "churchianites")—that pale in comparison to the genuine faith we see preached, practiced, and portrayed in the New Testament.

Revelation's consistent message, along with all the books of the New Testament, is that we are responsible to God to reign and rule, here and now—not just someday in the great by-and-by. The New Jerusalem at the center of the new heaven and new earth and in all its fullness is the final outworking of God's New Covenant community (Heb. 8:7-13; 9:10). All believers are invited to enter and become part of this city and bring healing to the nations, as we participate with the historical and greater Jesus Who is "making *everything* new" (Rev. 21:5).

Revelation's consistent message, along with all the books of the New Testament, is that we are responsible to God to reign and rule, here and now—not just someday in the great by-and-by.

Yet, most Christians, whom I believe are being sat on by the great prostitute, won't have anything to do with this high level of Christianity. They'll term it too radical, perhaps heretical, and a new idea, even though it's been around for over nineteen hundred years. They'd rather hang onto their short-term, pessimistic view of the end of the world and await their hope of going to heaven someday. Meanwhile, they are content and quite comfortable sitting in their pews, looking up into the sky, and hoping for Jesus to come back to earth and straighten everything out—after they have been removed of course. It's the sad and reductionistic focus of their faith. Most likely, they will never accept the biblical truth and reality that He never left, exactly as He said, and wants us to co-reign and co-rule with Him in this present world. Yes, they have been seduced and deceived (Matt. 24:23-26). The good news is, they are still the elect.

Other reasons many Christians shirk these God-given responsibilities is quite frankly because they are so tired of struggling with a less-than-rewarding life that subduing the power of the flesh is too painful or inconvenient, that fighting against the beast system, the dragon, and the harlot church is too bloody, and all this seems to be just too much for them to bear. Besides, their identity is so wrapped up in their church and its reductionistic practices (lesser versions of Christianity) that forging a new identity in the greater Jesus Christ is too emotionally challenging, if not intimidating and/or threatening.

For these reasons and more, I believe it is vital to invest this message into the next generation. Maybe we can catch them before they get too prostituted or too tired of our compromised versions of the faith; or before they become too anesthetized by and comfortable with worldly pursuits that they become too timid to force their way into the kingdom (Matt. 11:12; Luke 16:16).

Thus, Richard Bauckham, and Howard-Brook and Gwyther as well, aptly summarize Revelation's tale of two cities in this manner:

> The fall of Babylon, which occupies so much of Revelation, is what human opposition to God must come to, but it is not celebrated for its own sake. Babylon must fall so that the New Jerusalem may replace her. Her satanic parody of the ideal of the city must give way to the divine reality. But . . . before this happens, not only his [John's] readers but even, through them, the nations, may be won from the deceitful charms of Babylon to the genuine attractions of the New Jerusalem.[58]

... people's experience of God depends on how they live in the midst of empire. Those who stubbornly refuse to repent will experience God as angry judge . . . . those who grant all authority to the One who is Holy and True . . . will experience God's and the Lamb's community of intimacy and compassion.[59]

What about You?

The prophecy of the Holy City is calling God's people out of mediocrity and into a fullness of life (see Rom. 12:1-2; Gal. 4:19; 6:15; Eph. 4:15; Col. 1:27-28). It gives us a great, high, and mountaintop view into how God desires us to live in his kingdom, in this world, here and now. It shows us something of our full potential in Christ.

Don't you find it somewhat difficult to believe that Jesus lowered Himself, came all the way down from heaven to be born into human flesh, suffered as He did, and finally hung on a cross and died, rose from the dead and ascended to the Throne at the right hand of God, all for the sake of creating the various, mediocre, and anemic brands of Christianity floating around today that have the seductive audacity to call themselves the Church? I do.

The word *mediocre* comes from two Latin words: *medi*, meaning halfway, and *ocris*, meaning a stony mountain. The Romans combined them to form an idiomatic expression which literally meant halfway up a mountain.

The prophecy of the Holy City is calling God's people out of mediocrity into a fullness of life . . .

In my younger days, I scaled some of the better-known mountains of the world: the Matterhorn, Kilimanjaro, Mount Kenya, Mount Rainier, and others. Then, I wrote a best-selling book about my experiences and the motivational and achievement principles I learned along the way.[60] I can tell you from those experiences that nothing is more demanding or exhausting than to keep climbing, higher and higher, when everything within you cries out for relief and rest. I can also tell you that nothing is more devastating to the human spirit than getting all primed to go to the top of a magnificent and lofty peak, only to get stranded, or give up halfway up that mountain.

My friend, God is calling us to the peak of his holy mountain—to be that city on a hill, the salt and light of the world (Matt. 5:13-14). Likewise, He is calling us to become kings and priests (Rev. 1:6; 5:10) of his holy mountain and that city. I believe the historical and greater Jesus came into this world to establish this city of the New Jerusalem as the earthly, universal, and New-Covenant-determined community of his overcoming saints and for the purpose of us converting, discipling, and transforming the entire world via our healing of the nations!

For too long now, however, we've been buying into the seductions and deceptions of the great prostitute that the great or greater things we are promised and called to do in the Revelation (and in the entire Bible) are yet to be fulfilled up in the sky, out in the future, in the great by-and-by, or after our death and in heaven.

The Apocalypse of Jesus Christ has unveiled and revealed the greater Jesus in both his Alpha and Omega form. Today, He stands atop his holy mountain and says, "Come unto me!" Live in this city with me—now! Its blessings are here and available—now! It's time to quit star-gazing off into the heavens looking for a physical city and enter into this spiritual/physical reality and begin co-reigning and co-ruling with Him, here and now and forever. How you and I will spend eternity depends on how we spend our time here on earth.[61]

Will you join me? Let's start our climb together—right now!

Jesus' Final Warning

The stated purpose of the Apocalypse (the unveiling and revealing) is to show that Christ is no longer the suffering servant and the Jesus of the Gospels who was rejected and abused by the authorities of this earth. It pulls away the veil of his earthly ministry and presents Him as the ascended, triumphant, and sovereign Lord of the universe—the greater Jesus—King of kings and Lord of lords. Thus, it is fitting and proper that He should sit on the highest Throne of authority and exercise universal judgment. But what is even more amazing is that this Jesus has invited us to sit on his Throne with Him, here and now.

WARNING — From this Throne at the very end of the prophecy of the Book of Revelation, the apocalyptic greater Jesus issues this most solemn warning and terrifying consequences for any disobedient believer who either adds to and/or subtracts from this prophecy (doctrinally or functionally):

"I warn everyone who hears the words of the prophecy of this book: If anyone adds anything to them, God will add to him the plagues described in this book. And if anyone takes words away from this book of prophecy, God will take away from him his share in the tree of life and in the holy city, which are described in this book" (Rev. 22:18-19; also see 1 Cor. 11:29-32; Deut. 4:2).

In my opinion, many Christian theologians, pastors, teachers, elders, deacons, authors, speakers, and laypersons, alike, over the centuries and certainly today have been and are guilty of disregarding and violating this warning. Don't be one of them (see again story in Chapter 2, pp-75-76). Why not seek God's best, here and now? And if and when you do, you'll discover what a wonderful city the New Jerusalem truly is.

The Apocalypse of Jesus Christ has unveiled and revealed the greater Jesus in both his Alpha and Omega form.

Conclusion

He Stands Up for Heroes—the Ultimate Honor

God the Father, through the historical and greater Jesus and the Holy Spirit, intends for every Christian to understand, obey, and apply the spirit-realm/physical-realm truths and realities the Book of Revelation unveils and reveals, and to receive its promises and blessings as well. The Jesus of the Apocalypse did not intend to confuse us or delay the fulfillment and ongoing applications of this pinnacle and climactic prophecy. This Jesus today also has no dimensional limitations, as did the historical Jesus. If we could renew our minds with this truth, it alone would transform our outlook and our lives.

But I further believe that the proper understanding and application of this final prophetic message from the Bible can usher in a tsunami of God's Spirit and the next Reformation of our faith. It can create a sense of freshness and a renewed sense of life and commitment that hasn't been present to such a degree before—with the possible and likely exception of Christianity's first few centuries. It can inspire us to reach out more broadly, to hunger for the Word of God more deeply, and to serve Him as never before.

Finally and conclusively, the Revelation of Jesus Christ shows us that God wants to encourage, empower, and bring victory to his saints, here and now and while we live on this earth. Oh, the victory will not come easily. Satan, his superhuman and human cohorts, as well as the beast, the great prostitute, and our flesh, always fight to try and keep this from happening—to keep you from becoming an overcomer. But here is the key question with which we shall conclude this book.

Will He Stand Up for You?

At the end of his life, Stephen, "a man full of God's grace and power" who "did great wonders and miraculous signs among the people" (Acts 6:8), was arraigned to stand trial before the Jewish Sanhedrin. He was being charged with blasphemy for teaching that "this Jesus of Nazareth" will come and destroy the city of Jerusalem and the Temple and change the customs delivered by God through Moses (Acts 6:14-15). This same age-ending coming was foretold by the historical Jesus while also standing trial before this same Sanhedrin (Matt. 26:64), as well as at numerous other times (see Matt. 24, Mark 13, Luke 21). (There are other types of comings, as we have seen.)

During the trial, the Sanhedrin became "furious and gnashed their teeth at him. But Stephen, full of the Holy Spirit, looked up to heaven and saw the glory of God, and Jesus standing at the right hand of God. 'Look,' he said, 'I see heaven open and the Son of Man standing at the right hand of God.'

"At this they covered their ears and, yelling at the top of their voices, they all rushed at him, dragged him out of the city and began to stone him. . . . While they were stoning him, Stephen prayed, 'Lord Jesus, receive my spirit.' Then he fell on his knees and cried out, 'Lord do not hold this sin against them.' When he had said this, he fell asleep," i.e., a euphemism for physically died (Acts 7:54-60).

In contrast to this singular account, all other scriptures state that Jesus is *sitting* at the right hand of God (Rom. 8:34; Eph. 1:20; Col. 3:1; Heb. 1:13; 8:1; 12:21; Acts 2:33-36; Psa. 110:1), Who is seated on his heavenly throne (Psa. 2:4; 11:4; 22:28; 47:2, 8; 103:19; Prov. 8:13; Isa. 66:1). But Stephen looked up and saw the greater Jesus *standing*. Why was He standing? I believe He was standing up in honor, respect, reverence, and appreciation as He welcomed one of his heroes home and rejoiced over a man completing his life of faithful obedience even unto death.

Many others throughout the New Testament and the history of Christianity have also served the ascended, exalted, glorified, transformed, transfigured, transcendent, apocalyptic, crowned, and cosmic Christ in this manner. For them, as with Stephen, they overcame "by the blood of the Lamb and by the word of their testimony; they did not love their lives so much as to shrink from death. Therefore, rejoice, you heavens and you who dwell in them!" (Rev. 12:11-12a).

So, at the end of your life, when you approach the judgment seat of Christ and see the greater Jesus face-to-face as He now is, will He stand up for you and you hear these words, "Well done, good and faithful servant" (Matt. 25:21a; 23a)? Or will He remain seated and not welcome you with these words but with something else? Many Christians who are casual, comfortable, and complacent with compromised and lesser versions of the Christian faith than what we see presented in the Bible, probably won't receive this standing-up and voiced honor.

But if He does stand up for you and speak forth these words, it will be *the ultimate honor*.

As always, the decision of how we will or won't serve Him, here and now, is up to each of us. Please be assured, there are eternal rewards and consequences for believers regarding this decision—and about which we should be very concerned.[1]

Repeatedly, throughout Scripture, we have been told we were created for great things by the Most High God and given the power and direction to do them. But we have to take the initiative and do our part. So will you and I, as the Bible says, finish our lives being "more than conquerors" (Rom. 8:37) or something less? Overcomers or less than? Kings and priests of the Most High God or less than? Sons of God or still children?

All Christians are called to co-reign and co-rule with the greater Jesus, implement his victory, perform God's will, and advance his kingdom on this earth as it is in heaven, here and now, and into every area of life and thought. Worldwide, we Christians have the numbers to do this. What we don't have is the will. It seems we have been prostituted, seduced, and tamed. Iconoclastically, Chilton characterizes our world today this way. "Our culture is not post-Christian – our culture is still largely *pre*-Christian!"[2]

But if He does stand up for you and speak forth these words, it will be *the ultimate honor*.

The sad reality is, as long as Christians continue to sit back comfortably in their pews, doing little, and waiting for Jesus to come back, not much will change. But the apocalyptic instruction is: "Come out of her, my people!" (Rev. 18:4). Awake! Stand up! Step up! Get going! Our world awaits! And it's not about to end, nor will it ever.[3]

Seriously, if we Christians want and hope to receive this ultimate honor someday, we are going to have to up our game. We are going to have to become much more involved in changing the world than we moderns have been in the recent past. But we must do it based upon a solid theological foundation and genuine substance. That is the overarching theme and purpose for all my writings (past and future).

Therefore, if you desire to be an overcomer in the full sense, as the Revelation presents it, then now is the time to start acting like it, talking like it, and seeing yourself as God wants you to be, rather than settling for anything less. God, through *both* the historical and the greater Jesus Christ, has made it all available to you and me. So what say you now?

What's Next?

Admittedly, I have left many portions and details in the Revelation untouched. And this book may have raised questions that you have never considered, let along answered. Much more needs done and will be forthcoming, Lord willing. But I hope what has been presented so far, and in my previous books, will compel you onto greater heights of study and application of our "once-for-all-delivered" faith and its established realities (Jude 3).

It is far past time to recognize that Christianity as it is largely preached, practiced, and perceived in our modern world is not nearly as authentic, strong, and effective as it should and could be. The reason lies in the widespread failure of most churches and Christians to understand, practice, and present the *real* Christian faith. Instead, we have settled for watered-down, diluted, devalued, and diminished versions, a gospel of death, pessimism, and retreatism. As a result, many moderns consider Christianity to be unattractive and irrelevant. And in my opinion that's a prime reason why we are losing our children from the faith in droves. They sense these discrepancies and the consequential emptiness.[4]

Something, indeed, is seriously wrong. It's time for a major change—the next reformation.

How about You?

Now that you know some of the truths and realities about the greater Jesus, I hope this vision has awakened something in you that will produce a catharsis and a new beginning. Which Jesus will be the Jesus you now follow? The historical Jesus? The greater Jesus? Or both and the same?

Yes, the problems facing humanity are so great, complex, and intimidating that anything short of the greater Jesus will make solutions inadequate if not impossible. But widespread change can only be possible through a revolution of God's people and a conversion to the genuine and radical Christian faith preached, practiced, and perceived by the early Church. Call it the Next Reformation or, perhaps, the Great Returning. But how can this happen?

It only can happen if the greater Jesus, at the least, becomes our equal focus. And not just Jesus someday in heaven, but Jesus today, in this world, here and now, and in all this glory and grandeur. Following this Jesus will take uncommon commitment. And the greatest enemy against this happening is us. But if this change does takes place, it could dwarf the 16th-century Protestant Reformation in its effectiveness and impact.

In this regard, Bass is right on target when she writes:

> When Jesus said, "Thy kingdom come, thy will be done on earth as it is in heaven," he was directing his followers to do something. God's reign does not fall from heaven to those who wait. The people of God must live the kingdom by purposefully *doing* actions that rehearse love, charity, kindness, goodness, mercy, peace, forgiveness, and justice. . . . Churches cannot be clubs for the righteous, institutions that maintain religious conformity in the face of change, or businesses that manage orthodoxy and personal piety. . . . They must grasp—in a profound and authentic way—that they are sacred communities of performance where the faithful learn the script of God's story, rehearse the reign of God, experience delight, surprise, and wonder, and participate fully in the play. . . . Experiential faith demands action. It is not enough to sit

quietly in private and pray or mediate. . . . . Spiritual transformation happens only as we jump in and make a difference.[5]

So, once again, how about you? Are you ready to jump in and begin making a difference—a big difference? Or will you continue being content to leave things the way they are? I believe it is time for you and me to step up and into the greater Jesus. It is He Who has "made us to be a kingdom and priests to serve his God and Father" and to "reign on the earth" with Him (Rev. 1:6; 5:10), here and now, for the betterment of the world, so help us God!

So now that you know some of the truths and realities about the greater Jesus, I hope this vision has awakened something in you that will produce a catharsis and a new beginning.

Lastly, here is my prayer, straight from Scripture, for you and me:

"With this in mind, we constantly pray for you, that God may count you worthy of his calling, and that by his power he may fulfill every good purpose of yours and every act prompted by your faith. We pray this so that the name of our Lord Jesus Christ [the historical and the greater] may be glorified in you, and you in him, according to the grace of our God and the Lord Jesus Christ." (2 Thess. 1:11-12).

In our being worthy, faithful, and obedient, may his name be lifted higher and higher!

Which Jesus will be the Jesus you now follow?

Appendix A

My Patmos Pilgrimage and Revelation

(March 26, 2006)

It was still dark at six o'clock in the morning of March 26, 2006 as I stood on the top deck of our cruise ship. Above me, stretched a star-filled sky, anchored by a perfect waning crescent moon on the horizon directly off the stern and above which sat the brightest star of all. Slowly, we approached the small and sacred Greek Island of Patmos, the one immortalized in the Bible's last book of Revelation. Below, my wife and eleven hundred other passengers slept or had just started their breakfast. I was alone in this awesome place with my thoughts, my prayers, my expectations, and my God.

For over twenty years I had longed for this day—ever since I began actively studying, teaching, and writing about the Book of Revelation and analyzing its various interpretive views. And today was my day!

A Personal Excursus
The Back Story and Highlights of My Thirty-Some-Year Quest for Truth and Understanding of the Book of Revelation

- **1983** – Called out by name and received a dramatic personal prophecy regarding my future teaching of Scripture at a revival meeting focused on the Book of Revelation and at which my wife and I knew no one and no one knew us, either.[1]

- **1986** – Began a serious study and analysis of the Book of Revelation and its various interpretative views.

- **1987-88** – Taught through the entire Book of Revelation in a home Bible study.

- **1991** – Based on the above, my book *The Apocalypse Conspiracy* is published by Wolgemuth & Hyatt / Word.

- **1993** – On March 8th, as the author of *The Apocalypse Conspiracy*, I appeared on CNN's *Larry King Live* show during the height of the Waco confrontation. I was invited to refute the claims of a fellow Christian, Harold Camping, whose book titled *1994* predicted the return of Christ and the end of the world in 1994.

- **2003** – Completed and successfully defended my Ph.D. in Theology dissertation in which a sizeable portion deals with a synthesized and better understanding of the prophecy of Revelation (and the rest of eschatology as well) than is presented by any of the four major eschatological views in the historic evangelical Church.

- **2004** – Introduced my new synthesized view of Revelation's past fulfillment and ongoing relevancy in a study group of conservative biblical scholars at the 56th Annual Meeting of the Evangelical Theological Society. Surprisingly, the leader recommends I write up my "new" view and submit it for publication in *JETS*—the *Journal of the Evangelical Theological Society*—along with his recommendation for publication (SEE APPENDIX B).

- **2005** – My *JETS* article is accepted and awaiting publication in the Winter, 2006 issue. It is titled, "An Exegetical Basis for a Preterist-Idealist Understanding of the Book of Revelation."

- **March 26, 2006** – Made my pilgrimage to Patmos and received my confirmation revelation of Revelation from God (see below).

- **December 2006** – My above article was published in *JETS*, Vol. 49, No. 4, 767-96.

- **August 2012** – The publication of this book, *The Greater Jesus*.

How Presumptuous?

Patmos was the prime reason I had journeyed these six thousand miles from America. But I was not coming as an act of religious devotion, as most on pilgrimages do. I was coming specifically to receive a revelation from God. So, once again, I was rehearsing in my mind how, over nineteen centuries ago, another John, the Apostle John, had entered this same harbor and later, while imprisoned and in exile for approximately two years and in a cave, received a revelation from the greater Jesus—the Bible's last Book of Revelation. But I would only be on Patmos today for little more than two hours.

How presumptuous, I thought, that God would give me a revelation while in this sacred place. Yet I had invested two months in prayer and publicly proclaimed that my purpose for coming to Patmos was to receive this revelation. My church, three Bible study groups, my family, and several other individuals were praying for me in this way. But what if nothing happens? Or what if I read too much into whatever does occur, given my high hopes and expectations? How would I face those people back home when they surely would ask, What happened? And if nothing of any revelatory significance happens, could I be honest and tell them so. Even worse I feared, was I actually guilty of testing God? After all, the Apostle John wasn't expecting to receive anything from God when he was forced into exile on Patmos. But it was too late now to turn back. And I had no idea of what, how, or even if God would do something for me significant enough of being characterized as a divine revelation.

Signs in the Sky?

As I peered out across the bow into the dark sky and oncoming sea, the shadowy bluffs of Patmos loomed ahead. Lights twinkling like stars lining the hilltop on which sit the two monasteries of the Apocalypse and of St. John the Theologian. These lights seemed to float in the sky several hundred feet above the harbor. On the crest of another hill to the right of the harbor was a large cross of white lights shining out to sea.

I felt a little disappointed, however. I had hoped to enter the harbor during daylight so I could see and have a better perspective of Patmos. Yesterday, at this same scheduled arrival time (6:30 A.M.) when we sailed into the Greek island of Rhodes, I could see everything quite well, since sunrise had been at 6:08 A.M. But the time had changed in Europe on the preceding night (one week ahead of America). We received a notice under the door of our cabin instructing us to set our clocks forward one hour. Hence, today at 6:00 A.M. it was still dark as we entered the harbor.

Interestingly in the sky above the hill behind the harbor, and on which is located "The Holy Cave of the Apocalypse," was the Big Dipper. It was directly in front of our ship and angled downward, left to right, handle to bowl, as if something was being poured out straight down. At 6:30 as we entered the harbor and anchored, the hill reached higher into the sky and almost touched the bottom stars of this well-known celestial formation. "Is this a sign?" I asked God in prayer. "And if so, what does it mean?" Once again, and as I have done so many times before, I prayed for "the Spirit of wisdom and revelation" (Eph. 1:17).

Next, I noticed that directly behind me straight off the stern of the ship and in the eastern sky hung the brilliant sliver of that perfect waning crescent moon. A moon-width distance directly above it was the brightest star in the sky. "What does this mean, Lord?" I asked again.

My initial thought was that these latter two "signs" might have something to do with Islam, since this phase of the moon, along with a star to its immediate right, is the internationally recognized symbol of the Muslim faith. And just over the eastern horizon, forty miles away, lay the mainland of the Muslim countries of Turkey, followed by and to the east Syria, Iraq, and Iran. But what sense would Islamic symbolism mean to me? And besides, this star was located above the crescent moon, and not off to its right. Hence, these perfectly aligned (bow-to-stern) celestial formations didn't seem to make any sense.

Oh, stop it, I cautioned myself. I was probably already trying to read too much into these natural coincidences. Anyway, my revelation from God most likely would occur in the cave where St. John received his revelation, I was thinking. But my spiritual antennas were already way up, so to speak, and I was actively looking for how God might give me the revelation for which others and I had been earnestly praying and I was seeking.

Signs at the Monastery and in the Cave

Around nine o'clock, groups began disembarked our cruise ship onto tender boats that ferried us to shore. On shore, we boarded buses that took us to the Monastery of the Apocalypse. This monastery, built around the 11th century, surrounds the cave, or the Sacred Grotto as the Greeks refer to it, in which St. John received the Book of Revelation. By the time my group arrived, several other tour buses had already unloaded, and a long line had formed waiting to enter the monastery.

While we waited, the young Greek lady who was our tour guide told us that "during the reign of the Roman Emperor Domitian in A.D. 95, the Apostle John was banished to Patmos, where he was held for two years. It was here that he received the inspiration for the Book of Revelation from his professor, Jesus Christ. It contains prophecies about the end of the world."

When she finished her prepared spiel, I stepped out of line, worked my way over to her and asked, "How do you know the prophecy of Revelation is about the end of the world?"

"This is the interpretation I was told," she frankly replied.

"Have you ever heard of the view that Revelation was written prior to the destruction of Jerusalem in A.D. 70 and was fulfilled, or mostly fulfilled, at that time and in this way?" I continued.

"No," she said bluntly.

"Well, many scholars are increasingly seeing it this way . . ." I followed up until I was rather rudely interrupted by a sixty-or-so-year-old American man standing next to us. He apparently had overheard our conversation.

"I don't agree with that," he barked out gruffly.

When I looked over at him anger raged across his face. So, I did not respond. After all, I was not here to engage in debate or get sidetracked into theological arguments with other Christians. I was here to receive a revelation from God and I didn't want anything to interfere or distract me from that. So I thanked my guide for her answers, dutifully went back to my place in line, and lifted up this silent prayer, "Lord, why did these two confrontations happen? What do they mean?" Yes, I was keeping a close mental track of every little thing.

Soon it was our turn. But our guide instructed us not to spend much time inside. Many others were in line behind us and we only had a limited amount of time before we had to be back on ship. She also said we should be quiet as we enter. Since it was the Lord's Day, a religious service was being conducted in the small Greek Orthodox Church of St. Anne immediately adjacent to the open cave.

Here we go, I thought, as I descended, in line, down a narrow and winding corridor of stairs into the monastery and toward the cave. This is why I came to Patmos. In the cave was where and when I was expecting God to reveal something quite significant and obvious to me. Yes, I was ready, super ready. Again, my spiritual antenna was way up and my radar on. I was in high alert and paying close attention to everything going on both around me and inside me.

When I reached the small church immediately adjacent to the opening of the cave, it was packed with local worshippers and Greek Orthodox priests chanting, reading Greek text, and shaking burning incense all around. The odor and smoke stung one's eyes. My wife could hardly stand it, and she left quickly. Plastered over every square inch of the walls were icons and frescoes of various saints. Ornate silver candelabras with burning candles hung down from the ceiling. It was like entering a mysterious and somewhat surrealistic world. But one thing was unmistakable. The Greek Orthodox people seriously revere and treat this place as sacred. I respected that. But the contrast, if not the irony, between their devotional rituals and the line of camera-laden, eye-gawking tourists parading through their service could not be missed. Moreover, the cave of St. John, could hardly qualify as a cave. It was only a smooth-stone indentation in the side of a hill, about ten feet deep and seven feet high. It left one with the sense of, "Is that all it is?"

I snapped five quick pictures. Then it happened. From behind, I felt a hand touching my shoulder. "This is it," I thought. I turned around expecting to see Jesus with a sword coming out of his mouth, or an angel, or something revelatory, or hear a loud voice like a trumpet as St. John did when he turned around to look in that same cave on the Lord's Day (Rev. 1:12). Instead, as I turned I saw a little old Greek lady wagging her index figure at me, shaking her head from side to side, and whispering, "no pictures."

After a brief few minutes, it was time to leave. Others behind were pressing their way in. On the way out, I turned to take one last look. It was then that I noticed a circular plaque above the entrance of this holy cave. It was written in Greek. I wondered what it said, but didn't think much of it at the time.

As I climbed back up the winding stairs of the monastery, it was with an empty feeling. After all, nothing happened—nothing of any revelatory significance whatsoever!

Outside the monastery, our group held a communion service and then we shopped in a small souvenir stand next to the buses. One of my purchases was a pictorial book titled "Patmos: The Island of the Revelation" since it contained numerous pictures and descriptions of the monastery and cave we had just visited.

After boarding our bus, we toured the Monastery of St. John the Theologian farther up the hill and then returned to our ship. All told, I had spent a little over two hours on the island of Patmos. True, my feet had stood were St. John's feet had stood—in the sacred cave of the Revelation, but I had received nothing, absolutely nothing, that I could recall. Or so I thought at the time.

When we arrived at Ephesus (in Turkey and one of the seven churches of the Revelation) for our tour that afternoon, however, I noticed a perfect waning crescent moon—like the one I had seen that morning—on Turkey's national flag. Interesting, I thought, and quickly moved on.

Signs Back at Home?

Our eleven-day tour of Greece, Turkey and Patmos lasted another five days. We visited Ephesus, Delphi, Kalambaka, Meteora,

Thessaloniki, and Athens before our long flight home. But I was so busy and tired that I really didn't think much more about my time on Patmos. After all, nothing revelatory had happened, right?

Upon landing in Chicago, and after having been up for twenty hours, my wife and I still faced a four-hour car drive home to Indianapolis. But traffic was backed up on the Interstate and we were delayed an extra hour getting out of Chicago. Finally, we reached Indiana and turned South onto I-65. In the sky on the horizon directly ahead loomed a massive and ominous-looking cloudbank. It appeared so solid that my wife commented that it actually looked like a mountain range. But the strange thing was, we never caught up to the cloudbank, even though we drove another 150 miles South at a seventy-mile-an-hour clip. As night fell, a constant rapid-fire lightning display emanated from the clouds to the ground and within the cloudbank. It was a spectacular light show. The radio was warning of tornadoes. So I didn't want to drive into it. But we never did and it never rained. The cloudbank was always just ahead down the road right in front of us all the way home and emanating its gigantic and forked lightning show. We joked that this must be like God leading the Israelites in the wilderness—they followed "the pillar of cloud by day" and "the pillar of fire by night" (Exodus 13:22). The awesome lightning display, however, helped keep us awake and attentive.

The next morning I awoke, unexpectedly, at 6:00 A.M. It must have been due to jet affect. So I decided to go ahead and go to the Saturday morning men's meeting I usually attend. As usual, we started by singing two praise and worship songs led by one of the men who plays a guitar. The words of the first song struck me as particularly relevant. We sang:

> Oh, God you are my God
> And I will ever praise You.
> And I will seek you in the morning
> And I will learn to walk in your ways
> As step by step you lead me
> And I will follow You all of my days

Interesting, I thought to myself as we sang. This is what I had done six days ago on the top deck of the cruise ship as we neared and entered the harbor of Patmos. I had sought God early that morning, even before the rising of the sun.

When the song ended, our worship leader rhetorically asked, "Where are all the signs and wonders?" Well, that's what I was still wondering. Then he started telling us about Gideon in the Old Testament book of Judges. It seems Gideon asked and wondered about this same issue. And what did Gideon do? He asked the angel of the Lord, Who was appearing to him, for a sign. Gideon asked, "If now I have found favor in your eyes, give me a sign that it is really you talking to me" (Judges 6:17).

I couldn't believe what I was hearing. Gideon was as presumptuous as I had been. But God gave him a sign as he requested (see Judges 6:18ff; also see Matt. 12:39).

The next morning, a Sunday, our pastor's sermon also cited Judges 6 and talked about Gideon's fear to undertake the task God had assigned him. I pondered, <u>Was this just another coincidence?</u>

Then It Hits Me

That Sunday afternoon I decided to look over my "Patmos: The Island of the Revelation" pictorial book I had purchased. And there it was, on page 18, a picture of "The Holy Cave of the Apocalypse" and at the bottom a picture of the circular, Greek-inscribed plaque I had seen above the entrance to the cave, as well as its English translation. It reads, *"This impressive place is nothing but the house of God and this is the door to the sky."*

Like a lightning bolt out of a cloudbank, that's when it hit me. The revelation I had sought from God did not come in the cave on Patmos as it did with John. It had come in the pre-dawn sky *above* Patmos! And why should I consider it unusual that God would choose to use signs and symbols in the sky to communicate to me a revelation about a prophetic book filled with signs and symbols?

Many times in the Bible God used signs and symbols in the sky as one of the ways He has communicated with us humans. For example:

- The sun and the moon were created to "serve as signs to mark seasons and days and years" (Gen. 1:14).

- The rainbow was given as "the sign of the [Noahic] covenant" (Gen. 9:13).
- One of the plagues in Egypt was of "total darkness" and "covered Egypt for three days" (Exod. 10:21-23).
- Once, "the sun stood still and the moon stopped" (Josh. 10:12-14).
- Many Christians believe and several books have been written demonstrating how the gospel is depicted in the stars, especially in the twelve constellations of the zodiac. Perhaps, this is one of the ways "the heavens declare the glory of God; the skies proclaim the work of his hands" (Psa. 19:1).
- When Jesus hung on the cross, there was an eclipse of the sun, "from the sixth hour until the ninth hour darkness came over the land" (Matt. 27:45).
- By inspiration, the Apostle Paul wrote, "For since the creation of the world God's invisible qualities—his eternal power and divine nature—have been clearly seen, being understood from what has been made, so that men are without excuse" (Rom. 1:20). This surely includes the sky and its contents.
- Jesus is termed "the sun of righteousness [Who] will rise with healing in its wings" (Mal. 4:2), "the sun, which is like a bridegroom coming forth from his pavilion" (Psa. 19:4-5), "a sun and shield" (Psa. 84:11), Revelation's "the bright Morning Star" (Rev. 2:28; 22:16), and Peter's "morning star" which "rises in your hearts" (2 Pet. 1:19).
- Joel prophesied that God would "show wonders in the heavens . . . the sun will be turned to darkness and the moon to blood before the coming of the great and dreadful day of the Lord" (Joel 2:30). Peter quotes this passage at Pentecost (Acts 2:19-20).
- Jesus said there would be "fearful sights and great signs from heaven" (Luke 21:11) and all this would take place before his contemporary generation passed away (Luke 21:32).
- 1st- and 2nd-century historians, Josephus and Tacitus, respectively, reported that great and awesome "signs . . . so evident and did so plainly foretell their future desolation" appeared over Jerusalem in the sky in A.D. 66 and prior to

Jerusalem's total destruction in A.D. 70 (Josephus, *Wars*, 6.6.3; Tacitus, *The Histories*, I.III).

So was the perfect, straight-line alignment (bow-to-stern) of the three celestial signs in the sky on the pre-dawn morning I arrived into the harbor merely coincidence? Perhaps. But, again, others and I had been praying for two months for a special revelation from God while I was on Patmos. And for more than twenty years one of my most frequent prayers has been for "the Spirit of wisdom and revelation" (Eph. 1:17).

Many times in the Bible God used signs and symbols in the sky as one of the ways He has communicated with us humans.

Furthermore, God's Word admonishes us that "If any of you lacks wisdom, he should ask God, who gives generously to all without finding fault, and it will be given to him. But when he asks, he must believe and not doubt, because he who doubts is like a wave of the sea blown and tossed by the wind. That man should not think he will receive anything from the Lord; he is a double-minded man, unstable in all he does" (James 1:5-8). And there was such a series of coincidences and a consistency I could not dismiss. So I prayed for this wisdom.

What's the Probability?

If you had been me, or with me, on the top deck of that cruise ship, seeing what I was seeing, and praying for "the Spirit of wisdom and revelation" (Eph. 1:17), what would you have thought? How would you have interpreted these happenings, or not? Or, would you have missed them entirely?

But what's the probability that all seven of these physical circumstances would be perfectly aligned—time, place, and position wise on planet Earth—especially on Patmos "The Island of the Revelation" during my visit on Sunday, March 26, 2006?

1). My wife and I would be invited to join a pre-set, eleven-day tour of Greece and Turkey that would put me on the island Patmos and in the cave where St. John received the Book of Revelation on "the Lord's Day" (Rev. 1:10).

2). The position of the Big Dipper in the sky would be straight in front of our approaching ship and directly above the harbor on Patmos, almost touching the hilltop of the cave of St. John. (The Big Dipper travels across the sky at night).

3). The position of a perfect waning crescent moon would be directly off the stern to the east. (It, too, moves across the sky at night but at a different rate of speed than the Big Dipper since it is closer to earth. (3/22/06 was the quarter moon; 3/29/06, the new moon).

4). Straight off the stern to the east was the nation of Turkey.

5). The brightest star in the morning sky was also in this same straight-line alignment and directly above the moon (it, too, travels across the sky at night but at a different rate of speed from the Big Dipper and the moon).

6). The time of day we entered the harbor and anchored was an hour before dawn, when on the previous day at that same time it was daylight. Had my ship entered in daylight, the three signs in the sky would not have been visible.

7). A sign on the entrance to "The Holy Cave of the Apocalypse," written in Greek, would eventually supply the interpretative key for putting everything together.

Then What Does It Mean?

The more I have reflected on and prayed about what happened that day on Patmos, the more I have gleaned.

Below is what I currently think these circumstances, or signs and symbols, might have meant. I ask you to judge my interpretations—like the Apostle Paul asked those in Jerusalem who he deemed to be leaders, "for fear that I was running or had run my race in vain" (Gal. 2:2; also see 1 Thess. 5:19-21):

The three relevant questions are:

1) Were the perfectly aligned and three celestial phenomena I had seen in the sky actually signs and symbols and God's way of communicating a revelation to me?
2) If so, what did they symbolize (point to)?
3) Would I allow Him to lead me this way and follow his leading?

Sign #1 – The Big Dipper in the Sky Directly above Patmos:
God poured something out at Patmos long ago, and is still pouring it out over the whole world. The next two signs symbolize what that something is.

Sign #2 – The Perfect Waning Crescent Moon:
A perfect waning crescent moon, i.e., the same width and shape, is featured on the national flag of Turkey. Nowadays, Turkey is the home country of the original seven churches of Revelation. Hence, this second sign signifies "the testimony for the churches" (Rev. 22:16; also 1:4, 11; Rev. 2 and 3) and that God has poured out and still is pouring out the prophetic contents of the Book of Revelation, and has been doing so for more than nineteen centuries.

Another possible interpretation of this sign is, and like a crescent moon, God's people are only receiving a sliver of Revelation's light and knowledge. Most are in the dark about this prophecy, which is God's ultimate, pinnacle, climactic, and final revelation to humankind in his plan of progressive revelation—from Genesis to Revelation. Hence, many of "my [God's] people are destroyed from lack of [this] knowledge. 'Because you have rejected [this] knowledge . . . .'" (Hosea 4:6). They are also missing out on Revelation's promised blessings—in this life and the next, because they shun the prophecy, or are confused by it, or improperly interpret it (see Rev. 1:3; 22:7), or add to or subtract from it (Rev. 22:18-19).

The Brightest Morning Star:
"The bright Morning Star" above the crescent moon symbolizes none other than Jesus Christ Himself (Rev. 2:28; 22:16). And Jesus Christ is what the testimony of the Book of Revelation is all about. As Revelation's first five words say, "the revelation (unveiling, revealing) of Jesus Christ" (Rev. 1:1). "For the testimony of Jesus is the spirit of prophecy" (Rev. 19:10b). Moreover, He is, indeed, above all things.

The Book of Revelation is not the revelation of the "end of the world" or "the Antichrist," or future events that have not happened yet. It's the revelation of Jesus Christ and events and realities that were "at hand" (Rev. 1:3; 22:10) and would and did "shortly come to pass" (Rev. 1:1; 22:6). And, it's more than that.

The Confrontations in Front of the Monastery:
Because of their erroneous, mostly futuristic, end-of-the-world mindset concerning the meaning and contents of the Book of Revelation, the Greek Orthodox people, my tour guide, and the angry American man who so abruptly disagreed and interrupted me, are not receiving the promised blessings of this prophetic book. Many others, who are afraid of or are intimidated by this prophecy, don't receive its blessings either.

The Revelation stipulates in both its first and last chapters that its blessings are given only to those who read it, hear it (with intended meaning and proper understanding), and obey it, all of it (Rev. 1:3; 22:7). It takes all three. How do we know it takes all three? Because the second prophecy-bracketing statement stipulating this fact does not mention the first two prerequisites, only the third, "Blessed is he who keeps/heeds/obeys the words of the prophecy of this book" [all of it] (Rev. 22:7). For the whole of the prophecy to be obeyed, it had to be keepable, heedable, and obeyable. Therefore, it had to be a present, available, and relevant reality, first and foremost, for this book's original audience—people in the seven original churches of Revelation located in what is now the modern-day nation of Turkey. But again, it is more than that.

Many others, who are afraid of or intimidated by this prophecy, don't receive its blessings either.

Then how do we break through the various negative, erroneous, and yet prevailing mindsets about the contents of the Book of Revelation as well as all the truth avoidance tendencies? The answer, I believe, I received in prayer—by emphasizing the promised blessings. People are drawn to blessings but repelled by fear and foreboding. And the biggest blessing of all, in my opinion, is this book's unveiling and revealing of the greater Jesus.

The Sign on the Cave Entrance:
This sign redirected me to the signs and symbols I saw in that pre-dawn sky. The revelation I had sought was given to me via the three signs in the sky *above* Patmos, and not in the cave *on* Patmos.

Further Confirmations:

- Beginning delayed an hour by heavy traffic and, consequently, having to follow the cloudbank on the drive home from Chicago that, again, redirected me to reflect on what I had seen in the sky above Patmos.
- The praise song reminded me that I had sought God in the pre-dawn hour of that morning on March 26, 2006.
- The Gideon comparative in Judges 6 gave me confidence that I had not been presumptuous about asking God for a revelation and looking for signs.

My Confirmation Revelation of Revelation!

I believe God did speak to me in a fairly dramatic way on that "Lord's Day," March 26, 2006, on the island of Patmos, and that I did receive a revelation. This revelation of Revelation, however, did not change the scholarly understanding I have evolved into over the past twenty-some years. Rather, it confirmed it. I also believe God is leading me in this Preterist-Idealist direction to:

- Emphasize the blessings—that's what the Book of Revelation does.
- Tell God's people why they are missing these promised and available blessings and how they can change this.
- Share, teach, and disseminate this climactic message of the greater Jesus, wherever a door is or doors are opened.
- "Go in the strength you have . . . Am I not sending you? . . . I will be with you" (Judges 6:14, 16).

But you be the judge.

Appendix B

My ETS Revelation Experience

(November 2004)

Most of the content of this appendix was originally published in an article in *Fulfilled Magazine*, Fall 2011, 6-7, 9.

At the 56th Annual Meeting of the Evangelical Theological Society held in San Antonio, Texas in November 2004, I was invited to participate in a special afternoon Group Study session on the topic of eschatology.

The session consisted of presentations from three speakers, which were followed by a response from Grant R. Osborn, Professor of New Testament at Trinity Evangelical Divinity School and author of the book *Revelation* (2002), part of Baker Books' *Exegetical Commentary on the New Testament* series.

After Dr. Osborn commented on the presentations, he opened the floor for questions and answers. One of the first questions was: "What do you think of the preterist view?" I braced myself for a typically dispensational and attacking response. Surprisingly, he said, "I think it makes a lot of sense."

Then, in reference to the Book of Revelation, he voiced the all-too-common perception: "But I still can't believe everything has been fulfilled and it's over." At which time, I immediately raised my hand and, after he called on me, queried, "What about the idea that the whole prophecy of Revelation has been *fulfilled* and it's *not over*?"

"I've never heard of that," he responded. "What do you call it?"

Caught somewhat off-guard, I quickly quipped, somewhat off-handedly, "How about *preterist-idealist*?" That was the first time I had ever connected or spoken these two words together.

"Tell me about that," he requested.

I mentioned that this understanding was part of my doctoral dissertation, and for the next ten minutes or so I highlighted an exegetical basis to support this preterist-idealist understanding. I began by advocating that a strong case can be made (and has been made) that the Book of Revelation was most likely written prior to the Jewish-Roman War of AD 66-70. As support, I cited both Kenneth L. Gentry, Jr.'s book *Before Jerusalem Fell* and John A. T. Robinson's *Redating the New Testament*.

"I think it makes a lot of sense. . . . But I still can't believe everything has been fulfilled and it's over."
Dr. Grant R. Osborn

Next, I presented the time statements in both Revelation's first and last chapters. I stressed how those time statements encompassed the entire prophecy and why this total bracketing demands that the fulfillment of all of this prophecy rises or falls together and cannot be bifurcated anywhere—not at the beginning of chapter 4 (as does dispensational premillennialism), not after chapter 19 (as does postmillennialism), nor in the midst of chapter 20 (as does amillennialism). Then I emphasized that another strong case can be made and has been historically documented that the fulfillment of this entire prophecy occurred during the 1st century in association with the Jewish-Roman War of AD 66-70 and the destruction of Jerusalem and the Temple—as according to the full preterist view.

Lastly, I laid out the exegetical basis in Revelation 10:9-11 for coupling the idealist understanding of ongoing relevancy of the entire prophecy with the full preterist understanding of its past fulfillment. Here, John was given a scroll and told to eat it. That scroll was the same scroll given to Jesus in Revelation 5 and from which came the seven seals, the seven trumpets, and eventually the seven bowls of God's judgment and wrath. In a book filled with signs and symbols, I contended that John's eating of this scroll was a dramatic and grotesque act. Therefore, it is not unreasonable to assume that his ingesting is also a sign and a symbol pointing to an actual reality, one which, I further related, is explained in the next two verses.

When John ate the scroll, "it tasted as sweet as honey" in his mouth because of the seven blessings promised in Revelation. It also "turned sour" in his stomach because of Revelation's soon-coming judgment events (v. 10). In verse 11, however, John was told that he "must prophesy again about many peoples, nations, languages and kings." I pointed out that this group is an entirely different group of people than to whom the Book of Revelation was given to in the first place, i.e., the seven churches in Asia Minor (Rev 1:4, 11, 20; 2 and 3), and a much broader group than this book's original recipients. Idealists focus on the very similar language used six times in Revelation (5:9; 7:9; 10:11; 13:7; 14:6; and 17:15) in order to justify universalizing the ongoing and timeless relevance of Revelation. I stated that I agree with this amillennialist-idealist paradigm; however, unlike the amillennialist-idealists, I place the idealist portion *after* Revelation's fulfillment, not *before* it as they do.

Of course, like almost everything in Revelation, as well as in the whole field of eschatology, this understanding and its textual support is contested. So I suggested that we take a quick look at this language's first use in Revelation 5:9: "And they sang a new song: 'You are worthy to take the scroll and to open its seals, because you were slain, and with your blood you purchased men for God from every tribe and language and people and nation.'" Most commentators agree that the lamb slain here is Jesus and those purchased by his blood "from every tribe and language and people and nation" applies to and includes you, me, and people all over the world from that 1st-century time period and onward. Not surprisingly, no one in the group objected.

Some preterists, however, do not want to admit that this same language applies in a similar manner to this prophecy's ongoing and timeless relevancy, as demonstrated in Revelation 10:9-11. They feel that such a view distracts from this book's circa A.D. 70 fulfillment. Even worse, they fear it allows for Revelation's many prophesied events to be reoccurring and its established realities to be experienced all around the world at different times and by many different groups and individuals.

But the exegetical basis for this preterist-idealist understanding is plainly provided in the text.

After my explanation, Dr. Osborn said this to me in front of the whole group: "I tell you what I'm going to do, John. I'm going to recommend that you write up your comments on your preterist-idealist understanding and put them in the form of an article and send it to the editor of the *Journal of the Evangelical Theological Society* along with my recommendation for publication."

John's eating of this scroll was a dramatic and grotesque act.

You could have blown me over with a feather. I thought for sure when the question about preterism was first raised, the preterist view would be bashed and trashed. But it wasn't. Just the opposite occurred. The preterist-idealist label and its scriptural support were compelling, respectfully listened to by the group, and publicly and positively responded to by Dr. Osborn.

After the session, several participants had many additional questions. Eight of them invited me to dinner for the purpose of continuing our discussion of the preterist-idealist view. When I returned home, I wrote up my comments in the form an academic journal article and submitted it with Dr. Osborn's recommendation. Two years later it was published.

This article is the most credible piece of writing (including all of my books) that I've ever had published. The reason is, it was published by a peer-review, academic, and prestigious journal.

If you would like to read this complete article, it is posted on PRI's website www.prophecyrefi.org. Or, you can check out a copy of the *Journal* (*JETS*) at your closest seminary library. The article title and reference information is: John Noē, "An Exegetical Basis for a Preterist-Idealist Understanding of the Book of Revelation," *Journal of the Evangelical Theological Society*, Vol. 49, No. 4 (Dec. 2006): 766-796.

More Books from John Noē

(Available on Amazon.com)

What are millions worldwide looking for today?

That's right! The perfect ending! Here it is!

Why All 'End-of-the-World' Prophets Will _Always_ Be Wrong!

The perennial prophets of doom have failed to recognize that our world is without end and "the end" the Bible consistently proclaims *for* the world is behind us and not ahead of us; is past and not future. This is the perfect ending! It's also the climax of the rest of the greatest story ever foretold. In this book you'll discover:

- ~ WHY THE WORLD WILL NEVER END.
- ~ HOW THE PERFECT ENDING FOR THE WORLD CAME RIGHT ON TIME.
- ~ DIVINE PERFECTION IN GOD'S END-TIME PLAN.
- ~ A NEW & GREATER PARADIGM OF THOUGHT AND FAITH.
- ~ OUR GREATER RESPONSIBILITIES HEREIN.
- ~ WHY THE FUTURE IS BRIGHT AND PROMISING.
- ~ THE BASIS FOR THE NEXT REFORMATION OF CHRISTIANITY.

"Noē's book just could be the spark that ignites the next reformation of Christianity." – Dr. James Earl Massey, Former Sr. Editor, *Christianity Today* Dean Emeritus, School of Theology, Anderson University & Distinguished Professor-at-Large

"Your treatment of the 'end of the world' is the best treatment of this idea . . . . Your book could really open the eyes of a lot of people." – Walter C. Hibbard, Former Chairman, Great Christian Books

"Noē . . . argues, with no little energy, against traditional views . . . [it] does have an internal logic that makes for exegetically interesting reading." – Mark Galli, Book Review Editor, *Christianity Today*

'*Hell Yes / Hell No: What really is the extent of God's grace . . . and wrath?*' –

This compelling and controversial book strikes at the heart of Christian theology and Christianity itself. It presents a balanced and scholarly re-exploration of "one of Christianity's most offensive doctrines"—Hell and the greater issue of the extent of God's grace (mercy, love, compassion, justice) and wrath in the eternal, afterlife destiny for all people. Inside, conflicting views are reevaluated, their strengths and weaknesses reassessed, and all the demands of Scripture are reconciled into one coherent and consistent synthesized view. The author further suggests that our limited earthly view has been the problem, re-discovers the ultimate mystery of God's expressed desire, will, and purpose, and transcends troubling traditions as never before. The bottom line is, God's plan of salvation and condemnation may be far different and greater than we've been led to believe. In a clear and straightforward manner, this book lays out the historical and scriptural evidence as never before.

Can We Really Be So Sure Anymore?

Battle lines are drawn. Sides are fixed. Arguments are exhausted. The majority proclaim, "Hell yes!" But growing numbers are protesting, "Hell no!" After nineteen centuries of church history, no effective resolution or scriptural reconciliation has been offered—until now!

So what really is the true Christian doctrine on this matter of hell and the greater issue of the extent of God's grace (mercy, love, compassion, justice) and wrath in the eternal, afterlife destiny for all people? The answer goes to the heart of Christian theology and Christianity itself. Has our limited earthly view been the problem? Could God's plan of salvation be far different than we've been led to believe?

In this book you'll discover:

- A balanced scholarly re-exploration of the mystery of God's desire, will, and purpose in the eternal afterlife destiny for all people.
- Re-evaluation of conflicting views.
- Re-assessment of the strengths and weaknesses of pro and con arguments.
- Synthesis of the strengths into one coherent and consistent view that meets all scriptural demands.
- Reconciliation of the greatest debate of 'all.'
- Transcending troubling traditions as never before!

(Available on Amazon.com)

Today's Dumbed-down Dilemma

Truly, have we Christians been led astray by our own leaders; dumbed down in our theology by ideas, interpretations, teachings, doctrines of men, and traditions that will not stand up to an honest and sincere test of Scripture; and consequently drawn off target in the practice of our faith?

This on-target, bull's-eye-aimed book re-explores what authentic Christianity really is versus today's institutionalized and substandard versions that we've comfortably come to know and accept. As you'll discover, beliefs do have consequences. This is why our modern-day versions pale in comparison with vibrancy and effectiveness of the Christianity that was preached, practiced, and perceived in the 1st century and turned that hostile world "upside down" (Acts 17:6 *KJV*). They also pale in contrast with the faith that brought our forefathers to America to found this country and establish its great institutions—most of which we moderns have given away to the ungodly crowd and without a fight. Bottom line is, we Christians are paying an awful price for our self-inflicted deficiencies.

Inside these pages we will reassess today's dumbed-down dilemma in these key 18 exposé areas:

More Books from John Noē

- Divine Perfection in Two Creations
- The Kingdom of God
- The Gospel
- Hell
- The 'Last Days'
- Second Coming / Return
- Rapture
- Antichrist
- The Contemporary Christ
- Book of Revelation
- Battle of Armageddon
- Israel
- Conflicting End -time Views
- Doing the Works of Jesus
- Doing Greater Works than Jesus
- Origin of Evil
- Eternal Rewards and Punishment for Believers
- Your Worldview

Revised edition – PEAK PERFORMANCE PRINICIPLES FOR HIGH ACHIEVERS *is a dynamic story of how one man transformed himself, sedentary and out-of-shape in his mid-thirties, into a dynamic leader – and how you can too.*

John R. Noē is using his mountain-climbing adventures as an allegory for the challenge of goal setting and the thrill of high achievement. He shows you how to choose accurate goals, how to reach them, how to remain committed to the accomplishment of a goal whether earthly or spiritual, and—in short—how to become a high achiever. To help you succeed, Noē offers a unique philosophy of reaching "beyond self-motivation" to the spiritual motivation that comes from God.

In this revised edition, Noē adds further insights and updates his reader on how these principles have fared in his life since the book's original writing in 1984—which was named one of Amway Corporation's "top ten recommended books."

Noē shows you how to learn the six essential attitudes of a high achiever:

1. High Achievers make no small plans.
2. Are willing to do what they fear.
3. Are willing to prepare.
4. To risk failure.
5. To be taught.
6. And must have heart.

"After reading this marvelous book I realized how little I have accomplished with my life . . . compared to what I could have done. But, it's not too late."

       Og Mandino, Author of:
       The Greatest Salesman in the World

"So many Christians are going through life settling for mediocre, settling for second best, and choosing the path of least resistance. Not Dr. John R. Noē, author of this old (1984) and new (2006) book, *Peak Performance Principles for High Achievers – Revised Edition*. He reminds us that the first mountain we need to conquer is that of ourselves and that God wants us to accomplish great things for His glory."

       Dr. D. James Kennedy, Ph.D.
       Senior Minister
       Coral Ridge Presbyterian Church

What's Next?

More pioneering and next-reformation titles are in development and forthcoming from John Noē and East2West Press. Tentatively titles and subtitles and their estimated publication year are:

UNRAVELING THE END
A balanced scholarly synthesis of four competing and conflicting end-time views—Unifying 'One of the most divisive elements in recent Christian history'
    (Est. 2012)

BEHIND 'UNRAVELING THE END'
The author's doctoral dissertation and more
    (Est. 2012)

A ONCE-MIGHTY FAITH
Whatever happened to the central teaching of Jesus?
    (Est. 2013)

GOD THE ULTIMATE COMPETITIVE EDGE
Why settle for anything less?
Transcending the limits of self-motivation, self-esteem & self-empowerment in a tough competitive world
    (Est. 2013-14)

THE ISRAEL ILLUSION
Pulling back the curtain on the 'land of God' (Oz)
    (Est. 2014-15)

THE ORIGIN AND PURPOSE OF EVIL
Solving the problem of the presence of evil
    (Est. 2014-15)

THE SCENE BEHIND THE SEEN
A Preterist-Idealist commentary of the Book of Revelation—unveiling its fulfillment and ongoing relevance—past, present & future
     (Est. 2015-16)

LIFE'S LAST GREATEST ADVENTURE
What really happens today immediately after you die?—you may be surprised!
     (Est. 2016-17)

'WARRIORS OF THE LAST TEMPLE'
The back story, theology, and script behind the movie

<u>Books Out-of-Print</u>

BEYOND THE END TIMES

SHATTERING THE 'LEFT BEHIND' DELUSION

DEAD IN THEIR TRACKS

TOP TEN MISCONCEPTIONS ABOUT JESUS' SECOND COMING AND THE END TIMES

PEOPLE POWER

THE APOCALYPSE CONSPIRACY

Scripture Index

OLD TESTAMENT

Genesis

1	77
1:1	61
1:3-5	185
1:14	52, 185, 405
1:14-19	185
1:16	185
1:26	366
1:28	342
1:31	323
2:7	307, 314, 323
2:9	342
2:14	239
2:17	342
2:23	245
2:24	245
3:1	342
3:5	115
3:8-10	242
3:10	327
3:19	314
9:13	406
11:1-9	269
11:5	129
11:8	129
12:1-4	150
12:7	39
15:18	239
16:7-14	39
17:1-2	35
18:1f	37
18:2	165
18:21	129
18:25	37
19:1	165
19:24	37
21:17ff	39
22:11ff	39
29:20	201
31:11ff	39
32:22-29	38
32:30	38, 38
34:12	201
35:9-10	38

Exodus

3:2ff	39
3:2-15	35, 38
3:7-8	128
3:8	129
10:21-23	406
13:22	404
14:22-26	xii
15:3	128
15:17	225, 229
16:7	163, 444
16:10	163, 444
16:14-36	211
17:1-7	36
19:4-6	150
19:11	129
19:21	33
20	145
20:24	184
23:19	311
24:9-11	36
24:10-11	33
24:16	163, 444
24:17	163, 444
25-40	209
32:35	246
33:11	33, 39
33:20	33
33:20-23	39
33:23	33
34:26	311
40:34	163, 444
40:35	163, 444

Leviticus

9:6	444, 454
9:23	444, 454

9:24	444	32:23	135	*1 Chronicles*	
17:14	271	32:32	95	5:9	239
26:13-21	247	34:10	33, 36	16:8-9	150
26:18	247			16:23-24	150
26:21	247	*Joshua*		16:33	176
26:23-24	247	5:13-15	38		
26:27-28	247	10:12-14	406	*2 Chronicles*	
				2:16	225
Numbers		*Judges*		4:2-5	349
5:27	246	4-7	225	7:12f	36
11:7-9	212	6:11ff	39	5:14	444, 454
11:16-17	129	6:11-26	36	7:1-3	444, 454
14:10	444, 454	6:14	411	7:14	36
14:14	33	6:16	411	7:19-20	36
14:21	454	6:17	405	35	225
16:19	444, 454	6:18ff	405		
16:42	444, 454	13:2ff	39	*Ezra*	
20:6	444, 454			1:3	225
26:53	239	*1 Samuel*		7:7	225
33:53	239	29-31	225		
34:29	239			*Job*	
		2 Samuel		33:4	323
Deuteronomy		4	225	34:14	323
1:8	239	7:11	197	39:22-28	123
1:38	239	19:34	225		
4:2	76, 248, 389	22:10-12	128	*Psalms*	
4:38	239	23:4	185	1:3	378
5:4	36			2:2	255
11:24	239	*1 Kings*		2:4	125, 392
12:32	76	2:2	314	2:9	123
17:16	122	7:23-44	349	11:4	124, 392
18:15-19	144	8:11	444, 454	11:14	125
18:21-22	138	9:15	225	16:10	314
29:29	178	12:28	225	18:9	129
31:16-17	196			18:9-12	128
31:16-18	252	*2 Kings*		19:1	64, 406
31:28	61	6:17	41	19:1-2	185
31:29	196	9:27	225	19:4-5	185, 406
32:1	61, 355, 356	9-10	225	19:4-6	196
32:2	129, 152	18:17	225	22:3	184
32:5	135	22	225	22:16	49
32:20	135, 135	25:13	349	22:27-29	180

22:28	125, 176, 392	125:1-2	29	13:10	226
23:5	196	138:5	444, 454	13:13	61, 72, 226
23:6	197	148:4	64	13:19-22	61
24:3-7	358	148:6	64	14:12	342
24:7	184			14:13	225, 225
27:1	185	**Proverbs**		19	153
31:16	375	2:1-6	187	19:1	128
34:6-8	36	5:1-5	253	19:20-21	142
36:9	185	7:1-27	253	20:1-6	128
43:3	185, 225, 229	8:13	125, 392	23:6-9	196
46:4	361	9:1-6	197	25:6-9	196
46:8-9	129	9:10	197	25:7-9	352
47:2	125, 392	12:28	327	25:8	313
47:8	125, 176, 392	13:12	154, 162, 186, 293	26:19	312
48:1-2	147	21:16	324	26:21	129, 176
49:9	314	30:6	76	27:9	152
50:3	129	33:10-11	176	29:5-6	129
67:2	150			29:11-18	449
68:4	128	**Ecclesiastes**		30:16	123
68:24	444	1:4	64, 181	30:26	78
78:23-25	212			31:1	123
78:69	64			31:4	129
84:11	185, 406	**Isaiah**		34:4	73, 226
89:36-37	64	1:2	356	34:5	73
90:3	314	1:2-3	61, 355, 356	35:1	78
90:4	52	1:10	95	35:2	444, 454
93:1	64	1:18	262	35:4-10	352
95:7-11	134	1:21	252	35:6	78, 361
96:10	64	2:2	352	37:16	176
96:13	129, 176	2:2-3	147, 225	37:20	142
98:3	150	5:16	144	40:4	73
103:14	357	6:1	33	40:5	444, 454
103:19	125, 392	6:5	39	40:10	129
104:3-4	128	6:9	187	40:15	176
104:5	64	6:9-10	16, 84	40:17	176
104:31	444, 454	9:6-7	42, 267, 313, 377, 446	40:23-24	176
105:2-5	142	9:7	181	41:22-23	147
110	125	13	153	41:22-29	200
110:1	34, 34, 34, 392	13:1	73	42:6	150
110:1-4	37	13:9-10	72	42:8-9	200
119:90	64			42:9	147
				43:8	150

43:10	150	*Jeremiah*		32:7	73, 226
43:12	150	1:6-10	370	32:8	73
44:3	361	1:12	370	36:26-27	27, 356, 450
44:6-8	147, 200	1:18-19	380	37:1-14	462
45:17	445	2:2	196	37:9-14	27
45:18-24	200	2:20	252	37:26-28	446
45:21	147	3:6-11	350	38:9	143
45:23	180	3:8f	196	38:16	143
46:9-11	200	4:13	128	39:21	147
46:10-11	147	6:20	234	39:29	27
48:3-6	200	10:7	176	40:4	16
48:4-6	147	26:18	313	43:5	444, 454
49:6	150	48:10	364	44:4	444, 454
51:13	61			44:30	311
51:15-16	61	*Ezekiel*		47:1-9	349
55:1	361	1:28	444, 454	47:12	378
56:7	197	2:8-3:7	449		
58:8	444, 454	3:12	444, 454	*Daniel*	
58:11	361	3:23	444, 454	1:1-2	270
59:17f	143	4:1	146	2:21	110, 159, 176, 184
59:20-21	152	4:3	146	2:22	185
60:1	444, 454	5:5-17	147	2:39	148
60:1-2	185, 186	5:8-17	147	2:44	181, 313, 446
60:19	185, 186	5:14-15	159	3:24-27	37
60:19-20	78, 374	10:4	444, 454	4:1	108, 148
61:2	143	10:18	444, 454	4:22	148
61:10	217, 351	11:23	444, 454	5:1-4	270
62:5	196	12:21-28	153	5:19	148
64:2	142	12:25	182	5:21	176
64:3	129	12:28	182	7	457
65:6-12	149	16	196	7:13	129
65:6-15	143	16:8-13	217	7:13-14	15, 313, 446
65:17	360	16:14-15	252	7:14	108, 181
65:17-18	62	16:44-58	95	7:23	148
65:17-19	347, 352	21:10	162	8:26	103
66:1	125, 392	21:15	162	9	37
66:15	129	21:28	162	9:24-27	40
66:15f	143	23	196	10-12	37
66:15-16	347	28:13	19	10:1-21	37
66:19	150	30:3	128	10:5-12	37
66:22	62, 347, 360	30:18	128		
		32:2	73		

Scripture Index

11:1-2f	37	1:5	73, 226	3:7	318
12	37			3:10	378
12:2	312, 313	**Habakkuk**		4:19	150
12:4	98, 103, 146, 312, 313, 449	2:3	153, 182, 268	5:3	92
		2:14	454	5:8	174, 216
12:7	146, 152, 312, 313, 360			5:9	368
		Zephaniah		5:11-12	281
12:9	103	1:14-15	128	5:13	378
		3:20	326	5:13-14	388
Hosea				5:14	298, 378
1:2	196	**Haggai**		5:17-18	353
1:4-5	225	2:6-7	61	5:18	348
2	203			5:29	83
4:6	409	**Zechariah**		5:30	83
8:1	129	1:10-13	39	5:44-45	368
9:1	252	3:1-2	39	6:6	33, 160
12:3-5	38	5:14	449	6:10	251, 358
		12-14	143	6:22	379
Joel		12:10	179	6:26	318, 333
2:1-2	128	12:10-14	49	6:31-33	205
2:10	226	12:11	225	6:33	378
2:28-32	27	13:1-2	179	7:15-23	380
2:30	73	13:6-9	179	7:16-19	114
2:30-31	146	14:17	225	7:20	114, 253
2:31	73			7:24	197
2:32	225	**Malachi**		8:11	198
3:15-17	143	3:6	175, 176, 247	8:11-12	194
3:16-17	225	4:2	185, 186, 406	8:20	318
		4:5-6	145, 162	8:22	365
Amos				8:29	140
6:1	364			8:30-31	240
8:9	226	**_APOCRYPHA_**		9:14-15	204
				9:15	185, 202
Micah		**2 Maccabees**		10:23	131
1:3	129	2:22	132	10:26	166
3:12	313			10:34	237
5:2	39, 40	**_NEW TESTAMENT_**		11:12	240, 344, 370, 386, 462
Nahum				11:14	162
1:1	73	**Matthew**		11:16-24	135
1:3	128	1:23	29	11:19	204
1:3-6	454	3:1-3	73	12:28	194

12:32	445	20:18	225	24:4-28	451
12:33	79	21:5f	450	24:8	138
12:39	134, 405	21:31-32	286	24:14	133, 133, 147, 148, 150, 267
12:45	135	21:37-39	196	24:15	133
13:8	263	21:43	150, 252, 280	24:15-16	96, 138, 275
13:10	16	21:43-45	203	24:15-21	285
13:11-17	91	21:45	135	24:16-20	133
13:13	85	22:1-10	198	24:21	133, 148
13:13-15	16, 84	22:1-14	194, 203, 216	24:23	161
13:19	462	22:11-14	194	24:23-26	230, 288, 386
13:22	445	22:23	318	24:24	55, 161, 133, 265
13:32	318	22:31	315	24:26	161
13:34-43	116	22:37	xii	24:27	47, 133, 162, 240, 453
13:39	445	22:41-46	34	24:29	74, 133, 333
13:40	445	23	134, 152	24:29-31	451, 451
13:49	445	23:1ff	202	24:30	127, 129, 129, 130, 133, 133, 146, 147, 160, 179, 226, 303
15:1	318	23:2	318		
15:6	xi, 31, 32, 54, 78, 139, 148, 269	23:13-14	88		
		23:17	92	24:31	184, 202, 295, 301, 326
15:24	381	23:27	365		
16:4	134	23:29-38	135	24:34	133, 137, 227, 281, 301, 309, 312, 313
16:6	318	23:32	149		
16:16	242	23:32-36	143		
16:17-19	379	23:33	134	24:34-35	353
16:18	314	23:34	313	24:35	61, 348
16:19	378	23:34-37	95, 280	24:36	138, 140
16:27	142, 151, 163, 226, 450	23:35	134, 135	24:42-44	178
		23:36	134, 227, 281	24:43	159
16:27-28	132, 202	23:36-38	348, 353	24:46	27, 28
16:28	42, 160, 181, 450	23:38	96, 135, 210, 228, 281, 313	25:1	185
17:1-3	42, 450	24	110, 134, 392	25:1-13	203, 216
17:2	185	24-25	133	25:1-28	443
17:2-3	144	24:1-34	143, 348, 353	25:5	185
17:5-8	144			25:6	185, 303
17:10-13	162	24:2	96, 133, 143, 145, 210. 313	25:10	185
17:17	134			25:13	138, 140
18:17	243	24:3	29, 133, 133, 137, 145, 160, 281, 312, 445		
18:18	379				
18:20	162, 229, 243				
19:3	318				
20:17	225	24:4	137		

Reference	Pages
25:21	15, 249, 393
25:23	15, 249, 393
25:31-46	264
25:34	239 370
25:37-40	217
26:18	448
26:35-45	242
26:45-46	448
26:46	102
26:64	127, 131, 226, 392
26:64-65	129, 130
26:64-66	151
27:22-25	135
27:24	179
27:25	49, 152, 179
27:45	406
27:51	209
27:51-53	311
27:52-53	304
28:18	125, 126
28:18-20	26, 150, 378
28:20	26, 26, 27, 445, 450

Mark

Reference	Pages
1:14-15	267
2:20	26
4:20	263
7:8	269
7:13	xi, 31, 32, 54, 78, 139, 148, 269
8:38	226
10:32	225
10:33	146, 225
12:12	135
12:35-37	34
12:37	139
13	110, 133, 392
13:27	301
16:12	173
16:15	378
16:20	30

Luke

Reference	Pages
1:17	162
1:32-35	313
1:33	181, 267, 446
1:52	176
1:78	186
2:1	148
2:9	444, 454
2:30-31	179
2:30-32	148
2:52	452
7:30	318
7:36-50	286
8:17	18
9:26	226
9:62	234
10:12	239
11:20	194
11:47-51	95, 280
11:50	135
11:51	135
12:36	443
12:37-40	218
12:40	43, 52, 53, 174
12:43	27, 28
12:47-48	365
13:29	194
13:33	95, 280
14:15	194
14:16-24	199
15:24	365
16:16	240, 344, 370, 386
17	158
17:5	xv
17:20	160
17:20-21	88
17:22	158
17:24	333
17:25	135
17:30	158, 166, 450
17:31	158
18:31	225
19:1-7	198
19:12	443
19:28	225
20:35	315
20:41-44	34
21	110, 133, 392
21:11	146, 202, 406
21:20	448
21:20-21	96, 138
21:20-22	143, 275, 348, 360
21:20-24	285
21:25	146
21:27-28	45
21:28	352, 360
21:32	348, 406
21:33	61
22:15-19	195
22:19-20	193
22:28-30	195
22:29-30	378
24:5	207
24:13-32	41
24:30-32	195
24:36-43	195
24:36-49	41
24:47	148, 378

John

Reference	Pages
1:1	244
1:1-2	xi
1:1-5	123
1:4	185
1:1-4	215, 441
1:9	185, 186, 186
1:12	366
1:14	123

1:18	33, 160	
2:1-11	204	
2:13	225, 448	
2:13-17	235	
3:1-13	84	
3:3	92, 116	
3:3-21	xiv	
3:5	92	
3:13	45, 313, 456	
3:16	64	
3:16-17	300	
3:17	64	
3:29	204	
4:4-26	117	
4:10	193, 361, 362	
4:14	361, 362	
4:21	228	
4:23-24	218	
4:24	86	
4:32	215, 216	
4:33	215	
4:34	215, 216	
4:52	443	
5:1	225	
5:17	175	
5:22	124, 142, 177, 184, 226, 247, 286, 353	
5:25	304, 324	
5:27	124	
5:28	304	
5:28-29	312	
5:39-40	92	
6:4	448	
6:15	462	
6:30-31	212	
6:32-33	212	
6:35	193, 213, 214	
6:39	202, 312	
6:40	202, 312	
6:44	202, 312	
6:47-65	87	
6:48	213	
6:51-58	213	
6:54	202, 312	
6:60-61	213	
6:63	213	
6:66	213	
7:2	448	
7:6	448	
7:33-34	444	
7:37-39	361, 362	
7:38	78	
7:39	78	
8:12	185, 378	
8:32	227	
8:51	327	
8:51-52	352	
8:58	35	
9:1-34	241	
10:10	323	
10:12	462	
10:28-29	462	
10:31-32	236	
11:24	202, 312	
11:26	352	
11:29	448	
11:31	448	
11:55	448	
12:34	30	
12:39-41	16	
13:27	448	
13:33	45, 313, 456	
13:36	45, 313	
14	27	
14:1-3	44, 45, 202, 301	
14:2	197	
14:2-3	456	
14:2-4	26	
14:3	27, 28, 28, 184, 202, 202	
14:12	55, 115, 215, 217, 218, 233, 236, 269, 320, 329, 337, 380, 380, 381,	
14:15-23	450	
14:15-29	27	
14:17	34, 160	
14:18	26, 29	
14:18-19	40, 41, 43	
14:18-23	45	
14:19	29, 161, 180	
14:20	372	
14:21	165, 174	
14:22	161	
14:23	174, 330, 351	
14:26	58	
14:28	27, 28, 28	
15:1-7	337	
15:1-8	219, 320, 363, 370, 378	
15:4-11	214, 216	
15:8	320	
15:19	287	
16:5	26	
16:5-16	87	
16:7	26	
16:13	61, 139, 141, 161, 268, 300, 309, 310, 313	
16:16	26, 29, 43	
16:28	27, 28	
16:33	298, 461	
17:14	287	
17:15	184, 188, 268, 298, 299, 300	
17:16	245, 287	
17:20	184, 188, 298, 299, 300	
17:20-21	245	
17:22	268	
17:23	298	
18:36	287	
19:2	262	
19:5	262	

19:30	360	2:40	135	17:11	xi, 82
19:34-37	49	2:47-4:4	116	17:24	229
19:37	179	4:2	315	17:32	312, 315
20:17	456	4:7	236	18:9-11	42, 42
20:19-31	46	4:13	57	21:12	225
20:19-21:14	183	5:1-11	235	21:15	225
20:22	323	5:30	374	21:17-18	42
20:24	29	6:8	392	22:18	448
20:26	29	6:14-15	392	22:23	335
20:26-29	41	7:28	443	23:6	312, 315
20:29	174	7:30-34	35	23:10	462
20:30	xi, 43, 164, 174	7:34	128	23:11	42
		7:44-50	348	24:5	148
21:1	29	7:48	229	24:11	225
21:4-14	41, 195	7:54-60	392	24:15	312, 315
21:12	205, 456	7:55	41	24:21	312, 315
21:14	29	7:55-56	25	25:9	225
21:22	132	7:60	324	26:8	312
21:22-23	25, 27, 28	8:26	43	26:12-16	41
21:25	26, 164, 174	8:39	305	26:23	312
		9:1-8	25	28:25-27	16
Acts		9:3	186		
1:3	41	9:3-6	172	**Romans**	
1:8	148, 150 381, 445	9:4-5	41	1:4	315
		9:9-16	42	1:8	148
1:9-11	46	9:10-16	42	1:16	63, 199
1:11	27, 28, 28, 163, 165	10:1-6	43	1:19-20	185
		10:13-15	41	1:20	406
1:21-22	172	10:39	374	2:9-10	199
2	26, 27	11:2	225	5:6	40
2:5	148	12:7	43	5:17	323
2:16-21	74	13:29	374	6-8	365
2:17	143	13:35	314	6:4	321
2:19-20	146, 406	13:47	150, 378	6:4-5	321
2:23	179	14:22	92, 244, 361	6:5-6	321
2:25	314	15:2	225	6:7-9	352
2:27	314	16:14	262	6:11-13	365
2:30-36	147	16:16-19	241	6:13	327
2:31	314	16:19	241	6:16-17	366
2:32-36	34	17:6	201, 282, 294, 360, 372	6:21-23	352
2:33-36	125, 392			7	329
2:36	49	17:6-7	125	7:4	201

8:1	237, 358	3:16	356	15:42	315
8:2	327	3:16-17	229	15:44	313, 313, 314, 322, 327
8:3-4	207	3:19	84		
8:17	321	4:1	198	15:47-49	359
8:14	368	4:1-2	267, 274	15:50	327, 361
8:15	368	4:19	448	15:50-57	455
8:18	166, 329	6:19-20	229	15:51	300
8:19	368	7:29	144, 448	15:51-52	300
8:21	366	7:39	196	15:51-57	325
8:23	368	9:1	172	15:51-58	298
8:24-25	184, 329, 376	9:26	335	15:54	313
8:29-30	369	10:4	36	16:22	157
8:34	10, 10, 15, 34, 125, 125, 392	10:6	36, 39, 246	**2 Corinthians**	
		10:6-11	159	3:17	27, 450
8:37	393	11:1	116, 322	3:18	444, 454
9:23	329	11:26	195	4:7	356, 357
9:25-26	203	11:27-32	76, 248	4:18	160, 160
9:33	229	11:29-32	389	5:4	327
10:18	148	12:1ff	236	5:16	16, 206, 207, 217, 363
11:15	321	12:10	266		
11:26	152, 229	12:27	243	5:17	357, 357
12:1	327	12:28	172	6:16	229
12:1-2	357, 357, 365, 368, 387	14:9	333, 335	6:18	366
		15	309	8:19	454
12:2	287	15:5-8	25, 40	10:3-6	322
12:3	379	15:6	324	10:4	384
12:19	143	15:12	312, 315	10:7-15	379
14:11	180	15:13	312, 315	11:2	200, 201, 201, 350
14:17	204, 205	15:14	310		
14:18	204	15:15	312	11:2-3	201
15:17	329	15:16	312	11:3	266
16:20	448	15:17	11	11:4	7
16:26	148	15:20	311	11:14	265
		15:20-24	310	12:2	304
1 Corinthians		15:21	315	12:4	304
1:18-25	84	15:22	327	13:5	320
2:7-10	189	15:23	311, 360, 455		
2:14	321	15:25	34, 125, 126	**Galatians**	
2:16	323	15:26	313	1:17	225
3:1	367	15:37	314	1:18	225
3:1-3f	211	15:38	313, 314, 322, 327	2:2	408

2:20	320, 321	2:20-22	351	1:17	177
3:1	266	2:21	229	1:18	311
3:7	150	2:21-22	356	1:23	148
3:15-19f	150	3:2-12	198	1:27	329
3:26	368	3:4-5	198	1:27-28	387
3:27	320	3:9	62	2:1	444
3:29	321	3:12	187	2:2-3	90
4-5	345	3:20f	313	2:3	112
4:1-2	367	3:21	62, 62, 63	2:9	88
4:1-7	321	4:1	322	2:12	321
4:3	367	4:4	322	2:12-13	321
4:4	40, 153	4:7	379	3:1	34, 125, 321, 392
4:6	450	4:13	379	3:1-3	321
4:5-7	369	4:13-15	367		
4:13-15	369	4:15	387		
4:19	387	4:22-24	357		
4:24-31	372	4:26-27	266		
4:21-27	196	5	220		
4:25-26	345	5:6-14	364		
5:19-21	370	5:14	186, 227, 322, 324, 326, 354		
5:21	239	5:22-23	200		
5:22-26	380	5:25-27	201		
6:15	387	6:12	241, 384		
6:16	229	6:17	124		

Ephesians

1:1	322
1:3-10	58
1:5	369
1:9-10	198
1:17	xiv, 58, 91, 238, 345, 400, 407, 407
1:18	xiv
1:18-23	321
1:20	34, 125, 392
1:20-23	11
2:1-5	321
2:2	318, 335
2:6	124, 321
2:6-7	321
2:20	350

Philippians

1:19	450
2:6-8	452
2:8-11	11
2:10-11	180, 323
2:19	448
2:24	448
3:10-11	326
3:11	315
3:14	322
3:16	323
3:21	315

Colossians

1:6	148
1:15-17	11

1 Thessalonians

1:4-8	116, 236
1:4-9	322
1:7	147
2:15-16	95, 280
4:13	310
4:13-17	202, 455
4:13-18	298, 304, 309, 317, 317, 318
4:15	300, 301
4:16	47
4:17	220, 291, 294, 295, 300, 303, 305, 306, 308, 323, 327, 329, 330, 335, 336, 363, 370
4:18	310, 314, 323
5:1	304, 325
5:1-11	300
5:2-4	159
5:4	300
5:6	300
5:19-21	408
5:21	ix, xi, 23, 61, 82, 297

2 Thessalonians
1:7	47, 144
1:7-8	152
1:7-10	143
1:11	322
1:11-12	396
1:12	329
2:1	295
2:1-3	450
2:2	142

1 Timothy
2:5	10
2:6	40
3:14	448
4:1	143
6:15	125
6:16	33

2 Timothy
1:10	165, 327, 352
3:1	143
3:5	234, 365
3:16	446
4:1	132, 165, 450
4:8	165, 174
4:9	448

Titus
2:7	322
2:13	155, 163, 163, 293

Hebrews
1:2	143, 227, 268, 312
1:3	126, 177, 441
1:4	11
1:8	445
1:13	34, 125, 392
1:14	44, 165
2:7	11
2:9	11, 125, 125
2:10	369
3:1	322
3:9-10	134
3:17	134
4:12	50, 124
4:13	124
4:14-15	10
5:11-13	367
6:1-6	211
6:2	315
7:18-19	207
7:25	10
7:27-28	25
8	25
8:1	20, 10, 34, 125, 392
8:5	348
8:7-13	385
8:8-13	203
8:13	105, 138, 210, 252, 348, 353
9	25, 213
9:2-4	214
9:6-10	153
9:8	203
9:8-10	210, 210, 348
9:9	207
9:9-10	252
9:10	105, 138, 385
9:10-11	353
9:11-12	210
9:11-15	25
9:26	210, 267
9:27	268, 299, 314, 327, 328, 360, 361
9:28	25, 45, 210, 352
10	25
10:4-5	55
10:10	267
10:11	207
10:13	34, 125, 126
10:14	207
10:20	206, 207, 217
10:25	450
10:37	153, 182, 268
11:1	160
11:16	372
11:27	33, 33, 36
12:1	29, 86, 159, 166, 210, 303, 316, 319, 320, 324, 324, 356, 372
12:5-6	236
12:5-8	369
12:21	34, 125, 392
12:22-23	229
12:22-24	29, 87, 159, 166, 210, 303, 316, 319, 320, 324, 324, 356, 372
12:26-27	61
12:28	193, 313, 446
12:29	186
13:2	48, 165
13:8	15, 443
13:9	55
13:14	372
13:20	446
13:23	448

James
1:1	149
1:5-8	407
2:5	239
4:4	196
5:2	370
5:3	143
5:8	144

1 Peter
1:5	45, 143, 352, 360

1:11	450	2:18	111, 141, 143, 144, 442		341, 409, 410, 446, 448
1:19	185	2:22	111, 442	1:1-3	58
1:20	143	3:1-2	366	1:3	9, 12, 15, 50, 88, 98, 98, 101, 103, 104, 111, 126, 224, 224, 231, 301, 341, 341, 385, 385, 409, 410, 410, 448
1:23	327	3:2	16, 115		
2:4-5	197	3:6	337		
2:5	351, 379	3:8	352		
2:9	252	3:23-24	320		
2:9-10	351	3:24	337		
2:10	203	4:1	266	1:4	101, 108, 159, 177, 409, 415
2:12	174	4:2-3	442		
2:24	374	4:3	111	1:5	89, 125
3:15-16	305	4:12	33, 160	1:6	89, 109, 116, 165, 231, 245, 252, 381, 388, 396
3:18	267	5:5-6	360		
3:22	126	5:18-20	352		
4:7	144			1:7	52, 127, 159, 178, 226
4:17	144, 235	**2 John**			
		7	111, 442, 443	1:7-8	48, 184
2 Peter				1:8	35, 117, 177
1:5-9	370	**3 John**		1:9-16	14
1:10	322	14	448	1:10	408
1:14	448			1:10-20	108
1:16	145	**Jude**		1:11	108, 159, 409, 415
1:16-18	42	3	148, 153, 190, 219, 268, 282, 304, 314, 352, 372, 394		
1:19	406			1:12	403
3	145, 446			1:12-16	114
3:2	74	4	324	1:12-17	37
3:3	143	12	303, 324	1:12-18	208
3:3-4	32, 143	14	47, 152	1:12-20	231
3:4	138, 145	17-19	32	1:13	28, 50, 156, 166, 229
3:8	52, 99	18	143		
3:10	74, 142, 159, 166	18-19	145	1:14	185
		23	217, 462	1:14-16	124
3:10-13	455	24	202	1:16	237
3:11	74			1:17	15, 43, 114, 207
		Revelation			
1 John		1	25, 231, 231, 244	1:18	313
1:5	185, 186	1:1	8, 50, 85, 98, 99, 101, 103, 103, 103, 112, 126, 166, 224, 231, 231, 252, 301,	1:19	17, 103, 103, 108
2:3	174				
2:5-6	214, 216, 320, 322, 337, 363, 370			1:20	28, 50, 113, 156, 166, 415
2:6	329				
2:15	287				

Reference	Pages
2&3	50, 51, 90, 159, 184, 214, 231, 232, 232, 235, 261, 261, 266, 275, 283, 302, 363, 409, 415, 457
2:1-3-3:22	101
2:1-7	233
2:7	51, 84, 116, 235, 362, 362, 363
2:8-11	233
2:10	249
2:11	84, 116, 235, 249
2:12-17	233
2:17	84, 116, 214, 235, 363
2:18-29	233
2:26	235, 236
2:26-27	321
2:27-28	363
2:28	185, 235, 406, 409
2:29	84, 116
3	103
3:1-6	233
3:3	159
3:4-5	363
3:5	235
3:6	84, 116
3:7-13	234
3:10	148
3:11	448
3:12	235
3:13	84, 116
3:14-22	234
3:20	188, 198, 235
3:21	235, 321, 363
3:22	58, 84, 116
4	17, 414
4-18	301, 302
4:1	302
4:1-2	108
4:8	35, 177, 184
5	17, 414
5&6	90
5:5	91
5:6	91
5:8	113
5:9	108, 109, 254, 415, 415
5:9-10	89, 252, 321, 372
5:10	109, 116, 231, 245, 323, 326, 381, 388, 396
5:13	180
5:19	363
6	103, 449
6:1-2	247
6:1-8	176
6:12	123
6:12-17	75
7	90
7:3-8	350
7:9	108, 254, 415
7:14-17	231
7:17	352
8:6	247
9:2	335
9:7	123
10	17, 107, 326
10:1	186
10:4	247
10:9	107
10:9-11	108, 414, 415
10:10	415
10:10-11	236
10:11	107, 109, 109, 158, 164, 254, 341, 415, 415
11	326
11-22	108
11:1	379
11:1-2	236
11:2-3	461
11:8	95
11:15	236, 326, 445
11:15f	446
11:15-19	232
11:16f	313
12	17
12:5	305
12:6	461
12:9	113
12:10-12	89
12:11	123, 236, 294, 363
12:11-12	393
12:12	461
13	457
13:1	252
13:3	58
13:5	461
13:7	108, 254, 415
13:9	302
13:16-17	458
13:16-19	350
14	17, 47
14:1	229
14:1-5	350
14:4-5	231
14:6	108, 111, 150, 254, 415, 446
14:12-13	110
14:13	314, 448
14:14	245
14:14-15	127
14:20	123
15:1	247
16-19	239
16:1	239
16:6	95
16:12	239, 239, 239, 240, 240

Scripture Index 439

16:12-16 239	18:17 96	20:13-14 313
16:12-21 238	18:18 95	21 339, 341, 344, 344, 345, 347, 375
16:13 240, 240	18:19 95	21&22 62
16:14 223, 226, 228, 228, 234, 241, 241, 241, 241, 254	18:19-23 96	21:1-4 340
	18:21 95	21:1-7 220, 346, 363
	18:23 185, 280	21:1-22:5 350
16:14-16 90	18:24 95, 280	21:2 196, 201, 252, 274, 274, 362
16:15 88, 159, 231, 241, 241, 448	19 17, 90, 103, 123, 158, 414, 449	
	19:1-3 254, 286, 350	21:4 327
16:16 223, 228, 242	19:4 207	21:5 385
16:17 319, 335	19:6-9 90	21:6 35, 327, 362
16:17-21 242	19:6-10 245	21:7 89, 201, 369
16:19 95	19:7 193, 350	21:7-10 209
17 254, 261	19:7-8 124, 201	21:8 375
17&18 90, 252, 253, 253, 375	19:7-9 200, 323, 350	21:9 201, 208
	19:8 215, 217, 236	21:9-10 196, 252, 274, 349
17:1 254, 367, 384	19:9 190, 193, 203, 208, 363, 448	
17:2 255		21:9-11 200
17:3 257, 305	19:9-10 34	21:10 339, 341
17:4 262, 266	19:10 90, 91, 147, 200, 380, 409	21:12 350, 373
17:5 242, 251, 269		21:12-14 373
17:6 95, 253, 271	19:11 47, 123, 130, 244, 244	21:14 350, 373
17:6-7 58		21:15 379
17:8 49	19:11-16 123, 244, 244	21:22 351
17:9 281		21:22-22:2 372
17:14 89	19:11-21 238	21:23 185, 186
17:15 108, 254, 367, 415	19:12 244, 245	21:27 274
	19:13 244	22 339, 341, 344, 344, 345, 347
17:16 273	19:14 47, 230, 244, 245, 363	
17:18 95, 274		22:1 91, 208, 361, 362
18 252, 254, 261	19:15 244	
18:2 96, 274	19:16 90, 124, 147, 245, 378	22:1-2 239
18:3 276		22:1-5 323, 374
18:4 96, 363, 394	19:18 124	22:2 362, 362, 378, 383
18:4-8 278, 285, 286	19:21 124	
18:7 196	20 17, 103, 414	22:5 323
18:8 96, 166	20:4-5 316	22:6 98, 101, 103, 103, 103, 126, 224, 252, 301, 341, 362, 410, 448
18:10 95, 96	20:5 304	
18:11 96	20:6 448	
18:12-13 278	20:7-10 456	
18:14 280	20:11 357	
18:16 95		

22:7   9, 12, 15, 49,
   52, 58, 98, 98, 101,
   111, 159, 184, 224,
   301, 341, 341, 379,
   385, 409, 410, 410,
          448, 448
22:8-9   34
22:9   108
22:10   98, 98, 101,
   103, 103, 104, 107,
   126, 165, 224, 224,
   301, 341, 341, 385,
         385, 410, 448
22:12 35, 49, 51, 52,
   98, 159, 184, 341,
             448
22:12-13   49
22:13   117
22:14 88, 323, 351,
       362, 362, 448
22:14-19   111
22:15   375
22:16 185, 406, 409,
             409
22:17 117, 361, 362
22:18   58
22:18-19   xiv, 9, 76,
   110, 248 286, 323,
         389, 409
22:19   22, 58
22:20   49, 98, 159,
   174, 184, 186, 188,
        341, 448

ENDNOTES

Author's Note

[1] John Noē, *The Perfect Ending for the World* (Indianapolis, IN.: East2West Press, 2011), *xv*.
[2] For more see ibid., chapters 1 and 2.
[3] Even now (before this date arrives), this prediction is being disputed by new information from the Mayan culture itself. *USA TODAY* reports that "Newly discovered wall writings found in Guatemala show the famed Maya culture's obsession with cycles of time. They also show a calendar that looks to a future well beyond 2012." (Dan Vergano, "Maya calendar goes beyond 2012," *USA TODAY*, May 11, 2012.)
[4] John Noē, "An Exegetical Basis for a Preterist-Idealist Understanding of the Book of Revelation," *Journal of the Evangelical Theological Society* 49/4 (December 2006) 767-796.
[5] For instance, the senior pastor at the church I attend and a spiritual advisor of mine, Dave Rodriguez, preached a sermon on May 6, 2011 on Jesus being the *Logos* (the Word – see John 1:1-4; also Heb. 1:3). He presented Jesus as "the supreme and ultimate power behind everything in the universe." The reference source for his statement further elaborates on Jesus being the *Logos* that He is "the power which extends throughout matter . . . and works immanently in all things. . . . the organic power which fashions unformed and inorganic matter, which gives growth to plants and movement to animals. . . . it gives men power of knowledge . . . . It is the son of God . . . . brings order and form into the world." (A. Debrunner, H Vleinknecht, O Procksch, G. Kittel, G. Quell, B. Shrenk, Gerhard Kittle, Ed., *Theological Dictionary of the New Testament*, Vol. IV, (Grand Rapids, MI.: Eerdmans, 1967), 85, 88.
[6] See John Noē, *Off Target: 18 bull's-eye exposés* (Indianapolis, IN.: East2West

Press, 2012).
[7] Cindy Jacobs, *The Reformation Manifesto: Your Part in God's Plan to Change Nations Today* (Minneapolis, MN.: Bethany House Publishers, 2008), 59.

Introduction

[1] Opening lines of PBS Special, *"From Jesus to Christ: The First Christmas,"* aired April 6, 1998.
[2] N.T. Wright, *Simply Jesus* (New York, NY.: HarperOne, 2011).
[3] Philip Yancey, *The Jesus I Never Knew* (Grand Rapids, MI.: Zondervan, 2002).
[4] PW Religion Bookline@email.publishersweekly.com, "Rabbi's Book About Jesus Stirs Controversy," 1/25/2012.
[5] In advertisement, *Charisma*, May 2012, 48.
[6] Yancey, *The Jesus I Never Knew*, 20 and in quotation of a scholar at the University of Chicago.
[7] Baker Publishing in its Spring 2012 Academic Catalogue prominently advertises four "Exceptional New Books on Jesus"—*Construction Jesus, A Hitchhiker's Guide to Jesus, Jesus and the Scriptures,* and *Jesus Among Friends and Enemies.* But they are just more books trying to figure out the historical Jesus.
[8] Brandon O'Brien, "A Jesus for Real Men," *Christianity Today*, April 2008, 49-50.
[9] Quoted in J.B. Phillips, *Your God Is Too Small* (New York, NY.: Touchstone Books, Simon & Schuster, 1952, 2004), 26-27.
[10] Ibid., 27-28.
[11] Ibid., 28
[12] Lee Strobel, "The Changing Face of Apologetics," *Christianity Today* (June 2009): 58.
[13] Yancey, *The Jesus I Never Knew*, 16.
[14] Ibid., 43.
[15] While the authorship and circumstances of John's stay on Patmos are contested, this is the most widely accepted understanding.
[16] Tim LaHaye and Jerry B. Jenkins, *Left Behind* (Wheaton, IL.: Tyndale House Publishers, 1995), back cover.
[17] See my exposé (chapter) titled "Antichrist" in my book: Noē, *Off Target*, 113-116. The only two places "antichrist" is mentioned in the Bible are in the New Testament epistles 1 John and 2 John. Here, John puts down the unbiblical idea of only one coming "the antichrist" and replaces it with "many antichrists," which were present back there and then (1 John 2:18). Then he gives descriptions of these people (see 1 John 2:22; 4:2-3; 2 John 7). "Any such

person is . . . the antichrist" (2 John 7). This is the biblical position regarding antichrist(s)—and there are many (past, today, and future) that fit these descriptions, not just one.

[18] T.M. Moore, "The Jesus We Preach at Christmas: The Truth about the Babe in the Manger," *BreakPoint Worldview*, December 2006, 8-11.

[19] The Greek word translated "yesterday" is *chthes*. For its two other uses, see John 4:52 and Acts 7:28. Hebrews 13:8 is literally correct as it reads.

[20] William Hendriksen, *More that Conquerors* (Grand Rapids, MI.: Baker Book House, 1940, 1962, 1982), 56.

Chapter 1

[1] To see a listing of this trail of failed predictions, see Noē, *The Perfect Ending for the World*, 26-47.

[2] From an advertisement for David M. Tyler's book, *The Second Coming of Jesus Christ* in *World* magazine (22 October 2011): 58.

[3] From an advertisement for end-time pundit John Hagee's book, *Earth's Final Moments*, Christianbook.com (Nov./Dec. 2011): 3.

[4] Billy Graham, "The End of the World," *Decision*, January 2004, posted on www.billygraham.org/article.asp?I=396&s=62, January 31, 2004.

[5] George Eldon Ladd, *The Blessed Hope* (Grand Rapids, MI.: Eerdmans, 1956), 69. Unfortunately, Ladd ignored his own and valid biblical insight by continuing to use these non-scriptural expressions and unscriptural concepts.

[6] For more on this, see Noē, *The Perfect Ending for the World*, 243-246.

[7] Henry A. Virkler, *Hermeneutics* (Grand Rapids, MI.: Baker Books, 1981), 150.

[8] Jesus did tell a parable once about a nobleman who *returned* after going into a far country to receive a kingdom (Luke 19:12; also see Jesus' parable in Luke 12:36). This nobleman certainly represents Jesus and this parable certainly refers to Jesus' departure and coming again. And this word is correctly translated as "return." However, neither this parable nor any others (see Matt. 25:1-28) can be employed to override Jesus' statements about Himself just because He used this word here. Especially note that the object of this parable is a nobleman who is a regular human being and as such is confined within an earthly body. He does not have the same transcendent, omnipresent, and spirit-realm ability as does the ascended Lord and which we will soon discuss further. Imposing that limitation upon the post-resurrected and ascended Jesus, Who is omnipresent, is reductionistic. This parable only foreshadows a period of time that will transpire between Jesus' physical departure (his death) and a special coming again that we shall cover in Chapter 4. Also notable, is the fact that this period of time would be within the lifetime of those mentioned in the parable, and not some future generation two-thousand years or so removed.

[9] Jesus' statements in John 7:33-34 cannot be used to lessen or dismiss this assertion.

[10] The four major evangelical positions are: premillennial, amillennial, postmillennial, and preterist.

[11] R.C. Sproul writes, "It has been argued that no less than two thirds of the content of the New Testament is concerned directly or indirectly with eschatology." From R.C. Sproul, "A Journey Back in Time," *Tabletalk*, January 1999, 5. Others have estimated that 25 to 30 percent of the whole Bible is so concerned.

[12] For more on this, see Chapter 5. But the fact is, "the glory of the Lord" appeared numerous times throughout the Old Testament. And never once was this a literal, bodily, visible, or physical appearance of the Person of God. Rather, the appearance of this "glory" took various forms: as a cloud, a consuming fire, fire, like a rainbow in the clouds, or radiance. (See: Exod. 16:7, 10; 24:16, 17; 40:34, 35; Lev. 9:6, 23, 24; Num. 14:10; 16:19, 42; 20:6; 1 Ki. 8:11; 2 Chron. 5:14; 7:1-3; Ezek. 1:28; 3:12, 23; 10:4, 18; 11:23; 43:5; 44:4; Also see: Psa. 104:31; 138:5; Isa. 35:2; 40:5; 58:8; 60:1; Luke 2:9; 2 Cor. 3:18).

[13] www.biblestudytools.com/lexixons/hebrew/nas/paniym.html, 4/10/12. For another Jewish example, compare how Paul's usage concerning himself in Col. 2:1 is translated in KJV ("not seen my face in the flesh") and NAS ("not personally seen my face") with NIV ("not met me personally").

[14] Eusebius, *Eusebius: The Church History*, Book 1.2, Paul L. Maier, trans. and comm. (Grand Rapids, MI.: Kregel, 2007), 24.

[15] Ibid., 31.

[16] Nor shall we have space to consider all the many possible comings of God the Father or of God's glory which are sprinkled throughout the Old Testament (Psa. 68:24).

[17] NIV translates this phrase as merely "origins." *Matthew Henry's Commentary (Electronic Database)* says it means Christ's "existence from eternity." But *Adam Clarke's Commentary (Electronic Database)* supports this understanding I am suggesting in commenting, "In every age, from the foundation of the world, there has been some manifestation of the Messiah . . . to his manifestation in the flesh . . . ."

[18] Nor shall we be considering the verses about Melchizedek that some scholars believe was Jesus incarnate.

[19] That is, occurred precisely on the timeline for the sequential unfolding and chronological fulfillment of Daniel's 70 Weeks prophecy. For more on this, see Noē, *The Perfect Ending for the World*, 109-126.

[20] I have written on this, extensively. See Noē, *The Perfect Ending for the World*, chapters 1-6 and following.

[21] Billy Graham, "My Answer," "God lives in us by the Holy Spirit," *The*

Indianapolis Star, 4/21/12, E-4 – "The Holy Spirit is God himself, as he comes to live within us when we give our lives to Jesus. . . . when we accept Christ and commit our lives to him, God comes to live within us by his Holy Spirit." Of course, this is true. But this particular coming is over and above and promises more than that.

[22] *Strong's Exhaustive Concordance of the Bible*, #2064. W.E. Vine: *An Expository Dictionary of Biblical Words*, New Testament Words, 195. Walter Bauer, F.W. Gingrich, and Frederick Danker, *A Greek Lexicon of the New Testament and Other Early Christian Literature*, 311.

[23] I have also written on this, extensively. See Noē, *The Perfect Ending for the World*, Introduction and chapters 5-8.

[24] Curtis I. Crenshaw and Grover E. Gunn, III, *Dispensationalism* (Memphis, TN.: Footstool Publications, 1985, 1986), 13, 8.

[25] See Acts 1:8 and note that the Greek word for "power" is *dunamis*, from which we get our word "dynamite."

[26] For more on my recommendation, see: Noē, *The Perfect Ending for the World*, 254-257.

[27] I have previously written on this topic of Christ's presence, which I do not plan on duplicating in this book. See Noē, *The Perfect Ending for the World*, 247-252.

Chapter 2

[1] Content here taken from my book, Noē, *The Perfect Ending for the World*, 82-83.

[2] Billy Graham, "My Answer," *The Indianapolis Star*, 11/17/07, E-7.

[3] Ibid., 6/17/98, 12/12/96 and 11/25/94, for example.

[4] Ibid., 10/7/05, E-2.

[5] Ibid., 4/20/05, E-6.

[6] The original King James Version of the Bible mistranslates the Greek word *aion* as "world" rather than "age" in the phrase "the end of the world (age)" in Matthew 12:32; 13:22, 39, 40, 49; 24:3; 28:20, for instance. Most Modern Bible translations, including the New King James Version, clear up this confusion and render it properly as "age." Those who use fear to hold on to people are hesitant, to say the least, to give up this translation weapon.

[7] See Noē, *The Perfect Ending for the World*, 279-319; 81-99.

[8] The Greek word *aion* is used for the Hebrew word *olam* in the Septuagint.

[9] Compare with similar idiomatic uses in Heb. 1:8, Rev. 11:15, and Isa. 45:17. A few scholars feel this double use of the idiom does not speak of eternity or endlessness, but of aggregated or compounding periods of time—until all ages

have run their course. Most, however, do agree with the explanation given here.
[10] As we shall continue to see (also see Isa. 9:6-7; Ezek. 37:26-28; Dan. 2:44; 7:13-14, 27; Luke 1:33; Heb. 12:28; 13:20; Rev. 11:15f; 14:6).
[11] Some Bible scholars maintain that the book of Ecclesiastes cannot be relied on because the arguments it contains are man's ideas and not God's. The New Testament book of 2 Timothy, however, asserts that "All Scripture [including Ecclesiastes] is useful for teaching, rebuking, correcting, and training in righteousness" (2 Tim. 3:16).
[12] For a discussion of 2 Peter 3's destruction of the present heavens and earth and burning up of their "elements" and why this, too, is not the end of the physical world, see Noē, *The Perfect Ending for the World*, 298-306.
[13] For more see, ibid., 101-106.
[14] Taken from ibid., 90-96.
[15] For literature concerning the further use of apocalyptic language in the Bible, see: John Joseph Collins, *The Apocalyptic Imagination: An introduction to the Jewish Matrix of Christianity* (Crossroad, 1984). *The Old Testament Pseudepigrapha, Vol 1* (Doubleday, 1983).
[16] For more on this, see Noē, *The Perfect Ending for the World*, 96-99.

Chapter 3

[1] Grant R. Osborne, *Revelation, Baker Exegetical Commentary on the New Testament*, ed. Moises Silva (Grand Rapids, MI.: Baker, 2002), 18.
[2] Many claim that Revelation's mysterious and symbolic language was use to prevent the Romans and apostate Jews from understanding and inflicting suppression of the prophecy and persecution upon Christians, which they did anyway.
[3] Throughout the book we will be using "spiritual" and "spirit-realm" terminology interchangeably. Too often in today's usage, "spiritual" is restricted to mean only a moral or ethical condition of the heart. This, of course, is true but much more is involved—specifically, the interaction of spirit beings in our physical universe.
[4] The Greek verb here is *semaino*. W.E. Vine's *An Expository Dictionary of Biblical Words* provides this definition: "to give a sign, indicate." In specific reference to its use in Rev. 1:1, Vine's adds: "where perhaps the suggestion is that of expressing by signs."
[5] The Greek verb here is *aletheia*. W.E. Vine's *An Expository Dictionary of Biblical Words* provides this definition: "the reality lying at the basis of an appearance; the manifested, veritable essence of a matter."
[6] The Greek word here is *antos* and can mean "within, among, or in your midst." Therefore, the proper meaning and translation must be determined by the

context in which it is used.

[7] For more on this aspect of divine perfection, see: Noē, *The Perfect Ending for the World*, 1-18f.

[8] More on this in my future book, *A Once-Mighty Faith*.

[9] Nancy Pearcey, *Total Truth*, (Wheaton, IL.: Crossway Books, 2004), 363.

[10] For an analysis of the dating evidence for both the early date (pre-A.D. 70) and late date (circa A.D. 95-96), and other source references, see my theological journal article: John Noē, "An Exegetical Basis for a Preterist-Idealist Understanding of the Book of Revelation" Also see endnote #12 below.

[11] Philip Schaff, *History of the Christian Church*, Vol. 1, (Grand Rapids, MI.: Eerdmans, 1910 [third revision]) *vi*, also 420, 834n.

[12] For good analyses of the dating evidence for both the early and late date but favoring the pre-A.D. 70 date see: Kenneth L. Gentry, Jr., *Before Jerusalem Fell* (Atlanta, GA.: American Vision, 1998), entire book; Foy E. Wallace, Jr., *The Book of Revelation* (Fort Worth, TX.: Foy E. Wallace Jr. Publications, 1966), 15-46; Milton S. Terry, *Biblical Hermeneutics* (Eugene, OR.: Wipf and Stock Publishers, 1890, 1999), 135-140 and *Biblical Apocalyptics* (Grand Rapids, MI.: Baker Book House, 1988), 256-260. For a countering analysis favoring the late date see: Leon Morris, *Revelation* (Grand Rapids, MI.: Eerdmans, 1987), 35-41; Robert H. Mounce, *The Book of Revelation* (Grand Rapids, MI.: Eerdmans, rev. ed. 1998), 15-21; Grant R. Jeffrey, *Triumphant Return* (Toronto, Ontario: Frontier Research Publications, 2001), 78-99; and G. K. Beale, *The Book of Revelation* (Grand Rapids, MI.: Eerdmans, 1999), 4-27.

[13] John A.T. Robinson, *Redating the New Testament* (Philadelphia, PA.: Westminster Press, 1976) 13.

[14] Ibid., 10, 352.

[15] For more see Don K. Preston, *Who Is This Babylon* (Ardmore, OK.: n.p. n.d.) 208-210. Also see, N.T Wright, *Jesus and the Victory of God*, vol. 2 (London, Great Britain; Society for Promoting Christian Knowledge, 1996) 323, 354.

[16] Eusebius, *Ecclesiastical History*, Book 3, chapter 5; from Edersheim, *Life and Times of Jesus the Messiah*, p. 138, Peabody, Mass.: Hendrickson; reprint of 1886 ed.

[17] David Chilton, *The Days of Vengeance* (Ft. Worth, TX.: Dominion Press, 1987), 363.

[18] Donald Guthrie, *New Testament Theology* (Downers Grove, IL.: Inter-Varsity Press, 1981) 816.

[19] Duncan W. McKenzie, *The Antichrist and the Second Coming* (n.l., Xulon Press, 2012), 30.

[20] In Chapter 8 we'll see that this call was more than a call to come out of the physical city of Jerusalem, which it certainly was. By extrapolation, it was also a

call for those Jews not only in Jerusalem but those scattered throughout Palestine and other nations of the Roman Empire to come out of the temple-system, which Jerusalem further represented—i.e., for all those under the Old Covenant.

[21] Gentry, Jr., *Before Jerusalem Fell*, 336.

[22] R.C. Sproul, *The Last Days According to Jesus* (Grand Rapids, MI.: Baker Books, 1998), 132.

[23] For instance, "shortly," [*en tachei*] "short," or "soon" [*tachos*] is consistent in its literal meaning everywhere else it is used in the New Testament (see for example: Rom. 16:20;1 Cor. 4:19; 7:29; Phil. 2:19; 2:24; 1 Tim. 3:14; 2 Tim. 4:9; Heb. 13:23; 2 Pet. 1:14; 3 John 14; Rev. 1:1; 22:6). Likewise, "quickly" has but one literal and consistent meaning everywhere it is used (see for example: John 11:29, 31; 13:27; Acts 22:18; Rev. 3:11; 22:7, 12, 20). "At hand" or "near" (*engus*) also has one literal meaning—i.e. close in relation to time or distance—(see for example: Matt. 26:18, 45-46; Luke 21:20; John 2:13; 6:4; 7:2, 6; 11:55; Rev. 1:3; 22:10). The various translators of the New Testament chose these English words as to best represent their Greek equivalents.

[24] Chilton, *The Days of Vengeance*, 52, 42.

[25] Gary DeMar, *Last Days Madness*, (Brentwood, TN.: Wolgemuth & Hyatt, 1991), 214.

[26] Ibid., 215.

[27] J. Stuart Russell, *The Parousia* (Grand Rapids, MI.: Baker Book House, From the 1887 edition issued by T. Fisher Unwin, 1983), 367.

[28] Many have contended that these seven churches should also be understood symbolically and in a wider significance since: 1) seven is the symbolic number of completion or perfection and is used often in the Revelation; 2) more than seven churches existed in Asia (what is western Turkey today) at that time; 3) they probably stand for the Church Universal, especially given the timeless application suggested herein.

[29] For the other six, see: Rev. 14:13; 16:15; 19:9; 20:6; 22:7; 22:14

[30] This portion of Daniel's prophecy was most likely fulfilled four hundred years later in the time of Antiochus Epiphanes in the 2nd century B.C.

[31] From the Product Description of this book on Amazon.com, 8/22/2009.

[32] From reviews of this book on Amazon.com, 8/22/2009.

[33] George Eldon Ladd, *A Theology of the New Testament* (Grand Rapids, MI.: Eerdmans, 1974), 672.

[34] "The Book of Revelation, written prior to the destruction of Jerusalem in AD 70 . . . describes events that were coming primarily upon the land of Israel in the first century—not subsequent generations" – Allyn Morton, general editor, "Preterist Bible Project," in "Cast Your Vote" mass email, June 19, 2012.

[35] So argues Ian Boxall, *The Revelation of St. John* (Peabody, MA.: Hendrickson

Publishers, 2006), 25; Grant R. Osborn, *Revelation*, 401; and many others. For other scriptures about eating scrolls and other scrolls, see: Ezek. 2:8-3:7; Zech. 5:1-4; Isa. 29:11-18; Dan. 12:4.
[36] Virkler, *Hermeneutics*, 25.
[37] "Asia Minor was a significant destination for two reasons: First, after the fall of Jerusalem the province of Asia would become the most influential center of Christianity in the Roman Empire . . . .with Ephesus as its radial point. Second, Asia was the center of Caesar-worship."—Chilton, *The Days of Vengeance*, 7.
[38] Russell, *The Parousia*, 531.
[39] William W. Klein, Craig L. Blomberg, Robert L. Hubbard, Jr., *Introduction to Biblical Interpretation* (Dallas, TX.: Word Publishing, 1993), 125.
[40] Beale, *The Book of Revelation*, 91, 45.
[41] ibid.
[42] Ibid., 45.
[43] See John Noē, "An Exegetical Basis for a Preterist-Idealist Understanding of the Book of Revelation."
[44] Hendriksen, *More Than Conquerors*, 10.

Chapter 4

[1] *The World Book Encyclopedia* (Chicago, London, Sydney, Tokyo, Toronto: World Book – Childcraft International, Inc., 1982), Horse, 308.
[2] Wikipedia.org/wiki/Horses_in_warfare, 1/19/2012, p-4.
[3] *The World Book Encyclopedia*, 308.
[4] Wikipedia, p-5.
[5] *The World Book Encyclopedia*, 309.
[6] Rousas John Rushdoony, *The Institutes of Biblical Law* (n.l., The Presbyterian and Reformed Publishing Company, 1973), 279.
[7] Although we are not told who this rider is, some commentators believe he is the same as the Rider in chapter 19, i.e., Jesus. But others think otherwise, preferring instead that his rider in Rev. 6 is the Antichrist or an angel.
[8] Hendriksen, *More Than Conquerors*, 93.
[9] McKenzie, *The Antichrist and the Second Coming*, 299.
[10] Ibid., 300, in quotation of Boxall.
[11] Ibid., 301.
[12] Tim LaHaye and Thomas Ice, *The End Times Controversy* (Eugene, OR.: Harvest House Publishers, 2003), 11.
[13] A. A. Hodge, *Evangelical Theology* (Edinburgh: Banner of Truth, [1980] 1976), 227.
[14] Authur F. Glasser, *Announcing the Kingdom* (Grand Rapids, MI.: Baker Academic, 2003), 253.

[15] Gary DeMar, "Giving Aid and Comfort to the Enemies of the Gospel," *Biblical Worldview* (December 2006), 23.

[16] Also, in the Old Testament, God dwelt in, or was present in, a physical and visible Shekhinah glory cloud. This is an entirely different matter and will not be addressed here. Our interest is how cloud phraseology is used in a symbolic manner in both prophetic and apocalyptic eschatology, namely that of swiftness and power of literal judgment.

[17] T. Everett Denton, *Hebrews* (n.l., n.p., 2012), 245.

[18] Some interpreters contend that this verse pertains to Jesus' ascension and not to his supposed "return to earth" or the destruction of Jerusalem in A.D. 70. But if this is so, how could Caiaphas et al. have seen the ascension? Others postulate that this "seeing" of the coming of Christ is in the "hereafter" and therefore doesn't demand a 1st-century fulfillment.

[19] Some contend that this verse has a more simple and obvious meaning, i.e. that Jesus is talking about rejoining them in their ministry trip. This contention is far too reductionistic in light of the eschatological wording used.

[20] Some feel Matthew 16:28 was fulfilled on the Day of Pentecost (Acts 2). But Jesus did not come in his kingdom at Pentecost. Nor was that "the day the Son of Man is revealed" (Luke 17:30). That day was still future and being waited upon thirty-some years after Pentecost (Heb. 10:25; 2 Thess. 2:1-3; 2 Tim. 4:1). Jesus had just gone away and had sent the promised Holy Spirit. But the Holy Spirit is not a Being separate from the Father and the Son (2 Cor. 3:17; Gal. 4:6; Phil. 1:19; 1 Pet. 1:11; John 14:15-23). The claim that it was only in this way and during this interim period that Jesus was said to be with them until the end of the age (Matt. 28:20). But the outpouring of the Holy Spirit was a separately prophesied event in the Old Testament (Ezek. 36:26-27).

Others claim that this verse was fulfilled at the transfiguration (Matt. 17:1-3), or upon his triumphal entry Matt. 21:5f), or at any of his post-resurrection appearances, or at his ascension, or even during his coming to John in the Book of Revelation. While the transfiguration was a temporary and partial glimpse of Jesus' divine glory granted to Peter, James, and John, the brother of James, it could not be the fulfillment of this verse. How could judgment and Jesus' rewarding of "every man," spoken of in the previous verse (Matt. 16:27), have taken place then? And where were "his angels" at either of those events, as stated in the previous verse? This same rejoinder is valid for all the previously suggested fulfillment explanations. Also, only six days had elapsed. That's not enough time for Jesus' "some...not taste death before..." statement to make any sense. The fact is, all inspired New Testament writers, some twenty and thirty years later, were still looking for a future but imminent coming befitting this description, as we'll see shortly. The fulfillment of this passage does not fit any of these previously noted events, nor was Jesus speaking of two different comings arbitrarily separated by a gap of time of at least two thousand years. Verses 27 and 28 are spoken by Jesus in the same breath and are indivisible! A forty-year interval better suits Jesus' prophetic words.

The wording "I tell you the truth" or "verily" is used some 95 times in the New Testament and never introduces a new subject. It always emphasizes something that has just been said.

The great preacher Charles H. Spurgeon said, "If a child were to read this passage I know what he would think it meant: he would suppose Jesus Christ was to come, and there are some standing there who should not taste death until really and literally he did come. This, I believe, is the plain meaning." Spurgeon later explained this imminency away by claiming, "this tasting of death here may be explained, and I believe it is to be explained, by a reference to the second death, which men will not taste of till the Lord comes." Spurgeon's view is an arbitrary and contrived way of looking at this passage. Why not stick to how a child would understand it? That's how Jesus' disciples understood his words. (Spurgeon's quotes are taken from pp-3-6 of Twelve Sermons on the Second Coming of Christ, edition 1976, Baker Book House.)

[21] For more on "Five Side-stepping Devices," see: Noē, *The Perfect Ending for the World*, 151-164.

[22] While some interpreters agree that "this generation" is a reference to Jesus' contemporaries, they also contend that "all these things" only cover verses 4-28, and that these events were the only ones which occurred at the destruction of Jerusalem. They point out that in verses 29-31 Jesus drops the use of the personal pronoun "you." Therefore, it's asserted, these events are for a different time, long after the destruction of Jerusalem. Obviously, this contention is an argument from silence. No textual justification exists for extracting verses 29-31 from the context.

[23] This judgment certainly came on that generation of Jews. Whether Jesus' "blood" and God's judgment is still "on us, and on our children" of subsequent generations of Jews post-A.D. 70 is arguable and debatable. I shall not be addressing this sensitive point in this book.

[24] Brian L. Martin, *Behind the Veil of Moses* (Napa, CA.: The Veil of Moses Project, 2004), 330.

[25] Some writers believe creation and the flood were also only local events. See: Timothy P. Martin and Jeffrey L. Vaughn, *Beyond Creation Science* (Whitehall, MT.: Apocalyptic Vision Press, 2007, Third Edition).

[26] For much more on this, once again, see: Noē, *The Perfect Ending for the*

World, 174-182.

[27] For much more on this, once again, see: Noē, *The Perfect Ending for the World*, 210, 240.

[28] C.S. Lewis, Essay "The World's Last Night" (1960), found in *The Essential C.S. Lewis*, Lyle W. Dorsett ed., (New York: A Touchstone Book, Simon & Schuster, 1996), 385. This is in reference to his made-up quotation of a skeptic.

[29] Theologians prefer the word "imminency" instead of nearness. But they disagree on what this means. Some say it means an event will take place very soon. Others maintain that it only means that it could happen at any moment or is certain to happen someday.

[30] See Noē, *The Perfect Ending for the World*, 229-235.

[31] As a man, Jesus did not know the "day or hour" nor everything. By lowering Himself (Phil. 2:6-8), He did not possess all the divine attributes of omniscience. Hence, Luke 2:52 tells us that as a man, "Jesus grew in wisdom and stature, and in favor with God and men."

[32] See Noē, *The Perfect Ending for the World*, 174-184.

[33] Sproul, *The Last Days According to Jesus*, 158.

[34] For more, once again, see Noē, *The Perfect Ending for the World*.

[35] For more about this sign, see: Noē, *The Perfect Ending for the World*, 241-242.

[36] For more on the exact, literal, sequential and chronological fulfillment of Daniel's two time prophecies, see Noē, *The Perfect Ending for the World*, 109-146.

[37] Some have suggested that these clouds of rising smoke compare with the cloud that hid Jesus from his disciples' sight upon his ascension (Acts 1:9-11). Therefore, in a similar manner, Jesus' coming here was hidden from sight. But I think not.

[38] Josephus, *The Wars of the Jews*, book 6, chapter 5, paragraphs 2-3, In William Whiston, trans. *The Works of Josephus* (Peabody, MA.: Hendrickson Publishers, 1987), 741-2. Also see Tacitus, *History*, v, 11ff.

[39] ibid.

[40] Eusebius, W.J. Ferrar, ed. *The Proof of the Gospel*, book 1, chapter 6, (Grand Rapids, MI.: Baker Books, 1981), 34-35.

[41] See Noē. *The Perfect Ending for the World,* 81-106.

[42] Klein and others, *Introduction to Biblical Interpretation*, 149.

[43] Ibid., 310.

[44] Moisés Silva, *Has the Church Misread the Bible?* (Grand Rapids, MI.: Zondervan, 1987), 8.

[45] For more, once again, see Noē, *The Perfect Ending for the World*, 109-202.

[46] For the fulfillment of Enoch's 70th generation prophecy, see Noē, *The Perfect Ending for the World*, 164-166.

Endnotes 453

⁴⁷ Eusebius, W.J. Ferrar, ed. *The Proof of the Gospel*, book 7, chapter 4, 147f, his discussion on Zechariah 14:1-5.
⁴⁸ Wallace, Jr., *The Book of Revelation*, 461.

Chapter 5

¹ A private email sent me (October 20, 2008) re the topic of this chapter from a cessationist preterist who believes that Jesus came in finality in A.D. 70.
² Rob Bell, *Love Wins* (New York, NY.: HarperOne, 2011), 158.
³ Some commentators maintain this is not the meaning. They claim Jesus was only warning his disciples of troublesome days ahead and these "days of the Son of Man" only refer to the peaceful days when Jesus was with them prior to His crucifixion. Or Jesus was speaking of those days before the fall of Jerusalem.
⁴ See endnote #28 in Chapter 3.
⁵ See Noē, *Off Target*, 101-112 and John Noē, *Shattering the 'Left Behind' Delusion* (Bradford, PA.: IPA, 2000 – out of print).
⁶ For more on this aspect, see: Noē, *The Perfect Ending for the World*, 203-217.
⁷ It was not until 1560 in the First Scottish Confession of Faith that an explicit declaration of a visible return is made in any of the historic creeds of the Church.

Many interpreters generally cite Jesus' comparison of his coming to "as the lightning comes from the east and flashes to the west" (Matt. 24:27), as proof of visibility. This, however, does not prove visibility or being "seen" everywhere all over the whole world. Instead, it is symbolic language and presents a better argument for invisibility than for visibility. Here are some reasons why:

- Lightning is associated with a localized weather system and is only seen in a specific locale and not everywhere all over the world at the same time.
- According to weather experts, lightning that flashes from "east to west" is the intra-cloud variety (within the cloud) or inter-cloud (between two clouds). These two types are different from the cloud-to-ground type of lightning, which we see most often. Cloud-to-ground lightning, however, only accounts for about one-third of all discharges. Sometimes a very active thundercloud produces hundreds of discharges without a single discharge to the ground. Therefore, intra-cloud lightning is the most common type. When this happens within the cloud, all that is usually seen, if anything at all, is a diffused brightening of the cloud and not the streak itself. Consequently, most lightning of this type is never seen directly on earth because it is obscured by the cloud.

- Perhaps by referring to this type of lightning, Jesus meant to symbolically illustrate the power and suddenness of his coming upon a particular people, in a specific locale, or to emphasize the darkness of thunderclouds passing in judgment over Israel, or to underscore that his presence would only be indirectly "seen" in the attending circumstances and results [sign] of judgment that fell.
- We should understand that lightning imagery is a common theme and manifestation of God in power and judgment and is used throughout the Scripture (see Nah. 1:3-6, for example).

---

[8] For more on lightning, see Noē, *The Perfect Ending for the World*, 255-257.

[9] According to Ron Allen, my friend, Greek consultant, and Professor of Preaching and Second Testament at Christian Theological Seminary, under certain circumstances a noun in a genitive construction can function as an adjective. But it usually functions as a noun. Therefore, the normal function of this noun in this verse is the more probable understanding of this expression.

[10] Yahweh and Jehovah are both phonetic transliterations of the four-consonant name of God in the Old Testament, YHWH, which was never pronounced by observant Jew out of deep respect.

[11] For other notable appearances of "the glory of the Lord" see: Lev. 9:6, 23; Num. 14:10, 21; 16:19, 42; 20:6; 1 Ki. 8:11; 2 Chron. 5:14; 7:1-3; Psa. 104:31; 138:5; Isa. 35:2; 40:5; 58:8; 60:1; Ezek. 1:28; 3:12, 23; 10:4, 18; 11:23; 43:5; 44:4; Hab. 2:14. Also see: Luke 2:9; 2 Cor. 3:18; 8:19. There are more. Also see endnote #12 in Chapter 1.

[12] Billy Graham, "My Answer," *The Indianapolis Star*, 3/5/11, E-4.

[13] Dallas Willard, *The Divine Conspiracy* (San Francisco, CA.: HarperSanFrancisco, 1997), 72.

[14] Ibid., 73.

[15] Chad Bonham, "He Dared to Touch the World," *Charisma* (January 2007), 60-62.

[16] Audrey Lee, "When Muslims See Jesus," *Charisma* (September 2011), 34-40.

[17] Jeff Swiatek, "A restaurateur's tale of growth, generosity," *The Indianapolis Star*, 11/5/ 2008, C-1, 3.

[18] Joel Osteen, *Become a Better You* (New York, NY.: Free Press, 2007), 296.

[19] See David E. Taylor, *Face-to-Face Appearances from Jesus* (Shippensburg, PA.: Destiny Image, 2009).

[20] Ladd, *A Theology of the New Testament*, 272.

[21] George Eldon Ladd, *The Presence of the Future* (Grand Rapids, MI.: Eerdmans, 1974), 48.

[22] But these post-A.D.-70 comings are for non-eschatological, non-revelatory, and non-redemptive purposes. By non-revelatory I mean not to reveal more Scripture. The canon is closed. Yet God can still reveal more from his revealed Word. By non-redemptive I mean not to fulfill his plan of redemption. It is fulfilled. Yet God can and does bring people to salvation in many ways.

[23] Chilton, *The Days of Vengeance*, 188.

[24] Willem VanGemeren, *Interpreting the Prophetic Word* (Grand Rapids, MI.: Zondervan, 1990), 386.

[25] Steven C. Roy, "God as Omnicompetent Responder? Questions about the Grounds of Eschatological Confidence in Open Theism," in David W. Baker, ed., *Looking into the Future: Evangelical Studies in Eschatology* (Grand Rapids, MI.: Baker Academic, 2001), 276.

[26] Ibid., 278.

[27] For more here, see John Noē, *Hell Yes / Hell No* (Indianapolis, IN.: East2West Press, 2011).

[28] Neither time nor space will permit us to discuss all the other so-called "Second Coming" and "day of the Lord" passages (1 Thess. 4:13-17; 1 Cor. 15:23, 50-57; 2 Pet. 3:10-13, particularly). For more on these see Noē, *The Perfect Ending for the World* and Noē, *Shattering the 'Left Behind' Delusion* (out of print).

[29] For more, see Noē, *Off Target*, 101-112 or Noē, *Shattering the 'Left Behind' Delusion* (out of print).

[30] Others feel the physical counterpart of "the bright Morning Star" is the planet Venus. During some seasons it appears first in the east, just before morning, as the harbinger of the dawn.

Chapter 6

[1] Hendriksen, *More than Conquerors*, 200.

[2] Rousas John Rushdoony, *Law and Society* (Vallecito, CA.: Ross House Books, 1982, 1986), 405-406.

[3] J. Daniel Hays, J. Scott Duvall, and C. Marvin Pate, *Dictionary of Biblical Prophecy and End Times* (Grand Rapids, MI.: Zondervan, 2007), 271.

[4] Brent Curtis and John Eldredge, *The Sacred Romance* (Nashville, TN.: ThomasNelson, 1997), 182-183.

[5] David Nasser, *A Call to Die*, (n.l., Baxter Press, 2000), 118.

[6] For more on the reality of the new heaven and new earth, see: Noē, *The Perfect Ending for the World*, chapter 13.

[7] Hays, Duvall, and Pate, *Dictionary of Biblical Prophecy and End Times*, 272.

[88] See Noē, *Off Target*, 37-51 and Noē, *The Perfect Ending for the World*, 272-273.

[9] For more, see Noē, *Off Target*, 37-51.
[10] Wallace, *The Book of Revelation*, 107-108.
[11] I won't repeat verses 11-14 since we covered them earlier in this chapter.
[12] Chilton, *The Days of Vengeance*, 33.
[13] For more, see my book, *The Perfect Ending for the World*, in which I have proclaimed and documented the past and perfect fulfillment for all end-time prophecies. I term this authentification and validation of our faith "divine perfection."
[14] Hendriksen, *More than Conquerors*, 179.
[15] Ibid., 179-180.
[16] Ibid., 180.
[17] Josephus, *The Wars of the Jew*, 6.5.3, 298-299.
[18] Chilton, *The Days of Vengeance*, 474.
[19] Ibid., 473.
[20] Wallace, *The Book of Revelation*, 388.
[21] Hendriksen, *More than Conquerors*, 181.
[22] See John 21:12
[23] Chilton, *The Days of Vengeance*, 472.
[24] David Chilton claimed that the Book of Revelation "is divided right in the middle between these two motifs. Thus: I. The Bridegroom, Chapters 1-11 . . . . II. The Bride, Chapters 12-22." (Chilton, *The Days of Vengeance*, 45.
[25] At this time in redemptive history heaven was not open yet (John 3:13; 13:33, 36). Jesus first had to go to heaven and prepare that place and then come and receive his disciples to "where I am" (John 14:2-3). This had not occurred even after his resurrection and during his many comings (appearings) prior to his ascension (see John 20:17). For more on this see: Noē, *Off Target*, 111.
[26] "8 Questions About Heaven," *Charisma*, July 2010, 32.
[27] Hendriksen, *More than Conquerors*, 79.
[28] Chilton, *The Days of Vengeance*, 477.

Chapter 7

[1] J. Daniel Hays, J. Scott Duvall, and C. Marvin Pate, *Dictionary of Biblical Prophecy and End Times*, 44. Dispensational premillennialists have this battle happening before their literal 1,000-year Millennium begins. But at the end of this Millennium is another and final rebellion, after Satan has been released from his prison. Then, he and his forces are defeated again and finally cast into the lake of fire (Rev. 20:7-10).
[2] Of course, it is not the end of the world. Our world is "without end." For more, see: Noē, *The Perfect Ending for the World*, 1-106.

[3] From advertisement – "Introducing the LaHaye Prophecy Study Group," *Christianity Today*, February 2003, 13.
[4] Joel C. Rosenberg, "War in November: A military showdown with Iran may be fast approaching," Washington, D.C., July 8, 2008, email, 7/9/2008.
[5] Most of the material in his section original appeared in Noē, *Off Target*, Exposé #11, 145-152.
[6] Josephus, *Wars*, 6.9.3, 420.
[7] Klein, Blomberg, and Hubbard, Jr., *Introduction to Biblical Interpretation*, 149.
[8] For more, see: Noē, *The Perfect Ending for the World*, 274-275.
[9] Chilton, *The Days of Vengeance*, 57. Others insist they "describe seven successive periods of Church history." To which Hendriksen replies: "hardly needs refutation. . . . there is not one atom of evidence in all the sacred writings which in any way corroborates this thoroughly arbitrary method of cutting up the history of the Church and assigning the resulting pieces to the respective epistles of Revelation 2 and 3. The epistles describe conditions which occur not in one particular age of Church history, but again and again." – Hendriksen, *More that Conquerors*, 60.
[10] Hendriksen, *More than Conquerors*, 163. But in typical amillennial fashion, he maintains that "the real, the great, the final Har-Magedon" is still future and will occur "just before and in connection with the last day" (ibid.) "at Christ's second coming [when] Satan's persecution of the Church and his power to deceive on earth shall cease for ever [sic]." (Ibid., 183).
[11] For more on this, see my future book, *A Once-Mighty Faith* and scheduled for publication estimate 2013..
[12] Ibid., 300, in quotation of Boxall.
[13] Ibid., 301.
[14] Chilton, *The Days of Vengeance*, 188.
[15] There are consequences to pay in both this life and the afterlife in heaven. See: Noē, *Off Target*, "Eternal Rewards and Punishment for Believers," 217-229 and Noē, *Hell Yes / Hell No*, "The Postmortem Experience," 329-363.

Chapter 8

[1] Revelation's beast is the same entity as Daniel's fourth beast (Dan. 7)—the Roman Empire. For more see, Noē, *The Perfect Ending for the World*, 136-137. Also, there are two beasts in Rev. 13 – one that arises out of the sea and one out of the land. I believe the first is Gentile, the Roman Empire, and the second is Jewish, Jerusalem's high priest and Sanhedrin in an illicit relationship with Roman rulers. As McKenzie states, "the high priest had become the puppet of Rome in the first century; the Temple leadership was in bed with Roman

appointed rulers of the land" (McKenzie, *The Antichrist and the Second Coming*, 221.

[2] I shall present this material as well as covering the fulfillment of two beasts in my future commentary on Revelation tentatively titled, *The Scene Behind the Seen* and schedule for publication estimate 2015-2016. For more on this now, see Chilton, *The Days of Vengeance*, 278-280; 325-352.

[3] Walter Brueggemann, *Out of Babylon* (Nashville, TN.: Abingdon Press, 2010), 109. This author identifies Babylon as being "empire" and particularly the contemporary United States (p-11).

[4] Ibid., 112.

[5] Admonishment to the jury by attorney Johnny Cochran during O.J. Simpson's murder trial in 1995 – "If the gloves fit you must acquit."

[6] Wes Howard-Brook and Anthony Gwyther, *Unveiling Empire* (Maryknoll, NY.: Orbis Books, 1999), 166.

[7] Ibid., 167.

[8] Ibid., 166 – these authors, however, see Babylon as empire—Rome in the 1st century. They also stress its ongoing character.

[9] Naomi Schaefer Riley, "Pastors Call a Truce on 'Sheep-Stealing,'" *The Wall Street Journal*, WSJ.com, May 3, 2012.

[10] Thomas E. Bergler, "When Are We Going to Grow Up?" *Christianity Today*, June 2012, 19, 24.

[11] Some believe this beast is evil world systems that fight against the kingdom of God and its ruler, Jesus Christ. Therefore, it would exercise control not only through governments but also through commerce, science, education, the arts, entertainment, media—everything that exists is the material realm, and even shows up in the Church. Hence, it lures people into giving it their allegiance by accepting its name and number (Rev. 13:16-17). Such people are sold out to their work, to money, or to some pleasure and have little or no place in their heart for God. That's bearing the name and number of the beast. More on this in my upcoming commentary on Revelation tentatively titled, *The Scene Behind the Seen*.

[12] www.irs.gov/newsroom/article/0,,id=161131,00.html, 3/9/12.

[13] ADF, "The Pulpit Freedom Initiative Executive Summary," 9/30/11).

[14] Howard-Brook and Gwyther, *Unveiling Empire*, 167.

[15] John L. Ronsvalle and Sylvia Ronsvalle, *The State of Church Giving through 2009* (Champaign, IL.: empty tomb, inc., 2011).

[16] Comments of a pastor friend of mine when we reviewed this report together.

[17] Ronsvalle and Ronsvalle, *The State of Church Giving through 2009*, 136.

[18] Ibid., 130.

[19] Ibid., 137.

[20] Ibid., 149.

[21] Ibid., 162.
[22] An un-footnoted quote in George Barna and Frank Viola, *Pagan Christianity* (n.l., BarnaBooks, an imprint of Tyndale House Publishers, 2002, 2008), 157.
[23] Diana Butler Bass, *Christianity After Religion* (New York, NY.: HarperOne, 2012), 72.
[24] Tony Evans, *What a Way to Live!* (Nashville, TN.: Word Publishing, 1997), 294.
[25] J. Lee Grady, "The Devil Is Religious" *Charisma* (October 2005): 8.
[26] Bass, 75-76.
[27] For more see: Noē, *The Perfect Ending for the World*, 201-206, 213-217.
[28] For more see: Noē, *Off Target*, 153-164.
[29] For more see: Noē, *Off Target*, 37-51, 231-236.
[30] For more see: Noē, *Off Target*, 53-59.
[31] For more see: Noē, *Off Target*, 181-204, 219-229.
[32] For more see: Noē, *The Perfect Ending for the World*, 216-217, 226, 232.
[33] For more see: Noē, *The Perfect Ending for the World*, 109-217f.
[34] For more see: Noē, *Off Target*, 91-99.
[35] For more see: Noē, *Off Target*, 77-90 and Noē, *The Perfect Ending for the World*, 171-202.
[36] Ed Stetzer, "Subversive Kingdom" in "Bits & Pieces," *Christianity Today*, May 2012, 56.
[37] For more see: Noē, *Off Target*, 181-188.
[38] For more see: Noē, *Off Target*, 181-204.
[39] James Robison and Jay W. Richards, "How to Restore America," *Charisma*, May 2012, 30-31.
[40] Footnote for Gen. 11:9 in *The Holy* Bible, New International Version, copyright 1978 by New York International Bible Society.
[41] Barna Group, "Most American Christians Do Not Believe that Satan or the Holy Spirit Exist," April 10, 2009, Barna.org. Also see George Barna, *Maximum Faith Live Like Jesus* (Ventura, CA.: Metaformation Inc. and Gendora, CA.: WHC Publishing, 2011), 37.
[42] Bass, *Christianity After Religion*, 83.
[43] John W. Chalfant, *American A Call to Greatness* (Longwood, FL.: Xulon Press, 2003), 142.
[44] Chilton, *The Days of Vengeance*, 446.
[45] Hendriksen, *More Than Conquerors*, 173.
[46] Howard-Brook and Gwyther, *Unveiling Empire*, 260.
[47] Richard Bauckham, *New Testament Theology* (Cambridge, NY.: Cambridge University Press, 1993), 130-131.
[48] Bass, *Christianity After Religion*, 161.
[49] Ibid., 162.

[50] Ibid., 167.
[51] "Easter Egg Hunts: 5 Places to enjoy the mad dash," *The Indianapolis Star*, March 22, 2012, Local Living, 3.
[52] "Easter egg hunt canceled because of aggressive parents," Zionica.com/2012/03/26/easter-egg-hunt-canceled-because-of-aggressive-parents, 3/26/12.
[53] Lori Walbury, *The Legend of the Easter Egg* (Grand Rapids, MI.: Zonderkids, 1999), last page, n.n.
[54] McKenzie, *The Antichrist and the Second Coming*, 61-62.
[55] Ibid., 246.
[56] Ibid., 247.
[57] Ibid., 252.
[58] Daniel de Vise, "Moving beyond lectures," *The Indianapolis Star*, 2/19/12, A-7.
[59] Barna and Viola, *Pagan Christianity*, 34.
[60] Ibid., 73.
[61] Ibid., 36.
[62] Ibid., 37.
[63] Ibid., 79.
[64] Ibid., 136.
[65] Ibid., 265.
[66] Hendriksen, *More Than Conquerors*, 174.
[67] Chilton, *The Days of Vengeance*, 585.
[68] Ibid., 586.
[69] For more see Noē, *Off Target*, 1-19.
[70] ibid.
[71] Chuck Colson, "A Sign for the Times: Repent!" newsletters@*BreakPoint*.org, 11/17/2010.
[72] McKenzie, *The Antichrist and the Second Coming,* 77.
[73] Hendriksen, *More Than Conquerors*, 174.
[74] Howard-Brook and Gwyther, *Unveiling Empire*, 184.
[75] To the best of my knowledge, no written reference can be found in Augustine's writing for these famous words. Some think this quote belongs to Martin Luther or Ignatius. But again, no written reference can be found. There are also minor variants.
[76] For more see: Noē, *The Perfect Ending for the World*, 274-275.
[77] Bass, *Christianity After Religion*, 94.
[78] Ibid., 98.

Chapter 9

[1] Much of the material contained in this chapter was originally published in my out-of-print book, *Shattering the 'Left Behind' Delusion*. But here, this material has been expanded and enhanced.

[2] *New York Times,* Front page, October 4, 1998.

[3] Focus on the Family *Citizen* magazine, December '98, 6.

[4] Edward E. Stevens disagrees. See his book *Expectations Demand A First Century Rapture* (Bradford, PA.: International Preterist Association, 2003).

[5] Concepts can be completely in line with the teaching of Scripture even though the term(s) used are non-scriptural.

[6] Some pre-tribulation-rapture proponents claim this ancient citation, ascribed to Ephraem of Nisibis (A.D. 303-373), first taught that believers in Christ would be raptured and taken to Heaven before "The Tribulation." The two sentences cited are contested by other interpreters who feel a two-staged second coming concept separated by some period of time is not mentioned. One thing is sure. If Ephraem believed and taught a pre-tribulation rapture, nothing of any significance developed from his or others' efforts until Darby.

[7] The key question that must be addressed by anyone teaching this "gap" theory today is, what is the scriptural justification for making this intrusion upon the text and interrupting the time frame? I know of none. It has just been assumed. It's necessitated. The interested reader is referred to the author's book, *The Perfect Ending for the World*, see chapter 5 (pp. 109-126) for the description of the literal, exact, chronological, sequential fulfillment—no gaps, no gimmicks, no twisted meanings.

[8] The Bible never mentions a 7-year period of tribulation. It's a contrived idea stemming from a misconception of Daniel's 70 week and/or the adding together of two 3½-year symbols in Revelation 11:2 and 3. But three more 3½-year symbols are mentioned in Revelation 12:6, 12; and 13:5. Why not add all five together and arrive at a 17½-year period? What's the scriptural authority for doing either? Zero. Jesus taught that "in the world ye shall have tribulation" (John 16:33). He didn't limit it to seven years or any time parameter, nor did any biblical writer and neither should we.

[9] See Noē, *The Perfect Ending for the World*.

[10] Leon Morris, *New Testament Theology* (Grand Rapids, MI.: Zondervan Academie, 1990, 1986), 89.

[11] Some rapture commentators explain this is a different group of "tribulation saints" who get saved during the seven years after the Church saints have been removed from earth.

[12] Not all Greek language resources recognize this distinction. See "An Academic Excursus on *Aer*" at the end of this chapter.

[13] McKenzie, *The Antichrist and the Second Coming*, 325.
[14] For other uses of *harpazo* that are translated differently see: Matt. 11:12; 13:19; John 6:15; 10:12; 10:28-29; Acts 23:10; Jude 23.
[15] Barbara Brown Taylor, "The Day We Were Left Behind," *Christianity Today*, May 18, 1998, 45-49.
[16] For more, see: Noē, *Off Target*, 1-19.
[17] Noē, *Off Target*, 108-112.
[18] The literal Greek (which has no punctuation) reads: "And behold the veil of the shrine was rent from above to below in two and the earth was shaken and the rocks were rent and the tombs were opened and many bodies of the having fallen asleep saints were raised and coming forth out of the tombs after the rising of him entered into the holy city and appeared to many."
[19] They claim they died again. But there is no scriptural support for that claim.
[20] Billy Graham, "My Answer," *The Indianapolis Star*, 1/23/06, E-2.
[21] Kenneth D. Boa & Robert M. Bowman Jr., *Sense & Nonsense about Heaven and Hell* (Grand Rapids, MI.: Zondervan, 2007), 37-38.
[22] The sacrament of water baptism (especially immersion) symbolizes this union with Christ in his death, burial, and resurrection. But what we are talking about here goes much farther than one symbolic act or event in one's life. All five "Co's" involve an almost, if not, daily identification and application.
[23] There is also what is termed the CBV – "Collective Body View" verses the IBV – "Individual Body View" being presented here. In the CBV, the "collective body" of the Church is seen as being raised out of the dead "body" of biblical Judaism and into the new "body" of Christ. This view arises from two primary sources: Ezekiel's prophecy of dry bones (Ezek. 37:1-14) and the New Testament use of the word "body." We shall not be presenting this aspect in this book. For those interested, see Noē, *Shattering the 'Left Behind' Delusion*, 111-115 (Out of Print).
[24] See Noē, *Off Target*, 219-229 and Noē, *Hell Yes / Hell No*, 329-363, 371-374.

Chapter 10

[1] G.R. Beasley-Murray, *The Book of Revelation, The New Century Bible Commentary,* ed. Ronald Clements and Matthew Black (Grand Rapids, MI.: Eerdmans, 1981), 315.
[2] Howard-Brook and Gwyther, *Unveiling Empire*, 184-185.
[3] Peter J. Leithart, *Defending Constantine* (Downers Grove, IL.: InterVarsity Press, 2010), 179. From Eusebius Pamphilius: Church History, Life of Constantine, Oration in Praise of Constantine, 3.33.
[4] Hays, Duvall, Pate, *Dictionary of Biblical Prophecy and End Times*, 309.
[5] Randy Alcorn, *Heaven* (Wheaton, IL.: Tyndale House Publishers, 2004), *xx*.

[6] Chilton, *The Days of Vengeance*, 537.
[7] N.T. Wright, *Surprised by Hope* (New York. NY.: HarperCollins, 2008), 101.
[8] Hays, Duvall, Pate, *Dictionary of Biblical Prophecy and End Times*, 176-177.
[9] Hendriksen, *More than Conquerors*, 196-198.
[10] From footnote in *The Holy Bible*: New International Version (Grand Rapids, MI.: Zondervan, 1978), 1155.
[11] For an extensive discussion see, Noē, *The Perfect Ending for the World*, "Why the World Will Never End," 81-106.
[12] Billy Graham, "My Answer," *The Indianapolis Star*, 11/21/05, E-2.
[13] For more, see Noē, *Off Target*, "Origin of Evil," 205-218.
[14] For more, see Noē, *The Perfect Ending for the World* and *Off Target*, 153-164.
[15] For this exposition, see ibid., 279-319.
[16] McKenzie, *The Antichrist and the Second Coming*, 428-429.
[17] Chilton, *The Days of Vengeance*, 545.
[18] Amillennialists, qualify this reality thusly, "all this is true in principle now but will be seen in perfection in the new universe of the future" (Hendriksen, *More than Conquerors*, 203).
[19] It would be impractical in this book, if not futile, to attempt a descriptive application of all the pieces comprising the structure of this city.
[20] Hendriksen, *More than Conquerors*, 208-209.
[21] Wallace writes that "the Jerusalem of the time of Christ and the apostles and people of the New Testament lies buried beneath the ruins of the succeeding centuries; and the Jerusalem which was the city of David is buried deeper below the surface of modern Jerusalem. In the fifteen centuries of its existence from its first appearance in Old Testament history until its destruction in A.D. 70 it had been besieged some fifteen or twenty times, was twice razed and burned, and twice its walls were crumbled by enemy attacks. There is not the slightest feature remaining today of its ancient glory." [Wallace, Jr., *The Book of Revelation*, 434-435.]
[22] Bauckham, *New Testament Theology*, 136.
[23] Hendriksen, *More than Conquerors*, 203.
[24] ibid.
[25] Ibid., 207. Unfortunately, and typical of the amillennial view, Hendriksen adds: "in the new universe. All these symbols apply, in principle, to this present age; and in perfection to the new universe."
[26] Billy Graham, "My Answer," *The Indianapolis Star*, 9/10/10, E5.
[27] Billy Graham, "My Answer, *The Indianapolis Star*, 12/9/11, E6.
[28] Eusebius, *The Church History*, 271.
[29] Bauckham, *New Testament Theology*, 88.
[30] For more, see Noē, *Off Target*, 53-59.

[31] Quoted in: Timothy Keller, *The Reason for God* (New York, NY.: Dutton, 2008), 66-67 from Dietrich Bonhoeffer, *Letters and Papers from Prison: Enlarged Edition*, Eberhard Bethge, ed. (Macmillan, 1971), p. 418.
For more, see Noē, *The Perfect Ending for the World*, 286-288.
[33] Taken from ibid., 286.
[34] Julie Ferwerda, *Raising Hell* (Lander, WY.: Vagabound Group, 2011), 113-114.
[35] For more on the Doctrine of Eternal Rewards and Punishment for Believers, see: Noē, *Off Target*, 219-229 and Noē, *Hell Yes / Hell No*, Appendix A.
[36] While some Bible versions make a few errors in this regard, the translators of *Today's New International Version* (TNIV) have obliterated the distinction between believers in Christ as children of God and as sons of God by failing to translate accurately the Greek words for *children* and *sons*, and thereby obscuring the difference and hinder the uniformed reader from understanding the crucial element of sonship in God's purpose. But as *Christianity Today* reported in 2009 "on more TNIV . . . the Committee on Bible Translation will discontinue the TNIV when an updated NIV is released in 2011" (Oct. 2009, 9).
[37] Ché Ahn, "Know Your Rights," *Charisma,* May 2008, 112.
[38] DeVern Fromke, "Ultimate Intention," quoted in "The Difference Between a Child of God and a Son of God" by Editor, in Discipleship, 2/27/2008, www.freethechurch.org/blog/?p=53, 12/20/2008.
[39] Myles Munroe, *Rediscovering the Kingdom* (Shippensburg, PA.: Destiny Image, 2004), 82-83.
[40] John Eldredge, *The Way of the Wild Heart* (Nashville, TN.: Nelson Books, 2006), 30.
[41] Ibid., 38.
[42] Ibid., 222-223.
[43] Rousas John Rushdoony, *Law and Society*, 269.
[44] McKenzie, *The Antichrist and the Second Coming*, 448.
[45] Chilton, *The Days of Vengeance*, 567-568.
[46] Hendriksen, *More than Conquerors*, 205.
[47] Wallace, *The Book of Revelation*, 452.
[48] For more on the lake of fire, see: Noē, *Hell Yes / Hell No*, 90-93, 329-332. We won't, however, be dealing in this book with all the various ideas about what this "second death" may or may not be.
[49] John Eldredge, *The Way of the Wild Heart*, 288.
[50] Billy Graham, "My Answer," *The Indianapolis Star*, 11/21/05, E-2.
[51] For more on this, see: Noē, *The Perfect Ending for the World*.
[52] For more on this, see Noē, *Off Target*, Exposé #14, "Doing the Works of Jesus," 181-188.
[53] For more on this, see Noē, *Off Target*, Exposé #15, "Doing Greater Works

than Jesus," 189-204.
[54] Taken from Noē, *Off Target*, 193-196.
[55] Chilton, *The Days of Vengeance*, 589.
[56] Ibid., 196-204. See Noē, *A Once-Mighty Faith*, 2013.
[57] Wallace, *The Book of Revelation*, 467.
[58] Bauckham, *New Testament Theology*, 130-131.
[59] Howard-Brook and Gwyther, *Unveiling Empire*, 210-211.
[60] John Noē, *Peak Performance Principles for High Achievers* (Hollywood, FL.: Frederick Fell Publishers, 2006, 1984).
[61] For more re: "Eternal Rewards and Punishment for Believers," see: Noē, *Off Target*, 219-229 and Noē, *Hell Yes / Hell No*, 329-363, 371-374.

Conclusion

[1] See Noē, *Off Target*, 219-229 and *Hell Yes / Hell No*, 329-363, 371-374.
[2] Chilton, *The Days of Vengeance*, 57 in quotation of Loraine Boettner, *The Millennium* (Philadelphia: The Presbyterian and Reformed Publishing Co., 1957), pp. 38-47, 63-66, and others.
[3] See Noē, *The Perfect Ending for the World*.
[4] See Noē, *Off Target*, 16-17.
[5] Diana Butler Bass, *Christianity after Religion*, 260-261, 266.

Appendix A

[1] For the full account of this personal prophecy, see: John R. Noē, *Peak Performance Principles for High Achievers*, Revised Edition (Hollywood, FL.: Frederick Fell Publishers, 2006), 166-169.

www.ingramcontent.com/pod-product-compliance
Lightning Source LLC
Chambersburg PA
CBHW020727160426
43192CB00006B/143